HOWARD MARKS

Howard Marks (1945–2016) was one of the
world's most wanted drug barons. An Oxford
nuclear physics and philosophy of science graduate,
he was famously acquitted at the Old Bailey of
cannabis trafficking, but was later convicted
in the US for his global cannabis network. He
served seven years in one of America's toughest
penitentiaries before being released and becoming
the author of *Mr Nice*. The autobiography has
sold over one million copies worldwide and was
adapted into a major film

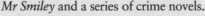

His public readings from *Mr Nice* received excellent
reviews throughout the national press. They quickly
evolved into the legendary one man comedy show,
An Audience with Mr Nice, which sold out at
venues throughout Britain and Europe for the rest
of his lifetime. Howard Marks also garnered critical
and popular acclaim for his travel journalism, *The
Howard Marks Book of Dope Stories*, *Señor Nice*,
Mr Smiley and a series of crime novels.

HOWARD MARKS

Mr Nice

WITH AN INTRODUCTION BY
Irvine Welsh

VINTAGE

To my son, Patrick Marks

1 3 5 7 9 10 8 6 4 2

Vintage
20 Vauxhall Bridge Road,
London SW1V 2SA

Vintage is part of the Penguin Random House group of companies
whose addresses can be found at global.penguinrandomhouse.com.

Penguin
Random House
UK

This edition published by Vintage in 2017
First published in Vintage in 1998
First published in hardback by Martin Secker & Warburg in 1996

penguin.co.uk/vintage

A CIP catalogue record for this book is
available from the British Library

ISBN 9781784705909

Printed and bound by Clays Ltd, St Ives plc

Penguin Random House is committed to a sustainable future
for our business, our readers and our planet. This book is made
from Forest Stewardship Council® certified paper.

Howard

Howard Marks was a supremely inspirational man. He sparked a tremendous devotion among the many people who met him. Countless more – who didn't have that privilege – still felt that they were his friends. To be held in such affection by strangers is generally something that only true outlaws attain. Olaf Tyaransen, the Norwegian-sounding Irish journalist, describes our mutual friend as a 'highly intelligent, erudite and charming man, who enjoyed life to the full – while running rings around law enforcement agencies for years'.

Yes, Howard certainly took the piss out of the authorities. His relish in flouting them fuelled his actions, just as much as his desire to turn profit. When he turned from drug smuggling to become a writer and anti-prohibition activist, he continued to be a thorn in their flesh. This was the quality that made him a true folk hero. Carl Loben, editor of *DJ* magazine, recalls a 1998 anti-drug prohibition demonstration they attended together. 'Howard was the de facto star speaker at the end of the demo. He hung around for a couple of hours after the speeches, chatting with people and posing for pictures. He always had time for everyone.'

So how did a kid born in 1945, to a merchant sailor
father and teacher mother, in the small coal-mining town of
Kenfig Hill, who spoke only Welsh till he was five years old,
become the world's biggest drug smuggler? Well, Howard
loved weed, and saw the lunacy of his tipple of choice being
illegal while all around him, in the booze-soaked pit towns
of South Wales, the destructive impact of alcohol was clearly
visible. The old maxim of 'don't get high on your own
supply' was never coined with him in mind. Although cannabis was a labour of love for him, Howard never judged
non-believers. Despite his zeal for pot and his intrigue at my
lack of interest, when I readily displayed an enthusiasm for
other substances, he never bothered trying to convert me.

He first began smoking hashish in 1964 at Balliol
College, Oxford, to which he won a scholarship from a Valleys grammar school. As often happens, he started dealing
small amounts to student friends to support his habit. Joshua
Macmillan, the grandson of former British Prime Minister
Harold Macmillan, was a close friend. He later died of a heroin overdose. This tragedy made Howard averse to trafficking
in hard drugs, despite the bigger money to be amassed in that
trade. He saw their potential for individual tragedy and social
destruction, and had no real emotional connection to them.

Leaving Oxford with a degree in nuclear physics meant
that the world was *almost but not quite* his oyster. Britain
is overly fond of its meritocracy myths: less academically
able but more connected rich kids could still harness family
networks to progress much further, much faster. Howard
could have established himself as an academic, but despite
brief employment in teaching, he was never cut out for the
straight life. International drug smuggling was more his forte
and he operated under multiple identities for many years, a
particular favourite, 'Donald Nice', establishing this book's title.

It was an exciting if precarious life, fraught with dangers
and stresses, yet Howard ducked and weaved with enormous

aplomb, as these pages recount. It took being grassed up
by a brothel-operating Tory peer and the obsessions of an
anally retentive DEA agent to change his luck, when, smack
bang in the middle of the acid house revolution of 1988, he
was arrested in Spain. Following extradition, Howard went
on trial in West Palm Beach, Florida, where the court heard
how he and his associates had smuggled thousands of tonnes
of processed marijuana into the USA since 1970, through a
criminal network covering many countries. He was sentenced
to twenty-five years in Indiana's Terre Haute Penitentiary,
one of the harshest death row prisons in America.

It was a tough call for anybody to survive such an environment, let alone a man whose wife and children were on the
other side of the ocean. Howard not only did so, he had the
audacity to actually thrive. His international notoriety was no
hindrance in helping him manoeuvre prison politics, but his
charm and intellect were even bigger assets. He taught many
inmates how to read and write, and, as a campaigning jailhouse
lawyer, facilitated the release of a few more. His 'exemplary
behaviour' and the zeal of the corrupt DEA to incarcerate
him, leading them to fabricate evidence, resulted in his release
through parole after just seven years. The global headlines that
followed assured that *Mr Nice* became an international best-
seller, shifting well over a million copies. It would later become
an acclaimed movie starring Rhys Ifans, and, of course, was
the subject of Howard's long-running one-man stage show.
On his release he campaigned for drug law reform and wrote
six further books – including 2015's follow-up autobiography,
Mr Smiley: My Last Pill and Testament.

I consider myself very fortunate to have been a friend of
Howard's. We were an unlikely duo to break into both the
best-seller lists and nineties celebrity, with *Mr Nice* coming
out around eighteen months after my first novel, *Trainspot-
ting*, through the same publishing group. As displaced
rock 'n' rollers who couldn't sing a note and who entered

pop culture through the back door of literature, we instantly hit it off, forming a kind of quiet, understated support system for each other. Both of us had been around the block enough to appreciate the gifts fame bestowed while retaining a certain ironic detachment, as we watched yet another Britpop star suffer a hotel-room whitey. Although Cool Britannia was fun, it wasn't our first rodeo. I had lucked out: here was a street-savvy big bro of infinite wisdom and huge heart to help me navigate those exciting but potentially treacherous waters.

The first thing that struck you about Howard Marks was his gaze. His eyes looked right into your soul and also presented his own beautiful one out on a platter for your consideration. It was always fair trade. That gaze and grin must have broken a few hearts, and, when coupled with the unsuspecting uppercut of his steely will, gotten him out of several scrapes with jailhouse bullies.

The second thing to hit you was that voice. His Valleys lilt, accentuated with a gravelly hue by smoking, was the dog whistle that drew the cool and the wannabe cool. If you went into a nightclub you would wonder who all those hot young women were huddled around, until those rich, Burtonesque tones gave the game away.

So to say that Howard was an impressive individual is a massive understatement. Charisma leaked out of him, and his mindset was one of natural extravagance, augmented with an understandable desire to catch up on life's good things after spending so long locked away. Yes, the cliché is true, he really did look like a sixties rock star. It was often said that he resembled a Rolling Stone, but the truth is that the only one that could ever come close to him in the coolness stakes would be Keith Richards. Dave Beer of Back to Basics nightclub in Leeds, a city Howard loved and where he lived the latter part of his life, told me: 'He was a real-life folk hero; a modern-day Robin Hood or, more true to his nature, a legendary highwayman such as Dick Turpin. Howard was a true outlaw and always considered himself a criminal, which he felt comfortable with. But most of all Mr Nice was the nicest man you would ever have the pleasure to meet.'

Howard was also one of the last of that great stratum of working-class intellectuals, who came out of the post-war era where education was greatly prized and fees and grants, rather than loans, were offered to those from modest backgrounds. It was a time when we still had a proletarian culture that hadn't been lain to waste by a declining capitalism, anxious to treat it like jam, and spread it as unthreateningly thinly as possible across its otherwise unappetising products, while reducing it to reactionary tabloid sound bites.

Unlike many working-class Oxford scholarship kids, blanding out his Valleys accent and muting his political radicalism was never an option. Howard Marks was a classic rebel. While he oozed charm and appreciated good conversation with people from all walks of life, the dumb, crass absurdities of the power elites offended his natural outlaw sensibilities. He didn't just disdain them, he fought a stealthy guerrilla war against them and their pathetic assaults on intelligence and freedom (disguised as a war against drugs), and he never let up on this crusade. More subversively, he fought this battle in the most personally charming and engaging way, generally by taking the high ground and playing the ball, never the opponent. One of the few exceptions was with the boundless hypocrite former Home Secretary Jack Straw. As he said at the 1998 anti-prohibition demo: 'If Jack Straw can't stop his own son doing it [smoking weed], how the hell does he think he's going to stop us?!'

Howard had a wise and wonderful way of simplifying matters and getting to the point. Artist Nick Reynolds, himself the son of an iconic working-class outlaw in Great Train Robbery mastermind Bruce Reynolds, recalls asking him to speak at an anti-death-penalty art exhibition in Brick Lane, with Paddy Hill and Gerry Conlan. 'Howard got up and boomed in an accusatory tone: "According to the Law, the most unacceptable and heinous crime a man can commit is premeditated murder. Premeditated murder – that means if you plan to kill someone at a specific time and carry it out, that's premeditated murder. So then, what may I ask is the death penalty? Is that itself not premeditated murder?" Classic Howard and spot on!'

Howard was portrayed as a superstar waster, and often he was – he saw no contradiction between fighting for a better world and basking in the joy of what life had to offer. He would laugh off sycophants' attempts to sanctify him as cheerfully as the media ones to demonise him. But he held his drugs well. James Brown, our editor at *Loaded*, remembers him as 'the one man in the room, whom, when everybody else was ranting shit on coke, you could still have a decent conversation with'. When those heavy eyelids did start to go, it was generally the best signal that the night, or morning, or afternoon, really had come to a natural close.

Howard's advice would often be counter-intuitive to most people. When Dave Beer stopped taking drugs and got a bit miserable as a result, everybody (including me) supportively told him he was doing the right thing. Howard took a differ-ent line. 'You don't look very happy to me,' he said to Dave. 'If I was you, I would get back on the drugs.' Dave laughed off this comment, but Howard's response was sincere. 'Don't laugh, it's true. It suits you and you're very good at it. Yes, people like you that way, you see, but it's not about everyone else, it's about you and what makes you happy.' Dave gave the matter some thought, later telling me: 'Only Howard would come out with that kind of advice. I didn't take it instantly, but after a while I realised that he was right, in that a little of what you like is good for you. It's all about being in control; using the drugs and not letting the drugs use you. After this perspective, I became in control of my own destiny and no longer a prisoner of my identity. I was happy in myself again.' Howard saw that Dave was essentially a creature of clubland, in all its psychic layers; it was wired into his DNA. To have him in such an environment without drugs was like having Tilikum the killer whale captive in SeaWorld or a polar bear pacing a small concrete enclosure in a zoo.

Thus Howard had little time for boring 'leftist' puritans, understanding how, in their stiff-arsed disapproving morose piety, they simply fuelled the right-wing reactionary forces they professed to despise. Yet he was well aware that his media portrayal as a supreme hedonist was often underpinned by a desire to neuter his campaigning edge. It never did. Whether through his natural raconteur's stage shows, or his journalism, his own voice was never muted or shorn of its critical intelligence in order to appease some lowest common denominator. I doubt if he'd have recognised such a concept.

Howard loved a good festival and nightclub, but was comfortable in any social situation. His spiritual home for a while was the legendary Tardis in Clerkenwell, a description-defying space run by George Parish and Nick Reynolds, where artists from all disciplines and gangsters of all levels of ambition merged happily, swapped tales, indulged in bad behaviour and put on weird shows. It was a journo-free zone, and the Fourth Estate had to content themselves with writing infinitely lamer tales about the Groucho, largely for each other's consumption.

On his last public appearance at Kentish Town's Forum, Howard, though in the throes of terminal cancer, was mesmerising and hypnotic, and most of all, beautifully angry. He evoked a latter-day Dylan Thomas, dismantling hypocrisy and vested interest with intelligence, passion and humour, almost literally until his last breath. A man who genuinely loved life so much was never going quietly: graciously, always, but never quietly.

It's rare to find a genuine intellectual and an incredibly warm person in the one package. The gift of abstraction that fuels the hungry, critical mind so often works against the expression of simple humanity and social engagement with others. Howard did both effortlessly. After the big Decriminalise Cannabis march in London in early 1998, the government did indeed relax the law on cannabis. As Carl Loben says, 'Not only was Howard a diamond geezer and great storyteller, he was also an activist who made a huge impact on the world.'

For a man who posited himself (as always with Howard, in self-deprecating humour) as an international master of disguise, he was paradoxically always himself. I've been in his company with writers, gangsters, publishers, labourers, schoolteachers, rock stars, scientists and even minor royalty, and I never saw him defer, condescend or dismiss a single one of them for a solitary second. He was always Howard Marks, and he took a great joy in them all. That was enough. God, that was so much more than enough. Howard's life is one of the few where fact impressively outstrips mythology, but it's all in here and he tells it better than I ever could. So it's probably time for me to shut up and let my old buddy take over. And for you to read the story of a remarkable life, lived by the very brilliant and exceptionally wonderful Mr Nice.

Irvine Welsh
January 2017

Contents

Acknowledgements

I would like to thank the following
for their assistance, support, and editing:
Ann Blain, David Godwin, Bee Grice,
Judy Marks, Amber Marks, Francesca Marks,
Geoffrey Mulligan, Mick Tyson,
and Helen Wild

Introduction

I was running out of passports, ones I could use. In a few weeks I intended to visit San Francisco to pick up several hundred thousand dollars from someone keen to exploit his connections, both with me and with a bent US Customs Officer working in the imports section of San Francisco International Airport.

A few years earlier, I had been declared the most wanted man in Great Britain, a hashish smuggler with documented links to the Italian Mafia, the Brotherhood of Eternal Love, the IRA, and the British Secret Service. A new identity was vital. I'd already gone through about twenty different identities, most of which had been backed up by a passport, driving licence, or other indicators of documented existence, but they'd all either been discovered by friends/enemies or compromised by featuring in some suspicious trail meandering through a recent scam.

We drove to Norwich. After a couple of awkward meetings with go-betweens, I was introduced to a gentle guy named Donald. I couldn't tell if he was a drinker, a stoner, or a straighter. His kitchen gave no clues. He looked normal, except that his eyes danced like those of a villain.

'We can talk privately out here,' he said and took me to a garden shed.

'I need a passport, Don, one that'll stand up to all checks.'

'You can have mine. I won't be needing one. But there's one problem.'

'What's that?'

'I've just done twelve years of a life sentence for murder.'

Convicted murderers, although clearly people with a criminal record, would rarely be declared as unwelcome at a country's borders. They were regarded as mere menaces to individuals rather than threats to the fabric of society. The latter attribute tended to be restricted to dope dealers and terrorists.

'I'll give you a grand for it,' I said, 'and a few hundred quid from time to time when I need more back-up.'

I was thinking of a driving licence, medical card, local library card. Just a passport with no supporting identification is suspicious. A membership card to the local billiards club, obtainable cheaply and without proof of identity, is enough to give the required credibility.

'That's the best deal I've ever been offered for anything.'

'What's your last name, Don?' I asked. I'd been lumbered with some terrible ones in the past.

'Neece.'

'How do you spell it?'

'N-I-C-E, just like the place on the Riviera.'

It was up to Don how he pronounced his name. But I knew I would pronounce it differently. I was about to become Mr Nice.

One

BRITISH

'Marks!' yelled the guard. 'What's your number?'

'41526-004,' I mumbled, still in a really deep sleep. My number was used more often than my name, and I knew it just as well.

'Get all your shit together,' he ordered. 'You're leaving.'

Slowly I woke up. 'Yeah, I'm leaving.' I was leaving El Reno.

El Reno, Oklahoma, houses the Federal Bureau of Prisons' transit facilities and is host to between one and two thousand federal prisoners, who are cajoled, bossed, and bullied by a few hundred guards. Every prisoner who is required to be moved from one US federal prison to another passes through El Reno. Even if the prisoner is being transported from North Dakota to South Dakota, he still has to go via El Reno. I had been through there five times. Some had been through more than fifty times. Expensive illogicalities and inefficiencies do not worry the monsters of American bureaucracy, and the taxpayers are enthusiastic and eager to spend fortunes in the name of fighting crime. Prison places cost the US taxpayer more than university places. The American belief that prisons are the best way to combat crime has led to an incarceration rate that is at least five times that of almost any other industrialised nation. Overcrowding is endemic. Conditions are appalling, varying from windowless, sensory-deprived isolation to barren and futile brutality.

Mostly, prisoners are taken to El Reno in aeroplanes confiscated by the US Government from the Colombian cocaine cartels, who have made billions of dollars out of America's War on Drugs. There are at least two large airliners, each seating well over one hundred prisoners, and numerous smaller planes carrying up to thirty passengers. Every day, between three and six hundred prisoners arrive and leave. Arrivals take place in the late afternoon and evening; departures take place in the early morning. Flying courtesy of the Federal Bureau of Prisons is a gruelling business. The only consolation was that this would be my last of over a dozen flights on this airline, known as Conair. I was going to be released in three weeks. My release date was the same as that of Mike Tyson. I had been continuously in prison for the last six and a half years for transporting beneficial herbs from one place to another, while he had done three years for rape.

'Getting my shit together' meant putting my dirty bedclothes in a pillow case. No personal possessions of any kind are allowed in El Reno. I got my shit together.

Along with about sixty or seventy others, I was herded into a holding cell to await processing. Our names, numbers, fingerprints, and photographs were carefully scrutinised to ensure we were who we said we were. Our medical records were perused to ensure that if anyone had AIDS, TB, or some other dreadfully contagious disease, the right space on the form was filled in. One by one we were stripped naked and minutely examined during the ritual known as 'shakedown'. In full view of, and in sickeningly close proximity to, three Oklahoma rednecks, I ran my fingers through my hair, shook my head, tugged my ears to show the wax, opened my mouth, pulled out my Bureau of Prisons denture plate, stretched my arms above my head to show my armpits, pulled up my balls, pulled back the foreskin of my dick, turned round to display the soles of my feet, and finally bent down, pulling the cheeks of my bum apart, so that the rednecks could treat my anus as a telescope. A federal prisoner has to perform this series of indignities before and after each time he is visited by his family, friend, religious counsellor, or lawyer, and each time he enters or leaves any prison. I had performed it thousands of times. The three Peeping-Tom rednecks made the same jokes that prison guards never tire of making when shaking down: 'I recognise that hole. Didn't you come through here three years ago?'

During the course of this departure process, I checked among the other prisoners where they were expecting to be transported to. It was important to establish that I was not about to be sent somewhere in error – a most common occurrence. Sometimes the error was deliberate – part of a practice known as 'diesel therapy'. This punishment of keeping one on the move and out of contact was frequently administered to troublesome prisoners. The 'treatment' could last up to two years. I was meant to be going to Oakdale, Louisiana, where criminal aliens (the word 'alien' is preferred to the word 'foreigner') nearing the expiry of their sentences began the gleeful process of being removed from the US and sent back to civilisation. I began to panic when some of my shaken-down companions mentioned they were going to Pennsylvania; others thought they were going to Michigan. Security reasons always prevent prisoners from knowing where (and sometimes when) they are going. Eventually I met someone who was also expecting to go to Oakdale. He was a gentle, bright marijuana smuggler, longing to finish his ten-year sentence and get back to his loved and longed-for native country of New Zealand. He told me that he knew it was just an hour's flight from El Reno to Oakdale.

We caught a glimpse of the time – 2 a.m. We were then outfitted with our travelling clothes: a sleeveless shirt with no pockets, a pair of trousers without pockets, socks, underwear, and a pair of very thin, beach-type shoes, which were made in China. Next came the part that everyone hates, even more than the shakedown: the adorning of heavy metal: handcuffs around the wrists, chains around the waist, chains from the chains around the waist to the handcuffs, shackles around the legs, and, if like me one is described as having a propensity for escape or violence, a 'black box'. This last lump of heavy metal is like a portable pillory without the hole for the head and renders the handcuffs completely rigid, preventing any independent hand movement. It is chained and padlocked to the chains around the waist. I have never attempted to escape from anywhere and have never physically harmed or threatened anyone. Nevertheless, according to information furnished to the US Federal Bureau of Prisons by Special Agent Craig Lovato of the US Drug Enforcement Administration, I'm an Oxford graduate and a British Secret Service operative, and, apparently, I can get out of places that Houdini couldn't even get into.

We were then placed in another holding cell. Two or three hours had passed since our awakening; two or three more would have to pass before we would leave by bus for Oklahoma City Airport. We sat around talking to each other, comparing conditions in different prisons in much the same way as I once discussed the pros and cons of various first-class hotels. Dog-ends that had been miraculously smuggled through the shakedown process were produced and fought over. At times like this I felt very glad I had given up smoking tobacco (after thirty-five years of fairly constant use). Prisoners clanked and jingled their chains as they shuffled to the solitary toilet bowl and performed the acrobatics necessary to unzip and undo.

Federal regulations require prisoners to be fed at least once every fourteen hours. Each prisoner was provided with a brown paper bag containing two hard-boiled eggs, a carton of 'Jungle Juice', an apple, and a Granola bar. People began to trade food items furiously.

The gates to the holding cell were opened, and we were led out into the sub-zero temperature in our sleeveless shirts and were counted and checked again against copies of photographs. We were then patted, as opposed to shaken, down and guided into a mercifully heated bus. A radio blared the two kinds of music with which Oklahoma rednecks are familiar: country and western.

The icy roads made for a slow journey to the airport. There was a long wait at the runway before we were finally handed over by the prison guards to the United States Marshals. None of them looked like Wyatt Earp. They handle interstate transportation of federal property such as prisoners. Some of them are female, kind of. Soon I would see real air hostesses – and then my wife.

After an hour in the air, we landed at a military airfield. Names were called, and some passengers left. My name was omitted. I panicked until I realised the New Zealander was still on board, but he looked worried too. Some different prisoners boarded and told us we were at Memphis. We took off again, and in an hour really did land at Oakdale airport. A bus took us to the prison, where we were dechained, shaken down, fed, and otherwise processed. I was beginning to look forward to the various facilities that every federal prison tends to have: tennis courts, jogging track, and library.

Processing is an irritating and lengthy process, but most of us had been through it dozens of times. Each newly arrived prisoner has to be seen and checked by a PA (physician's assistant) and a screening counsellor. Each prisoner also has to be fed and given clothes that fit at least approximately. These seemingly straightforward activities take several hours to complete.

The screening counsellor's function is to decide whether or not the prisoner may be allowed to be accommodated in the general prison population. If not, the prisoner is locked up in the prison's 'hole', a very uncomfortable prison within a prison. There are a number of reasons why a prisoner would be separated from the others. Occasionally, the prisoner would himself request segregation: he might have been warned that someone at this new prison was out to get him to settle some old dope or gambling debt. He might be terrified of being raped, extorted, or discovered to be a snitch. Sometimes, particularly if release was imminent, the prisoner would wish to be isolated merely to diminish the chances of getting into any trouble inadvertently. One had to do one's best to decrease the frequency of random cock-ups. Moreover, there is an obligation for prisoners to be gainfully employed, and one of the very few methods of avoiding work is to be locked up in the hole. Accommodation in the hole could always be requested: checking-in was easy, checking-out extremely difficult. More often than not, it's the screening counsellor who determines who goes where, and the most scanty of reasons are used to justify placement in the hole: a history of violence, escape, connections with gangs, and high profile would almost always ensure at least a limited spell inside. My file was littered with absurd allegations of escape attempts, but I did not expect problems from that quarter because of the short time I had left to serve. It was March 3rd, and my parole release date was March 25th. Not a sensible time to attempt to leg it, but American law enforcement is prohibited from making common-sense assumptions.

Despite valiant attempts, I hadn't pissed for over twelve hours. The toilets in the holding cells are always crowded by smokers, and I've never yet been able to piss covered in chains and sharing a pressurised airplane cabin with a redneck marshal whose job is to stare at my dick to ensure it doesn't turn into a dangerously offensive weapon or dope stash. I was bursting. My name was the first called. I went into the screener's office and immediately noticed on his desk a piece of paper referring to me with the word ESCAPE highlighted in yellow.

'Oh no!' I thought. 'They can't be that insane.'

But I knew they could be.

They didn't use my so-called escape history against me, but I was put into the hole anyway. The screening counsellor informed me that as I had less than thirty days of my sentence left, it would be pointless for the prison to go through the time-consuming charade of admitting and orientating me. The screener didn't care who I was. It was policy.

'How am I going to see Immigration and get deported? How can I get my passport? How can I get the airline ticket that will take me out of this horrible country if I can't telephone or write?'

'Don't worry,' said the screener. 'They'll come to you, tell you what's happening, and arrange for you to have all the calls and stamps you need.'

They lie so easily.

The New Zealander saw my solemn face as I returned to the holding cell.

'That's too bad. Nice to have met you, British. Take care of yourself.'

I was so angry. I went to the toilet, now really crowded with dick-staring smokers.

'Fuck them,' I thought, and I let loose a stream of vile-smelling dark green liquid.

That was the last time I had any problem pissing. After a few hours, I was called out of the holding cell, handcuffed behind my back, and marched to the hole.

The Oakdale hole contained about forty cells. Everyone coming into the hole has to be showered under supervision in a cage; submit to mouth, anus, and foreskin search; and be given a pair of underpants, socks, fairy slippers (Chinese made), and a sterilised, oversized jump-suit. Nothing else could be acquired without a struggle. I had long ago reached the point where degrading rituals ceased to matter. Had they taken away my dignity, or was my dignity too formidable to be dented or diminished?

Most of the prison officers in Louisiana are Black. A Black duty officer took down my particulars. Custodians of the hole have no interest in why someone has been placed there. There was absolutely no point trying to explain that I had committed no disciplinary infraction, that I was only in this punishment block because I was almost free. They'd heard it all before. Sometimes it was true, sometimes not. Instead, I did my usual trick of being excessively friendly and polite. This was the only way I could begin to get the essential books, stamps, paper, envelopes and pencil. The duty officer liked my accent and did an almost recognisable imitation of John Gielgud. I laid on my best Oxford inflection and called him 'Milord'. He loved it. Sure I could have some books to read.

He locked me for one hour in the library cell. I rummaged around and found *Lord of the Flies*, *1984*, a Ken Follett novel, the inevitable Bible, a Graham Greene novel, and a textbook on calculus. These would last a few days, much longer if my cellmate turned out to be a jabbering Yank or loony. I got some paper, pencils, and envelopes. Stamps and phone calls were issued only by counsellors and lieutenants.

I was taken to a fairly clean and mercifully unoccupied cell, which contained the usual fixtures and fittings: steel bed, frayed and stained mattress, continuously flashing neon light, and a filthy, malfunctioning WC and washbasin. It had been an exhausting day. The time was almost 10 p.m. I read and slept.

'You're in the jailhouse now,' sang a tone-deaf Irish hack as he passed coffee, cereal, and other quasi-edibles through three-inch slits in the cell doors.

I knew it had to be 6 a.m. Breakfast in bed. If it wasn't for time zones, well over a million American prison inmates would be consuming the same fare at the same time. It was cold.

*

Special Housing Units, euphemism for holes, were always deliberately maintained at discomforting temperatures in case one or more of the prisoners were there to be punished. One of the hole's inmates was assigned the job of orderly. He came round and took the breakfast waste back through the slits. The orderly's other official duties included keeping the areas outside the cells clean and supplying prisoners with toilet requisites. Unofficial duties, 'hustles' that he could maybe make some money from, included distribution of contraband (non-generic coffee, stamps, and cigarettes) and liaising between buyers and sellers of the same.

'Got a stamp?' I asked as he retrieved an empty box of raisin bran.

'Maybe,' he said, 'but I'll need two back.'

This was the standard prison loansharking rate for almost everything.

'Give me two, and I'll give you five back.'

He looked as if he trusted me and nodded assent.

The cells were patrolled every couple of hours. When anyone other than the orderly passed by, I banged the door and demanded to make a phone call, to contact my lawyer, to contact my family, and to contact the British Embassy. Chaplains (authorised to listen to prayers), psychiatrists (authorised to listen to everything else), and medical officers (authorised to distribute Tylenol) are required by law to make daily rounds of the hole. They cannot supply stamps or arrange phone calls, so one is kept insane, stressed, and in need of help from above. I would have to be patient. Now that there was no one to watch my bumbling attempts to rescue my body from ugly deterioration, I could resume my yoga and callisthenics. And I had my books. Someone would come sometime and let me make a call. The orderly would bring some stamps. Relax. There wasn't long to go until I became free. What was Special Agent Craig Lovato of the Drug Enforcement Administration doing? Was I in the hole again because of him? Was he going

to be able to stop my release? He had ruined so much, so
very, very much.

Craig Lovato's ancestors were rich Spaniards. They emigrated to America from Spain about 250 years ago and were
given 97,000 acres of what became New Mexico in a land
grant from the Spanish throne. By the time Craig Lovato was
born, his family had lost most of their fortune, and he had to
work for a living. He missed both the Vietnam War and the
Sixties movements which opposed it and joined the Las
Vegas Sheriff's Department as a deputy. He learned about
street life as a patrolman and 'goon squad' officer chasing
undesirables out of town, about dope as a narcotics detective, and about life and death as a homicide detective. In
1979, he yearned for a new way of life and joined the DEA.

The DEA has offices in sixty-seven of the world's
countries. It has more power than the KGB ever had. One of
its offices is in the United States Embassy, Madrid. In
August 1984, Craig Lovato went to work there. At the same
time I was living in Palma peacefully carrying on my
international drug-smuggling business. Lovato found out I
was not only smuggling dope but actually enjoying it. God
knows why, but this made him lose his marbles, and he has
been hounding and persecuting me ever since.

The weather in Louisiana comprises rain, light or heavy,
and thunder, loud or very loud. Although quite early in the
evening, it suddenly got very dark, and a torrential down-
pour began. Four hours later, the rain was still tamping
down. I went to sleep. In a few hours, I was woken by
thunderclaps and observed about three inches of water on
the floor. Strange creatures were swimming in the water, but
I was too sleepy to be scared. I went back to sleep and was
vaguely aware of the rain ceasing.

In the distance I heard, 'You're in the jailhouse now.'

I looked at the floor. The water had disappeared, and in
its place was a writhing mass of hideous Louisiana insects:
multicoloured spiders, grotesque underwater cockroaches,

large worms, and giant beetles. All my carefully cultured Buddhist beliefs on the sanctity of all life quickly evaporated, and I set about systematically murdering the creatures of the night by whacking them with my Chinese fairy slippers before accepting my breakfast. The corpses filled two empty cartons of raisin bran. The air-conditioning was on full. It was very cold. I did more yoga, callisthenics, and reading, but I couldn't get my mind off the primitive life-forms. Did Tibetans really ensure they killed no insects when building their temples?

'Put your hands behind your back and through the slit,' ordered two hacks in unison from the other side of the cell door.

One of them was the Irish crooner. They slipped on the handcuffs. I retrieved my hands. It was now safe for the hacks to open the door.

'The Immigration want to see you.'

This sounded good.

'Can I wash, change, shit, shave, and shampoo?'

'No, they want you now.'

The crooner and his buddy led me out into the blinding sun, across several yards of squelching swamp, and into a building labelled INS. I sat down. The handcuffs were removed.

I heard a voice in the background say, 'Well, he was extradited, so is he going to be excluded, deported, repatriated, expelled, or permitted to depart voluntarily?'

Since at least 1982, I have been prohibited from entering the United States. I did not have a visa, and in order to gain entry when I was extradited in October 1989 I was paroled (a strange use of the word) by the United States Attorney General to satisfy the public's interest in prosecuting, convicting, sentencing, and incarcerating me. Paroling is not entering, and I was not to be considered as having entered the United States despite having been conspicuously present here for well over five years. Legally, I was to be treated as still just outside the border, and no decision regarding my deportability or excludability could be made until the reason for my being paroled into the United States no longer applied, i.e., until my release from incarceration. Given I was a felonious, criminal alien, I could not in any circumstances be allowed to walk the streets of the Land of the Free. Given I had not applied for entry, I could not be excluded. Given I had not entered in the way the law understood the meaning of the word, I could not be deported. Given I was soon to finish my sentence, I could not thereafter be held in prison.

I had read all the relevant law in the law library of United States Penitentiary, Terre Haute. As a consequence of the Sixth Amendment to the US Constitution, freedom of access to the courts had to be available to all prisoners. This was achieved by putting law books and typewriters in every prison and allowing prisoners to litigate to their hearts' content. For years, articulating other prisoners' legal presentations to the US courts had been my 'hustle'. I had achieved a few successes and was quite a respected jailhouse lawyer, but I had no idea what on earth the Immigration authorities could or would do. I didn't know of anyone else in the same position. I was very scared of law enforcement bureaucrats. Anything could happen. I could become a Cuban illegal.

'Come in, Marks. Can you get a passport and pay for your own ticket? If so, you can avoid all court proceedings and leave the United States as soon as you finish your sentence on March 25th.'

What a very nice man.

'Sign this, Marks.'

I had never signed anything so quickly. I read it later. I had waived all court proceedings provided I got my passport and ticket within thirty days. I knew Bob Gordon of the Chicago British Consulate had already sent an emergency passport, and there were plenty of family and friends prepared to pay for my ticket.

'Get yourself an open, one-way, full-fare ticket from Houston to London on Continental 4.'

'I'm in the hole and not allowed to make telephone calls,' I said, 'and I can't get any stamps.'

'Don't worry. I'll speak to the lieutenant of the hole. Your phone calls will save the United States Government several thousand dollars. He'll agree. Ask for him when you get back.'

Since when were these people into saving money?

'Will you please take some passport photos?' I asked. Maybe the ones I'd sent Bob Gordon wouldn't be suitable. Spares would always be handy.

Armed with photographs and a signed waiver form and feeling happier than I had for a good few days, I was handcuffed and marched back to the hole. I was greeted by the lieutenant.

'Listen up, British. I don't give a motherfucking fuck what those motherfuckers at Immigration said. I run this motherfucking place, not them. This is my motherfucking hole. You get one motherfucking call a week, and your first will be next Sunday. On Monday, you can ask the counsellor to give you some stamps. I'm not authorised to. Now fuck off.'

Angry and frustrated, but not really surprised, I returned to my cell. The orderly gave me a couple of stamps. I wrote to the consul.

After another two days of yoga, meditation, and callisthenics, I again heard from the other side of the door, 'Put your hands behind your back and through the slit.'

'Where am I going?'

'Oakdale Two.'

'Where am I now?'

'Oakdale One.'

'What's the difference?'

'Oakdale Two is run by Immigration. That's where you'll be deported from.'

This news made me feel on top of the world. There were

still two weeks of my sentence to go. Were they trying to get
me out of the country as soon as possible?

I was halfway through being handcuffed when the foul-
mouthed lieutenant came tearing along, yelling, 'Put that
motherfucker back in his motherfucking cell. The Warden's
Executive Assistant wants him.'

After a few minutes I spotted a human eye at the door's
spyhole.

'Some journalists from an English newspaper want to
interview you. Yes or no?' barked the Warden's Executive
Assistant.

'Oh! No!'

How did they know I was here? Did they know I was about
to be released? If they knew, who else knew? Would there be
an international storm of protest from the DEA, Her
Majesty's Customs and Excise, Scotland Yard, and all the
other law enforcement agencies that had struggled so hard to
get me locked up for the rest of my life? The Warden's
Executive Assistant pushed a piece of paper under the door.

'Sign this. It states you refuse to be interviewed.'

I signed. I had to keep a low profile, but I felt bad about
it. On the whole, journalists had written sympathetically
about my incarceration in America. Their sympathy,
however, might galvanise the authorities into preventing my
release. I couldn't risk it. I slid the paper back under the
door. Footsteps receded.

Two sets of footsteps returned.

'Put your hands behind your back and through the slit.'

Handcuffed and chained, I was dumped in a holding cell
for six hours, taken to a van, and driven by two hacks
sporting automatic rifles to another prison a hundred yards
away. There I was dumped in another holding cell for a
further four hours, but this time I shared it with eight other
dumpees: an Egyptian, a Ghanaian, four Mexicans, and
two Hondurans. The Ghanaian and the Hondurans were
ecstatic. Never again would they have to endure the brutality

of the United States Justice system. The Egyptian and the Mexicans were subdued, as each had been deported from the United States at least once before and had re-entered illegally. It was a way of life. Cross the border, get an illegal job, get busted, spend a few weeks, months or years getting fit and fed while incarcerated at the American taxpayer's expense, get deported, and start the cycle all over again. I'd forgotten. Most people don't want to leave America.

'What's it like here?' I asked my fellow criminal aliens.

'Just like any other federal joint,' replied one of the Mexicans.

'I thought this was run by Immigration,' I protested.

'No, it's run by the Bureau of Prisons. You're lucky if you see an Immigration Officer. It's just another joint, man.'

Handcuffs were removed, dozens of forms filled in, photographs and fingerprints taken, medical examination given, body and orifices searched, prison clothes issued, and cell assigned. My roommate was a Pakistani, fighting deportation by seeking political asylum. There were almost a thousand inmates of all nationalities: Nigerians, Jamaicans, Nepalese, Pakistanis, Chinese, Indians, Sri Lankans, Vietnamese, Filipinos, Laotians, Spaniards, Italians, Israelis, Palestinians, Egyptians, Canadians, Central and South Americans. Most were convicted dope offenders and spent all their free time discussing future dope deals. 'We're not bringing any more stuff to this country' was often voiced. 'Europe and Canada are where it's at. They don't give you much time if you're busted. They're not all snitches like Americans.'

Many deals were hatched. Many, I'm sure, will come to fruition.

The Mexican was also right about the difficulty in seeing an Immigration Officer. I tried relentlessly. We were able to phone, so I called the British Consul.

'Yes, Howard, your passport has been sent. Your parents, who send you all their love, paid for your open ticket, and that's also been sent.'

I finally found an Immigration Liaison Officer.

'Yes, we've received your passport and ticket, but they've been mislaid. Don't worry. We're all on the case. We'll find them.'

Apparently everyone's ticket and passport got mislaid at some stage. We just had to wait patiently. There was nothing we could do.

A Walkman was permitted. I bought one and spent every day walking twenty miles around the jogging track listening to the oldies' station. During my years inside, my daughter Francesca, now fourteen, had regularly written to me of her fondness for my record collection. Little Richard, Elvis Presley, Waylon Jennings, and Jimi Hendrix were among her favourites. Soon we could listen to them together, and she could educate me on the new music I'd missed. I became sun-tanned, nostalgic, and bored. Three days before my supposed release date of March 25th, I was pacing the track listening to a New Orleans disc jockey raving about the latest and greatest British band, the Super Furry Animals. They were from the Welsh valleys. I was listening to them calling me home when the prison loudspeaker cracked.

'Marks, 41526-004, report to the Immigration Office.'

'We've got your passport and your ticket,' said the Immigration Officer. 'Everything's ready for you to leave. We can't tell you precisely when, of course, in case you initiate plans to prevent it. But it'll be soon.'

My release date came and went, and a week or so passed by. 'Lovato's doing it,' I thought. 'He's persuading his buddies in the DEA to stop me leaving.'

On Thursday, April 7th, Komo, a Thai who'd been fighting deportation for seven years and who'd not been outside of a prison for seventeen years, came running towards me.

'British, British, you're on the list. Leaving tonight. About 1 a.m. Please leave me Walkman.'

Komo's prison job was cleaning and tidying the offices of

the administrative staff, so he had access to confidential information. He also had about twenty Walkmans, which he would attempt to sell to new arrivals. Every long-term prisoner has to have a solid hustle. But it was such good news that I immediately handed over my Walkman.

'Good luck, Komo. Maybe see you in Bangkok one day.'

'Me never go Bangkok, British. They kill me there. Me American. Stay here.'

'They'll kill you here, too, Komo,' I said, 'but much slower and more painfully.'

'Slow is okay, British, and very slow is very good.'

I couldn't risk telephoning anyone with the news. It might not be true, and besides, the phones were tapped. If the authorities discovered that I was leaving, they just might change my travel plans.

There were eight others leaving that night: an Americanised Nigerian of British nationality and seven South Americans.

'Is this all your property, Marks?'

I had approximately one hundred dollars, a pair of shorts, nail-clippers, comb, toothbrush, alarm clock, papers confirming my 'release' date of two weeks ago, a credit card I could use in prison vending-machines, and five books, including one written about me, *Hunting Marco Polo*.

'Yes, that's it.'

I put the money in my pocket. It felt strange. First time for over six years. How often was I going to be thinking that? First time for over six years. Money, sex, wine, a joint of marijuana, a bath, an Indian curry. All around the corner.

My other belongings were put into a cardboard box. I was given a pair of blue jeans with legs about a foot too long and an extremely tight white tee-shirt. This was called being 'dressed out', a gift from the United States Government for those re-entering the free world.

We were handcuffed, but not chained, and squeezed into

a small van. Then we picked up two other guys from another prison exit. One seemed Hispanic, the other seemed northern European. Everyone was silent, excited by his own thoughts. The van's engine made a terrible racket as it headed towards Houston and the dawn, just beginning to break. By nine o'clock, it was like sitting on a rock in a sardine can on fire. By ten o'clock, we were sitting in an enormous holding cell at Houston International Airport, along with over fifty other criminal aliens.

The northern European asked the Nigerian, 'Where do you live?' His accent was strong South Welsh. I had never met a Welshman in an American prison, nor heard of one. I'd met very few Americans who'd heard of Wales.

'Are you Welsh?' I interrupted.

'Aye,' he said, looking at me with deep suspicion.

'So am I.'

'Oh yeah!' Deeper suspicion.

'Which part are 'ew from?' I asked, laying on the accent a bit.

'Swansea,' he said, 'and 'ew?'

'Twenty-five miles away from 'ew in Kenfig Hill,' I answered.

He started laughing.

'You're not him, are you? God Almighty! Jesus wept! Howard bloody Marks. Marco fucking Polo. They're letting you go, are they? That's bloody great. Good to meet you, boy. I'm Scoogsie.'

We had a chat, a long one. Scoogsie explained how he, too, had just finished a drug sentence, and he told me of his early days in the business.

'My wife has worked for a long time in a drug rehabilitation centre in Swansea. Not a bad partnership, really. I get them hooked; she gets them off. We keep each other going, like.'

Memories of South Welsh humour had often helped me through the bad times in prison. Now I was hearing it for real. I was heading back towards my roots, and they were reaching out for me.

Looking confused, the Nigerian belatedly replied to Scoogsie's original question.

'I live in London. I am being deported there. I am never coming back here. They took away my money, my property, and my business. Just because someone I didn't know swore in court that I sold him some drugs.'

An all too familiar story.

The number of deportees in the converted aeroplane hangar was dwindling. 'Anyone else going to London?' Scoogsie asked.

No one.

Soon, there were just the three of us left. We'd found out that the Continental Airlines flight to London should be leaving in an hour. An Immigration Officer came in holding a gun.

'This way, you three.'

A small van took us to the gangway. With his gun, the Immigration Officer indicated we should climb the steps. The Nigerian led the way. Scoogsie followed and spat dramatically on American soil.

'None of that!' ordered the immigration man, waving the gun.

'Don't mess it up now, Scoogsie. You know what they're like.'

'I know what the fuckers are like, all right,' said Scoogsie. 'I hate them. I wouldn't piss in their mouths if their throats were on fire. I'm never going to eat another McDonalds. No more cornflakes for breakfast. And pity help any Yank who asks me the way anywhere. Let anyone dare try to pay me in dollars. God help him.'

'Take it easy, Scoogsie. Let's get on board.'

Walking into the aeroplane was like entering the starship *Enterprise*. Passengers with spacey haircuts and clown clothes took out computers of all shapes and sizes. Had things really changed that much, or had I forgotten what it was like? Lights flickered on and off. Glamorous and smiling women, the like of whom had existed only as photos on a prison cell wall, walked the aisles. One actually talked to me.

'Mr Marks, your seat number is 34H. It's in the aisle. We shall hold your passport until London. Then we'll give it to the British authorities.'

I didn't like the sound of that, but I was too mesmerised to pay much attention. Scoogsie and the Nigerian were placed out of sight. I sat down, gloated over magazines and newspapers and played with knobs adjusting seat position and volume of canned entertainment, like a child on his first flight. I had flown on commercial airlines thousands of times before, but I remembered none of them. Take-off was magic. I saw Texas disappearing. Then, all of America vanished. There is a God.

'Would you like a cocktail before your meal, Mr Marks?'

I had drunk no alcohol and smoked nothing for three years. I was proud of my self-discipline. Perhaps I should carry on as a teetotaller.

'Just an orange juice, please.'

A tray of food was placed in front of me. In the old days, I would rarely eat while flying: apart from the caviare and foie gras given to first-class passengers on long-haul flights, it was all fairly disgusting and well below the cordon bleu standard to which I had become accustomed. Prison fare had cured me of that bit of pompous pseudery. This meal was the best I could remember, and I loved fiddling around with the little packets of condiments. There was a very small bottle of red wine on the tray. Surely, I could drink that. It was exquisite. I ordered six more.

I began worrying about the remark made by the air hostess. Which British authorities? There were so many I'd upset and so much they could still do me for. While I was spending the last six years in prison, the British authorities had obtained evidence that I had been involved in countless

other marijuana and hashish importations to England, ones
that I hadn't been charged with. They'd also found more of
my false passports. There are no statutes of limitation in
British law. They could bust me if they wanted to.

Two books had been written about me, each making it
clear that I was an incorrigible rogue with nothing but
contempt for the forces of law enforcement. Fourteen weeks
earlier, at the end of a high-profile, colourful, nine-week
trial, I had been acquitted of being the ringleader for the
largest-ever importation of marijuana into Europe – fifteen
tons of Colombia's best. The charges had been brought by
Her Majesty's Customs and Excise. It had been their
biggest-ever bust. They would never forget me.

A chief inspector of police had committed suicide after
being blamed for leaking my involvement with the British
Secret Service to the press. Scotland Yard had lost a good
man because of me. There wouldn't be many friends there.

MI6 weren't too happy with me either, smuggling dope
with the IRA when I was supposed to be spying on them.

Ten years ago, after assessing me as having earned two
million pounds from cannabis smuggling, the Inland
Revenue reluctantly settled for a total tax liability of sixty
thousand pounds. As a result of public proclamations by the
most senior of DEA staff, it was now accepted as a matter of
fact that I had well over two hundred million pounds in
Eastern bloc bank accounts. The tax man would want some,
no doubt.

Even if the British felt I had been punished enough,
Special Agent Craig Lovato was bully enough to change
their minds. During the mid-1980s, he'd almost single-
handedly mobilised the law enforcement agencies of
fourteen different countries (United States, Great Britain,
Spain, Philippines, Hong Kong, Taiwan, Thailand,
Pakistan, Germany, the Netherlands, Canada, Switzerland,
Austria, and Australia) to band together in unprecedented
international co-operation to get me locked up forever. He

would be bound to take my premature release as a personal
failure and suffer extreme loss of face. He'd get the British to
arrest me on arrival. He'd get tough with them and promise
them helicopter rides, computers, and days shopping in
Miami malls. What was waiting for me at London's Gatwick
airport?

A large-scale map appeared on the screen and indicated
we were descending over the Welsh mountains. Kenfig Hill
seemed a long time ago.

Two

MASTER MARKS

My earliest memory is of throwing a cat into the deep ocean from the deck of a ship. Why did I do it? I swear that I expected the cat to go for a swim, catch fish, and return triumphantly. So, I didn't know any better and mustn't blame myself. But maybe consigning Felix to a watery grave was symptomatic of a character far from nice. If it's any comfort to cat lovers, the image still haunts me. Whenever my life flashes before me, which happens not only when I'm about to die, that cat's face is the first I see.

We were on the Indian Ocean. The ship was the *Bradburn*, a 10,000-ton freighter owned by Reardon Smith and Co., Cardiff. The cat belonged to the Prince of Siam, and was the darling of the rough-and-ready ship's crew. My father, Dennis Marks, son of a boxer/coal miner and a midwife, was the skipper of the *Bradburn*, and he was coming to the end of his twenty-one years' service in the British merchant navy. He had been allowed to take my mother, Edna, schoolteaching daughter of an opera singer and a coal miner, and me on various lengthy sea journeys. Between 1948 and 1950, I went everywhere. I remember very little, just the cat. Perhaps the reason this cat is indelibly imprinted on my psyche is that when my murderous actions were discovered my father was constrained to give me a spanking in front of the crew, who were seething with hate and developing murderous intentions of their own. He has never hit me since.

The incident did not turn me into an animal lover (though I do like cats best), but it has made me very hesitant of consciously inflicting pain on any creatures. Even cockroaches in prison cells do not have to worry for their lives (except in Louisiana). And if I do have to admit to any religion, I risk the hot flames of a Christian hell and say I'm a Buddhist, especially in Bangkok.

Although most inhabitants of the South Wales coalfield spoke Dylan Thomas English rather than Welsh, my mother was an exception. Her mother hailed from the Druidic wilds of West Wales. For the first five years of my life, I spoke only Welsh. The next five years, I attended an English-speaking primary school in Kenfig Hill, the small Glamorganshire mining village where I was born. Apart from my sister, Linda (a few years my junior), I had just one real friend, Marty Langford, whose father not only owned the local ice-cream shop but also had won a nationwide competition for the best ice-cream. Marty and I were bright infants and most of the time could hold our own in schoolyard scraps.

While waiting for my 11-plus results, I decided to fall ill. I was very bored with school and needed some attention and sympathy. I had previously discovered that the mercury in a regular clinical thermometer could be flicked up almost as easily as it could be flicked down. So long as no one was watching, I could decide what temperature to be. It's true that near the thermometer's bulb a gap in the mercury line was visible, but no one examines the end. Occasionally, I could not risk flicking it up without being caught, so I shamelessly fabricated symptoms such as sore throat, dizziness, nausea, and headache, while my temperature when I was unobserved would seemingly oscillate from just below normal to 104 degrees Fahrenheit.

Very few diseases produce roller-coaster temperature graphs. One is rather unimaginatively called undulant fever, although it is sometimes referred to as rock fever or even Gibraltar fever. It tended to occur in the tropics. Apparently St Paul had it. My father had certainly had it, unless he, too, was scamming. Although the local doctor was sceptical (he knew I was at it), he had little choice other than to agree with the medical specialists' diagnosis that I, like Dad and St Paul, had contracted undulant fever. I was placed in an isolation ward in the nearest general hospital at Bridgend.

This was great stuff. Dozens of confused and interested doctors, nurses, and students surrounded my bed and were incredibly kind and considerate to me. They gave me all sorts of dope and all sorts of tests. My temperature was taken several times a day, and, unbelievably, I would sometimes be left alone with a thermometer, so I could engineer another fever. I would also take sneaky looks at enormously bulky files labelled, rather unjustly, 'Not to be Handled by the Patient'. I developed a genuine interest in medicine and an even more genuine interest in nurses. I suppose I must have had erections before, but I certainly hadn't associated their onset with leering at women. Now I did, but I still had no idea that these sensations were intimately linked with the survival of the human species.

After a few weeks of sex and drugs, I became bored again. I wanted to go home and play with my Meccano set. I stopped flicking up the thermometer and complained no more. Unfortunately, in those days hospital, like prison today, was much harder to get out of than to get into. My anxiety to leave the hospital bed took away my appetite. Accordingly, I was presenting the specialists with yet another symptom for them to log and ponder over. Eventually, by drinking gallons of Lucozade, my appetite returned, and I was discharged to undergo convalescence. My first scam was over.

In South Wales, there were more pubs than chapels and

more coal mines than schools. The local education authority sent me to a school named Garw Grammar School. Garw is the Welsh for rough, presumably referring to the terrain rather than the inhabitants. An old-fashioned co-educational grammar school, it lay at the dead end of a valley which was an eleven-mile, forty-five-minute, fun-filled school bus journey away from my home. Sheep were often to be seen wandering through the schoolyards, and occasionally they would attempt to graze in the classrooms.

I received an intensive crash-course in the facts of life, which form the first few lessons of the unofficial syllabus of any Welsh grammar school. I was told that a carefully handled erection could produce intense pleasure through ejaculation and that a well-guided ejaculation could produce children. The techniques of masturbation were painstakingly explained. In the privacy of my bedroom, I tried. I really did. Over and over again. I tried very hard indeed. Nothing. This was terrible. I didn't mind not having kids. I just wanted to come, like everybody else, and my inability to do so plagued and depressed me. I had yet to realise that if one had to fail at anything, one would choose failing to become a wanker.

I had stopped scrapping and fighting, partly because I had lost the knack, i.e., I was getting beaten, and partly because I couldn't stand physical contact with boys. The nurses had spoiled me. God bless them.

Mutual masturbation in the sports and physical training lessons was not unknown, and the idea of being coerced to participate and admit my shortcoming (and demonstrate my no-coming) terrified me. Relying on my increased medical knowledge and, once again, flicking the mercury thermometer, I developed a mysterious illness and was excused from all school physical activities. This rendered me a wimp (though the word then and there was sissy) in the eyes of my peers. My ability to do well in school examinations made me into a swot, which in some ways was worse. My life was not going the way I wanted it to: girls ignored me and boys made fun of me. Some radical changes were necessary.

Elvis Presley clearly suffered from none of these problems. I watched his movies and listened to his records endlessly. I read everything about him. I copied his hairstyle, tried to look like him, and attempted to sound and move like him. I failed. But I was getting there, or so I thought. After all, I was slim, tall, dark-haired, and thick-lipped; and by standing up straight I could even lose my round shoulders and pot-belly. Also, since the age of six, I had been taking twice-weekly piano lessons at a neighbour's home. To my parents' dismay, I now stopped practising *Für Elise* and the 'Moonlight' Sonata in the early morning and directed my talents towards giving note-perfect renditions of *Teddy Bear* and *Blue Suede Shoes* to an imaginary audience.

At school, I decided to become really mischievous. This, I hoped, would make me unpopular with the staff and popular with my classmates. To a large extent it did, but my lack of physical toughness continued to bestow upon me an aura of wimpishness, and I was subject to occasional bullying. I didn't yet have sufficient pluck to pull out my Elvis card. What I needed was a bodyguard.

There were no organised extra-curricular activities at the Garw Grammar School because most of the pupils lived in scattered and fairly isolated mining communities. Each village had its own social life and its own youth, only a few of whom attended a grammar school the other end of the valley. Each village also had its tough kid. Kenfig Hill's was Albert Hancock, an extremely wild and strong James Dean look-alike, a few years my senior. I used to see him around, but I was scared stiff of him. So were most people when they were sober. It was impossible to conceive of a better bodyguard. How on earth could I befriend him? It was easier than I thought. I supplied cigarettes and asked him to show me how to inhale. I made myself available to run errands for him. I 'lent' him money. A long-lasting alliance began to develop. My schoolfriends were too intimidated to taunt me further: Albert's fierce reputation was known for miles around. When I was fourteen, Albert took me to a pub to sample my first pint. There was an old piano in the bar. With alcoholic courage, I strolled over and accompanied myself singing *Blue Suede Shoes*. The clientele loved it. The good times had begun.

The good times ended about a year later when my father discovered the diary in which I had foolishly recorded the cigarettes I'd smoked, the beer I'd drunk, and my sexual adventures. He grounded me. I could go to school, but nowhere else. He insisted I cut off my Teddy Boy hairstyle. (Fortunately, Presley had just had his hair cut for the United States Army, so I used this punishment to some advantage.)

My 'O' levels were six months away. There was nothing to do but study for them, which I did with surprising obsession and tenacity. I passed all ten subjects with very high grades. My parents were delighted. The grounding was lifted. Astonishingly, Albert was also over the moon about my results: his best friend was a combination of Elvis and Einstein. The good times began again.

My new-found freedom coincided with the opening in Kenfig Hill of Van's Teen and Twenty Club. Visiting bands would play at least once a week, and more often than not, I was invited to sing a few numbers. I had a very small repertoire (*What'd I Say*, *Blue Suede Shoes*, and *That's All Right Mama*), but it always went down well. Life became almost routine. Weekdays at school were devoted to the study of my 'A' level subjects of Physics, Chemistry, and Mathematics. Week nights from 5.30 p.m. to 9.30 p.m. were similarly devoted. All the rest of my waking time was spent drinking in pubs, dancing and singing in Van's, and taking out girls.

Early one spring evening, at the request of several Chubby Checker imitators, I was trying to play *Let's Twist Again* on the piano in the lounge bar of The Royal Oak, Station Road,

Kenfig Hill. The already fading light was suddenly further darkened by the arrival of five large local policemen who had come to check the age of the pub's customers. The landlord, Arthur Hughes, was never very good at guessing ages. I was not yet eighteen. I was breaking the law. One of the policemen I recognised as PC Hamilton, a huge Englishman who had recently taken up residence in the village. He lived a stone's throw from my house. Hamilton walked up to me.

'Stop that racket right now.'

'Carry on playing, Howard. It's not illegal. It should be, mind,' said Albert Hancock.

I played a little slower.

'I've told you once to stop that racket,' snarled Hamilton.

'Bugger 'im, Howard. He can't stop you playing. Fancy doing the twist, Hamilton, and get some of that fat off?'

The pub cackled with laughter at Albert's audacious wit.

'Watch it, Hancock,' warned Hamilton. 'I've got a Black Maria outside just waiting for you.'

'Well, bring her in, Hamilton. There's no colour bar here.'

To the accompaniment of more laughter, I started to play the first few bars of Jerry Lee Lewis's *Great Balls of Fire*. I played loud and fast. Hamilton grabbed my shoulder.

'How old are you, son?'

'Eighteen,' I lied confidently. I had been drinking in pubs for over three years, and no one had ever questioned my age. To add some insolence, I grabbed my pint of bitter and drank some of it. I was already too drunk.

'What's your name, son?'

'Why do you want to know? If I'm eighteen, I can drink here whatever my name is.'

'Come outside, son.'

'Why?'

'Just do as I say.'

I carried on playing until Hamilton dragged me outside. He took out his notebook and pencil, Dixon of Dock Green style.

'Now, give me your name, son.'

'David James.'

To my knowledge, there was no such person.

'I thought I heard your friends call you Howard.'

'No. My name's David.'

'Where do you live, son? I know I've seen you around somewhere.'

'25, Pwllygath Street.'

There was such an address, but I had no idea who lived there.

'Where do you work, son?'

'I'm still in school.'

'I thought you looked young, son. Well, I'll just check on this information you've given me. I'll find you if it's wrong. Goodnight, son.'

I went back inside and got bought loads of drinks.

It wasn't until I got up the next morning that I realised how stupid I had been. Hamilton would quickly find out that there was no David James at 25, Pwllygath Street, and I was as likely as not to run into Hamilton the next time I ventured out of the house. I began to get worried. I was going to get caught and be charged with drinking under age and giving the police false information. There would be a court case. It would be written up in the *Glamorgan Gazette* alongside Albert Hancock's latest vandalous exploit. I would certainly be grounded, maybe worse.

Although my father disapproved of smoking, drinking, and gambling, he always forgave any of my transgressions if I told him the truth. I confessed to him the events of the previous night. He went to see Hamilton and told him what a good boy and clever student I was. Hamilton expressed scepticism, citing Albert Hancock as an unlikely source of good influence. Somehow or other, my father won the day. Hamilton agreed not to pursue the matter any further.

My father delivered me a serious lecture. I learned a few things: I, like most people, behaved stupidly when drunk, policemen could cause problems, my father was a good man, and criminal charges could be dropped.

King's College, University of London, had invited me to be interviewed for a place to read Physics. I looked forward to the trip, the first one I had ever undertaken alone. Physics was still coming easily to me, and the interview presented me with no worries. My mind was more concerned with visiting Soho, a place Albert had discussed at length with me on several occasions.

After a four-hour train journey terminating at Paddington, I bought a tourist map, caught a tube to the Strand, and dealt with my interview at King's College. The questions had proved to be straightforward. I worked out which underground stations were close to Soho Square and killed time so as to arrive there by nightfall. I walked down Frith Street and Greek Street. I couldn't believe it. The place really was like Albert had said. There were strip-clubs and prostitutes everywhere. I had never seen either before. I saw the clubs and bars I had read about in the *Melody Maker* and the *New Musical Express*: the Two I's, the Marquee, the Flamingo, and Ronnie Scott's. Then the sexiest girl I had ever seen asked if I wanted to spend some time with her. I explained I didn't have much money. She said not to worry. I told her my name was Deke Rivers (the name of the character Elvis played in *Loving You*). She was called Lulu. Through Wardour Street I accompanied her to St Anne's Court, and we went into a flat. I gave her everything I had – two pounds and eight shillings. She gave me just a little bit of what she had, but it was more than enough. I walked to Hyde Park, then to Paddington. After a couple of hours' passenger-spotting, I caught the two o'clock 'milk train' back to Bridgend. I had lots to tell my friends.

King's College accepted me on the understanding I would get good enough 'A' levels. I'd make sure I'd get them. I couldn't wait to get back to Soho. I got Grade A in each subject. Herbert John Davies, headmaster of Garw Grammar School, had other ideas. It was an overwhelming surprise when he took me aside one day and said that he wanted me to sit the Oxford University Entrance Scholarship Examination. It had been at least eight years since anyone from the Garw Grammar School had attempted to get into Oxford. He had been successful and was, in fact, the headmaster's son, John Davies, who read Physics at Balliol College. The headmaster suggested that I try to do precisely that. I had not actually heard of Balliol. The headmaster suggested that I read Anthony Sampson's *Anatomy of Britain* in order both to learn something of Balliol and to increase my general knowledge. The section dealing with Balliol was very impressive and intimidating. The list of Balliol men included far too many Prime Ministers, Kings, and eminent academics to warrant my even conceiving of being admitted. Still, what was there to lose? If I failed I could always get a place at King's College, London, and go to see Lulu.

Sometime during the autumn of 1963 I sat two examination papers sent from Oxford to the grammar school. One was on physics, which was no problem, and another was a general paper, which was virtually incomprehensible. One of the questions was: 'Is a copy of *The Times* more useful than a Thucydides or a Gibbon?' I had heard of neither Thucydides nor Gibbon and had never seen a copy of *The Times*. This question remained unanswered, as did most of them. In answer to one of the questions, I did attempt to write some justification of why pop singers earned more than hospital ward sisters, based on the fact that pop singers had no minimum wage guarantee, but I doubt if it was convincing.

Preparing for the preliminary interview at Balliol was a nerve-racking experience. My hair was extremely long, larded with Brylcreem, and combed in a Teddy Boy style with a quiff over my forehead. My parents insisted it be cut, and I reluctantly complied. I had, at last, finished reading

Anatomy of Britain, and, again at the advice of my headmaster, was struggling with Hemingway's *The Old Man and the Sea*. At that point, the only works of classical or contemporary literature that I'd read, unless one counts those of Leslie Charteris and Edgar Wallace, were *Oliver Twist* and *Julius Caesar*, both of which had been included in my 'O' level English literature syllabus, and *Lady Chatterley's Lover*, which had not. In physics I had not read anything outside the 'S' level curriculum and was dreading being asked about relativity or quantum mechanics, which to this day I cannot fully understand.

The Old Man and the Sea was abandoned when the Bridgend to Oxford train reached Cardiff, and I settled down in the buffet carriage to drink numerous cans of beer. We had to change trains at Didcot. I sat opposite a man holding a pair of handcuffs, and I saw Oxford's dreaming spires for the first time.

A couple of hours later I was in Balliol College waiting outside the interview room. Also waiting was another interviewee. I put out my hand.

'Hello. My name's Howard.'

He looked puzzled and put his hand in mine as if he expected me to kiss it.

'Which school are you from?' he asked.

'Garw.'

'What?'

'Garw.'

'Where's that?'

'Between Cardiff and Swansea. Not far from Bridgend.'

'I'm sorry. I don't understand you.'

'Glamorgan,' I answered.

'Oh, Wales!' he said disdainfully.

'Which school are you from?' I asked.

'Eton,' he said, looking down at the floor.

'Where's that?' I couldn't resist asking.

'The school! Eton. The school!'

'Yeah, I've heard of it, but where is it?'

'Windsor.'

The Etonian was the first to be interviewed, and I pressed my ear against the doorframe to hear his long, articulate recital of various sporting accomplishments. I felt apprehensive. Despite being a keen rugby fan, I had not participated in any physical exercise or sports since I was twelve years old, when I was mistakenly picked to play as a second-row forward for the school 'B' team. Any confidence I had in handling this interview disappeared.

After about twenty minutes the door opened, the Etonian exited, and the doorframe was filled with the imposing figure of the Ancient Greek historian Russell Meiggs. He had magnificent shoulder-length greying hair, and I now regretted acquiescing in my parents' insistence on my visiting the barber before I left Wales. Russell Meiggs made me feel completely at ease, and we talked at length about Welsh coal mines, the national rugby team, and the Eisteddford. I made him laugh on a number of occasions, and the interview was over in no time. The physics interview was a much more sombre affair, and I quickly realised that I could not joke my way through this one. Luckily, the questions were all based on the 'A' level curriculum. Overnight accommodation had been secured at a bed-and-breakfast in Walton Street, where I had deposited my suitcase after arriving at Oxford railway station. My straight suit was hurriedly exchanged for my Teddy Boy outfit, and I dashed into the nearest public house to drink myself stupid.

A couple of months later, I was again summoned to Balliol. This time the reason was to sit a number of Entrance Scholarship examinations. These were spread over a period of a few days, and we were expected to reside in the College. I had explained in full detail to my parents the nature of Russell Meiggs's hairstyle, but to no avail: the mandatory haircut was again imposed.

On arrival at Balliol, I joined the other candidates, who

were gathered in the Junior Common Room. The Etonian was nowhere to be seen. I felt shy and inhibited. Each attempt I made at conversation was greeted with mocking laughter aimed at my Welsh accent. Eventually, I talked to another grammar school boy, who was from Southampton. He too intended to read Physics and also seemed to feel as out of place as I did. His name was Julian Peto, and he has remained absolutely my best friend to this day. We dutifully attended the Examination Schools every morning and afternoon and, equally dutifully, got completely drunk every evening. A few more interviews were somehow managed, and I returned home without making any further friendships and certainly not expecting to visit Oxford again.

Sometime during the first half of December 1963, a letter from Balliol arrived at my home in Wales. I gave it to my father to open. The expression of delight on his face conveyed the letter's contents. Contrary to numerous reports which later appeared in newspapers during the 1970s and 1980s, I had not been awarded a Scholarship. I had, however, been granted a place.

The news that I had been successful in my attempt to enter Oxford University swept through Kenfig Hill. Balliol College had just won *University Challenge*, which increased the awe and respect that I was accorded. I couldn't walk down the street without being congratulated by everyone I met. I was made Head Prefect of the school. My success went completely to my head, and I have been living off it to some extent ever since. The rest of the year was spent basking in the glory of my surprising achievements. I kept my eyes open for mentions of Balliol in the media but saw only one article. It described the new Balliol fad of smoking marijuana, about which I then knew nothing, and the concern of the Master of Balliol, Sir David Lindsay Keir, about its propensity for encouraging idleness.

Before attending Balliol as a freshman, I had to acquire various items that had been suggested in lists sent by college tutors and officials. These included a cabin trunk, college scarf, books, and gown (short). Accompanied by two very proud parents, I spent a few days in Oxford purchasing these articles. We visited Balliol College, of course, but it was deserted and lifeless apart from the odd American tourist staring, with unconcealed disappointment, at the gardens. All our purchases were neatly packed into the cabin trunk except the college scarf, which I retained to improve my chances while hitch-hiking through Europe.

In early October 1964, I began life as a Balliol undergraduate. I was assigned a small, drab room on the ground floor, overlooking St Giles' and vulnerable to inspection by passers-by. The traffic noise was the worst that I had ever encountered in sleeping quarters, and the window provided me with the first, though unfortunately by no means the last, opportunity of looking at the outside world through bars. An elderly gentleman wearing a white jacket knocked on the door, opened it, walked in, and said, 'I be your scout, George.'

I had not been forewarned of the existence of scouts and had no idea what function this kindly gentleman served. My first thought was that he was something to do with sports activities. George and I spent a long time talking to each other, and he explained that his duties included making my bed, cleaning my room, and washing my dishes. I found this information totally astonishing. Up to that point, I had never eaten at a restaurant with waiter service, had never had my bag carried by a porter, and had never stayed at a hotel.

Dining in Hall was quite frightening. I had no idea what to talk about and was very concerned about exhibiting bad table manners. I felt very out of place and quite miserable, but Julian Peto, who had been admitted to Balliol as a Scholar, would always pull me out of it.

A Freshman's Fair was held at the Town Hall. Julian and I attended to see what was on offer. None of the various societies and clubs appealed to us. Three pretty girls approached and invited us to join the Oxford University

Conservative Association. Julian, a member of CND, and a sincere socialist born to humanist parents, walked off in disgust while I lingered, overcome by feminine charm. To prolong this enjoyable encounter, I agreed to become a member and parted with a few shillings for the privilege of doing so. My parents, on later hearing of this treachery, were absolutely livid. I did not attend any of the Party's meetings and never again set eyes upon those three beautiful ladies. The only possible repercussion of this impulsive foolishness was the probability of its documentary record being favourably regarded by those ultimately responsible for recruiting me as an agent for MI6, the British Secret Service.

I wandered along to the Oxford Union. Having attended a dance at Swansea University Union some months earlier, I presumed that if there was any action, rock music, alcoholic frivolity, promiscuity etc., it would be found at the Union. I paid approximately eleven pounds for a life membership and have not been there since. My life membership card, however, remained in my wallet until confiscated by the United States Drug Enforcement Administration in July 1988.

The Physics tutorials that I was obliged to attend were surprisingly relaxed affairs, and I managed to keep my head above water. I abandoned university lectures when I realised that they were not in any way compulsory. Physics students, however, were expected to spend inordinately lengthy periods of time at the Clarendon Laboratories, performing a seemingly interminable series of mindless experiments with pendulums, lenses, and resistors. I loathed this part of the course and dreaded the time spent there. Soon, I abandoned that too.

Although I had little, possibly nothing, in common with my fellow Physics students (excepting, of course, Julian Peto), there was certainly no feeling of animosity towards me. Other Physics freshmen were courteous towards me and seemed now to be able to comprehend my heavy Welsh lilt.

I gradually met Balliol students outside of the Natural Science faculty and formed the opinion that arts undergraduates, particularly historians and philosophers, were a far more interesting and non-conforming bunch than scientists. Some of them even had long hair and wore jeans. I developed a nodding acquaintance with them.

My sexual adventures were confined to females not attached to the university. I assumed that university girls were not the type to go to bed with me or anyone else. This ridiculous assumption was the result of my Welsh coalfield upbringing, where there was no overlap whatsoever between girls who studied and girls who would 'do it'. The ones that 'did it' would invariably be girls who had left school as soon as they could, and they would tend to work in Woolworth's, betting shops, or factories. Consequently, my first sexual liaisons in Oxford were initiated in the Cornmarket Woolworth's store and the odd street encounter. Most of the latter seemed to be with foreign students attending nursing and secretarial colleges. The illusion of British blue-stocking celibacy became further entrenched.

Halfway through my first term a notice appeared in the Porter's Lodge at Balliol College announcing: 'The following gentlemen will read essays to the Master on . . . The subject will be "The Population Problem".' My name then followed along with six others whose surnames also began with L, M, or N. I was not aware there was a population problem. About a week's notice was given, and I was very nervous. I hurriedly withdrew some books from the college library, and shamelessly copied huge chunks. Someone informed me that Sir David Lindsay Keir, Master of Balliol, used these essay readings to determine how well freshmen could hold their sherry. This gave me some comfort.

Fortunately, I was not one of the three gentlemen chosen to read an essay. I drank an enormous amount of sherry and had a long conversation with Sir David about the origins of the Welsh language and its grammatical peculiarities. He was of the belief that Welsh was a purely Celtic language with grammatical features akin to those of Gaelic and Breton. I, on the other hand, steadfastly maintained that the aboriginal Welsh was pre-Celtic with unique grammatical oddities such as the regulated mutations of the beginnings of nouns. A few weeks later, he told me that I might have been right. Sir David had not, up to the time of our conversation, been aware of the admittedly disputed fact that America had been discovered in AD 1170 by Prince Madoc ab Owain Gwynnedd, whose followers bequeathed elements of the Welsh language to the Padoucas Indians. Keeping my sherry glass full, Sir David listened with polite interest to my detailed account of this esoteric history.

Also present at this essay reading (or, in my case, non-essay reading) were freshmen John Minford and Hamilton McMillan, each of whom had a very significant effect on my life. John Minford was immediately convinced that I was a talented actor and persuaded me to join the Balliol Dramatic Society. Hamilton McMillan, years later, was convinced that I would make a talented espionage agent and persuaded me to work for MI6. It is strange to think that had my surname not begun with M, I would have suffered neither the glare of stage lights nor the attention of the world's media.

To entice me into participating in Balliol Dramatic Society activities, John Minford asked if I would be prepared to play the part of First Yob in the Balliol College/Lady Margaret Hall Christmas pantomime, *The Sleeping Beauty*. It was a small part, which consisted of uttering a few appropriate, timely obscenities and lying around looking either vaguely menacing or perversely seductive. I agreed on condition that Julian Peto be persuaded to play the part of Second Yob.

My membership of the Balliol Dramatic Society led to my befriending other members, and I soon became adopted into a group of largely second-year Balliol undergraduates, often

referred to as 'The Establishment'. These included Rick
Lambert, the current editor of the *Financial Times*, and Chris
Patten, currently Governor of Hong Kong. They were all
heavy drinkers and very entertaining. 'The Establishment'
also formed the core of the Victorian Society, and I was
invited to become a member. It was a strange society, to say
the least, but again the main requirement was to down large
amounts of drink, this time port, which I had never tried.
Each member was obliged to sing a Victorian song to the
audience of other members, and further obliged to sing
different Victorian songs at subsequent meetings. The
officers of the society permitted me to sing the same song on
each occasion. The song was a Welsh hymn, *Wele Cawsom Y
Mesiah*, sung to the tune of *Bread of Heaven*.

The pantomime went well, and a cast party was held. I
made a disgusting exhibition of myself by attempting to
imitate Elvis Presley while the main vocalist of Oxford
University's most illustrious rock group, The Blue Monk
and His Dirty Habits, was taking a break. As a consequence
of this, I began my first affair with a university undergraduate, the rivetingly glamorous Lynn Barber of St Anne's
College. No more Woolworth's girls for a while.

The room next door to me was far more spacious and
attractive than mine. I would sometimes spend time there,
often accompanied by Harold Macmillan's grandson,
Joshua Macmillan, who was a very close friend of the
occupant. For some reason, the room became vacant, and I
took it over.

My new quarters considerably enhanced my potential for
entertaining guests. A few days after I moved in, Joshua
visited and warned me that I would be likely to get lots of
visitors in the middle of the night, particularly at weekends.
The reason for this was that the bars of the window were
removable, thereby giving an extraordinarily easy access to
the street. The secret was known by a dozen or so friends of
Joshua, and they would like to continue to make use of the

facility. The removable bars also dramatically facilitated my nocturnal entries and exits as well as those of my friends, all of whom soon shared the secret. My room became a popular late-night venue. Interruptions at 4 a.m. by others seeking access were occasionally inconvenient, but they gave rise to the broadening of my circle of adventurous Balliol students and loose women.

At the beginning of each term, returning students would have to sit 'collections', examinations designed to test the previous term's progress. The examination papers were very likely to be lying around one of the physics tutors' college rooms. A preview of the papers would solve the problem of how to make a satisfactory showing at the examination. This, of course, would require clandestinely entering the tutors' rooms and searching through their desks. A couple of days before the beginning of my second term, I made a tour of inspection of the exterior of the rooms of Dr P. G. H. Sandars and Dr D. M. Brink. They were locked, but Dr Sandars' room was on the ground floor. The following night, at about 3 a.m., I crept across the deserted college grounds, opened the window, and, armed with a torch purchased that afternoon, proceeded to search Dr Sandars' desk. After about half an hour, I gave up. There were no collection papers to be seen. Prowling around was relatively safe, so I had a look at Dr Brink's room. This, too, was on the ground floor, but the window was inaccessible and tightly shut. I wandered around trying to figure out a way of getting into Dr Brink's room, in which I was convinced the elusive collection papers would be found. It then came to mind that Wally, the venal night porter, kept in the Porter's Lodge what appeared to be a full set of duplicate keys. I strolled across the quad to my room, got out of my window into St Giles', walked to the Porter's Lodge, and asked Wally to let me in. Once inside I told him that I had locked myself out of my room with the key still inside. He asked for my room number, and I gave him Dr Brink's. He handed me the key to Dr Brink's room and asked me to return it to him when I had retrieved my original. I proceeded to Dr Brink's room, opened the door, immediately found a stack of collection papers, took one, and returned the key, together with another half-crown tip, to a very grateful Wally. I passed the collection examination with flying colours.

Balliol undergraduates often spoke of a character named Denys Irving, who had been rusticated from Oxford and had sensibly spent his period of banishment from the city walls visiting exotic parts of the world. He had recently returned from his voyages of discovery and was about to visit, presumably illegally, his friends at Oxford. I was invited to meet him. Denys had brought with him some marijuana in the form of kif from Morocco. Up to that point I had heard the odd whisper of drugs being taken at the university and was aware that marijuana was popular with British West Indian communities, jazz enthusiasts, American beatniks, and the modern intellectual wave of Angry Young Men. I had no idea of marijuana's effects, however, and, with a great deal of enthusiastic interest, I accepted the joint that Denys offered and took my first few puffs. The effects were surprisingly mild but quite long-lasting. After just a couple of minutes, I started having a sensation akin to butterflies in the stomach but without the customary feelings of trepidation. This led to a desire to laugh followed by my interpreting most of the conversation as amusing enough for me to do so. I then became acutely aware of the music that was being played, James Brown's *Please Please Please*, and of the aesthetic qualities of my immediate environment. Each of these experiences was completely new to me and highly enjoyable. My next sensation was of the slowing-down of time. Finally I became hungry, as did everyone else, and invaded the premises of what later became the Sorbonne French restaurant, but was then the Moti Mahal, in a street appropriately named The

High. This was my first experience of Indian food, and I became addicted to it for life.

After endless bhajis, kurmas, pilaos, doopiazas, and other curries, the effects of the marijuana gradually wore off, and I invited the entire group to come back to my room, where we smoked numerous joints and listened to doo-wop music on my rather antiquated tape recorder. One by one, we passed out.

The next morning was George's day off. He was replaced by a scout who did not share his liberal attitude to carryings-on in college rooms and, on seeing the battlefield that was my room, promptly threatened to report it to the Dean. My newly found friends decided to headquarter themselves in my room for the day. Further friends of theirs from all over Oxford were invited to join the gathering. Someone turned up with a record player and a box of records. Others turned up with different types of marijuana and hashish. Loud Rolling Stones and Bob Dylan music blared, and cannabis smoke poured out into St Giles' and into the Elizabethan section of Balliol's back quad. During the early evening, Denys Irving returned to London, and the 'happening' slowly faded out.

The next day, Joshua Macmillan died from respiratory obstruction, resulting from an overdose of Valium and alcohol. I saw his body being carried down the stairs. It was the first human corpse I had ever seen. Joshua's death was tragic in every respect. Although people speculated that it might have been suicide, this was entirely inconsistent with his recent behaviour. He had taken a cure for heroin in Switzerland and claimed not to be using it any more. He also maintained that he only ever took barbiturates or alcohol when there was no marijuana to be found. Joshua and I were by no means close friends; we were simply acquaintances. His death, however, had a profound effect on me and forced me to carefully examine my attitudes to drug-taking.

Shortly after Joshua's death, my pigeon-hole contained a summons to see the Dean, Francis Leader McCarthy Willis

Bund, as soon as possible. He came straight to the point. As a result of Joshua's death, there would be inquiries by the police and Proctors (university police) regarding drug-taking in the University, with particular emphasis on Balliol. The Dean was making his own preliminary investigation and he had good reason (information from George's stand-in) to start this investigation by asking me some questions. Did I take drugs? Who else did? Where were they taken? I explained that I had smoked marijuana a couple of times but that I was not prepared to give him names of others who might have also done so. The Dean seemed greatly relieved at my refusal to name others, and I've not forgotten the look on his face, which has since carried me through all sorts of unpleasant interrogations. He finished the meeting by asking me to have a quiet word with anyone I knew who did smoke marijuana, begging them not to do so on the college premises.

The following weekend, the *Sunday Times* review section featured an article headlined 'Confessions of an Oxford Drug Addict', which was mainly an interview with a close friend of Joshua's. A number of articles with similar themes appeared in other newspapers as a result of the University having been invaded by journalists wishing to write a story following up the death of Harold Macmillan's grandson. The most unlikely students were bending over backwards to confess to some reporter their flirtation with Oxford's drug culture. Marijuana smokers were popping up all over the place, and it was considered fairly unfashionable not to be one. Having fortuitously penetrated the drug culture a couple of days prior to the national exposé, I was accorded the status of one of its pioneers. I did absolutely nothing to dispel this misconception. It was, therefore, no surprise to anyone else, but slightly surprising to me, that I was issued with a summons to appear before the Proctors 'in connection with a confidential matter'. I immediately sought the advice of the Dean, who was now getting very concerned at all the unwelcome attention Balliol was attracting. We spent quite a long time together in his room, and I must have given him my life story. During our conversation, I developed the beginnings of an enormous liking and respect for him, and it seemed that he had a fatherly type of affection for me. He spoke quite a lot about his life, taking care to mention his former position as Junior Proctor, and how Proctors generally were a bad lot. He advised me to behave with them in precisely the same way as I had done with him when first questioned.

I turned up to see the Proctors. The Senior Proctor was David Yardley, a stern, police-interrogator type of individual. I refused to answer all questions on the grounds that it was against my ethical code to incriminate other people. I was dismissed with a 'You'll hear from us later.'

I walked out of the building, and the Dean was waiting outside. He asked, 'Did you stand up to that damnable pair?'

I told him that I had, but expressed my concern that they were likely to punish me for my silence. The Dean reassured me by saying that if that should happen, they would have to cope with his resignation. I believed him, and, from that day on, we had an unbreakable bond of friendship.

I determined to become a dedicated beatnik (the word 'hippie' had not yet been invented). Brylcreem was abandoned, and my hair just flopped onto my shoulders. Drainpipe trousers were exchanged for frayed jeans, winkle-pickers for Spanish leather boots, long velvet-collared jacket for a short denim one, and a white mackintosh for a sheepskin coat. I smoked as much marijuana as I could get my hands on, read Kerouac, listened to Bob Dylan and Roland Kirk, and attended French movies I didn't understand. My whole life seemed to have changed dramatically except for my promiscuity and avoidance of academic work.

On June 11th, 1965, a bunch of us went up to London to attend Wholly Communion at the Royal Albert Hall. This was a modern poetry conference featuring Allen Ginsberg,

Lawrence Ferlinghetti, John Esam, Christopher Logue, Alexander Trocchi, and other notables. It turned out to be the largest audience ever assembled to hear poetry in this country and the first genuine large-scale 'happening'. Peace and love, getting stoned and making love. A new generation was taking over. I wanted to be part of it.

I spent Oxford's very long vacations in filthy clothes hitch-hiking fairly randomly around Great Britain and Europe in the belief that I was somehow 'On the Road'. My European travels included a visit to Copenhagen, where I ran out of money. Luckily, I had made friends with members of a Danish rock-and-roll group, who very kindly allowed me to sing with them on a few occasions, thereby earning enough to leave the country. The route back to the United Kingdom took me through Hamburg, where my friend Hamilton McMillan lived. Mac had given me his address, and I telephoned him from a sordid bar in the Reeperbahn. I was looking for the Star Club, where the Beatles had been discovered. Mac was delighted to hear from me, insisted I stay a few nights at his home, and came to pick me up.

Mac assumed that I would be unlikely to be mistaken for a city gent, but even he was noticeably shocked at my outrageous, dishevelled, unkempt, long-haired, dirty appearance. He was also slightly disconcerted by the ever-increasing crowds of curious and intrigued Hamburgers who were staring fixedly at the degenerate specimen of humanity I presented. The possible reception that we both might encounter at his parents' home was filling Mac with understandable apprehension. We sat down for a few beers and his fears gradually lifted. He felt confident that after seeing me, his parents would, at least, refrain from nagging him about his lamb-chop sideburns. In fact, his parents turned out to be the most accommodating and generous hosts, although a long hot bath and a quick laundering of the dirtiest of my clothes had no doubt helped. Mac and I had a great time. He loved to display my shoulder-length hair to his friends, and I loved to be so displayed. We cemented our friendship and remained very good friends until British Intelligence and Her Majesty's Customs and Excise terminated our relationship.

For a period of about two weeks I slept rough outside the Shakespeare Memorial Theatre in Stratford-on-Avon. This meant that I was invariably first in the queue when the box office opened to sell the forty tickets it withheld until the day of performance. I would buy four tickets, the maximum that could be sold to any one person. One ticket was kept for my own use, as I had become quite a genuine Shakespeare fan by then, two would be sold at vastly inflated prices to American tourists, while one would be given, or sold at a very cheap price, to an attractive single female. She would, of course, be obliged by her ticket to sit next to me during the performance, and conversation was easy to start up. I wondered if other people played these kind of games.

During my hitch-hiking escapades, I picked up a varied assortment of ethnic rubbish, pretentious *objets d'art*, gimmicky knick-knacks, and other hippie trinkets with the intention of using them to decorate my college room. They included a 400-square-foot net used to protect fruit trees from birds, a road sign stating 'Mind the Hose', a very large Cézanne poster, and rolls of aluminium foil. I suspended the net from the room's ceiling, papered the walls with aluminium foil, and nailed the Cézanne poster to the floor. Lamps made of orange-boxes containing low-wattage coloured bulbs were carefully placed in corners, and my newly acquired record player was set up with extension speakers dotted around the walls. All and sundry were welcome to visit my quarters and bring their friends, records, alcohol, and supplies of marijuana and hashish. The rooms rapidly became the location of a non-stop party, with music continually blaring and dense clouds of marijuana smoke clouding out of the door and windows. I dropped out completely from all college activities and would rarely

venture out of my room other than to eat lunch at George's
workers' café in the market or dinner at the Moti Mahal in
The High.

The fame of this dope-smoking haven, enshrined and
protected by College and University, had spread far
and wide. The occasional student visitor from the Sorbonne
or Heidelberg would show up, as would the odd member of
the embryonic London underground. Marty Langford, who
was studying art, and a few other Kenfig Hill friends
dropped in. Even John Esam, one of the beat poets who had
performed at the Royal Albert Hall's Wholly Communion,
graced the premises with his presence. He turned up
unannounced in my room and offered to sell me some LSD,
which I had never heard of. Each dose was in the form of a
drop absorbed by a sugar cube. The cost of each treated
sugar cube was £3. John Esam told me that it was like
hashish, but infinitely more powerful and not the least bit
illegal. He was telling the truth on both counts. I purchased
a few cubes and stored them away for use on another day. I
made enquiries among my friends. A few had heard of LSD,
but none had taken it nor knew anyone who had. It was all
very mysterious. Someone said that LSD was like mescaline,
which Aldous Huxley had written about. Someone else said
that a Harvard scientist, Timothy Leary, had experimented
with LSD and written about it.

About a week or so later, I was invited by Frances Lincoln,
a vivacious Somerville student, to come to her rooms for tea.
On the strangest of impulses, I decided that this would be an
opportune moment to take one of the sugar cubes, and I ate
one about an hour or so before my appointment. No
discernible effect had occurred by the time I left Balliol, and
when I reached Somerville I concluded that I must have been
well and truly conned into the purchase of this so-called
wonder drug. Halfway through eating my teacake, the effects
suddenly hit me. The pictures on the wall came to life, the
flowers in the vases breathed heavily and rhythmically, and

the Rolling Stones record that was being played sounded like a Handelian heavenly choir singing to the accompaniment of African tribal drumming. It was impossible to explain to Frances what was happening inside my head, but she was politely intrigued by my descriptions. When the four Beatles on the front of the album cover of *Please Please Me* jumped up and played, I said I ought to leave. Frances escorted me back to Balliol and left me at the front gate. I wandered around the quads and the Junior Common Room in a giggling stupor. Fellow students were used to seeing me in various states of intoxication, and I doubt if my condition occasioned any alarm. At about midnight, a full eight hours after ingesting the sugar cube, the effects wore off, and I went to bed.

The next few weeks, spent partly in Oxford and partly in Wales, were devoted to finishing off the sugar cubes. Several friends joined me in this experimentation. John Esam came again, and I purchased more sugar cubes. I took one which resulted in what came to be generally known as the 'horrors'. These are extremely difficult to describe. Instead of finding the LSD experience an amusing, interesting, thought-provoking state of instant Zen, replete with benign and wondrous hallucinations, one finds it frightening and grave, and one experiences instant psychosis. Flowers no longer gently breathe. They turn into werewolves and bats. The hallucinations turn into menacing demons. It's not funny, and I became uncharacteristically depressed and perturbed about the meaning of life, its futility, and my identity. Although the severe effects wore off after the usual time period, the problems they caused remained. I was convinced that the only way to resolve these problems was to take more LSD and try to come to grips with whatever was disturbing me. This didn't work. The 'horrors' continued to manifest themselves in diverse forms. Between acid trips I read anything I thought remotely relevant to the LSD experience: Aldous Huxley's *Heaven and Hell*, *Doors of Perception*, and *Island*; Evan Wentz's translation of *The Tibetan Book of the*

Dead; Sydney Cohen's *Drugs of Hallucination*; and Timothy Leary's *The Psychedelic Experience*. None of these did anything to dispel the intense depression I was suffering. I became unusually introverted, morose, suicidal, and probably crazy. My miserable demeanour did nothing to deter people from maintaining the almost non-stop 'happening' at my college rooms, but it seemed to have less and less to do with me. I just sat discontentedly in the corner, occasionally smiling weakly at whoever came in.

In those days it was not, for some extraordinary reason, against college rules to possess an air-rifle. I did not have one myself, but there was one lying around in my room. One evening, alone in my room, I was leaning out of the window, pointing the air-rifle at passers-by in St Giles' and yelling mindless platitudes at them. Most of those who noticed me simply ignored this puerile behaviour, but one man took particular exception. He too started yelling, saying that I had no idea what real war was like and that if I did find myself face to face with an enemy, I would be too scared to pull the trigger. I pulled the trigger. The rifle was not loaded, but the noise startled the man at whom it was carefully aimed. He set off in the direction of the Porter's Lodge with the obvious intention of grassing me. I still possessed enough good sense to dash down to the cellars, run through them, and emerge into a remote area of the College grounds. The Dean was striding purposefully from the Porter's Lodge. He saw me, and asked me to accompany him as there seemed to be some problem in the vicinity of my room. We both entered and beheld the air-rifle lying conspicuously on the floor. The Dean said that someone in the street had been shot at with this same air-rifle, and although I was clearly elsewhere and not responsible for this particular outrage, this was just one of a number of worrying instances concerning my room. He asked me to report to him in one hour.

After listening to a quick reprimand about the company I was keeping, I explained my feelings of futility and depression and their likely cause, the still not illegal use of LSD. I brought up my total neglect of studies, but the Dean seemed completely unworried by my lack of academic progress and felt it important that I should not worry about this either. He insisted that I took off the last six weeks of that particular term, concentrate on some meaningful extra-curricular work, and seriously consider a change of subject in which to take finals. He would sort things out with my tutors. The Dean had always been a keen supporter of the Dramatic Society and suggested that I re-involve myself with their activities.

I went to see John Minford to see if he knew of any openings in forthcoming drama productions. At the same time he was working on a treatment of Peter Weiss's *Marat/Sade*. There weren't any obvious parts for mind-blown Welsh hippies, but as virtually all the characters were lunatics, he was confident he could accommodate me. He gave me the part of The Singer, which entailed my looking stoned, unkempt, and menacing, and behaving like a sex maniac. I was required to sing four songs. Minford composed the music. Two were in the style of Elvis Presley and two in the style of the Rolling Stones. The part was tailor-made.

The final rehearsals and public performances took place at the Great Tithe Barn just outside Faringdon. Learning my lines, perfecting my performance, and travelling daily from Oxford to Faringdon took up many hours of each day. There was little time left for sitting around moping. Although a few of the cast cracked up under the strain of continually acting as if completely mad, I found that pretending to be crazy for much of the time prevented me from going insane the rest of the time. I ceased being morose, reverted to my previous heavy indulgences in sex, alcohol, and marijuana, and did not take LSD again for a number of years.

In the light of the Dean's advice to me, a number of my friends had suggested that I consider switching from Physics

to either Politics, Philosophy, and Economics (PPE) or
Philosophy, Physiology, and Psychology (PPP), paying
particular attention to philosophy. I talked to the Dean
about it and he arranged for me to speak with Alan
Montefiore, a PPE tutor, who gave me a short reading list
and asked me to write, before the end of term, an essay on
the definition of 'good'. Approximately eighteen hours of
each of seven days were spent struggling through a series of
texts in moral philosophy before I realised that I would
neither be able to fully understand the subject nor be capable
of contributing to it. Years later I found out that no one
completely understood moral philosophy and that non-
comprehension was by no means a bar to contribution.
Sheepishly I attempted to explain this seemingly serious
inability to Montefiore, who seemed confused by my
problem but was also extremely kind and considerate. He
offered to give his advice and assistance to me any time I
thought I might need them. I didn't change courses. I stuck
with Physics.

I was elected to organise the entertainments for the
forthcoming 700th anniversary Commemorative Ball. My
primary duty was to engage groups to supply the musical
entertainment. I had a budget of £1,000. The entertainment
manager's main goal was to try to spot talent likely to
become famous within a short period of time and book them
while they were still at a relatively low price. A daunting
precedent had been set by Magdalen College a couple of
years earlier. They had booked the Rolling Stones for a mere
£100 just before they became superstars. My knowledge of
pop music was then as good as anyone's, and I booked the
relatively unknown Spencer Davis Group and the Small
Faces for a mere pittance. Within weeks of being booked,
they both had Number One hits. Their respective managers
wanted to withdraw from the Balliol booking as this would
clash with recently offered lucrative tours. Contractually
they were obliged to appear and could be heavily sued for

not doing so. The agent suggested a solution: if I let the Spencer Davis Group and the Small Faces off the hook, I could choose artists normally costing up to about £2,500 but would only have to pay the cheap prices agreed for the original two groups. I agreed. As a result we engaged the Kinks, the Fortunes, Them, and Alan Price, all of whom were already top names. There was still money left over from the original £1,000, so I engaged an Irish showband, a string quartet, and a professional all-in wrestling bout. On the night of the ball, I smoked marijuana with Them and Alan Price and drank whisky with Ray Davies.

Final-year undergraduate students were required to live out of College in lodgings. Julian Peto, Steve Balogh, and I tried to find some. During our searches we encountered a Canadian postgraduate named Gilbert Frieson. He was living in one room of an otherwise empty house, 46, Paradise Square. He was a heroin addict with strong suicidal tendencies. He made countless suicide attempts and actually succeeded sometime during 1968 or 1969. Gilbert had absolutely no money and was about to be evicted unless he could find tenants who were prepared to rent the whole house and allow him to continue living rent-free in his room.

The house was in an atrociously bad state of repair, had once been rented by William Burroughs, and stood in the shadow of Oxford prison, a much more externally attractive penal institution than any I've since encountered. A few yards away from the house was a wonderful pub called The Jolly Farmers, which was more than prepared to serve regular drinks after time.

One morning my late lie-in was rudely disturbed by dense clouds of smoke pouring through the floorboards. Within minutes, visibility was reduced to zero. Dashing out of my room, I discovered that Gilbert's room on the first floor was on fire, with flames licking through various holes in the walls. Julian and Steve were still asleep. I kicked down Gilbert's door and became engulfed in smoke. I was unable to see

Gilbert. I was unable to see anything. After some kamikaze forays into the room, I assured myself that Gilbert wasn't there. The telephone was situated downstairs and for the first and only time in my life, I dialled 999. A number of fire engines rolled up in Paradise Square, and a large squad of firemen charged into the little terraced house, extinguished the fire, and flooded the premises. It took about two weeks to get the house back into anything vaguely resembling the appalling state it was in when we first rented it.

The news of the fire spread far faster through the University than did the fire itself through the house. The matter came to the attention of the Proctors. We were informed that our house was not a registered lodging, and unless it somehow became one we would have to seek alternative accommodation. An official deputation from those responsible for determining which lodgings could be deemed registered would be visiting within a few days. Registered lodgings required a landlord or landlady to be living on the premises, whom the deputation would have to be able to meet. For a great multitude of reasons Gilbert was not thought by us to be a suitable candidate for presentation. To solve the problem we asked the friend of a friend to pretend to be the landlady for the day that we were expecting to be visited. She was a single parent with a baby daughter, and we made up the spare room to look like the home of such a mother and child. To our great surprise, the officials were quite satisfied with what they found and accepted our premises as registered lodgings.

People were always on the look-out for cheap rooms to rent in Paradise Square, and shortly after we became registered, a couple of pleasant long-haired hippies knocked on our door and asked if we had any space to let. We rented them the 'landlady's room'. They had a great many town friends, who gradually took over the house, filling it with delightful marijuana smoke and music from Joe Cocker and Cream. Julian, Steve, and I had no objection to this development, and once again my home turned into a place where people from far and wide came to smoke marijuana and generally hang out.

The best girl I knew was a St Anne's English student, Ilze Kadegis. She was a beautiful, fiercely witty, golden-haired Latvian. She had an exotic past, present, and presence. We had dated each other off and on for about a year and spent about half our time at her lodgings, which were very close to St Anne's, and half the time at Paradise Square.

In Paradise Square Julian and I kept noticing strange people sitting in cars for long periods of time outside our house reading newspapers. One day, while I was eating lunch at Ilze's lodgings, a plain-clothes policeman came round and informed me that Oxford drug squad officers were searching my home and my presence was required. I was driven to Paradise Square, where about a dozen or so of Oxford's finest were tearing the place to bits. Steve Balogh had already been taken to the police station in St Aldate's for having a sugar cube in his jacket pocket. The police presumably thought it was LSD (now illegal). In fact it was a lump of Tate & Lyle that Balogh had appropriated from Balliol Junior Common Room. In my room the ceiling, which had been in an extremely fragile state since the fire, had collapsed, and all fittings had been wrenched from the wall. One of the policemen was proudly displaying a marijuana roach, which he claimed he found lying in the ashtray. I feigned an expression of complete surprise. The policeman told me that he was taking the roach for forensic analysis. Both my and Julian's particulars were laboriously recorded, and we were told that the police would be in touch after conducting laboratory tests on the roach and various culinary items that they had wrapped up in plastic bags.

The Dean managed to get Balogh out of custody and demanded to see the three of us. We trooped sheepishly into the Dean's room and were told that as nothing incriminating had been found on the premises, other than the roach, the drug squad would not press charges provided we were prepared to be questioned by the police in the presence of a chosen representative. The Dean strongly advised that he should be our chosen representative. We agreed and marched off to the investigation rooms in St Aldate's Police Station. We denied all knowledge of everything, including the roach. The police seemed disappointed but let us go. The Dean told us that we'd all had a very narrow escape and, given that we were taking our Finals within six months, we should knuckle down, study, and refrain from smoking marijuana with town hippies.

The Dean's counsel was sound and his words of advice were sincerely taken. We resolved to study. This resolution was facilitated by the sudden departure from Paradise Square of the hippie tenants. They were lucky enough not to have been present when the police carried out their raid and were not keen on pushing their luck any further. Julian and I began studying in earnest. I can't remember what Balogh did. Ilze joined our intensive studying programme. We were so committed that we spent the entire Easter vacation in Oxford revising, or more accurately, learning for the first time, our degree courses. We even gave up smoking marijuana on weekdays.

The work for tutorials I was now coping with easily, but somehow or other, I had to complete many months of practical physics experiments in the eight weeks that were left for me to use the Clarendon Laboratories. Not completing them severely limited the chances of getting a worth-while degree. With the assistance of the loan of practical physics workbooks completed by other students and a friendly Clarendon Laboratory Demonstrator/ Examiner who looked the other way while I stole my record card and filled in the blanks, the work was successfully completed within two weeks.

This period of study continued until Finals. Julian and I would occasionally take breaks to play table football or get drunk in The Jolly Farmers. On one occasion, about three days before Finals, our break took the form of a water-pistol fight. New machine-gun water-pistols had just come on to the market, and we had each purchased one. While tearing barefooted around the house, brandishing one of these new models, I stepped on a rusty nail protruding from a plank of wood. The pain was excruciating, and within an hour or so my leg turned purple. Julian and Ilze took me to the Radcliffe Infirmary, where I was given a series of penicillin overdoses, painkillers, and a pair of crutches. I left there unable to either think or walk, and could not study to save my life.

On the first day of Finals I was carried to the Examination Schools and given a specially located desk and chair which enabled me to maintain my leg in a horizontal position. I struggled through the first three papers but felt fairly certain I'd made a mess of them. The pain suddenly eased, and I found the next three papers much easier. I felt I'd at least passed.

Soon afterwards, we all drifted back to our various parents' homes, taking our possessions with us. After a few weeks I was summoned for a viva, an oral examination, normally used to decide borderline cases. I was not told which borderline I was straddling.

At the same time, my sixteen-year-old sister was run over by a car while on holiday with my parents in Stratford-on-Avon. My father saw her lying on the street with blood oozing from her. Whatever faith he'd had in God, it left right at that moment. Linda had survived but was critically ill with multiple injuries. She'd be lucky to make it. A miracle would be required for her ever to walk again. I rushed from Wales to her bedside at Warwick Hospital and wept bitterly at the sight of her fragile and crippled ghostliness. My parents and I have never recovered from the despair and sadness that tortured us during that summer of 1967. Nothing hurts like the pain of someone you love. With superhuman resilience and determination, my sister pulled through. After months on crutches, Linda defied predictions and walked. She bore her burden so nobly.

The degree results were displayed in the Examination Schools in The High and indicated that I had obtained a second-class honours degree. I was delighted. Ilze and Julian were also given Seconds. Strangely enough, no Balliol Physics student of that year obtained other than a second-class honours degree. This made my rather mediocre achievement seem more impressive than it was. I was probably the only Balliol physicist who was delighted with having a Second. I was pleased I had straightened out in time. Maybe I should stay straight.

Three

MR MARKS

Looking back, it seems ironical that I should have gone temporarily straight just when the rest of the country realised that England was some kind of headquarters of Sixties culture and creativity. The death penalty had been abolished; incitement to racial hatred had been outlawed; mini-skirts had become fashionable; sex had become okay; poets smoked dope, and Dylan had played electric at the Royal Albert Hall. Carnaby Street and the King's Road had become world fashion centres with Twiggy as supermodel. Mick Jagger, with support from *The Times*, had beaten a drugs charge. Students, particularly those from the London School of Economics, wielded power. Thousands of people demonstrated against war and for the legalisation of marijuana. The Duke of Bedford had hosted a Festival of the Flower Children at Woburn Abbey. British music dominated the world. Many prominent members of whatever was happening had passed through my Oxford rooms. Some had smoke their first joints there. Instead of trying to get up there with them, I decided to become a physics teacher.

Ilze, equally strangely, decided to become an English teacher. We had both been enrolled by London University to do the Postgraduate Certificate in Education and expected to gain teaching positions in London during the subsequent years. We took up residence in a spacious third-floor flat in Notting Hill. The first term of the teaching course was anything but demanding, and in my spare time I read the books that all my contemporaries had talked about during my undergraduate years. One of the first was Bertrand Russell's *History of Western Philosophy*. It was the most interesting book that I had ever read, and it led to my reading a variety of works by Plato, Aristotle, Lucretius, Locke, Berkeley, Hume, Aquinas, Leibniz, and Spinoza. This reading provoked my sincere and lasting interest in the history and philosophy of science. It dawned on me that I'd wasted all the facilities available to me at Oxford, and I longed to return there to make use of them. I wrote to those who administered the postgraduate History and Philosophy of Science courses at Oxford, expressing my interest in the subject, and they suggested I came to Oxford to be inter- viewed. I was accepted to study for the Diploma in History and Philosophy of Science (a year's course).

During late December of 1967, Ilze and I became married at my parents' local Welsh Congregational chapel. Although we revelled in each other's company, I still have no idea why we took such an extraordinarily impractical step. We had no intention of having children. We had no money. Ilze was destined to become a poorly paid primary school teacher. I was destined for goodness knew what. We took a one-night honeymoon at a bed-and-breakfast establishment in a place called Ogmore-by-Sea.

One of our wedding presents was a Go set. Go has been Japan's most popular board game for about 1500 years. Playing it well demands great skill, strategy, and patience. It is capable of infinite variety. Yet the rules and pieces are so simple that children can play. Easy handicap rules allow players of unequal skill to play together. Japanese war leaders throughout history have studied Go. Originally, it was a

Chinese game dating back at least four thousand years, when the rectangular board on which it was played was marked out on sandy beaches. Ilze and I had both played chess at an elementary level but no longer enjoyed doing so. Go was different. It was aesthetically so much more pleasing, as if one was dealing with the basic structures of life and thought.

I became very bored with the teaching course. Although I was leading a straight life, I still liked to wear my hair long and dress like a hippie, and the staff were constantly berating me for doing so. I withdrew from the course and, naturally, lost my grant. To make ends meet, I took a five-hour-a-day teaching job at a London crammer college and did some private tuition in the evenings. I befriended one of my young fellow teachers, a Welshman named Dai. We would drink at the Princess Royal in the Hereford Road, a favourite haunt of some Black South African musicians and entertainers, whom I also befriended.

A few of my Oxford undergraduate friends had also moved to London. One who had done so was Graham Plinston, a PPE student, one year my junior, who, well equipped with kif and hashish, had often frequented my Balliol rooms in 1966 before he set up his own communal dope-smoking rooms in a small village between Oxford and Woodstock. The police raided them and found some LSD. Graham was fined £50 by the police and rusticated for a year by the University.

'Howard! Hello. What are you doing in London?'

'I'm living here now, just round the corner in Westbourne Grove.'

'Really! I thought you had stayed in Oxford or gone back to Wales.'

'I guess I should have, Graham. But I'm going back to Oxford next year to do some postgraduate work.'

'That's a coincidence. I'm going back there myself next year to finish my degree. This rustication has been a bit of a pain. What are you doing with yourself these days?'

'I've got a teaching job. The rest of the time, I usually play Go.'

'What! These coincidences are getting ridiculous. I learned Go a few months ago, but now I have no one to play with. Shall we have a game?'

There were many hippie pads in London, but Graham's Lansdowne Crescent flat was an expensive hippie pad. There were not only the usual kilims on the floor and kaftans hanging off pegs, but also priceless porcelain on shelves, stacks of perfume and after-shave in the bathroom, and up-to-date gadgetry squatting in corners. It was a flat one would expect to find belonging to a successful rock singer.

Graham laid out the Go board, put on the Rolling Stones' *Their Satanic Majesties Request*, and handed me a sticky lump of aromatic Afghani hashish. I didn't hesitate. I rolled a joint. I jumped right back into it. I smoked hashish every day for the next twenty-two years.

Back at the Westbourne Grove flat, another Oxford friend, Humphrey Weightman, showed up. He had just come into some money, bought a new expensive stereo, and wanted to leave it, along with his extensive record collection, with us for safe keeping. We set it up, rolled some joints, and played the latest albums. It was great. Tensions began unwinding.

Ilze and I were natural hosts, and with the help of Humphrey's stereo and Graham's Afghani, Westbourne Grove quickly became a natural successor to Balliol and Paradise Square. Most evenings and weekends, the flat was full of people, including some newly-met Black South African musicians and minor celebrities of the time. Graham and I usually huddled in the corner playing Go, while everyone else either danced or lay down on mattresses or cushions. There was an endless supply of marijuana and hashish.

I was comforted to discover that although I found reading mathematical physics more difficult when stoned, I found reading philosophy easier. It is not that philosophy is any easier than mathematical physics. It's just that reading philosophy was actually what I wanted to do. When one is stoned, it is very hard to do what one really doesn't want to do.

My freelance tuition work required me to visit students at various times of day and night at their homes and teach on an individual basis. Such irregular schedules, combined with my increased marijuana use, inevitably led to occasions when I would be required to teach when very stoned. The first time this happened, I was asked by a nineteen-year-old Arabian student to explain to him the theory of permutations and combinations, a part of school mathematics at which I was never very proficient. Until this point my teaching abilities had not been particularly remarkable. I was far too impatient with my pupils when dealing with subjects I knew well, and I deviously avoided other subjects. Under marijuana's influence, however, I now found I was extremely painstaking with my explanations and extraordinarily patient with my pupils' progress. I ceased to feign knowledge when I had none and would honestly admit that I had forgotten everything and would have to work things out from scratch. I found it easy to put myself in the students' positions and appreciate and solve their difficulties. From then on, I made a point of smoking marijuana before teaching, and my students made excellent progress.

London was definitely an interesting place to be in 1967/1968: the Beatles provided singalong psychedelia with *Sergeant Pepper's Lonely Hearts Club Band* and established their Apple boutique, while their manager, Brian Epstein, died from an overdose of sleeping pills. The Rolling Stones took a shot of rhythm and blues out of their music and produced love and peace singles like *We Love You* and *Dandelion*, while their leader and founder, Brian Jones, struggled to get released on bail for a drug charge. Procul Harum's *A Whiter Shade of Pale* made an appropriate anthem for the junkies and housebound. Eighty thousand people (including me) marched on the American Embassy to protest against the war in Vietnam. But the dreaming spires of Oxford were too much to resist. A delightfully stoned academic career was at hand.

There was a problem with respect to how my diploma course would be financed. In those days there were two main grant-giving bodies funding postgraduate study: the Department of Education and the Science Research Council. The former limited its grants to graduates in non-scientific subjects while the latter would only fund students undertaking research degrees in the pure sciences. These regulations precluded my Philosophy of Science studies being funded by either body. A thick publication gave a complete listing of organisations that funded postgraduate study and the conditions under which they did so. I scoured through this book and discovered the Thomas and Elizabeth Williams Scholarship, which was restricted to applicants who lived in a small area of Wales which included the village in which my family lived. My mother's brother, Uncle Mostyn, was then Chairman of Glamorgan County Council. I approached him about the possibility of being awarded the Thomas and Elizabeth Williams Scholarship, and he arranged for me to be interviewed by the trustees. They agreed to pay all course fees and awarded me a maintenance grant.

Ilze and I decided that while I resumed my studies at Balliol, we should live in a romantic country cottage outside Oxford. A third-year English undergraduate, Bill Jefferson, whom I liked very much, and his girlfriend, Caroline Lee (daughter of Anthony Lee, our man in Anguilla), had similar intentions. Bill Jefferson and I combined forces to scour the countryside for suitable cottages. We became well known at an enormous number of country pubs but were making little progress at finding a place to live. Eventually, while getting drunk at a pub called The Plough in Garsington, we discovered a cottage for rent not one hundred yards from where we were drinking. The landlords were egg producers called Jennings of Garsington, and we rented the cottage for a twelve-month period. Ilze found a teaching job at a primary school in Didcot. My father had given me a beaten-up Hillman, and I would get up extremely early to drive Ilze to Oxford railway station in time for the Didcot train. The drive took place in total darkness. I would then breakfast at either Balliol, if my stomach felt strong, or at George's workers' café in the market, if feeling queasy or hungover. I usually ate at George's.

Just after my postgraduate term started, the Dean spotted me hanging around the Porter's Lodge and invited me to come and see him for a chat. He said he needed my help in sorting out what was, in his eyes, becoming a very serious problem at Balliol and, indeed, at most of the University's colleges. I fearfully assumed the problem being referred to was drug use and that the help the Dean was seeking was my becoming some sort of grass, keeping the college authorities apprised of the identities and habits of drug users. I could not have been further from the truth. The problem was not drugs but left-wing revolution. My assistance was not to become a mole but merely to refrain from participation in protests etc. and persuade the cronies that I would inevitably attract to do likewise.

Balliol had certainly become quite revolutionary by October 1968. Although the attire and appearance of student revolutionaries were almost identical to those of 1966 hippies, the attitudes were poles apart. Smoking marijuana was now regarded as some sort of stupefaction imposed on the working classes by the bourgeoisie. There didn't seem to be any revolutionary music as such, and Top Ten hits had deteriorated from *2,000 Light Years from Home* to *Me and You and a Dog Named Boo*.

During the 1960s, Balliol College life was essentially determined by the whims, preferences, and behaviour of the second-year undergraduates. First-year students were too meek to set the trends, and third-year students were apt to become distracted by Finals. During 1968, the trend was definitely one of revolutionary activity. One topic on which I agreed completely with the revolutionary students was that of racial equality. The Right Honourable Enoch Powell, MP, was giving an anti-immigration speech at Oxford Town Hall, and I participated in what turned out to be quite a violent demonstration. A few fellow participants had been brutally assaulted by police and, to add insult to injury, been charged with assault themselves. The next morning, I missed my tutorial with Michael Dummett, a chain-smoking, Go-playing, devout Christian, who later became Oxford University's Wykeham Professor of Logic but was then a Fellow of All Souls and taught me in mathematical logic. I missed the tutorial in order to make myself available at court to speak on my injured and arrested friends' behalf. I hadn't let Mr Dummett know and was feeling a little guilty. Also feeling a little guilty for missing our appointment was Mr Dummett, who had presented himself at the same court to speak up for someone else who had also been arrested during the previous night's demonstration. We burst out laughing at the sight of each other. The same day, he invited me for lunch at All Souls, where I had the privilege of sitting next to the Warden, John Sparrow. After lunch, Mr Dummett had to hurry off somewhere, and I was taken for a walk around the grounds of All Souls College by John Sparrow. Like the Dean of Balliol, he was concerned about revolutionaries and unconcerned about marijuana smoking.

One evening, Ilze and I went to a dinner hosted by one of her colleagues who taught at the school in Didcot. There were two or three other couples present, including John and Fanny Stein. John at that time was a general medical practitioner about to become a Fellow of Magdalen, while Fanny was a housewife. About halfway through the dinner, I discovered that Fanny's maiden name was Hill and that she was the daughter of Christopher Hill, David Lindsay Keir's successor as Master of Balliol. Fanny and I struck up a strong friendship. We fancied each other like mad, but newly-entered marital obligations prevailed, and we didn't have an affair with each other until long after.

Shortly after my first meeting with Fanny, I ran into Christopher Hill at a function held in the Balliol students' bar. We hardly knew each other but quickly became engaged in earnest conversation, which we both wished to continue when the function drew to a close. The Master asked if I would be prepared to buy a bottle of whisky on my account at the students' bar and bring it up to his lodgings, where he would immediately reimburse me and continue our discussions. I was delighted to do this. We got on remarkably well, and by the end of the evening Christopher had accepted my invitation to have dinner in Garsington.

Ilze was very nervous at the prospect of entertaining such distinguished guests and had no idea what kind of meal to prepare. During the previous year in London, I had befriended the chef of the local Indian restaurant and had become reasonably proficient at cooking curries. Christopher had mentioned to me how much he had enjoyed Indian cuisine while he was in India. I agreed to cook the food, which Christopher and his wife, Bridget, gratefully devoured.

Christopher had tremendous sympathy both with revolutionaries and with those who wished to smoke marijuana. He was also a source of an immense amount of information about Garsington. He mentioned that Russell Meiggs (my long-haired hero) lived only a hundred yards away from us (I had never seen him in the village) and that across an adjacent field, tucked in a hollow, was Garsington Manor, the one-time residence of the Morrell brewery heiress, Lady Ottoline Morrell, whom Christopher referred to as Lady Utterly Immoral. Apparently, Bertrand Russell, Aldous Huxley, Lytton Strachey, etc. had all been frequent guests at the manor. Weeks afterwards, after a night tripping out on the first LSD I had taken for years, I embarrassed myself by knocking on the door of Garsington Manor and asking the occupants if Aldous Huxley could come out to play.

There were isolated pockets of marijuana smokers, mainly postgraduates. One of these was at our cottage in Garsington. One regular visitor was Graham Plinston, now completing his final undergraduate year. He was always keen to play a game of Go and always brought with him a few ounces of excellent hashish. I would sometimes buy more than I needed and sell off the surplus at enough profit to pay for my own absurdly heavy consumption, which was about twenty joints a day. Bill Jefferson was close behind.

I got down to my philosophy reading. A common difficulty encountered by those beginning to study philosophy is that whatever is read appears totally convincing at the time of reading. Smoking marijuana forced me to stop, examine, scrutinise, and criticise each step before proceeding. It assisted me not only in pinpointing the weaknesses of certain philosophical theories, but also in articulating alternative philosophical viewpoints.

As part of the course, I was asked to deliver a paper to learned men assembled in an ancient seminar room at All Souls College. My assigned topic was the difference in views of space and time held by Isaac Newton and Leibniz. Newton seemed to hold that solid things existed through absolute time in absolute space, which could be considered as God's sensorium, sniffing out trouble everywhere. Leibniz, in many ways a precursor of Einstein, was a lot more hip and a lot more baffling. He seemed to maintain that space and time were shifting around out of control and that each bit of stuff had everything else in the universe as part of it. Writing about it was difficult, but I muddled through.

I became interested in confirmation theory: what evidence do scientists need to end up believing the things they do? A paradox arises when considering hypotheses of the general form 'All X are Y', for example, 'All ravens are black', together with what sort of evidence would tend to make them believable. One could begin by looking at a raven to see if it is black. If it is black, then this observation confirms the hypothesis to a limited extent. If one looked at thousands of ravens, and they were all black, then these observations would further confirm the hypothesis. 'All X are Y' is logically equivalent to 'All non-Y are non-X.' The two propositions 'All ravens are black' and 'All non black things are non-ravens' state the same fact. Therefore, observations of non-black non-ravens would confirm the hypothesis 'All ravens are black' just as much as they would 'All non-black things are non-ravens.' This leads to the counter-intuitive conclusion that observations of such things as red noses, white swans, etc. confirm the statement 'All ravens are black.' Everyone knows, of course, that they do not.

Bill Jefferson was an English literature student from Yorkshire, and he would sometimes organise poetry readings. He organised one at some college in Oxford, and brought two of the poets, Christopher Logue and Brian Patten, together with some of their entourages, back to the cottage in Garsington. A second, more informal, poetry reading took place, followed by a mammoth drinking and smoking session lasting at least a day. This, however, was quite a rare occurrence, and the cottage in Garsington never achieved the status of my previous accommodations in terms of hosting debauchery and culture.

The preponderance of student revolutionaries dominating the quadrangles and bars, the lack of both fellow marijuana smokers and fellow philosophers of science, and the paucity of books on History and Philosophy of Science in the Balliol library led to my spending less and less time in College and becoming rather disaffected with it. I was visiting Balliol no more than once a week. Ilze was most unhappy with her teaching job in Didcot, and we both thought seriously of leaving Oxford once I'd completed my diploma course. The expectation was for me to continue at Balliol with a B.Phil.

or D.Phil. course, but this could easily be done at another university. I decided on the University of Sussex, which in those days was referred to as Balliol by the sea. Brighton looked like fun. Ilze obtained the promise of employment at a convent school in Worthing. My diploma was acquired without too much difficulty, and I was beginning to feel reasonably secure about my ability to pursue an academic career. At the end of the diploma course, Christopher Hill asked if I would be interested in participating in a summer school that Balliol was organising for the benefit of teenage boys who came from deprived backgrounds. I was glad to help, and I really enjoyed my every involvement with the venture. Part of my task was straightforward teaching. Part of it was socialising with the young men with the intention of convincing them that university men were not all stuffed shirts. This was easily achieved by a pub crawl followed by the viewing of a pornographic film at the Scala cinema in Walton Street.

Ilze and I moved to Brighton and found a cheap sea-front flat. Through Christopher Logue, who rented a room in their house, we met Johnny Martin, an anthropology lecturer at the University of Sussex, and his wife Gina. We all had similar interests: marijuana, LSD, rock music, and after-eight philosophy, and we spent much time together.

I hated Sussex University. By this time, I had a firm idea of what a university should be like, and Sussex didn't come up to it. Every room had a number rather than a name. There was no romance about studying in an office-block library. One couldn't lie back and think that this was where, in the past, great minds produced great ideas. My supervisor was a Polish logician named Jerzy Giedymin. He was reckoned to be brilliant, but only in areas that no one else could test. I found him very difficult to understand, whatever he was talking about. He made it plain he had no interest in irrelevancies such as confirmation paradoxes. I made it plain I had no interest in studying his irrelevant obsessions. He said I should never have left Oxford. I said he was right.

I was still getting the Thomas and Elizabeth Williams Scholarship and spent the first term's instalment on a new stereo system. The next few months were devoted to listening to Led Zeppelin, Blind Faith, Jethro Tull, and Black Sabbath. I decided to give up academic life and withdrew from the University of Sussex. Ilze's schoolteacher's salary was barely enough to live on, but I managed to make up the shortcomings to almost survival level by getting more hashish from Graham Plinston, who often came down to Brighton for a weekend by the sea and a game of Go, at which we were both now becoming proficient.

Graham had visited Morocco, where he met Lebanese Joe. Joe's mother was an entertainer in Beirut. Joe knew Sam Hiraoui, who worked for the Lebanese airline, Middle East Airlines. Sam also had a textile business in Dubai, the great Middle East gold- and silver-smuggling port on the Persian Gulf. Sam's partner in Dubai was an Afghani named Mohammed Durrani. Graham explained that through these people he was being delivered fifty pounds of black Pakistani hashish every month or so. For the first time, I imagined what an interesting and rewarding life a smuggler's must be. But Graham was merely treating me as a confidant. He was not making me any propositions. I was just another provincial dealer selling a couple of pounds a year to survive and not wanting to do too much other than survive.

There were one or two ex-Oxford students attached to the University of Sussex. One was a brilliant mathematics lecturer, Richard Lewis, who would often visit Ilze and me along with Johnny and Gina Martin. Richard came from a relatively wealthy family, owned property in Brighton and London, drank like a fish, smoked everything at hand, thought mathematical profundities, and was a keen and talented chess player. He had heard of Go, was interested in the game, but had never played. I taught him. After a dozen games, he beat me. He still beats me.

Richard had a beautiful wife, Rosie. I couldn't take my eyes off her. At the same time, Ilze couldn't take her eyes off Johnny Martin. In no time, all six of us had grounds for suing for divorce, all three marriages were breaking up, and Richard and Rosie's daughter, Emily, was calling me Uncle Howie.

Graham Plinston's wife, Mandy, telephoned. She asked if I could come up to London to see her as soon as possible. When I got there, Mandy was distraught and crying.

'Howard, Graham has disappeared. There's something wrong. I think he's been busted. Can you go and find out? You can have all the expenses you need.'

'Where is he, Mandy?'

'He's got to be somewhere in Germany.'

'Why do you want me to go?'

'You're the straightest of Graham's friends. You don't have a record or a file on you. Can you imagine what our other friends are like? Graham was meant to meet this German guy Klaus Becker in Frankfurt. He'll probably be able to help you find Graham.'

'All right, I'll go.'

I had never flown before, and I was excited throughout the flight. At his house, Klaus told me that there'd been a bust in Lorrach, a Swiss–German border town near Basle. He suspected the person busted was Graham. I flew from Frankfurt to Basle on a scary propeller plane. Not speaking a word of German hindered progress somewhat, but I was eventually able to get newspaper back-issues from the Basle public library and found a report of the bust. Graham had been driving a Mercedes from Geneva to Frankfurt. A hundred pounds of hashish had been stuffed under the back seat and in the door panels. At the Swiss–German border, the car had been searched and the hashish found. Graham was in Lorrach prison.

I took a cab to Lorrach and walked around the streets until I found a lawyer. He went to see Graham in prison and agreed to defend him. Graham had no messages.

When I arrived back at London airport, I telephoned Mandy and gave her the Lorrach lawyer's particulars.

'Is he all right, Howard?' Mandy asked.

'The lawyer said he looked fine.'

'Did he have any messages for me? Anything he wants me to do?'

'He didn't have any messages for anyone, Mandy.'

'Howard, would you mind going over to see a friend of Graham's and telling him what happened on your trip? He's a good guy, but he's a bit concerned about what's happened and wants to hear everything from the horse's mouth.'

'I don't mind, Mandy. Where do I go?'

'Mayfair, 17, Curzon Street. His name's Durrani.'

Mohammed Durrani was the grandson of the brother of the former King of Afghanistan. Educated in Delhi, he served eleven years on the Hong Kong Police Force and had several shady businesses throughout the East. One of them was supplying Pakistani hashish to Europe. Durrani let me in to his Mayfair flat. He had a hawk-like face, Savile Row suit, beautifully manicured fingernails, and wore strong after-shave. He poured me a Johnnie Walker Black Label whisky and offered me a Benson & Hedges from his gold, monogrammed cigarette case. He lit my cigarette with a Dupont lighter, introduced me to Sam Hiraoui, his Lebanese partner, and said, 'Thank you, Howard, for agreeing to come. We have simple question. Has Graham talked?'

'He said he didn't have any messages for anyone,' I answered.

'We mean to the German police.'

'I don't know.'

'The reason we ask, Howard, is that we have merchandise in pipeline which might be compromised by our friend's arrest. You are best friend, Mandy says. Do you think he would let police know anything about our operations?'

'Not deliberately, obviously, if that's what you mean.'

'That is what we mean.'

'In that case, no. He hasn't talked. But here's all the newspaper reports, lawyers' papers, etc. Maybe these will help you.'

'You have been very efficient, Howard, very efficient,' said Durrani. 'We are much in debt to you. It is possible, *inshallah*, that we may have merchandise to sell in England when Graham is in German prison. Are you interested?'

'I don't have any money, but I am honoured you ask me.'

'We would give you 100% credit,' said the Lebanese Sam. 'Simply sell it, keep your commission, and give us the agreed amount of money.'

'I'm not really that kind of dealer, Sam. Graham would give me a pound or two to sell every couple of weeks. That's it. I've never done any real business of any kind.'

'Surely you must be knowing people who are buying merchandise?' Durrani asked.

'No, I don't.'

'But you were at the Oxford University with Graham, no?'

'Yes, we were at Oxford together, but it's not much of a business school.'

'It is world's best, Howard. Graham sells his merchandise to people from the Oxford University.'

'That's very probable. Can't you get hold of any of them to sell your stuff?'

'We know only David Pollard, and he is now crazy man.'

I knew David Pollard. He was an exact contemporary of mine at some Oxford college other than Balliol. He too read Physics and was by no means crazy, though he was a little eccentric and had recently suffered tragic circumstances. In fact he was brilliant and invented all sorts of things from kidney dialysis machines to LSD manufacturing accessories, as well as pioneering the first British joint-sized rolling papers, Esmeralda. His girlfriend, Barbara Mayo, had gone hitch-hiking on the M6 motorway, and had been raped and murdered. The police never found the killer, but David was routinely grilled and treated as the prime suspect. The police finally let him go, and he threw his LSD manufacturing plant into the Thames. I had no idea he was Graham's main wholesaler.

'Jarvis once came out to Beirut to see me,' said Sam, 'but I have no idea where to get hold of him. Neither does Mandy. I don't think he was at Oxford University, but Graham sells to him.'

I had met Jarvis a few times with Graham. He was a state-of-the-art London Sixties dealer: shaded glasses, pop-singer clothes, model girlfriends, and lots of new vocabulary. He hailed from Birmingham but spoke Chelsea.

'No, he wasn't at Oxford, but I could probably track him down.'

'Good,' said Durrani. 'We look forward to good business. I will ask Mandy to call you when we are ready.'

The German and Mayfair experiences filled me with a new kind of energy and excitement. So much of me longed for more of this adventure. I thought of things I could buy with a lot of money.

Back in Brighton, I saw lots more of Rosie and little of anyone else. I told her about my recent adventures and the proposition I'd been made.

'That's wonderful, Howard,' said Rosie. 'That's obviously what you should do. Get out there and be somebody in your one and only life. I think selling Durrani's hashish in London is a brilliant idea. It's what you've been waiting for, isn't it?'

'I don't know. I just don't have any money to set myself up. I'd need a flat in London, a car other than my beaten-up Hillman, operating expenses, all kinds of things, let alone money to live on.'

'Howard, I don't know about you and Ilze. But Richard and I are not going to carry on pretending to be living with and loving each other. We're separating. My family has money. His family has a lot more, and they will certainly make sure that Emily, their granddaughter, will be properly provided for. I'm going to move to London. My parents will rent me a flat and buy me a car. You can stay there anytime you want, use the car, and if you need to borrow a couple of hundred pounds to set up a business, I couldn't think of a better investment for me to make.'

In a whirlwind of love, romance, and unlimited possibility, Rosie, her baby daughter Emily and I moved to a maisonette in Hillsleigh Road in the expensive part of Notting Hill. Richard would visit and play Go. We have remained very good friends. Ilze would also visit, and although we both felt somewhat betrayed by each other's infidelity, we remained on the very best terms.

During my postgraduate year at Oxford, I had met and liked a friend of Graham's called Charlie Radcliffe. He was from an aristocratic background, had an enormous collection of blues records, chain-smoked marijuana, belonged to the Campaign for Nuclear Disarmament, and had been busted for forging a staggering quantity of first-class counterfeit United States $100 bills with the words 'In God We Trust' replaced by an anti-Vietnam war slogan. He worked then for Robert Maxwell's publishing company, Pergamon Press, in Headington, just outside Oxford. Now Charlie, too, was living in London, and when he heard of Graham's bust, he tracked me down to get what news he could. I told him what I knew and mentioned the possibility of my being asked to sell Graham's hashish in his absence. I asked if he could help me out by either selling some or getting hold of Jarvis, whom Charlie knew quite well. Charlie was eager to make some money but explained that he had a partner, Charlie Weatherley, who would have to be involved. I had met Charlie Weatherley a few times when he was an undergraduate at Christ Church. He was now a heavy hashish-consuming biker and, when not pushing his

Norton Commando to the limit, listened continually with amusement to the Grateful Dead. He was a joy to be around. Charlie Radcliffe and I decided that the simplest and fairest arrangement for all concerned was that Jarvis, the two Charlies, and I form a syndicate to market Durrani's hashish. My initial responsibility would be to receive the hashish from Durrani and store it at Hillsleigh Road. Jarvis and the two Charlies would sell the hashish to their various dealer connections. I would then be expected to take the money to Durrani after splitting the profit four ways. We were ready. All we needed was the hashish.

No hashish materialised. Durrani never got in touch, and Graham was released after serving a six-month sentence. Throughout that six-month period, however, partly because of the conveniences provided by the Hillsleigh Road maisonette and partly, I'm sure, by the continual hope of Durrani coming through with large amounts, our newly formed syndicate operated as arranged with hashish from other sources. Through these dealings, I became acquainted with Duncan Laurie, a major hashish importer who had set up the Forbidden Fruit chain of Sixties boutiques in the King's Road and Portobello Road, Lebanese Joe, the person responsible for Graham's knowing Durrani, and James Goldsack, David Pollard's dealing partner. Essentially, I was making money and connections by sticking Rosie's neck on the line and mercilessly using her accommodation, car, and telephone. But I was also able to buy a few pounds of hashish at the best prices, and these I would sell in quarter-pounds and ounces to university dealers and friends in Oxford, Brighton, London, and Bristol, where my sister was doing a French degree. My new career had begun. Trading in cannabis would remain my active profession for the next eighteen years.

My views on cannabis differed in some ways from those of Jarvis and the two Charlies. They were far more radical than I and tended to see hashish as a new meaningful currency capable of overthrowing the fascist overlords. They wished hashish to remain illegal. It gave us a means of living and salved our rebellious consciences by fucking up the establishment. We were true outlaws: we didn't really break laws, not real ones; we just lived outside them. We didn't pay tax because we didn't want our money being used by the armed forces to kill innocent foreigners and by the police to bust us. We just wanted a good time, and we worked hard and took risks to get it by supplying a badly needed service. I went along with most of this but couldn't begin to condone the punishing of those who wished to smoke marijuana and, therefore, could not logically condone the illegality of the hashish trade.

Graham had hatched up several plans while incarcerated. Some were hindered by his inability to enter Germany without first paying his rather hefty fine. I agreed to take £5,000 of Graham's money to Frankfurt to give to Lebanese Sam. He would then take care of the fine. Currency restrictions made it illegal to take more than £25 out of the country, so I stuck the money down the back of my trousers and checked in at Heathrow. A couple of policemen did an unexpected anti-terrorist passenger search. Before I had time to realise the danger I was in, I had been incredibly inefficiently searched and motioned through the boarding gate. I didn't feel relief. I just felt a bit dazed and confused.

On the way back the next morning, I hid the receipt for the fine payment and £300 generously given me by Sam in my sock. I bought some duty-free perfumes for Rosie. Customs stopped me at Heathrow.

'Where have you come from, sir?'

'Frankfurt.'

'Is this all your luggage?' he asked, pointing to my small briefcase and plastic bag of perfume bottles.

'Yes.'

'Did you buy these perfumes duty-free?'

'Yes, at Frankfurt airport.'

'Do you realise, sir, that it is illegal to buy duty-free items if out of the country for less than twenty-four hours?'

'Yes,' I lied.

'How long have you been abroad?'

'Two days,' I lied again.

'Would you mind opening your briefcase, sir? I would just like to have a quick look.'

The briefcase contained only my used airline ticket, a toothbrush, and a book appropriately entitled *The Philosophy of Time.*

'Travelling light, sir?'

'I stayed at a friend's house. I didn't need to bring anything.'

The Customs Officer picked up my used airline ticket and looked at the dates.

'I thought you said you had been gone for two days. This ticket shows you left London last night.'

'Yes, two days: yesterday and today.'

'Would you come this way, sir?'

The Customs Officer led me to a cold, breeze-blocked room.

'Let me see your passport. Thank you. Would you mind taking off your clothes?'

'Of course I mind.'

'Mr Marks, if you have no contraband, you have nothing to fear.'

'I have no contraband, and I have nothing to fear. But I'm not taking my clothes off.'

I was beginning to worry about the £300 in my sock. If it was illegal to take £25 cash out, then it surely must be illegal to bring in twelve times that amount, or was it?

'Then you leave me no choice. I will hold you both for attempting to smuggle perfume into the United Kingdom and on suspicion of carrying other contraband. You either let me strip-search you now or the police will do so when I put you in their cells.'

'I'll take the second option.'

'That's up to you. There is another alternative. You declare what contraband you have to me and hand it over. If I accept your declaration as true, we'll deal with the matter without strip-searching.'

'I've got £300 in my sock,' I stupidly confessed.

'Show me.'

I took off my shoe and sock and gave him the bundle of fifteen £20 notes and the fine-payment receipt.

'Did you take this money out of the country, sir?'

There didn't seem much point admitting that fact.

'No. A friend gave it to me in Frankfurt. I didn't know what else to do with it. Is it illegal to bring back money, too, if I've been away for just a short time?'

'No, Mr Marks, bringing sterling into the country is not illegal, but taking more than a certain amount out of the country is. Why did you put it in your sock? So we wouldn't see it?'

'Just for safe-keeping, I suppose.'

'Is this receipt also in your sock for safe keeping? What is your occupation?'

'Well, I'm sort of unemployed at the moment, but usually I'm a teacher.'

'Who is Kenneth Graham Plinston?' he asked, looking at the name on the receipt.

'Just a friend, really. He owed some money in Germany and asked me to sort it out.'

'You always pay off his debts? Are you that well paid a teacher?'

'No, I used his money. It was his friend who gave me the money in Frankfurt.'

'What was his friend's name?'

'Sal.' I knew I had to lie on that one.

'Italian, is he?'

'I think so.'

'Just one moment, Mr Marks.'

The Customs Officer left with the receipt. After several minutes, he returned with a senior official-looking man in plain clothes.

'Good morning, Mr Marks. I'm with Her Majesty's Customs and Excise Special Investigative Branch. We are going to charge you the duty on the perfume you bought. In the matter of the £300, we can't touch you. Here it is. We know your friend Mr Plinston. We know how he makes his money. We trust you aren't going the same way. Stick to teaching.'

Graham seemed totally unperturbed when I got to his house and gave him the receipt and report of my brush with the law.

'I don't think there's much to worry about there, Howard. We're friends, and that's that.'

'I'm not worried about it,' I said. 'I'm just telling you what happened. I really couldn't care less.'

'That's good. Howard, something's just come up. Would you like to make quite a decent sum of money by doing a couple of days' work in Germany driving some hash around to various friends of mine?'

'Graham, I've never driven abroad. I can't imagine driving on the wrong side of the road.'

'There's always a first time.'

'Maybe, but it shouldn't be when I've got dope in the car.'

'Couldn't you hire someone, Howard, to be your driver? I'll be paying you plenty.'

'Yeah, I'm pretty sure I could do that.'

'Okay, Howard, I'll call you from Frankfurt in a few days when I'm ready.'

Neither Jarvis nor the two Charlies were interested in venturing from the Royal Borough of Kensington and Chelsea. It was too much of a disruption. However, Charlie Radcliffe's attractive lady, Tina, had a New Zealand friend called Lang. He had years of all kinds of smuggling experience and was in London looking for work. He was more than happy with the German proposition. We agreed to split profits.

Lang and I met Graham in Frankfurt airport. Graham explained that a ton of Pakistani hashish was in a lock-up garage. The assignment was to rent an appropriate vehicle, go to the garage, load up the hashish, deliver some to a group of Californians in a predetermined lay-by, some to a couple of Germans in Frankfurt, and the rest to a group of Dutchmen at a pre-arranged location in the middle of the Black Forest. Lang and I would be paid £5,000 between us.

We rented an Opel estate car with massive space for baggage. The lock-up garage was in an expensive suburb of Wiesbaden. Inside the garage were twenty 50-kilo wooden boxes with 'Streptomycin, Karachi' stencilled on each. The smell of hashish was overpowering. We loaded up the Opel, covered the boxes with a rug, and drove to the lay-by. A couple of Cheech and Chong look-alikes were waiting in a large saloon car. We pulled up alongside. One of the Californians jumped out and opened the boot. Lang and I opened the back of the Opel, and the three of us transferred five of the twenty boxes to the saloon. We shook hands. The saloon car drove off.

The Dutch and Germans were not ready to receive their hashish. Lang and I had to kill a few days. We drove the Opel from Wiesbaden, along the banks of the Rhine, to a village called Osterich. There we checked into a hotel, curiously named, in English, The White Swan. We wined and dined and broke into one of the boxes. We got stoned.

The day before the rendezvous with the Dutch, we took a boat down the Rhine to Wiesbaden. Lang wanted to get some English newspapers. While we were crossing one of the city's main streets, a car came quickly round the corner, shot the red pedestrian light, and almost knocked Lang over. In a moment of understandable anger, Lang hit the back of the car with a rolled-up newspaper. The car screamed to a halt. A huge red-faced German jumped out of the car, ran over to

Lang, gave him a tremendous thump across the head sending his glasses splintering on the road, ran back into the car, and drove off. It was all over in seconds. Lang was barely conscious and was blind without his glasses.

'You'll have to drive tomorrow, mate,' was all he said.

The rendezvous with the Dutch was at a remote but accessible clearing in the Black Forest. With fear and apprehension, I drove the hashish-filled Opel into the country's wooded depths. It took no time to adjust to driving on the other side. We got to the clearing. There was no one there. After twenty minutes, two Volvos arrived. Inside one was Dutch Nik, whom I'd once met at Graham's. Inside the other was a man who introduced himself as Dutch Peter. We gave them thirteen boxes.

At an efficient German chemist's, Lang soon fixed himself up with a pair of new prescription glasses and was able to drive the Opel into Frankfurt for the final drop-off to an unnamed German in the car park of the Intercontinental Hotel. It passed without incident.

Graham had been supervising matters from his room in the Frankfurter Hof. He had bought a new BMW. He asked if we wanted to keep him company for a few days, after which he would pay us off. Lang wanted to get back to London and was happy to be paid there. I stayed with Graham, who was collecting bags of money. After a couple of days, we hid the money, a mixture of United States dollars and German marks, in the BMW, and drove to Geneva. Graham banked large quantities of German and American cash in his Swiss bank account after first giving me our payment. I asked what happened to the hashish we had distributed and was told that the German would be selling his hashish in Frankfurt, the Californians would buy brand-new European cars and ship them stuffed with hashish to Los Angeles, while Dutch Nik and Dutch Pete would be driving the 650 kilos of hashish they received to England. I asked who would be selling the hashish once it got to

England. I presumed Graham would now revert to using David Pollard and James Goldsack. Graham smiled.

'You will be, Howard.'

'But I know that in the past you've used Dave Pollard and James. I don't want to cause problems.'

'Howard, I also used to use Jarvis and the two Charlies. London dealing is musical chairs. Anyway, David Pollard is out of business. You can keep James happy by letting him have some hash to sell at a good price.'

Jarvis, the two Charlies, and I sold the 650 kilos of hashish and made about £20,000 profit between us. I had made £7,500 in just one week. For the first time ever, I felt rich and gradually began to get used to a lifestyle of fast cars, expensive restaurants, and gadgetry. I bought a brand-new BMW, record and cassette-playing equipment of all descriptions, and a water bed. Rosie suggested we rent a flat in Brighton to use at weekends and other periods when I wasn't tied up moving hash around London. She still had friends in Brighton and missed the proximity of the sea. We rented a ground-floor flat at 14, Lewes Crescent. One of Rosie's friends was Patrick Lane, ex-Sussex University English Literature graduate working as an accountant for Price Waterhouse Ltd. Patrick and I got on well with each other. He introduced me to his seventeen-year-old sister Judy. Her smile, her waist-length hair, and her long legs tantalisingly stayed in my mind. It wasn't long before I invited Patrick to participate with me in Graham's next proposal.

Mohammed Durrani had a variety of ways of getting hashish into Europe. The most common was in the personal effects of Pakistani diplomats taking up positions in Pakistani embassies and consular offices throughout Europe. Durrani would arrange with the diplomat to put about a ton of hashish into the diplomat's personal furniture and belongings before they left Pakistan. A diplomat's personal effects would be unlikely to be searched on arrival, and he could always claim diplomatic immunity or blame it on the Pakistani shippers if the dope was accidentally discovered. On this occasion, the personal effects had been delivered to the diplomat's residence in Bonn. Patrick and I had to rifle through the cabin trunks, remove the hashish, and drive it to a disused gravel pit near Cologne, where Dutch Nik, Dutch Pete, and other Dutch would pick it up and smuggle it to England. Everything went without a hitch, and after taking care of sales in London, I'd made another £7,500.

Graham had made a great deal more and was intent on legitimising his hard-earned money in the form of respectable London businesses. He had met Patrick and liked him. He needed a bent accountant and felt Patrick would be ideal. I could see no disadvantage. Soon Graham and Patrick had established a carpet shop, Hamdullah, and a property company, Zeitgeist, at 3, Warwick Place, Little Venice. They carried appropriate business cards which they flashed at every opportunity.

My lifestyle went from expensive to outrageously flamboyant. In London, Brighton, Oxford, and Bristol, I would pick up the tab at every bar and restaurant I visited. Any of my friends who wished to merely smoke hashish rather than sell it would be given as much as they wanted free of charge. There are few things that give me more pleasure in life than getting people very stoned and giving them good food and wine, but meanwhile I could see very well the sense of using some of my money to set myself up in the way Graham was doing. It would have to be on a smaller scale, but in principle it could be done.

Redmond and Belinda O'Hanlon were undergraduate friends of mine at Oxford. Redmond was now at St Anthony's doing a D.Phil. on Darwin's effect on nineteenth-century English literature while Belinda was running a small dressmaking business with Anna Woodhead, the Spanish wife of Anthony Woodhead, another Oxford undergraduate friend. Their clientele were largely Oxford University ladies

looking for suitable ball dresses. Anna and Belinda were
badly under-capitalised. I gave them the impression that I
had recently inherited some money. We agreed to go into
business together from small, tucked-away premises near
Oxford railway station. Using cash, I bought a bunch of
sewing-machines and formed a company, AnnaBelinda Ltd.
It immediately did well, and we looked for suitable street-
front rental premises to open up a boutique. We found them
at 6, Gloucester Street, where AnnaBelinda still stands.

A few more Durrani scams occurred, but they involved
significantly smaller amounts. Occasionally I would drive a
stashed car across a European border. I'd get a religious
flash and an asexual orgasm every time I did. Marty
Langford and a couple of other Kenfig Hill school friends,
Mike Bell and David Thomas, were also living in London
doing boring and menial jobs. I gave each the opportunity
of working for me moving and stashing hashish, taking
telephone calls, and counting money. Each took it, and I
was no longer exposing the London flat to the dangers
inherent in street dealing: they were exposing theirs. The
four of us were probably London's only Welsh criminal
gang, and were jokingly referred to by our fellow dealers as
the Tafia. It was dangerous fun. But I was spending almost
as much as I was earning. Thousands of pounds a month
were not enough.

Four

MR McCARTHY

Charlie Radcliffe, Graham, and I were smoking joints and counting money in Graham's Marylands Road flat. We were bemoaning our poverty. Although we were grateful to Mohammed Durrani's Pakistani diplomats for smuggling hashish into Europe and giving it to us to sell, we were jealous of the amount of money they were making. We would make about 20% of the selling price in London. The diplomats and Durrani made the rest. We, or the Dutch, had to drive the dope into England and then deliver it to wholesalers in London. It was a risky business, particularly with road blocks now being set up all over the place to catch IRA activists. We were taking all the chances, while the Pakistanis were taking none. There was no chance of getting the hashish for a better price in Europe. The Pakistanis knew full well that there were plenty of buyers more than willing to pay at least as much as we were. We couldn't beat them down.

'If only we could find our own way of getting hash in,' said Graham, 'we would become so rich. Don't either of you know anyone who works in a key position in an airport or in the docks somewhere?'

I didn't.

'I could try Cardiff, Graham,' I suggested. 'There are probably some old school friends of mine working in a freight department somewhere. I could go drinking in the pubs where dock and airport workers hang out. I'll find someone who needs to supplement his income, I'm sure.'

'Good idea,' complimented Graham, but without much enthusiasm.

Charlie spoke up. 'I've just met someone who I'm sure will be able to bring in some hash. I interviewed him for *Friends*. He's an IRA guy. If he can smuggle in guns, he can smuggle in dope.'

Friends was an underground magazine. Its editor was a South African named Alan Marcuson. Charlie and his lady, Tina, lived in Alan's Hampstead flat. Together with Mike Lessor's *International Times* and Richard Neville's *Oz*, *Friends* catered for the tastes and beliefs of 1960s drop-outs, dope dealers, rock musicians, acid-heads, and anyone with a social conscience. The underground press was unanimously opposed to the British presence in Northern Ireland. The IRA's struggle was seen as championing the causes of the world's downtrodden and poverty-stricken Catholics. How could one not sympathise? There were increasing doubts and worries, of course, about the violent methods used by the IRA, particularly the Provisional IRA, which had recently broken away from the Official IRA to form a terrorist splinter group. There was also discomfort about the IRA's rather puritanical stance on smoking dope.

The current issue of *Friends* carried a very lengthy piece on the IRA, which included an interview with a Belfast member, James Joseph McCann. In the interview he admitted to a petty-criminal childhood in Belfast which led to an involvement during the 1960s with South London's most powerful and feared gangster, Charlie Richardson. A spell in Her Majesty's Prison, Parkhurst, Britain's heaviest nick, had converted McCann into a poet and proponent of Irish nationalism. His poetry sucked, but his rhetoric seemed quite persuasive, especially when it took the form of explicit threat. McCann missed the criminal glamour and clearly felt there would be an even greater opportunity for money, deviousness, and deceit in becoming an Irish folk hero. He achieved this longed-for status by throwing Molotov cocktails at Belfast's Queen's University, declaring himself as an IRA man, giving himself up to the authorities, and subsequently escaping from Crumlin Road prison. It was the first escape from there since World War II. He was now on the run in Eire, presenting himself to press photographers in badly fitting military wear and brandishing a variety of lethal weapons, claiming to have smuggled them into Dublin. Belfast schoolchildren mocked and jeered at British soldiers patrolling the Andersonstown streets yelling, 'Where's your man McCann? Where's your man McCann?' He was a hero all right.

'Would he go for it, though, Charlie?' I asked. 'You know what these guys are like about dope. They'd tar and feather someone for smoking a joint. They think it pollutes their youth. They aren't going to help anyone bring it into Ireland, that's for sure.'

'Howard, Jim McCann actually smokes almost as much dope as we do. He's got no problems with it.'

'It's a first-class suggestion,' said Graham, this time with enormous enthusiasm. 'Can you set up a meeting?'

A week later Graham and I landed at Cork airport, our first visit to Southern Ireland. We went to the car hire desk. It was called Murray Hertz.

'Now! What are you?' asked the Murray Hertz employee.

'What do you mean?' asked a very puzzled Graham.

'Your profession. I'll be needing it for my files.'

'I'm an artist,' stammered Graham.

'Now! Tell me. Why would an artist be wanting a car on a day like this? And what about your man there? Will he be holding your brushes?'

We gave up and went to the Avis desk, where they tried

harder. They gave us a car, and we drove through the misty night to Ballinskelligs, where some time ago Alan Marcuson had rented a fisherman's cottage and placed it at McCann's disposal. Its telephone number was Ballinskelligs 1, and it lay next to a former lunatic asylum for nuns.

'Thank God you've arrived,' said Alan, 'but you mustn't do anything with Jim, whatever Charlie said. The man's a dangerous lunatic. He's got a boot full of explosives in a car parked right outside, he's stashed guns in the nuns' nuthouse, he's got me looking after this dog, he's stoned or drunk all day, he keeps bringing IRA guys here, and every policeman in Ireland's looking for him. I've never been so scared in my life. Humour him when he comes back from the pub, but don't think of doing business with him. He'll be busted in a flash.'

Jim McCann, drunkenly reeling and staggering, fell through the door and gave the sleeping dog a hefty kick up the arse. He ignored me and Graham, farted loudly, and stared at the dog.

'Look at that fucking dog! What about you? You don't give him any exercise, Alan. It's wrong, I'm telling you. Look at that fucking dog!'

Alan, Graham, and I stared blankly at the still sleeping mongrel. So this was your man McCann. An Irish freedom fighter.

McCann's eyes shifted from the dog to me. 'You from Kabul, are you?'

'No, I'm Welsh, actually.'

'Welsh! Fucking Welsh! Jesus Christ. What the fuck can you do? Why are you here?'

'I've got to help decide whether you could be of any use to us.'

'Use to you!' McCann screamed. 'Listen. Get this fucking straight. I'm the Kid. The Fox. I decide if youse any fucking use to me. Not the other fucking way round. And youse better be of some fucking use. We need some arms for the struggle. You hear me, do you? Youse were followed from the airport by my boys. This place is fucking surrounded by the IRA. Any fucking around, and you're gone, brother, gone.'

He turned and addressed Graham, 'Are you from Kabul, then?'

'Well, not exactly . . .'

'Why have you brought me these two wankers, Alan? I thought you were going to bring me someone who could get me arms from Kabul.'

'I've been to Kabul,' said Graham, attempting to save the situation.

'Can you get me some guns from there, then? Yes or no. Either shit or get off the pot. I've got John Lennon coming round here this evening. Time's short.'

'Kabul is not a place that sells arms,' Graham explained.

'What the fuck do you mean? Sell arms? I don't buy fucking arms. I get given them for the struggle by people who want to insure their future when we finally kick you fucking Brits out of my country. What's a fucking Welsh cunt doing selling arms anyway? You should stick to painting road signs.'

'Jim,' I said, 'we're a couple of hash smugglers. We want to know if you're able to get the stuff in for us. We'll pay you a lot for doing it.'

'Where's the hashish coming from?'

'Kabul.'

'Where the fuck's that, you Welsh prick?'

The conversation was in danger of getting out of control. Graham came to the rescue.

'Kabul is the capital of Afghanistan. But we can also get it out of Karachi, Pakistan. Do you have any suggestions of how we could get it into Ireland?'

'Put it into a coffin. You understand me, do you? They never search those. I'll give youse the address to send it. My brother Brendan knows the priest. Our Gerard can drive the hearse, and our Peter will make sure no one touches it.'

Not the best scam. Not even original, but at least we were talking the same language. I brightened up a bit, but Graham seemed unimpressed.

'Handling coffins has its problems in places like Kabul, Jim. It really does. There'd be all sorts of paperwork to do. They'd want to know the identity of the corpse, etcetera.'

'Alan fucking told me youse could do anything from Kabul. Youse can't get ahold of any guns there. Youse can't even get ahold of a dead fucking body. I'll send youse a dead fucking body with a fucking passport tied round his neck so those idjits in Kabul know who the fuck he is. Where the fuck's John Lennon? He's late again. Go upstairs and call him, Alan.'

Alan disappeared up the stairs, scratching his head.

'He's not getting a fucking penny,' said Jim, pointing up the stairs. 'That's my first condition. Charlie Radcliffe doesn't get a fucking penny either. That's condition number two. Condition number three. I want £500 cash, now, to set everything up, and I want £5,000 for doing it.'

I spoke up, 'Jim, if we just sent you some boxes, not a coffin, just some boxes, to the airport, would you and your brothers be able to get them?'

'Of course we could, you Welsh arsehole. What do you think I've been telling youse for the last ten minutes? We run this fucking country. Give me some of that fucking joint.'

Graham, getting noticeably tired, reached into his pocket and said, 'Okay, Jim, here's £500. Let us know when you have an address for us to send you some boxes. I'm going to bed now.'

Graham and Alan passed each other on the stairs. Alan yawned and told Jim, 'There was no answer from that number you gave me for Lennon.'

'He must be on his way. You fancy a pint of Guinness, H'ard? Alan will wait here for John Lennon. A couple of the boys might be coming, too, so they'll keep John company when we're having a wee drink.'

We walked in total silence to a shop a hundred yards away. It was about 2 a.m., dark, and foggy. Jim banged at the door hard and long. It was opened by an elderly farmer, who led us through the shop into a bar at the back. About a dozen people of assorted sizes and professions were downing pints of Guinness and breaking into song. Jim had left just a couple of hours ago and was greeted by warm cries of 'How about yer, Seamus.' We sat at a table and were brought several pints of Guinness. Jim began telling me his life story – or someone's life story. Essentially, his account was the same as what had appeared in *Friends* with even further embellishments. He asked me details of my past. I told him.

'So, youse a fucking Oxford academic, are you? The fucking brains of this fucking crazy gang from Kabul. The Welsh wizard. Oxford? You're not British Intelligence, are you? Coming to catch the Kid? Who do you sell all the dope to? Other fucking academics and hippie shit? Do you just carry a fucking bag down to Brighton seafront and go to Hyde Park for big deals? I know people who can sell dope in Brighton. You know the Weavers, don't you? Or Nicky Hoogstratten? You must know him, for Christ's sake?'

'I know of them, Jim, but don't really know them.'

The Weavers were Brighton's best-known criminal family. The *capo* was James Weaver, who had been sentenced to death for murder and kidnap but who had later been reprieved. The family were known for taking a dim view of any of its rank and file who succumbed to the temptation of selling recreational substances. Nicholas Hoogstratten was Brighton's millionaire slum landlord. His heavies were continually evicting impoverished, dope-smoking hippies.

'I could sell the dope for you. I could sell it here in Ireland. There was a bust in Dublin last week.'

There had indeed been a bust in Dublin. It was of half a pound of hashish, and a Dublin police chief had described it on television as Ireland's biggest 'burst'. I wasn't at all sure if any dope-smuggling venture with McCann could possibly work. But if it did, it would definitely be a bad idea for him to be hawking our hashish around the streets of Dublin, gathering all the cash and probably getting 'bursted'.

'Jim, surely it would be better that none of the gear gets sold in Ireland. We don't want the cops thinking that the dope's being imported into this country. Once you get the gear, give it to me, and I'll take it over on the ferry to Wales, drive it to London, and sell it. In a couple of days, I'll drive back on the ferry with the money, if you want it here.'

'I want my money in Amsterdam.'

'That's fine, Jim.'

'Can you get me any guns, and bring those over on this fucking Welsh ferry? It would help the cause.'

'No, Jim.'

'What about pornographic movies? Bring all you can.'

'Yes, Jim, I can do that.'

A record player was turned on, and some of the other drinkers began dancing an Irish jig. Jim joined them. I went to the bar and bought drinks all round. There was a telephone on the counter. Its number was also Ballinskelligs 1. The revelry continued until dawn. Jim and I were the last to leave.

We walked across soaking wet fields. The sea was a few yards away. Through patches in the early morning mist, we could see nearby small islands.

'That's Scarriff Island. John Lennon's buying it. We probably missed him when we were in the pub. Still, it was a good crack. Better than a fucking Welsh pub, I'm sure.'

Back at the fisherman's cottage, Graham and Alan were still soundly asleep. There was no sign of John Lennon. Jim and I smoked some joints.

'You know condoms are illegal in Ireland, Howard. But they won't be for long. Once we get the Brits out, we're getting rid of the fucking priests, and people will be able to fuck each other without having wee kids to support. It's a British conspiracy to keep us poor. Charging us for sex, a kid a fuck. I'm forming a company called Durex Novelty Balloons, so Durex will have to call their condoms some other fucking name, and they won't sell any. You hear me? Dan Murray did the same with Hertz. We'll screw those fucking capitalists. But I have to get some money first. I might need you there, H'ard. Let's go to the shop and buy something to eat. I'm fucking starving.'

We traipsed back over the wet fields, this time passing the nuns' lunatic asylum. 'That's our arms dump,' said Jim. 'We could hole up here for months.'

The same shop/bar we had not long left had now opened for its breakfast trade. A kindly lady was serving customers enormous breakfasts, and a young lad was selling groceries. At the back, last night's mess remained uncleared at the bar, but five characters were propping it up and swallowing Guinness. The bar phone rang. It was for Jim. I looked aimlessly at the groceries, then sat down at a table in the bar. Jim walked back.

'Was it John Lennon?' I asked.

'No, it's Graham and Alan. They're coming over now for some food. Don't say a fucking thing about what we've been talking about. That's important. You hear me.'

I was wondering how Ballinskelligs 1 could dial Ballinskelligs 1. Jim ordered four large breakfasts and four pints of Guinness. They were ready when Graham and Alan arrived. They said it was too early for them to drink, so Jim and I drank their Guinness.

'Jim, we have to fly back to London today. Is there anything further to discuss?' asked Graham.

'No. I'll see you in seven to ten days. I'm away.'

With that, Jim got up, shook our hands, and walked out of the shop.

'So, what do you think?' I asked Graham and Alan.

'You've got to forget it,' said Alan. 'The man's nuts. All this John Lennon nonsense. And he's got no idea where Kabul is.'

'I think he can do it,' said Graham. 'He's the kind of
person who can get away with things. Look, we should leave
now and get on the road. I have to get to London.'

On the way back to Cork airport, we passed near Blarney.
I wanted to stop and kiss the stone to get some luck. Graham
said there was no time. This was the area where my great-
great-grandfather, Patrick Marks, then McCarthy, spent his
young life. How Irish did this make me?

At Cork airport, I picked up a payphone and asked the
operator for Ballinskelligs 1. A beautiful Irish voice said,
'Now, who would you be wanting: Michael Murphy's, the
shop, the farm, or the strangers? Two arrived last night, but
they've gone early this morning.'

'To whom am I speaking?' I asked.

'Why now, I'm the Ballinskelligs operator.'

It all made a bit more sense now, but it was still weird.

There were things to do back home. The new
AnnaBelinda premises included a self-contained flat. Rosie,
Emily, and I were leaving both our Brighton and our
London flats to go and live there and open the planned-for
up-market boutique. I supervised, or rather smoked joints
and watched, the extensive refurbishing of the one-time
transport café. The dress-shop front was beginning to look
good and was already attracting a great deal of the city and
university's interest. Pattern-cutting and other workshop
rooms sprouted out of the timber and sawdust. The flat was
comfortable, and there were separate offices. In one of these
I had an interior decorating company which, with an
accommodating local builder, Robin Murray, I'd formed
primarily for the purpose of being able to fiddle the accounts
when refurbishing the premises. Although money-laundering then was nothing approaching the problem it is these
days, one still had to be a little devious if one ventured from
underground. I definitely didn't want the authorities to
know how much money I had. Accordingly, I paid a lot of
money in cash for the refurbishing, but the accounts showed

an expenditure of considerably less. Another office was set aside to convert my hobby of collecting stamps into a philatelic business. My plan was to buy in my own name massive quantities of unsorted stamps, known in the trade as kiloware, at cheap prices. At the same time, expensive rare stamps would be bought anonymously by me for cash from reputable dealers in the Strand. My business records would state that these valuable stamps had been recovered from the kiloware after a painstaking, time-consuming search. I would then sell the valuable stamps to stamp dealers in the provinces and appear to be shrewdly making legitimate money. There would be some financial loss, but who cared? 6, Gloucester Street, Oxford, was shaping up to be a great headquarters. Only the large, empty cellar remained without a function.

A week after my return from Ireland, Alan Marcuson rang saying that McCann had set everything up. He said he had totally underestimated McCann's abilities. He really had got it together. Graham and I should come over to Dublin right away. I pictured McCann standing behind Alan at some Ballinskelligs 1 location, threateningly prompting Alan's every word.

Graham couldn't make it; he was too tied up with his property and carpet businesses. I flew alone to Dublin and checked in at the Intercontinental Hotel. It overlooked the Lansdowne Road rugby ground, where just the year before the Irish had cruelly robbed the Welsh of the Triple Crown. There was a package waiting for me at the reception desk. An attached note said: 'Read this. Seamus.'

I opened the package. Inside was a mass of detail about an airport I had never heard of. It was called Shannon and was situated on the Atlantic coast just outside Limerick.

The airport boasted a number of unique characteristics. It was the closest European airport to North America, and, as such, was a connection and refuelling point for European and Asian airlines on long hauls across the Atlantic. In 1952,

Irish government and individual entrepreneurs, doing their utmost to exploit Shannon's position as an airways crossroads, invented the first ever duty-free shop where transit passengers could purchase alcohol, cigarettes, perfumes, and watches at bargain prices. The area surrounding Shannon airport had been declared a freeport, to which raw materials and other bonded goods could be shipped for use for manufacturing purposes provided the finished products were exported from Ireland and not offered for sale within the country. A massive trading estate housing numerous businesses anxious to take advantage of this incentive spread around the airport. Every day, several hundred cars and trucks drove in conveying factory employees and locally built machinery. I began to see the point. Gear could be sent into Shannon Trading Estate from abroad without going through customs checks and would, somehow or other, be taken out of the trading estate camouflaged by the exodus of factory workers leaving at the end of their shift. There were maps of every inch of the estate and airport and a variety of air-freighting/importation forms. I was very, very impressed.

The hotel room door opened, and Jim walked in accompanied by a hotel employee carrying a bottle of Paddy Irish whiskey and a bucket of melted ice.

'You're a good man, Damien,' said Jim. 'Sign the bill, H'ard, and give your man here a twenty-pound tip. He deserves it.'

I gave the whiskey-bearer his money.

Jim put his arms around me and squeezed tightly. I was very startled.

'What do you think of the Kid, then? I've done it. I've cracked it. Send all the fucking dope you want.'

'How did you do it, Jim?'

'I pretended I worked for *Fortune* magazine and rang up the airport manager to ask for an interview. I went from him down, you understand me, till I got the man I wanted. Anything can be taken out of that trading estate there. Any fucking thing. As long as you got one of these.'

Jim grabbed hold of the pile of papers I'd been reading and displayed one entitled 'Out of Charge Note'.

'You can get these copied, can't you?'

'I should think so, Jim. Charlie Radcliffe worked in the printing and publishing business for years. He'll know how to get it done.'

'Don't you tell Charlie Radcliffe what they're for. You hear me.'

'Well . . . Okay. Maybe I'll use someone else. Who examines them?'

'You wired up, H'ard? I just fucking told you I got the man I wanted. He fucking examines them. And, if he values his fucking Guinness, he'll pass them. His name's Eamonn. He's a true Republican.'

'Does he know we're going to bring in dope?'

'Of course he fucking doesn't, you Welsh arsehole. He thinks he's bringing in guns for the cause. He's against dope.'

'Where's Alan, Jim?'

'I've just sacked the no-good fucker. Him and Radcliffe had better watch out for their lives. And that fucking John Lennon. You ought to get rid of Soppy Bollocks, too.'

'Who is Soppy Bollocks?'

'That fucking Brit that was with you last week.'

'Jim, we need Graham. I don't know anyone else who can send stuff from Pakistan and Afghanistan.'

'Well, fucking find someone, you hear me. You and me can go to Kabul. Did you bring those pornographic movies you promised?'

I had forgotten.

'I didn't want to bring them on the plane, Jim. I'll get them brought over on the ferry very soon. This plan of yours seems brilliant. When do you want to start?'

'Fucking now. I'm ready. I got it all together.'

'How much shall we send?'

'I'll let you know, H'ard.'

'What address shall we send the stuff to?'

'I'll let you know, H'ard.'

'What goods shall we pretend to be shipping?'

'I'll let you know, H'ard.'

Jim clearly didn't have it all together, but it did sound most promising. I wanted to see Shannon for myself. We rented a car and drove via Limerick to Shannon airport. The countryside was spectacular, a large and beautiful estuary surrounded by gentle rolling hills. In the middle of this idyllic setting lay a large industrial estate and airport. Jim was driving. He parked right outside the passenger airport terminal in an obvious no-parking area.

'You can't be parking there,' said a quietly spoken Irish airport official.

'It's a fucking emergency. I'm picking up my boss's luggage,' said Jim in his loudest and most aggressive Belfast accent.

'That'll be grand. I'll keep an eye on it for you.'

Jim then took me on a guided tour of the airport, including the Aer Lingus cargo terminal. Various employees nodded to him. He escorted me as if he owned the place. Then he got an Aer Lingus van driver to take us to the industrial estate. There appeared to be no check on anyone or anything. Jim asked a supervisor to tell me how the freeport worked.

'This is like its own country,' explained the supervisor. 'No goods are allowed to leave this estate unless, of course, they've been specifically cleared to do so.'

'What if someone tried to take them out?' asked Jim, playing a bit close to the bone.

'They can't without one of these,' said the supervisor, displaying an 'Out of Charge' note.

'See what I mean, H'ard,' said Jim as we were dropped off back at the terminal, where the obliging official was still keeping an eye on our car. 'This place is wide fucking open.'

It was.

'You'll have to give me some more money, H'ard, to rent an office in Limerick and a small workshop in Shannon Trading Estate. How will you take the hash to London and Brighton? You want our Brendan to take it over for you? He needs to work and make some money, that's for fucking sure.'

'I'll get friends to drive it over the ferry to Wales, Jim. We have a lot of experience driving across the European borders.'

'Do you just put the gear in the boot and pray?'

'No. We hide it in the door panels and under and behind the back seat. You'd be surprised how much you can get in. I'll need a place, a cottage or something, or a garage, where I can stash the car before putting it on the ferry.'

'I'll get you one. Just give me the money to do it.'

'Jim, if I give you another £500, will that cover down payments on the office, workshop, and a place for me to stash?'

'It might just be enough, H'ard.'

We checked into the Shannon Shamrock, a kind of motel popular with airline pilots. The lobby smelt of peat and Guinness. I used my real name. Jim used the name James Fitzgerald. We had a drink. The pilots were narrating horrifying tales of near misses and bad landings.

'You must never use your real name again, H'ard. It's too dangerous. It's fucking dumb.'

The next morning there was a direct flight from Shannon to Heathrow. I took it. An 'Out of Charge' note was in my pocket. I went straight to Graham's. Charlie Radcliffe was there. One of Dutch Nik's firm had brought over a hundred kilos of Lebanese from Sam Hiraoui. It had to be sold. That would give me and Charlie another £1,500, Graham £5,000, the Dutch £2,000, and Lebanese Sam, whose diplomats brought it to Holland, £20,000. If Shannon worked, we stood to make so much more.

'Howard, we'll have to do a dummy first. I can't risk my Middle East connections just on McCann's say-so.'

'I don't think Jim will go for that, Graham. He's anxious to do the real thing.'

'He's got no choice.'

Charlie Radcliffe said he'd have no trouble making copies of the 'Out of Charge' note.

After Charlie Radcliffe, Charlie Weatherley, Jarvis, and I sold the Lebanese, which merely entailed giving it to James Goldsack and waiting for the money, I drove to Brighton. Although no longer living there, I'd kept on the flat and had given McCann its address and phone number. There was a telegram waiting for me. It was from Limerick. Jim had sent it about an hour after I'd left him. It stated: 'Send sporting goods to Ashling Distribution Services, Shannon airport. I need more money. Fitzgerald.'

I had no direct way of getting hold of Jim by telephone. There was just a mail drop in Ballinskelligs. I phoned Graham, who suggested we just went ahead and sent a dummy consignment once the 'Out of Charge' notes were printed but not to tell Jim it was a dummy until the last possible moment. I didn't like it. But it made sense. Graham got Patrick Lane to put a stack of London telephone directories in a box and air-freight it to Shannon. I telegrammed the eleven-digit air waybill number to Jim's Ballinskelligs address and express-mailed some perfectly forged 'Out of Charge' notes. Jim telephoned many hours later.

'Those fuckers in Kabul have ripped you all off. Fucking telephone directories. Don't ever fucking bother me again, you Welsh arsehole. I'm going to Kabul myself. Fucking telephone directories. They could have at least sent some dirty magazines for the boys. Tell Soppy Bollocks his days are numbered. You hear me. Fucking telephone directories.'

'Jim, we had to do a dummy first, and there was no way of letting you know. I couldn't say in a telegram that this was a dummy, could I? You must give me a better way of getting hold of you.'

'I want another £500 tomorrow, without fail. Soppy had

better be on the next fucking flight to Kabul, and he'd better send something other than fucking telephone directories, otherwise he'll be without his fucking kneecaps. What's his fucking phone number?'

'I'm not giving you his phone number, Jim, but I will be over tomorrow morning with the money. Did you find me a cottage or something?'

'It's all together, man. I do what I fucking say. I deliver. I'm the Kid.'

I reported to Graham. He agreed to go out to Pakistan in the next couple of days. I flew back to Shannon, rented a car, and, as arranged, waited in the lobby of the Shannon Shamrock. Jim came in accompanied by what appeared to be a giant all-in wrestler.

'This is Gus, H'ard. He's a member of the Belfast Brigade's assassination squad. I want him to know your face. Okay, Gus, you can fuck off now. Don't forget to get John Lennon's London address. I'll teach that fucking arsehole a lesson he'll never forget. H'ard, I don't want any more fucking games, you understand me, do you?'

'It was a simple communication breakdown, Jim. There were no games. Here's your £500. Where's this cottage?'

We drove to a village called Ballynacally. At one of the pubs, we picked up a farmer with whom Jim had negotiated a rental the day before. The three of us drove up a winding road to a burned-down and abandoned stately home.

'This is Paradise,' said the farmer.

I mumbled puzzled agreement.

'Are we renting that, Jim? There's no roof.'

'Colonel William Henn used to live in that very house,' the farmer continued, 'but it's the cottage nearby you'll be renting. I didn't get your name, by the way.'

'His name's Brendan,' Jim quickly interjected.

'Brendan what?' asked the farmer.

'McCarthy,' I said. 'My family were originally from Cork.'

'Welcome to Paradise, Mr McCarthy.'

We drove to the remote cottage. There was absolutely no passing traffic. It would suit our purposes admirably.

'What's the address of this place?' I asked the farmer.

'Paradise Cottage, Paradise House, Paradise. But if I were you, Mr McCarthy, I'd also put on the envelope that it's near Ballynacally.'

Driving back in the direction of the Shannon Shamrock, I asked Jim why he had chosen the name Ashling for the Limerick company.

'Can't you even work that out with your fucking Oxford brain? Ashling means vision in Gaelic. It's also a combination of hashish and Aer Lingus. We could go and see the Limerick office if you like.'

The rented office was squashed between a small car-rental company and a do-it-yourself shop. Jim unlocked the door. It was a simple room with a desk and a phone. The phone worked, but Jim did not know its number. It had been the previous tenant's private line.

'Has Soppy Bollocks gone to Kabul?'

'Yes, he left this morning,' I lied.

'How long will it take him to send me the nordle?'

'What the hell is nordle, Jim?'

'You have to use codes, you stupid Welsh cunt. Codes and false names. Nordle is hashish.'

'Oh! Okay. Well, Soppy will take about a week to send you the nordle.'

'A week! A fucking week! Why so fucking long?'

'I don't know, Jim.'

We continued on our journey back to the Shannon Shamrock. There was plenty of time for me to make the flight back to Heathrow, so we had a meal in the hotel's restaurant. Jim made a phone call, and a few minutes later Gus came in. He took a seat at another table in the corner. He ignored us. We ignored him.

'Remember, H'ard, no fucking games. Codes and false names. Then it will all flow like the grace of a Mozart concerto. You're with me, kid. No one will bother you in Ireland. Anytime you want to get hold of me, call this number in Dublin. Don't give it to anybody. I mean anybody. See you next time.'

A few days later, Graham still hadn't left for the Middle East. The connection of his most suitably equipped to air-freight hashish was a man named Raoul, Mohammed Durrani's man in Karachi. I had met him several times at Graham's. He was a small, bespectacled, slightly overweight Pakistani about ten years my senior. Whenever I saw him, he was smiling broadly and counting large stacks of money. Graham and his Californian connection, Ernie Combs, a member of the Californian dope-dealing organisation, the Brotherhood of Eternal Love, had often sent vehicles of various descriptions to Pakistan to be filled up with Raoul's hashish. They were then driven overland to Europe, and, in some cases, put on ships to be taken across the Atlantic. Raoul was a rich man and owned cinemas and numerous other businesses in Karachi. All Graham had to do was give Raoul instructions for air-freighting or sea-freighting, and the job was done. He could do what he wanted in Pakistan when he wanted, except in times of natural disaster and war. India was threatening to invade East Pakistan and free it from West Pakistan's yoke. Serious war was inevitable. Visitors to Pakistan were discouraged. Raoul was unable to operate.

At least once every day, a very impatient Jim McCann rang up asking, 'How much fucking longer are you going to take?'

'Jim, there's a war on out there. Karachi airport is surrounded by soldiers. It's impossible to get anything out of there at the moment.'

'A war! What the fuck do you think is happening in my country? I'm surrounded by fucking soldiers everywhere. It doesn't stop me from fucking operating.'

'Well, it stops some people, including our man in Karachi.'

'Fucking Welsh academics. Can't you get the nordle from somewhere else?'

'Hopefully, yes. Graham's got people in Beirut and Kabul.'

'Kabul! You just said there's a fucking war there and you can't fucking do anything. Don't play fucking games, H'ard. I warned you about that.'

'Jim, the war is in Pakistan, which was where we were going to send the sporting goods from.'

'What fucking sporting goods?'

'The nordle, Jim. You know what I mean. Anyway, there's no war in Afghanistan. So Graham should be able to do it from there.'

'Tell Soppy Bollocks he's got three days to deliver or he's got a pair of busted kneecaps.'

'Okay, Jim.'

There were several similar conversations. Eventually Mohammed Durrani said he could send an air-freight consignment from Kabul within a week. On the strength of this, I flew back to Shannon, taking with me Marty Langford, who had agreed to live in Paradise Cottage until the hashish arrived and then guard it until it was ready for onward transportation to Britain. Jim met us at the Shannon Shamrock. He was very subdued but still a bit scary. He addressed Marty.

'This had better fucking work if you want to see Wales again. You hear me?' Then he left.

'I don't want to be a hostage, Howard. I don't mind sitting in a cottage all by myself, but I don't like all this heavy stuff like Niblo's on about, you know.'

'Don't worry, Marty. Niblo, as you call him, just talks threateningly. He never does anything.'

We drove a hired car to Paradise. Marty liked it. He was a widely read man of simple pleasures and looked forward to a period of reading books and pottering about. I left him there and flew back to London to see Graham. Jim had found out Graham's number (probably by ringing directory enquiries but claiming he had done so through his Kilburn investigation unit), so Graham was not answering the phone. His wife, Mandy, dutifully informed Jim every time he rang that Graham was in Kabul.

While I was at Graham's, Mohammed Durrani phoned. The consignment had left Kabul for Frankfurt, where it would be placed on an Aer Lingus flight to Shannon, and one of Durrani's men had arrived in London with the air waybill. Graham and I went to a flat in Knightsbridge to pick it up. We examined it closely. The consignment was described as being one of antique carpets being sent by an Ali Khan in Kabul to a Juma Khan in Shannon. It did not look good. I called Jim's Dublin number and left a message for him to call me at Graham's in a couple of hours. He did so.

'Well, it's left, Jim. It'll be with you tomorrow.'

'About fucking time.'

'There's a few problems, though, Jim.'

'What?'

'It's not sporting goods.'

'You mean it's not nordle?'

'No. It is nordle, but the paperwork doesn't describe it as being sporting goods as we instructed. It's described as antique carpets.'

'That's no fucking problem. I don't care what it's fucking described as. It's sent to Ashling, right?'

'Well, that's the other problem, Jim. It's addressed to Juma Khan, Limerick.'

'You stupid Welsh cunt. What did you put my fucking name on it for?'

It wasn't until then that I realised the similarity in pronunciation between the names Jim McCann and Juma Khan. This was too ridiculous for words.

'Have you got no idea about security? False names and codes. I fucking told you that a hundred fucking times, and you put my fucking name on it. What you fucking think this is? Amateur night?'

'Jim, Khan is like Mister in the Middle East. And it's Juma, not Jim. Juma means something like Friday in their language.'

Explanations to Jim fell on stony ground.

'Jim McCann might fucking mean Man Friday in Kabul, but in Ireland Jim McCann means it's fucking me, the Kid. I'll still get the nordle, but because of your fucking cock-ups, it'll cost me an extra £500. I need it right now.'

Early the next morning, I flew back to Shannon. This time Jim was waiting at the airport. He was fired up. He took the £500 and ran, screaming at the top of his voice, 'Wait for me in Paradise or the Shannon Shamrock. Check in as McCarthy.'

I hired a car and drove to Paradise. Marty was standing outside looking very relieved.

'Thank God it's you, Howard. I thought it was those Pakistanis again.'

'Pakistanis? What Pakistanis?'

'Two days ago, I heard a car pulling up. I thought it was you or Niblo from the IRA. The car stopped outside the gate, and two Pakistanis got out. You'd told me something about some Pakistani dope coming, and I remembered you telling me something about a pretend dead body or something coming from Pakistan, so I thought they were something to do with that, like. I thought they would either give me some dope or a coffin or something. In fact, they were selling shirts. Yeah, shirts! Then I figured you sent them as a joke. Then I thought Niblo had sent them to freak me out. Then I thought they were undercover Pakistani cops. I bought a couple of shirts off them. There they are. Not bad really for what I paid for them.'

The coincidences were beginning to get out of hand.

'You've had any other visitors?'

'No, that's it. Everything has been as quiet as a mouse, except for the rats. Rats freak me out.'

We had a cup of tea and some egg, peas, and chips. Marty always made the best. I'd brought over a little hash, and we had a smoke. I drove back to the Shannon Shamrock and checked in as Stephen McCarthy. My mother had seriously thought of christening me Stephen, and my ancestor Patrick Marks used the surname McCarthy. I hadn't yet graduated to using only false names that have absolutely no connection to one's past. These were early days.

I had dozed off for a few minutes when the phone rang. It was Jim.

'Come down right away, H'ard. Since when do antique carpets fucking rattle when you move them around?'

In the lobby, Jim was all smiles. I followed him to the hotel car park. In the middle was an unlocked, beaten-up Ford with a sack-covered cabin trunk on the back seat and a similar one in the boot, which, because of the size of the cabin trunk, had been left wide open. It stank of hashish.

'You see, H'ard, the Kid's done it. The Kid delivers with the grace of a Mozart concerto. I want my two grand, and another five hundred for extra expenses. And next time I don't want my fucking name on the paperwork, and I don't want fucking carpets that rattle, and I want some pornographic movies. But between me and you, Howard, it was a fucking good job the carpets did rattle. It convinced them they were bringing in guns. They knew they weren't fucking carpets. You understand me, do you? Here's the keys. Take this shit to Paradise. When do I get my fucking money?'

'Do you still want it in Amsterdam, Jim?'

'What the fuck use is it to me there, H'ard? You say some fucking stupid things sometimes. I want it here.'

'I've got a couple of hundred on me which you can have right now. The rest will arrive tomorrow.'

'Give it to me, and give me the keys of your car, H'ard. I'll drive it over to Paradise in about an hour. I've got to see some of my people. Don't open those fucking boxes till I get there.'

Jim tore off in my rented Volkswagen. The old Ford he'd left me was difficult to start. The gauge registered less than an eggcupful of petrol. The body of the car almost touched the ground. I drove to a nearby petrol station and was comforted to discover that most other vehicles on Irish roads also look suspicious. No one gave me a second glance on my journey to Paradise. Marty and I unloaded the car and, abiding by Jim's instructions, left the trunks unopened. Soon the aroma of the packaged hashish filled Paradise Cottage. Jim wasn't long. The three of us unpacked the trunks. There were two hundred pounds of the finest hand-pressed Afghani hashish. We smoked joint after joint. Marty and I giggled nervously as Jim tore around the room screaming, 'I've done it. I've done it. The Kid's done it.'

Marty and Jim collapsed into a deep sleep. I drove the hired Volkswagen a few miles to the nearest phone box and telephoned Graham with the good news. He was pleasantly surprised and told me that Patrick Lane would drive over right away with the balance of the money owed McCann and drive back with the hashish. Leaving the phone box, I noticed that the boot of the car was very low. I opened it. Inside were stacks of London telephone directories and boxes of plastic-covered chemicals. A little confused, I drove it back to Paradise. Jim was waiting outside the cottage door.

'You didn't go over any bumps, did you? That car's full of fucking explosives.'

'Well, take them out of there, Jim. Stick them in your wreck.'

'What's wrong with you? You only deal in fiction. Nordle is fiction. Fucking explosives and arms are non-fiction. That's reality, man. I deal in non-fiction. Not this fucking hippie shit.'

He threw away his half-smoked joint into the Irish night,

transferred his odd cargo of telephone directories and explosives from my car to his, and drove off.

Twenty-four hours later, Patrick Lane checked into the Shannon Shamrock. I was waiting in the lobby. I took the keys of his rented Ford Capri and drove it to Paradise while he had a sleep. Marty looked agitated and said, 'Niblo's just been here. He took away about twenty pounds of the hash. He said he'd be back very soon. He wants his money. And some dirty movies. He's a bit funny, Howard.'

We stashed the rest of the dope into the car, in the front door panels, the rear panels, and under the back seat. It fitted in easily enough, but the stench was overpowering. Jim arrived.

'Where's my fucking money?'

'You just took it, Jim. Twenty pounds of nordle is worth about £2,000. You've been paid.'

'You can have all of that hippie shit back right now.'

He went to his car, pulled out a bag, and gave it to me.

'That's only about ten pounds, Jim. Where is the rest?'

'That's all I fucking took.'

Then I realised I had forgotten to get the money off Patrick. I tried to explain to Jim, but he was most unreceptive.

'I'm getting it myself right now. This had better not be another of your fucking games. Wait here till I get back.'

Several hours later, Jim and Patrick arrived at the cottage. They were drunk and extremely angry with each other. Patrick had refused to pay Jim without my authorisation. Jim had threatened Patrick with Gus and other assets of the Belfast Brigade. Patrick, for the first time realising that there was a possibility of IRA involvement in the scam, had exploded. His grandfather, Patrick Murphy, a Catholic policeman in Belfast, had been murdered by the IRA. Jim said he must have deserved it. They were a hair's breadth away from coming to blows. Patrick gave me the money. I gave it to Jim.

'H'ard, I'm holding you personally responsible to make
sure this man never comes to Ireland again. He's got an
amnesty to drive back tonight, but that's it. I'll be in touch.
I'll be in touch with you, brother.'

Patrick was still fuming but insisted on leaving
immediately for the ferry. Within a day, Jarvis and the two
Charlies had sold all the hash and had collected over
£20,000. A number of people had to be paid. Given all the
expenses, particularly Jim's, no one had made a fortune. But
Jim, undoubtedly, could deliver the goods. It was we who
were experiencing problems sending them. We'd have to get
our act a bit more together to take advantage of this
extraordinary opportunity.

On January 1st, 1972, Graham made a New Year's
Resolution. He was going to get things together and personally oversee matters in Karachi in readiness for the next load
to Shannon. The intention was to do a ton, a big increase.
This time there'd be no mistakes.

Marty Langford had two old art college friends who
owned a car repair and sales business in Winchester. With
their assistance, we examined various cars to see how much
hashish could be safely stashed in each. The two-door Ford
Capri was perfect. It could hold at least 200 pounds just in
the rear panels and under the back seat. We bought a few.
There never seemed to be any eyebrows raised when cars
were paid for in cash.

There was tremendous wrangling about how the next deal
would divide up. McCann was getting wise to how much
money could be made in this business. Finally, it was settled
that he would be paid £30 for every pound of hashish he
imported.

Durrani and Raoul's costs in Karachi amounted to £35 a
pound. We would pay £10 a pound to anyone prepared to
drive a stashed Ford Capri on and off the Irish Channel
ferry. There would be some other small expenses. Hashish
was selling in London for about £120 a pound. On a ton

load, Graham and I should make £50,000 each. McCann would make more, but that was a pain we had to suffer.

Pretending to be arranging a farm-equipment salesmen's conference, McCann rented a remote farmhouse near Newmarket-on-Fergus, about twenty miles from Limerick. Shannon airport could be seen from some of the bedroom windows. I bought a stack of pornographic films and loaded them into one of the doctored Ford Capris. I drove from London to Swansea, on to the British & Irish ferryboat to Cork, and from Cork via Limerick to the Shannon Shamrock, where a room in the name of Stephen McCarthy had been booked. I was at the check-in desk about midday when a loud Belfast accent screamed in my ear, 'Don't fucking bother. We can stay at the farm. We'll go in your car. Gus has just taken mine to Dublin. We're going to burn down the British Embassy.'

We got into the car.

'So, how's about you? Did the academics on Brighton seafront like the nordle the Kid brought in?'

'They'd never heard of you.'

'You didn't fucking tell them I brought it in, did you? You fucking Welsh arsehole.'

'I'm kidding, Jim.'

'I got no time for games, H'ard. You know that. There's a fucking war on. Last Sunday, youse fucking Brits killed thirteen innocent Irishmen in cold blood. You think you got problems, man. I'll give you some fucking problems. And that fucking John Lennon is dead meat.'

'What's he done, Jim?'

'He promised to give a free concert in Derry, and I set it all up. Now, after last Sunday, he says he won't fucking do it. He's just going to write a fucking song about it. We got enough fucking songs, for fuck's sake. It makes me look bad, man. All the kids on Derry's streets were looking forward to it. I'm sending our Brendan to John Lennon's house in St George's Hill, Weybridge, to burn the fucker down. No one messes with the Kid. When's Soppy Bollocks sending the nordle? What's the fucking hold-up? What the fuck does he think this is? Amateur night? I got things to do, man. I just got back from Amsterdam buying some guns for the Provos. That's pressure, you understand me, a lot more fucking pressure than selling stamps and dresses.'

'I don't sell stamps and dresses. They're fronts to satisfy the authorities.'

'Fuck the authorities. Where the fuck are you at, H'ard?'

'It's security, Jim. It keeps them off my back. When I arrived at Cork today off the boat, I was asked what I was doing in Ireland. I said I was a stamp dealer specialising in 1922 overprints. It's like using a false name or cover. You told me that was important.'

'You're right, H'ard. Security's very important. Take one of these.'

He brought out a hand-held walkie-talkie.

'This time we do things to military precision with the grace of a Mozart concerto. When I pick up the nordle from Shannon, I want you to be alone in the farmhouse with one of these walkie-talkies. When I'm on my way to you I'll send you a coded radio message like "I've got the nordle."'

'What's the point of that?'

'So you'll know precisely what time I'll be delivering the nordle, you stupid Welsh cunt.'

'Why do I have to know precisely? If I know to the nearest few hours, I'll just stay at the farmhouse until you get there.'

'H'ard, just do as you're fucking told. I'll be calling you on one of these walkie-talkies.'

Following McCann's erratic directions, I drove us into the farmhouse grounds. The property was ideal for clandestinely stashing cars. We got out of the Ford Capri. McCann looked at it in disgust.

'That fucking car sticks out here like a pork chop at a Jewish wedding.'

'What did you expect me to come over in, Jim, a fucking tractor?'

'Don't be fucking facetious, H'ard. I told you this was a farming front operation.'

'Well, the Ford Capri is an excellent car for hiding things. There are about fifty dirty movies under the back seat.'

'About fucking time, Howard. I've been asking you for ages. Let's take them into the house. We can watch one now.'

'Do you have a screen and projector?'

'Of course I fucking don't. Since when does a farmhouse have those in it? You mean you didn't bring any?'

'I didn't know you wanted to watch the movies here. You can buy them in Limerick, can't you?'

'I've told you before, H'ard, pornography is illegal in Ireland.'

'Projectors aren't pornographic. But if you have a problem, I'll get one put in the next car to come on the ferry.'

'See that you do that, H'ard. It's important.'

I left Jim looking at the lavishly illustrated film boxes and drove to the nearest phone kiosk. I called Mandy. Graham had sent the ton load from Pakistan on Pakistan International Airways from Karachi to London, where it was booked on an Aer Lingus flight to arrive in Shannon that day. I took down the air waybill number. I went back to the Newmarket-on-Fergus farmhouse. McCann was holding up one of the 8mm pornographic films to the light trying to figure out the images. I gave him the particulars of the air waybill for the hashish load.

'I'll call you on the walkie-talkie at exactly 10 p.m. tonight,' screamed Jim, and climbed into my Capri.

'Don't you fucking leave here, mind,' he yelled out of the car window.

'I can't, Jim. You've got my car.'

Nothing happened at all until just after 10 p.m., when an inaudible crackling emitted from the walkie-talkie followed by a gentle Dublin accent whispering, 'I can't hear you, Jim. I'm not used to these gadgets.'

Then silence.

I heard vehicles in the far distance and opened the farmhouse door. Across the dark, deserted Irish landscape, I heard McCann's voice yelling, 'Pull the fucking aerial out, you idjit.'

My Capri was the first to pull up. Inside was an unassuming young man fidgeting with the controls of a walkie-talkie. Then a Volkswagen van pulled up. Inside was McCann, still yelling into a switched-off walkie-talkie, sitting in front of a ton of boxed-up Pakistani hashish.

'Nothing but idjits, the fucking both of you. Let's get these guns unloaded,' ordered McCann.

We took the boxes into the farmhouse. McCann's assistant drove off in the Volkswagen. Jim and I unwrapped a box. The hashish was excellent. We switched on the television. It was the news. The British Embassy in Dublin had been burned down.

'Told you,' said McCann.

Then it was *Gardai Patrol*, the Republic of Ireland's equivalent to *Crimewatch*, the public's chance to grass. A stern-faced Irish policeman appeared on the screen: 'Some household equipment, electric kettles and toasters, have been stolen from O'Reilly's in Sean MacDermot Street . . .'

'Can you believe that, H'ard? We're sitting on a ton of nordle worth a few hundred grand, and the cops are looking for fucking pots and pans.'

There were matters I now had to attend to in England: sending over empty cars and making arrangements for receiving full ones. I drove to the phone box and asked Marty to drive over another Ford Capri, bringing a projector and screen. McCann would wait guarding the hashish until he arrived. I flew from Shannon to Heathrow.

Apart from the members of the Tafia, other friends of mine had agreed to drive hashish from Ireland to England for a £2,000 fee. They included Anthony Woodhead, Johnny Martin, and several other university friends and their wives. I sent two such academic couples over to Ireland to be met by Marty. I prepared the Winchester car repair shop and garage to receive and destash returning cars and flew back to Shannon.

When I arrived back at the Newmarket-on-Fergus farmhouse, two university lecturers and their spouses were sitting in the darkened living-room staring with horrified expressions at a projection screen displaying a farmgirl having intercourse with a pig. Standing just off-screen was McCann. He had his dick out and was masturbating. After vainly attempting to persuade my Oxford friends that the world hadn't gone mad, Marty and I stashed their cars, and they set off. I flew back to Heathrow to supervise the destashing at Winchester. Graham had sensibly advised that I should no longer be actively involved in selling in London. I was already doing too much. He wanted James Goldsack to sell this load. I felt this was a bit unfair to Charlie Radcliffe, who had been instrumental in our meeting McCann and should, therefore, at least have some hashish to sell, but I went along with Graham. All 2,240 pounds of hashish were safely brought to Winchester and sold in London. I was £50,000 the richer, and everyone who had worked for me felt suitably rewarded.

My crude money-laundering structure in Oxford was cranked right up. AnnaBelinda 'sold' vast quantities of dresses every day. Dennis H. Marks, International Stamp Dealer, kept getting the most extraordinary good luck with 'finds' in his kiloware. Mythical individuals paid cash to Robin Murray Ltd., for their interior decoration. I had credit cards, life insurance, and many other trappings of an upwardly-mobile prick. To many, my parents included, I was a hard-working and successful straight businessman who had come back to his Alma Mater to make his fortune.

Friends now asked me for bigger loans. They claimed to have wonderful business ideas: all they needed was the capital. I was persuaded to pay for the purchase and shipping from Rotterdam to England of ten tons of Dutch candles. As a result of the coalminers' strike, there were severe power cuts and candles were at a premium. By the time the candles were ready to hit the streets, I had decided that my ethics would not allow me to weaken the impact of the coalminers' strike. Virtually all the male members of my family either worked or had worked underground in the South Wales coalfield. There was a conflict of interest. The candle entrepreneurship lost, and ten tons of plain Dutch candles occupied the otherwise empty space in the basement under AnnaBelinda.

I was, however, sincerely attracted by one of my friends' ideas. Denys Irving, the Balliol man who gave me my first-ever joint, had spent the last few years living in New York's Greenwich Village, San Francisco's Haight-Ashbury, and other Meccas of the hip and cool. He had now married Jamaican actress Merdelle Jardine, and they lived in London in an enormous warehouse in St Katherine's Dock. Denys had one clearly definable short-term goal: to produce a hit song entitled *Fuck You*. He'd already written the lyrics, the chorus of which was:

> Arse and cunt
> Back and front
> I just want to fuck you,
> Baby.

None of the existing record companies would consider it for a second, so we formed our own record company called Lucifer. We made a single and an LP. The LP tracks other than *Fuck You* were entitled *P-R-I-C-K*, *Puke on Me*, and suchlike. The music was a blend of the Who at their destructive best and raw Little Richard. No record shop or distribution centre would touch either single or LP. We ended up selling the single by mail order through *Private Eye*. We sold 1,500 copies. I had spent £15,000. London wasn't ready for Denys's punk; it waited for Johnny Rotten's.

Behind the candles under AnnaBelinda, I set up a hydroponic marijuana cultivation research centre. Robin Murray Ltd., built the growing tables. Anthony Woodhead took care of the nutrient solutions and lighting. Apparently, a friend of his worked for BOSS, the South African secret service, and had obtained research documents relating to United States government hemp production. The research concentrated on what chemical nutrients would make good rope and bad dope. Woodhead reasoned that by appropriate inversion, he could determine which chemicals would make good dope and bad rope. The electricity bills were enormous, but tolerable marijuana was grown.

Rosie became pregnant. Although each of us was still formally married to someone else, Rosie longed for a sister for Emily and longed again to be the mother of a baby. I knew Rosie was the lady for me. We were delighted. I bought her a quaint little cottage in Yarnton, a small, sleepy village outside Oxford, to enshrine our domestic bliss. We celebrated with a fortnight's luxury holiday at the Dome Hotel, Kyrenia, Cyprus. At the end of August 1972 I attended the maternity ward of Headington Hospital to witness the birth of my daughter Myfanwy. I have loved her dearly since the second she was born.

Myfanwy was two months old when the next Irish scam took place. The Newmarket-on-Fergus farmhouse had been abandoned because McCann had drawn attention to its location through his involvement with the dirty movies I had brought him. He had turned the farmhouse into the only place in the Republic of Ireland where one could participate in orgies and watch and buy pornographic movies. The Limerick police had stopped and searched a car leaving the vicinity of Newmarket-on-Fergus, frightened the occupants into disclosing the source of the pornography, and busted the farmhouse. McCann somehow gave them the slip, but the newspapers carried the story the next day, claiming that the Limerick police had the pornographic movies 'under observation' at the police station. McCann had found a replacement for the farmhouse in a curiously shaped country house situated in a tiny village with the unlikely name of Moone.

I still wanted to use my odd collection of Welsh drop-outs and Oxford academics to drive the hashish over from Ireland to England, but Graham was keen to use his Dutch connections. There hadn't been much work for the Dutch lately, and Graham felt that to keep them loyal, dedicated, and available, they should be given the chance to earn. I didn't argue.

According to McCann, there was some complication regarding shift changes at Shannon airport, and the next load from Pakistan had to arrive on a specific Aer Lingus flight from Frankfurt. McCann and I were in a bar in Moone. I was talking to Mandy in London on the phone. She told me the load had left Karachi but would probably be delayed a couple of hours en route to Frankfurt.

'Jim, it's not going to get to Frankfurt in time to be loaded on to our Aer Lingus flight.'

'It's got to be, H'ard. I've told you that a dozen times.'

'Well, it isn't going to be, Jim. Are you going to do anything about it, or shall I go home and write this one off?'

'Are you fucking crazy? I'll get the fucking nordle. But I want £50 a pound, £30 a pound won't even cover the Kid's expenses given the extra hassle you and Soppy Bollocks have caused me and the boys.'

'Forget it, Jim.'

'Put it this way, H'ard. You either pay me £50 a pound, or I'll rip off the fucking lot and become a legend. Give me the fucking phone. What's the number for international enquiries? I need to get hold of Aer Lingus in Frankfurt. Get me some coins, H'ard.'

I wondered what on earth he could be up to.

'Aer Lingus, this is yer man Jim McCann of the Provisional IRA. My boys have just put a bomb on your next flight to Shannon. You've got twenty minutes.'

Jim put the phone down with a broad beam of self-congratulatory delight.

'That should slow them down, H'ard, and give time for the nordle to arrive from Kabul and be loaded. You understand me, do you?'

'It's from Karachi, not Kabul. But they'll know it's a hoax, surely, Jim?'

'I used the code, H'ard. I'm authorised to use the IRA code. They know it's not a hoax.'

'What do you mean, Jim? That a bunch of Provos and British Army Intelligence guys secretly sat down and agreed that if the Provos began a bomb threat with the words "This is yer man", the Brits would take the threat seriously; otherwise, they wouldn't?'

'Don't be facetious, H'ard. It's a bad fucking habit.'

Whether or not the Karachi to Frankfurt flight was critically delayed and whether or not McCann's hijack threat was taken seriously remain unknown. My own belief is that there never was any vital requirement for the load to come into Shannon on a specific flight. This was all part of McCann's theatre, as indeed was his call to Aer Lingus in Frankfurt. He was probably talking to the speaking clock.

The load arrived, and the Dutchmen's cars were stashed in Moone. Dutch Nik took the first of several Volvos on the ferry and on to the Winchester stash. Dutch Pete followed. Then other Dutchmen. Then Dutch Nik again. The final load was brought over by Dutch Pete.

James Goldsack and Jarvis were about a third of the way through selling the hashish when Marty called me from Winchester. It was early in the morning, and I was feeding Myfanwy a bottle of milk.

'Howard, this is going to blow your mind, right?'

'Go ahead, Marty.'

'All the nordle has gone. Someone has stolen it.'

I drove to Winchester. Marty was, of course, right. Well over half a ton of dope had disappeared from the garage. Bits of door locks and latches lay on the ground. In my mind there was only one possible explanation. Graham's Dutchmen had come in the middle of the night and ripped it off. Graham wouldn't accept this and suspected everyone else. After a few days of stunned inactivity, McCann rang.

'Where's my fucking money?'

'The nordle's been ripped off, Jim.'

'By who? Those fucking Dutch hippies?'

'Yeah.'

'I told you, man, not to trust those Dutch cunts of Soppy's. They're treacherous. In future only your Welsh road-sign painters and academics can come over here. You understand me? But don't worry, H'ard. No one fucks with the Kid. I'll get the nordle. I've got the registration numbers of all those Dutch cunts' vehicles, and I've got their passport numbers. Gus and a couple of the boys from Belfast will track them down.'

'Jim, we don't want anyone getting hurt.'

'Who said anything about anyone getting hurt? I just want what's mine. I'm taking it.'

The only accounts I've heard of what then transpired have been those of McCann, and each one differs greatly from all preceding ones. It is certainly the case that McCann ended up with significant Dutch assets. It is very likely, of course, that McCann himself had persuaded Dutch Pete to do the Winchester rip-off in the first place, paying him a pittance to do so. He's that kind of guy.

Five

MR HUGHES

By the end of 1972, the Shannon scam had turned into an immense money provider. Admittedly, it was erratic and irregular. It was inescapably infested with McCann madness and the accompanying fears, whether real, contrived, or imaginary, of IRA participation. Nevertheless, many had made small and large fortunes as a result and were busily squandering them on fantasy fulfilment. Junior university lecturers could buy expensive cars that worked; those who'd always wanted to run a bar, café, or other small business could at least make a start; and I had boxes of money that I didn't know what to do with.

It was odd: I would still have recurring dreams of winning the football pools even though I had more than the prize money lying idly under the bed. I had more than enough money to retire for the rest of my life, but I wanted more, lots more. I wanted an inexhaustible supply. My lifestyle was becoming unacceptably flash, and Oxfordshire family country life lost its charm. London clubs took the place of Oxford pubs. I determined to expand my legitimate business activities as well as my dope-smuggling antics, and envisioned an AnnaBelinda boutique in each of the world's major cities.

At this point I was recruited to work for the British Secret Service. Hamilton McMillan (Mac), whom I had not seen since my postgraduate days, appeared one day at AnnaBelinda. We had a few drinks and a chat about old times. He had changed very little, still sporting his lamb-chop sideboards and blustering with mischievous arrogance. The Foreign Office were his current employers. For a while we kept up the charade of two Oxford chums, a junior diplomat and a small businessman, nostalgically mulling over the good old days. Then he admitted he actually worked as a spy for MI6, the security department of the Foreign Office. I admitted, without divulging any detail, that some of my money resulted from hashish smuggling. A general discussion of cannabis took place. Yes, of course it should be legalised. I pointed out that cannabis tended to be cultivated in countries particularly susceptible to political turmoil: Afghanistan, Pakistan, Lebanon, Colombia, and Morocco, to name but a few, and that those able to export it were invariably powerful individuals within their societies. He was fascinated with the amount of European travel I had done and with my plans for AnnaBelinda expansion.

'Howard, I'll come straight to the point. I haven't just turned up on your doorstep without doing my research. Will you help us?'

'You want me to be a spy, Mac?' I asked, clearly very surprised.

'It's not a word we use. But there are a number of areas where someone like you can be of immeasurable assistance to us. I still remember your extraordinary ability to pick up girls. You will always meet interesting people. Your legendary charm has not diminished.'

I liked what I was hearing. Was he going to throw me into bed with beautiful spies? The idea of screwing some voluptuous Mata Hari behind the Iron Curtain had its attractions.

'Keep talking, Mac.'

'At first, we just want to use some of your business establishments.'

'As what, Mac?'

'Letter drops, safe houses, that kind of thing. We would encourage you to open businesses in Romania and Czechoslovakia. Then, more interesting work would be unavoidable. I know you, Howard. You'll love it.'

'Sign me up, Mac. Just tell me what you want me to do.'

'At the moment, just carry on expanding, and keep your eyes and ears wide open.'

Mac left me with his home phone number, and with his office number, which I'll never forget – 928-5600.

'It's listed in the London telephone book under Her Majesty's Foreign Office, Parliamentary under-secretary. Ask for me by name, if you come across anything you think I should know. In any event, I'll contact you within the next few months.'

Mac's overtures had really got me going. What a front! A secret-service agent. James Bond. Not a licence to kill. I didn't want or need anything like that. But could it be a licence to smuggle hashish? Now, that I could definitely use. I'd better not tell McCann. The British Secret Service weren't too popular in Belfast. I'd better not tell anyone.

In early 1973, I decided to invest some of the cardboard boxes of money in dope deals that didn't involve McCann. An old Oxford acquaintance had a friend, Eric, who claimed he could smuggle suitcases from Beirut to Geneva through a personal connection in Middle East Airlines. Eric needed to be supplied with the hashish in Beirut. Furthermore, if given a boatload of hashish on a Lebanese beach, Eric was prepared to sail it to Italy. I discussed these possibilities with Graham, and we agreed to begin work on them. We gave Eric a couple of hundred grand and told him to get on with it.

Graham also mentioned an idea he had been presented with. A friend of his, James Morris, was responsible for manufacturing and arranging the transport of pop group equipment to and from the United States. In those days, British pop was at its peak of excellence, and groups such as Pink Floyd, Genesis, and Emerson, Lake and Palmer would frequently tour America with container trucks full of enormous speakers and amplifiers. The equipment, because it was only temporarily imported into America, underwent minimal examination by United States Customs. If the paperwork was in order, the equipment went straight through. Although source countries like Pakistan and Lebanon were not hosting British pop concerts, European countries were. Hashish was three times more expensive in America than in Europe. The scam was obvious. Fill the speakers with hash in a European country. Air-freight them across the Atlantic. Take the hashish out in America. Put bricks back in the speakers to avoid the possibility of weight discrepancies appearing on air waybills. Bring the speakers back across the Atlantic, and wait to get paid. Let's do it.

Mohammed Durrani was still coming up with Pakistani and Afghani diplomats who were moving several hundred kilos of hashish with their personal effects as they took up their positions in various Middle Eastern embassies throughout Europe. Lebanese Sam was doing the same thing with Lebanese diplomats, and, of course, he was only too glad to supply Eric with any of his needs in Lebanon. One of Sam's contacts had just smuggled a few hundred kilos into Paris, and in March 1973 the first transatlantic rock-group scam took place. None of James Morris's rock groups were actually due to tour America at the time, so four out-of-work musicians were hurriedly banded together to form a group called Laughing Grass and behave as if they had an engagement in California. Rock bands were continually splitting up and reforming with slight personnel modifications: there should be no grounds for suspicion.

The speakers were loaded with hashish in the remote French countryside and air-freighted from Paris to Los

Angeles, via New York. It worked like a dream. Graham's Brotherhood of Eternal Love contact, Ernie Combs, sold the hashish in California. I occasionally talked to him over the telephone when Graham was unable to. Ernie was invariably happy, witty, and extremely sharp. We developed an excellent telephonic rapport with each other.

A few weeks later, Mohammed Durrani came up with some Pakistani hashish in Vienna. This time we didn't even take the precaution of finding or creating a suitable touring British rock group. A name was written in the appropriate place on the customs form; that was all. The hashish was again sent to Philadelphia. No problems.

Eric was as good as his word and turned up at Geneva airport with a hundred kilos of Lebanese hashish that Sam had provided outside Beirut airport. It wasn't enough to justify a rock-group scam, so I asked Anthony Woodhead to drive it from Switzerland to England. He did so without a hitch. I paid everybody off and asked them to do the same again. This they did several times, until Eric had to concentrate on his Mediterranean boat scam. He was now in a position to pick up hashish off Lebanese Sam at the port of Juni, Lebanon.

During Eric's air-freight scams, I occasionally monitored his passage through Geneva airport. I noticed that some international flights had stopped in Zurich before the last leg to Geneva, and further noticed that suitcases checked in at Zurich emerged on arrival at Geneva on the same carousel as suitcases checked in at airports outside of Switzerland. This was worthy of focused investigation, and I was delighted to discover the existence of a Swissair flight whose itinerary was Karachi–Zurich–Geneva. I flew the flight's Zurich–Geneva leg. At Geneva airport the immigration police asked to see my ticket. They gave a cursory glance and let me through to pick up my luggage. There was no customs check after baggage pick-up.

Graham and I sent Anthony Woodhead to Karachi and

asked him to catch this potential goldmine of a Swissair flight just to see what would happen. I waited at Geneva airport. When Woodhead showed his ticket, they took him to the luggage carousel to identify his suitcase, which they then thoroughly searched. We sent Woodhead back out to Karachi and arranged with Durrani and Raoul to fill Woodhead's suitcase with hashish. Woodhead got on the Zurich–Geneva flight. In Zurich, I got on the same plane with another suitcase, which had previously been filled with Woodhead's effects. I got off the plane first and showed my ticket to the Geneva immigration police, who waved me through. I picked up Woodhead's suitcase of hashish from the luggage carousel and carried it out. Woodhead showed his ticket. Swiss Customs wanted to see his suitcase. He showed them mine and displayed its innocent contents. Later on, I gave him back his suitcase, and he drove the hashish to London. We repeated this a few times until the Swiss changed their customs procedures, rendering the scam impossible.

My first assignment for MI6 was to seduce a female employee of the Czechoslovakian Embassy. Mac's bosses thought she was a KGB agent. She was known to be attending a forthcoming birthday party, and it had been arranged for invitations to be issued to me and Mac. I was shown a few photographs. She looked nice. The party took place in Highgate. I didn't know anyone there other than Mac. The girl didn't show up, and I wasn't even offered expenses. This business was clearly a test of one's patriotism and patience. No wonder they kept it secret.

Much as Graham and I were enjoying the lack of business with McCann, it was difficult to resist. We planned to send 1,500 kilos, our biggest load yet, to Shannon and deliver it to Moone. Some we would move in the usual way on the ferry to England. The rest we would take to another house in County Cork, rented by Woodhead, whose location was unknown to McCann, and air-freight it from Dublin to New York in James Morris's Transatlantic Sounds rock-group equipment. We could take care of paying McCann and the Pakistanis out of the British sales, and McCann wouldn't know we were making heaps more money by selling hashish in California. I was soon sitting on a ton and a half of Pakistani hashish in the curious Moone property, loading up the first drivers for the ferry before dashing to catch the next flight to London.

We couldn't use the Winchester garage as the British destashing point after the Dutch fiasco. James Goldsack had his own facilities, so the first two carloads were sent across on the ferry to him while a few other carloads went to the place in County Cork. While selling the first carload, James Goldsack was busted. The second carload of hashish had been parked outside Hammersmith Police Station. James was being grilled inside the police station. In an extra-ordinary display of pure courage, Patrick Lane broke into the car and retrieved the hashish. I took it from Patrick to Rosie's cottage in Yarnton. I repackaged the hashish from its plastic wrappings into suitcases and threw the plastic wrappings on to a pile of litter on the country roadside.

Transatlantic Sounds rock-group equipment was sent from London to Cork, filled up with hashish at Woodhead's Irish country place, and air-freighted from Dublin to the United States.

We badly needed a new destashing premises in England, so Marty rented a farmhouse near Trelleck in Monmouthshire. Hashish from Ireland and Oxford accumulated in Wales. Jarvis sold enough to pay off McCann, Pakistan, and the drivers. The rock-group equipment was destashed in California by Ernie Combs and the Brotherhood of Eternal Love. Ernie sold the lot at three times the price we would have got in London in just one day. Greatly impressed, we filled some more Transatlantic Sounds speakers with what hashish was left in Marty's Trelleck farmhouse and sent them from Heathrow to Phoenix. We took a week's breather.

There were worries whether James Goldsack would talk. Would he blow the Irish scam? In fact James was as solid as a rock. He admitted being a hashish dealer and refused to testify against anyone else. Nothing seemed to be compromised. The Irish scam was still unknown to the authorities.

During the week's inactivity, I invited my parents and grandmother to visit Rosie, me, and the children at the cottage in Yarnton. It was a warm spring Sunday afternoon. My grandmother was doting over little Myfanwy. Emily was playing dressing up with my father. Rosie and my mother discussed maternal matters. I was trying to stabilise. A police car drove up the little lane and pulled to a halt outside the cottage. Two members of the Thames Valley Constabulary emerged holding a few of the plastic wrappings I had just discarded on the roadside. I remained seated, paralysed. My mother looked at me, puzzled and worried. She could tell I was uneasy.

'Does someone called Emily live here?' asked one of the policemen, unexpectedly.

'Yes, that's my daughter. Why?' Rosie was unshaken.

'Is this envelope hers?' asked the policeman, pulling out a small envelope addressed to Emily at Yarnton.

I then realised what must have happened. Emily, in childish innocence, must have stuffed one of her letters into the waste-bag containing the hashish wrappings. Instead of taking the wrappings to a rubbish dump or burning them, I had stupidly thrown them away at the roadside. Someone had discovered them. The wrappings were full of crumbs of cannabis, covered with my fingerprints, and accompanied by an envelope which had been in my house. This could be serious.

'Yes, it is. Where did you get it?'

Rosie was still completely unshaken. Did she realise the danger we were in?

'It was with these, ma'am,' said the policeman, holding up some plastic wrappings.

'Have you seen these before?' the second policeman addressed the family group as a whole.

'Well, no,' said my mother.

'We've just arrived from South Wales, Officer,' said my father. 'How would we know anything?'

Dad was always firm with police.

My grandmother kept playing with Myfanwy as if the policemen did not exist. The first policeman looked me directly in the eyes.

'What about you, sir? Familiar to you, are they? Obviously, they came from here, didn't they?'

'No, I've never seen them before.'

'Oh! Now I remember,' interjected Rosie with first-class criminal inspiration. 'The man who came to fix the damp course last week had a big bag of these wrappings left over when he'd finished doing his work. I suppose all the chemicals he used must have been in them.'

'I don't suppose you have his name and number, ma'am.'

'I certainly do. I was going to call him anyway. His work was so shoddily done.'

Rosie gave the policemen the name and number. They shot off to harass some poor damp-course man. I excused myself on the pretext of having to attend to important matters at AnnaBelinda, sped off down the M40 to London, and checked into Blake's Hotel, Roland Gardens, under the name of Stephen McCarthy.

I was sure the police would return to Yarnton and was haunted by images of Rosie in a police cell and two little girls crying in intense fear and sadness. Rosie was easily persuaded to leave the country, and in my BMW, she, the two little girls, and a wonderful nanny named Vicky drove to Ibiza and rented a house in Santa Eulalia. I stayed at Blake's.

I had to find out what was going on and thought maybe Mac would help. I called the Foreign Office and arranged to

meet him. I told him what had happened at Yarnton. Later
on the same day, we met again.

'Did you find anything out, Mac?'

'I certainly did. You can rest assured that the police are
not minded to arrest you. Feel free to go home. But I want
you to meet one of my superiors, tomorrow, if possible. He
has some questions for you.'

'What kind of questions?'

'He mentioned Ireland.'

'Mac, I can't talk about that. It involves my dope-dealing
business.'

'Howard, I assure you we are not interested in your
smuggling of cannabis. That is of no concern to us. Other
matters in Ireland may be.'

'Like what?'

'Donald will explain to you tomorrow.'

Donald, a stern-faced, well-dressed spy, Mac, and I met
for lunch at the Pillars of Hercules, just off Soho Square.
Donald came to the point.

'We know you have been meeting a member of the
Provisional IRA who supplies them with arms and know why
you have been meeting him. We would like you to carry on
meeting him to get some information from him.'

'Well, I have no plans to see him again right now.'

'That's fine. But when you do, let McMillan here know.'

'Sure.'

Mac and I went to his home in Putney. We had a whisky
each in his sitting room.

'Howard, this might clear up any uncertainties,' said Mac,
producing a photograph. I looked at it. It was a picture of
McCann with his name underneath. Mac took it back from
me and went into his study to make a phone call.

There was no doubt in my mind that I had to let McCann
know MI6 were on his case. If MI6 knew he was dope-
dealing, the IRA would soon get to know, and McCann
might get executed. No more Shannon deals. They had to

stop. It was just too dangerous, too heavy. Where had all that peace and love stuff gone? Arms smuggling, Bloody Sunday, executions, and knee-cappings. Ernie's Brotherhood of Eternal Love came far closer to traditional dope-dealing values of sex, drugs, and rock 'n' roll; and they could make far more money. No more McCann. I would warn him of the danger, then get out of his life. I wanted that photograph of him so he would know I wasn't playing games.

Mac returned. I asked if I could telephone AnnaBelinda. He motioned me towards his study, and I made my phone call, letting my eyes roam over Mac's bookshelves. A book named *The Unconscious Mind* snatched my attention. I picked it up, opened it, and the photograph of McCann fell out. I put it into my pocket. That has remained the most inexplicable event in my life.

Feeling noble and resolute, I left Blake's and went back to Yarnton. I cabled Rosie to call me and told her it was safe for her to come back. She said she didn't want to come back. Life in Ibiza was far more meaningful: sun, stars, beaches, and lots of dope to smoke. She suggested that before I turn into a money-making megalomaniac and lose all my friends, I should join her in Ibiza. But I should promise not to bring with me any of my fucked-up lifestyle. She'd made some wonderful friends who wouldn't appreciate it. I could tell I was losing her. I went to visit Fanny Hill and began a very clandestine affair with her. At the same time, she was having a less clandestine affair with Raymond Carr, the Master of St Anthony's College, Oxford's CIA annexe.

I went to Ibiza and thought it would make a good neutral venue to meet McCann.

'Why the fuck have you dragged me here, H'ard, in the middle of all this hippie shit? You know I'm busy. Why couldn't you have come to Ireland? This had better be important.'

'It is, Jim. MI6 are on to you.'

'Who the fuck cares? There's a war going on. And what the fuck's MI6 got to do with you, you Welsh cunt?'

'An old Oxford friend of mine works for them. They know you and I have been dope-dealing. If they know, other people know, like maybe the IRA.'

Jim went white.

'Fuck off! Fuck off, will you! You're playing fucking games.'

I showed him the photograph.

'You and Soppy Bollocks, I knew you were fucking Brit agents. I knew it. How can I know you haven't been setting the Kid up all along?'

'Try thinking, Jim.'

'Fuck you!'

'This is it, Jim. No more deals for a while.'

'Okay, H'ard. But I'm staying here in Ibiza for a while for a holiday. My new Dutch girlfriend, Sylvia, and my old Irish girlfriend, Anne, are coming over. We'll stop with you.'

'I thought you were busy, Jim.'

In a couple of days, Rosie's Santa Eulalia holiday house had turned into a madhouse. McCann was playing musical beds with Sylvia and Anne, unsuccessfully encouraging Rosie and Vicky to do the same, and forever filling the house with various odd characters he picked up in the bars in Ibiza. He was making me laugh, so I didn't mind. I called AnnaBelinda in Oxford. There was a message to phone Eric in Athens. I knew Eric had picked up the hashish from Lebanon. He must have already landed it in Italy, where Johnny Martin had rented a villa in preparation to receive both the dope and Transatlantic Sounds rock-group equipment. Great!

It wasn't great. Eric said that there'd been a slight problem. I should come to Athens now. I packed my bags, and Rosie exploded.

'That's right. Leave me in the middle of all this chaos you've brought to ruin my holiday. I told you not to do this. Where are you going?'

'Athens. Fancy coming? Vicky can look after the children.'

The 'slight problem' was that Eric had temporarily

stashed 700 pounds of Lebanese hashish on a remote Greek island. A herd of goats had unearthed the dope, which was spotted by some Greek sponge fishermen. The sponge fishermen had taken the hashish to Crete and were selling it at absurdly cheap prices. I knew Eric was telling me the truth. Eric's solution was to launch a commando-style attack in Crete and recover the hashish. I told him to forget it, but if he ever did get it back, I'd like some. After a quick tour of the Acropolis, Rosie and I flew back to Ibiza.

Graham favoured a commando solution and wanted to proposition McCann. I persuaded him not to. With no other means at his disposal, he sent Patrick Lane to Heraklion. A week later, Patrick returned with a sun-tan, lots of tall stories, and no dope, but I'm sure he did his best.

Graham told Ernie that the Italian speaker shipment was off. Ernie said it wasn't: some friends of his were soon to arrive in Italy having driven from Kabul in a camper stashed with Afghani hash. One of his friends was a draft-dodging Californian scientologist named James Gater. James Morris and I met Gater at Johnny Martin's rented villa in Cupra Maritima, near Ancona, on the Adriatic coast. We destashed the camper that had come from Afghanistan, put the hashish into Transatlantic Sounds speakers, and air-freighted it to Los Angeles from Rome. James Morris and I caught a flight from Rome to Zurich, where he introduced me to his Swiss banker. I opened up an account at the Swiss Bank Corporation. The banker assured me there would be no problem in my depositing large amounts of cash. Ernie gave me $100,000 for my assistance. Graham said I could keep it all. He wouldn't interfere with any deal I made with Ernie as long as I did not interfere with deals he intended doing with McCann. We would remain partners on all other deals and could invest in each other's individual deals without participation. I agreed but couldn't help worrying about Graham. He was changing from a bourgeois, middle-class monarchist buccaneer to the exact opposite. That was okay, but he was doing it too quickly and doing it under the influence of McCann. God knows what McCann had in mind, but it wouldn't have been Graham's political development.

In Ibiza, Rosie had given up the Santa Eulalia holiday house and rented a *finca* in the middle of nowhere. She was going back to nature. There wasn't even a bathroom or toilet, and it was several miles from a telephone. I put up with it for a while. Rosie and I were getting on well again. We had confessed our infidelities and were pretending they didn't matter. She introduced me to one of many Dutchmen who had places on the island. His name was Arend, and he was a heavy-drinking, fun-loving dope dealer from Amsterdam. I asked him what sort of prices and quantities normally prevailed in Amsterdam. I reported them to Ernie. He sent over Gater and another friend of his, Gary Lickert, to Amsterdam with several hundred thousand dollars, and Arend and I invested some money of our own. Gater rented a flat in Maastricht, near Utrecht. A hired truck full of Transatlantic Sounds speakers was parked outside. Arend and I purchased 700 pounds of Lebanese hashish from an Amsterdam wholesaler friend of his. Gater and I stashed the speakers, and one of James Morris's people drove the truck to Schiphol Airport and air-freighted them to Las Vegas via New York.

It was early September 1973, and Ernie had invited me to come over to California once the Dutch load had been sent. I could pick up my own profit and maybe spend some of it. I was in Los Angeles before the speakers arrived at Las Vegas. Ernie and James Morris met me at the airport. Ernie was tall, thin, bearded, bespectacled, long-haired, and sun-tanned. He was Californian.

'Hi. How you doing? Have a good flight?'

'Yeah. It was long, though.'

Ernie thought for a second, then machine-gunned a few sentences.

'Shit! I used to do that son-of-a-bitch once a week when I was working with Graham in the early days. What's his beef, these days? He's been really kinda rude to me. I get pissed with that. Well, we should pick up our load from Las Vegas airport tonight. You're booked into the Newporter Inn, an old Richard Nixon hangout. Nixon cracks me up. What you like to do for fun? There's real good surf here. I got a shed full of surfboards.'

'I've never tried surfing, Ernie.'

'How about sailing?'

'Never tried that either.'

'Not an ocean lover, huh? Okay. You want to go motorcycle riding in the desert? I got a bunch of real nice bikes.'

'That's another thing I've never done. I've been a passenger, but I've not ridden one. Not even a pushbike.'

Ernie started laughing uncontrollably. I joined in.

'I guess it seems strange to you, Ernie, yeah?'

'You got that right. So what do you do when you ain't working, watch television?'

'Sometimes. But usually I just get stoned, read books, and listen to music.'

'You'll like California,' said Ernie.

I did, or what I saw of it, which was mainly the inside of a hotel room in Newport Beach. I wandered around the hotel complex, the bars, swimming pools, and other public areas, and realised that American movies weren't about fantasy: they were documentaries about Hollywood. There were hundreds of radio stations and dozens of TV channels. In Britain we had only three. The radio stations were fantastic. I listened to a few hours of doo-wop and golden oldies before the commercials drove me mad. All the TV channels were showing sport, cop shoot-outs, sit-coms, game shows, or news. I watched the news. A reporter said, 'Hey, one of you guys out there has just lost $5,000,000. Today, law enforcement officers seized Nevada's biggest ever haul of illegal drugs. Hashish, highly concentrated cannabis from the Middle East, almost half a ton of it, was discovered hidden in speaker cabinets. Over to Las Vegas . . .' On the screen came pictures of the Lebanese hashish and the speakers Gater and I had stashed in Holland.

In the movies, the crook, usually a fugitive, always immediately switches off the radio or television when the relevant news bulletin finishes. I didn't. I stared at it blankly for at least an hour. Was this really happening? I was very jet-lagged from my first-ever long flight, and Ernie had given me the most varied collection of hashish and marijuana imaginable. I was as stoned as I'd ever been. This was Hollywood. It probably wasn't happening.

There was a knock on the door. It was Ernie, and it was happening.

'Well, we lost that one. The cops . . .'

'I know, Ernie. I just saw it on TV.'

'No kidding. That was quick. What you figure on doing next?'

'I think I ought to leave.'

'That's smart. Here's $10,000. I guessed you didn't bring a bunch of money over with you. It'd be kinda dumb if you were coming to pick some up. Here's my new phone number. Call me.'

'Thanks, Ernie. How did the load get busted? Do you know?'

'Sure I do. Didn't it say on TV? The load transited in John F. Kennedy Airport, New York. When the airport loaders put it on the plane to Vegas, they fucked up and left one speaker behind, which they stuck in some shed in Kennedy overnight, and a dog sniffed it. The DEA took the dope out of the speakers once they were in Vegas and let my guy, Gary Lickert, the kid you met in Amsterdam, pick it up so they could see where he was taking it to. I had that covered. I was watching Gary from a distance. I saw him being followed, overtook him, gave him the signal, and haularsed outa there.'

'What did Gary do?'

'Drove in circles around the airport until the cops stopped him.'

'Will he tell the cops about you and me?'

'No. He did a tough stint in Vietnam. He won't crack. But we should play it cool for a while, like a few days. I got friends in the FBI. I'll find out what they got on us. Take a limo from here to LA airport. When you get there, buy a ticket in some dumb English name like Smith for a flight to the East Coast, somewhere like Philadelphia, then fly in your own name to anywhere you want.'

I flew to New York and stayed at the Hilton overnight, visiting Greenwich Village, Times Square, and the Statue of Liberty. Then I flew to London. Mac wanted to see me. We met at Dillons bookshop and took a cab ride to nowhere in particular.

'Howard, you know that recently we have had to suffer some embarrassment over the Littlejohn affair.'

'Yes.'

Kenneth and Keith Littlejohn were bank robbers who had claimed to be infiltrating the IRA at the behest of MI6. The claims had been substantiated, and the British public expressed outrage at their Secret Service's employing of notorious criminals for undercover work in the independent Republic of Ireland.

'For that reason, and that reason alone, you and I have to terminate our relationship. We can no longer liaise with criminals.'

'Dope smuggling is hardly a crime, Mac.'

'Of course it is, Howard. Don't talk rot. It's illegal.'

'I thought you agreed hashish shouldn't be illegal. It's the law that's wrong, not the activity.'

'I do. But until the law changes, you're a criminal.'

'Don't you think, Mac, there's a duty to change laws which are wrong, evil, harmful, and dangerous?'

'Yes, but by legal means.'

'You would use the law to change the law.'

'Of course.'

'I suppose you would recommend saving a drowning man by telling him to drink his way out of it.'

'That's sophistry, Howard, and you know it. This end to our relationship is not my decision. I've been ordered to tell you this.'

I felt curiously cheated. My career as a spy was over without my having derived any benefit from it.

'Mac, if by abiding by my own decisions and beliefs, rather than those of others, I come across something which affects the security of this country, do I take it that I should now no longer bring it to your attention?'

Mac smiled. I've not seen him since.

After the Greek sponge fishermen fiasco, Eric was determined to make amends; he went to Beirut. He found his own source of supply who was prepared to give him 100 kilos of hashish on credit. Eric offered to extend this credit to us and bring another suitcase to Geneva. The deal went ahead smoothly. Anthony Woodhead drove the hashish from Geneva to England.

One of Mohammed Durrani's diplomats turned up in Hamburg with 250 kilos of Pakistani hashish. Graham and I sent out one of the Tafia, who rented a car and a lock-up garage in the outskirts of Hamburg to store the dope.

James Morris rang from Los Angeles. Three of his workers had been arrested in London. He didn't know why. Neither did Graham or I. We knew American law had been broken, but we couldn't see how anyone involved had been guilty of breaking British law. Graham didn't want to bother to find out. He'd been to prison once; that was enough. He wanted to go to Ireland under a false identity to join McCann and supervise matters from there. It was safer. McCann had got him a false Irish driving licence. He left London that night.

Graham was right. Whatever reason was used to bust James Morris's workers could be used to bust us. I didn't want to rejoin McCann so soon after breaking from him, but Ireland was the only foreign country one could travel to from England without showing a passport. If there really was a danger of being arrested, I clearly shouldn't travel around under my own name. I had no choice but to seek refuge with McCann. I borrowed Denys Irving's driving licence, hired a car, stashed my passport, some dope, money, and bits and pieces in the back panels, and drove to Fishguard. On the ferry I drank several pints of Guinness at the bar before it docked at Rosslare. Once I reached open country, I stopped and rolled a very stiff joint of Afghani. As night fell, I drove towards Drogheda, where McCann was now based. Cruising along at 50 mph, I totally missed a right-angled bend and crashed through a hedge into a field. I lost consciousness.

'Will he be needing a doctor or a priest?'

Two carloads of people surrounded the steaming, dripping vehicle. Although I was lying awkwardly, I felt no pain and could move all my muscles.

'I'm all right,' I said.

'Don't you be moving now. We'll have an ambulance and tow-truck here in no time. No time at all.'

I thought of the dope and my inconsistent identity documents.

'No, look, I'm perfectly all right,' I said, leaping out of the wreck. 'If someone could give me a lift to the nearest telephone, I'll be able to take care of everything myself.'

'That'll be at Bernard Murphy's down the road. Jump in.'

Bernard Murphy's, which was actually named something like the Crazy Horseshoe, was heaving with serious Irish Saturday-night revelry. A large group were energetically performing an Irish jig around the telephone. A few young lads were holding the phone and sticking fingers in their ears. I made a reversed charges call to McCann at Drogheda and told him I was stuck in the Crazy Horseshoe about ten miles outside Rosslare. Would he please come and get me? He arrived in a couple of hours.

'Some fucking operator you are. Can't drive a fucking car. Got nowhere to go. Can't even go back to selling dope on Brighton seafront, or dresses to fucking academics. Like a rolling fucking stone. Why don't British Intelligence help you out? You can't do things without the Kid, can you? This is war, H'ard. Soppy Bollocks has joined the struggle. You fucking better, too. You got two fucking choices: I'll lend you £500 and you fuck off, or, with a new passport that the Kid'll give you, you handle these two deals from Kabul and Lebalon, or whatever the fuck that place is called, that Soppy Bollocks told me you and him are in the middle of.'

'What you mean by handle?'

'Soppy told me the Lebalon nordle is in London. Sell it. The Kabul nordle is in fucking Nazi land. I've already blown up a British Army base in Mönchengladbach, and the Baader-Meinhof gang eat out of my fucking hand. I want you to give the Kabul nordle to my man in Hamburg. He'll sell it.'

'How much do we all make?'

'We're partners, H'ard. Me, you, and Soppy. Equal shares after everyone else has been paid off.'

'That's fair enough for the dope in Hamburg if your guys are selling it. But why should you get anything from the Lebanese deal?'

'Soppy's already agreed, H'ard.'

We picked up my belongings from the wrecked car and drove to McCann's Drogheda hideout. The false Irish passport took a few days, during which time McCann constantly berated me for incompetence. It looked perfect and was in the name of Peter Hughes.

'Is this a real person, Jim?'

'Peter Hughes is fucking real all right. He's a member of the Provos, and he's interned by the Brits.'

'In that case, it doesn't seem to be a particularly good idea for me to pretend to be Mr Hughes,' I said.

'Well, the cops are not fucking looking for him. He's in Long Kesh, and they fucking know that. They're looking for you, H'ard. Think, you stupid Welsh cunt.'

McCann took me to the airport.

'Let me give you some advice, H'ard. Never fly to where you're really going. Do the last bit by train, bus, or car. See, there's an Aer Lingus flight to Brussels. Go on it, then take a train to Hamburg.'

On my arrival in Brussels, the Immigration Officer looked carefully at my Peter Hughes passport. He looked up.

'Howard?' he asked.

I froze. I'd been found out. But the Immigration Officer was smiling. Then I realised he was merely making a joking reference to billionaire Howard Hughes.

'You have a famous name, Mr Hughes.'

After several hours on the train, I checked into the Atlantic Hotel, Hamburg, where I was meant to stay until McCann called with his friend's whereabouts. I had the keys to the car and garage. Meanwhile, Marty Langford had checked into the International Hotel, Earls Court, London, with a carload of Lebanese hashish in the hotel car park. Charlie Weatherley was going to sell it. I called Marty. He wasn't in his room. I left my number with reception. I called again after a while. Someone else answered the phone in his room.

'Could I please speak to Marty?' I asked.

'Yes, this is Marty, go ahead.'

The voice wasn't remotely like Marty's.

'This is Marty. Who are you?'

I put the phone down and rang again.

'Could you put me through to Mr Langford's room, please?'

'Hello, hello, this is Marty speaking.'

It was now obvious to me what had happened. Marty had

been busted, and the police were in his room finding out what they could. I had stupidly left my hotel number in Hamburg with the receptionist at the International Hotel, Earls Court. It was time to check out and scarper.

On the flight schedule board at Hamburg airport there were two flights leaving almost immediately, one to Helsinki and one to Paris. I couldn't remember in which country Helsinki was situated, so I bought a ticket for the Paris flight. At Paris I was able to get a flight to Barcelona, and from there to Ibiza. By the time I landed, I had a heavy fever. For the next two days, I stumbled around Rosie's primitive *finca* deliriously searching for a telephone and a toilet. Rosie ignored me. When I recovered, I went straight to Ibiza airport and called Marty's, Weatherley's, and a host of other London numbers. No answer. I called McCann's in Drogheda. No answer. I caught the next flight to Amsterdam and went to Arend's flat. I called McCann's again.

'Don't you ever call this fucking number or show your fucking face in my country again. My Anne is in prison because of your fuck-ups. She's with those fucking Nazis, man. Marty and his two friends are over here. I've given them sanctuary. You promised them riches and gave them fucking ashes, you Welsh cunt.'

The torrent continued. I was able to piece together what had happened. Charlie Weatherley had gone to Marty's rooms to get a sample of the Lebanese. He was stopped by a hotel security man on the way out, and when asked which room he had come from, gave Marty's. The security man hauled Charlie up to Marty's room to check. Marty, thinking that Charlie must have been busted, denied all knowledge of him. Marty panicked, packed his clothes, left his room, left the carload of Lebanese, and fled to Ireland, taking the rest of the Tafia with him. McCann had no idea what had happened to me. He sent his girlfriend, Anne McNulty, and a Dutchman to Hamburg to pick up the car from the lock-up garage with the spare keys that Graham had. They got busted by the Hamburg police.

'Jim, I'm genuinely sorry about Anne. Is there anything I can do?'

'I don't need your fucking help. I've already personally declared war on those fucking Nazis. They know what the Kid's capable of. Unless they want a fucking reminder of World War II, they'd better let Anne go.'

I called up Ernie. He said he'd come over to see me in Amsterdam during the next few days. The Paradiso, Amsterdam's first legal joint-smoking café, had just opened. I was beginning to like the city with its pretty canals, hooker window displays, and liberal dope-smoking policy. Perhaps I should settle here. One evening, I went to the Oxhooft, a night-club, and ran into Lebanese Joe.

'Hey, Howard, man, it's good to see you. What are you doing here?'

'I might be living here from now on.'

'Same as me, man. It's a cool place. Give me your number. Here, have a smoke.' He put a piece of Lebanese hashish in my top pocket.

Ernie arrived and checked in under a false name at the Okura Hotel. I told him my tales of woe.

'Hey, don't worry. We're going to do something from this Amsterdam place real soon, even if we go back to our old way of taking new European cars to the States. It made me a bunch of money, I'll tell you. Here's $100,000. Start buying. And here's a sole of Afghani. I know there ain't nothing good to smoke in Europe. Can I give you a lift anywhere? I got a rent-a-car.'

'Yes please, Ernie. I think I'll open up a bank deposit box to put this money in and then get to Arend's.'

Ernie drove me to the Algemene Bank Nederland. I opened up a safe-deposit box in the name of Peter Hughes and placed the $100,000 and the Irish Peter Hughes passport inside. Arend was overjoyed at the idea of buying some more hashish in Amsterdam. We made a pipe out of Ernie's Afghan. There was heavy knocking on the door. It burst open, and six Dutch police swarmed through the flat. I got up to leave.

'I don't live here. I have an appointment. I have to go,' I stammered.

One of the police stopped me and searched me. He found the piece of hashish Lebanese Joe had given me. He asked for my passport. I still had my own. I gave it to him.

'Are you Dennis Howard Marks?'

'Yes, I am.'

'We are arresting you and will now take you to the police station.'

Three of them marched me downstairs and put me into the back seat of a car before climbing in. At the police station, they went through my pockets again and took everything away. They took down my particulars and led me towards the cells. Mick Jagger was singing *Angie* on the police-station radio. I was busted.

Six

ALBI

In April 1974, almost six months later, I was sitting in a flat
near the top of a high-rise building in the Isle of Dogs,
overlooking the River Thames and Greenwich naval station.
I was skipping bail. Over my Amsterdam lawyer's protests,
the Dutch police had put me aboard a BEA flight to
Heathrow. Her Majesty's Customs and Excise Officers came
on the plane at Heathrow and took me to Snowhill Police
Station, where I was charged under the hitherto unenforced
Section 20 of the Misuse of Drugs Act, 1971, with assisting
in the United Kingdom in the commission of a United States
drug offence. Californian James Gater, who had been
arrested at Heathrow airport a couple of days before my
arrest, and a few of James Morris's workers were my co-
defendants. After three uneventful weeks in Her Majesty's
Prison, Brixton, I was granted bail for sureties totalling
£50,000. On bail, I lived with Rosie and the children at 46,
Leckford Road, Oxford, premises formerly rented and
occupied by William Jefferson Clinton, who was to become
the President of the United States. The evidence against me
was strong, partly because I had been daft enough to admit
to Her Majesty's Customs and Excise my documented

illegal activities in Holland in the hope that my offence would be treated as a Dutch rather than a British one. That strategy had backfired, and my solicitor, Bernard Simons, was certain I would get convicted and was not too optimistic of my getting less than three years in prison.

The East End flat belonged to Dai, my old school-teaching companion. Thames Valley Police must obviously have made some enquiries into my whereabouts, but no one seemed to be getting very excited. I had written a note to Bernard Simons so that everyone could know that nothing untoward had happened. I had just skipped bail. The trial had started without me the previous day, May 1st, 1974. My co-defendants pleaded guilty and got sentences ranging from six months to four years. Ernie had promised to pay off any sureties demanded by the judge as the result of my skipping bail. He felt indebted to me because at the time of my arrest in Amsterdam I was the only person in the world who knew his whereabouts, and I had not disclosed them to the authorities. I was biding my time.

Dai had woken me up early before going to school.

'Howard, you've been on the news.'

'What! What did it say?'

'Well, there were only three headlines: one about Prime Minister Harold Wilson, one about President Nixon, and one about you. I couldn't take it all in. Something about MI6 and the IRA. I'll go out and get the newspapers.'

The *Daily Mirror*'s entire front page was devoted to a story about me headlined WHERE IS MR MARKS?, describing how I was an MI6 agent, with arrest warrants out for me in seven countries, who had been kidnapped, beaten up, told to keep my mouth shut, and persuaded to become an IRA sympathiser. There was no clue as to how the *Daily Mirror* had got hold of the information that I had worked for MI6. There were general statements claiming that I had told some friends I was a spy. In fact I had told only Rosie, my parents, and McCann. Rosie, when interviewed by the press, categorically stated there was no connection between me and the IRA or the security services. Her Majesty's Customs and Excise had been made aware of my MI6 involvement: Mac's telephone number had appeared in the telephone records of an Amsterdam hotel, and I had successfully used my promise of not mentioning MI6 in court as a lever to secure bail. HM Customs would have been unlikely to spill all to a *Daily Mirror* reporter. The *Daily Mail*'s front-page headline was YARD FEAR NEW IRA ABDUCTION, and the text claimed that I had last been seen in the company of two Customs Officers and that police were now investigating the possibility that I had been executed by the IRA. Later the same day, Thames Valley Police vehemently denied that I had been an MI6 agent spying on the IRA, and Bernard Simons kept saying he'd heard from me, and that I was not being held against my will. But the media took no notice. That was too boring. In fairness, the *Daily Mirror* felt obliged at least to present an alternative theory: the next day's front page was headlined THE INFORMER, and the report stated that I had been kidnapped by Mafia drug smugglers to prevent me from appearing at the Old Bailey and grassing them up. Other reports suggested I had staged my own kidnap. The public, though, preferred the spy/IRA theory, and that's what the television and radio news stations gave them. Who were my enemies? – the police because they were being forced to look for me everywhere, the IRA because I'd smuggled dope, the Mafia because they thought I was going to talk about them, Her Majesty's Customs and Excise because I didn't turn up to get my conviction, Her Majesty's Secret Service for my switching of loyalties, or the media for reasons I didn't understand? Did it matter? All I had intended to do was change my appearance and carry on scamming. I already had a bit of a moustache. All this off-the-wall publicity would just make me more careful. Still, it all felt rather unreal and occasionally scary.

*

The media circus stopped as suddenly as it had begun. The Old Bailey trial judge deferred any decision regarding the estreatment of the bail sureties. I might have been abducted, he said, and therefore could not be termed an absconder. My main duty was to ensure that my family knew for certain that I was unharmed. Dai was not keen on my using his telephone for any purpose, and I assumed that most of my family's telephones were tapped as a result of the nation-wide search for me. Through circuitous and complex manoeuvres involving conversations with my sister in Wales, I was able to have clandestine meetings with Rosie, Myfanwy, and my parents while I continued perfecting my disguise. After about two months, I looked very different and felt no fear walking the streets. Each morning, I would buy a few newspapers and have a coffee at a dock-workers' café. One hot early July morning, I was at the newsagent's and saw a *Daily Mirror* front-page headline, THE LONG SILENCE OF MR MYSTERY. Underneath was a photograph of me. I bought a copy. The report stated that Thames Valley Police had called off the search for me and that my disappearance had been the subject of discussion in the Houses of Parliament. Another blaze of publicity followed in the *Daily Mirror*'s wake.

'You need another name and more disguise,' said Dai. 'Everyone's talking about you on the Tube. I'm not calling you Howard any more. And I'm not calling you Mr Mystery either.'

'Call me Albi,' I said, partly in deference to my old friend Albert Hancock and partly because it was an anagram of bail.

'All right,' said Dai. 'Why don't you get yourself a pair of glasses?'

'From whom?'

'I think they're called opticians, Albi.'

'But there's nothing wrong with my eyes, Dai. They won't give me a pair.'

'You walk into a dentist; he'll say you've got bad teeth. You walk into an optician, and he'll say you need glasses. That's the way they make money. Anyway, I read the other day that the stuff you keep smoking causes long sight. Why don't you smoke a load and go to an optician?'

Dai had probably read one of those absurd scare stories of marijuana causing just about everything from sterility to nymphomania. But there might be something to it. I knew marijuana had some effect on intraocular pressure. I smoked several joints and had my eyes tested. I needed glasses, and a special pair was made. They dramatically changed my appearance, but made things rather blurry, except when I was stoned.

Intermittent press speculation on my whereabouts continued for over a month. The FBI feared for my life. A West Country man, of whom I'd never heard, confessed to murdering me and burying me beneath a motorway bridge near Bristol.

'You'll have to go, Albi. This is driving me, Jane, and Sian nuts.'

'Okay, Dai. I'm sorry. I never thought I'd be staying here this long, and I never thought all this madness would happen.'

'Why don't you leave the country?'

'I haven't got a passport, Dai. I don't know where to start.'

'Take mine.'

Normally, Dai and I looked a bit like each other. We were tall, dark, blue-eyed, clean-shaven, and heavily featured. Now, with my moustache and stoned glasses, we didn't, but the photograph could easily be changed; the Foreign and Commonwealth Office embossed stamp covered just a minute part of the corner. Its absence on the replacement photograph would not be noticed. Dai gave me his driving licence as well. He was anxious that nothing hold me up.

I decided to go to Italy. There were two main reasons. A large Winnebago motorised caravan lay in a camping site in

Genova. I had bought it a year previously for Eric to use, had
he landed the Lebanese in Italy rather than made it available
to Greek sponge fishermen. Living in it appealed to me.
Also, my sister was about to start a teaching course in
Padova, so I had an easy way of keeping in touch with the
family. Apart from the Winnebago, my assets were about
£5,000 cash. Everything else had gone. While I was on bail,
Ernie had sent someone to Amsterdam to try to get the
$100,000 and the Peter Hughes passport from the safe-
deposit box in Algemene Bank Nederland, but the cupboard
was bare. The authorities had got there first. The guy Ernie
had sent, Burton Moldese, apparently had some Los
Angeles Mafia connections, and I'm sure that this is what
gave rise to the *Daily Mirror*'s Mafia theory. Ernie would
lend me some money, I was sure, particularly if, as seemed
increasingly likely, there would be no estreatment of bail
sureties. I had a mailing address for Ernie, but was unsure
how he would have reacted to all the weird publicity. I'd
contact him when everything was settled.

Remembering McCann's advice, I didn't fly directly to
Italy. I took a ferry to Denmark and caught a flight from
Copenhagen to Genova. The passport stood up. The
Winnebago started first time, and I cruised around the
camping sites of the Italian Riviera. I stopped wearing my
glasses and began a period of debauched promiscuity,
driving up and down Italian roads picking up female hitch-
hikers. The Winnebago had a kitchen, sitting room, shower,
loud stereo, and comfortably slept six. I would usually pick
up just one hitch-hiker, but occasionally as many as fifteen
or sixteen. From Como to Napoli, the autostradas became
my home. I had to pay for petrol, but dope, sex, food, and
drink seemed to be free.

Rosie brought out Myfanwy to see me for a couple of
weeks. They had now sold the Yarnton cottage and, together
with Julian Peto and his family, had bought a large house at
Northleigh, outside Oxford. I kept in touch with Rosie

through Fanny Hill. In September, I called Rosie at Fanny's and mentioned that my parents were hoping to come out to see me. It later emerged that this conversation had been overheard on another extension by Raymond Carr, Master of St Anthony's College, who was still having an affair with Fanny. It is not certain that Raymond Carr passed on this information to the authorities, but it is likely. My parents did come out and shared with my sister and me a two-week holiday touring Northern Italy in the Winnebago.

After they left, I hung around at a camp site in Padova. My sister came to see me in a panic. The *Daily Mirror* were trying to interview her. They knew I was in Italy and knew my parents had been to see me. I had to assume the authorities also knew. Where could I go now? I had almost no money. The police would not be looking for me in England. That would be the last place they'd expect to find me, and there I could find at least a floor to sleep on.

On October 28th, 1974, I drove the Winnebago to the Genova campsite I had collected it from three months earlier. I put yet another photograph in Dai's passport and booked a seat on a British Caledonian flight to Gatwick.

On arrival at Genova airport, I had several glasses of *grappa* before passing uneventfully through the passport check, and settled down to some serious drinking in the departure lounge. At the duty-free shop, I bought some cigarettes and a few bottles of *sambuca negra*. During the flight I ordered several more drinks and even began drinking from the *sambuca negra* bottles. Newspapers were distributed, and I took a copy of the *Daily Mirror*. On the front page was a photograph of me under a blazing headline HE'S ALIVE. The article was several pages long and stated that Mr Mystery was living as a guest of the Mafia in Padova. Mr Mystery's hideout was known only to the Mafia and my sister. Mr Mystery was living undercover as a student, shielded and protected by Mafia gangsters. The aeroplane was full of people reading this exclusive. Ably assisted by the *sambuca*

negra, I was again losing touch with reality. By the time we
disembarked, I was giggling uncontrollably and cannot even
remember any confrontation with Immigration or Customs. I
followed the passengers through to Gatwick railway station
and got on a train to Victoria. I was still drinking *sambuca*
negra when the train arrived. I took a Tube to Paddington
and, following my drunken homing instinct, took a train to
Oxford, arriving about 9 p.m. I walked from Oxford railway
station to the police station in St Aldate's. When I got there I
was extremely confused. I could not bring myself to believe
that the last six months had actually happened. I wanted to
rewind my life back to when I was signing on for bail in
Oxford. I had understood everything until then. A policeman
walked out of the station. I asked him how I could get a bus
to Northleigh. He said it was too late. I would have to take a
taxi. I went into a telephone box to call Rosie at Northleigh.
No reply. I walked to Leckford Road, where I had last been
seen by the sane world. The pub around the corner, the
Victoria Arms, one that I and friends of mine had often
frequented, was still there. I walked in. There was a deathly
silence. Almost everyone recognised me. Julian Peto was there
and exploded into helpless laughter. I asked where Rosie was.
She and Myfanwy were at a party, to which he was now going
himself. Rosie and Myfanwy had left by the time we arrived. I
drank some punch and smoked some joints. Julian and I drove
to Northleigh. Rosie was in a state of shock. Chief
Superintendent Philip Fairweather of the Thames Valley
Police, the man in charge of investigating my disappearance,
had just left. Rosie put me to bed. The next morning's news
reported that Mohammed Ali had regained the world
heavyweight championship from George Foreman and that
an Old Bailey judge had decided not to forfeit any money
from those who had stood bail for me, despite the police's
knowing my whereabouts in Italy. Police inquiries were at an
end. It was not in the 'public interest' to disclose where I was.
But I was alive. At least I had stopped being a dead spy.

Judy Lane, now all of nineteen, was paying a social visit to Northleigh. We hadn't forgotten each other, and I did not have to be persuaded to accept her kind offer of accommodation at her flat in Brighton. Judy had five brothers and sisters. At that point, I had only met Patrick, who for the last year had been living in self-imposed exile in the Dordogne, growing snails. Judy's mother had recently died from cancer, and her father had a new young girl-friend. All her brothers and sisters lived away from home or in boarding-school. The former family flat in Brighton was at Judy's disposal. Judy and I have been together ever since.

Again, the media furore died as quickly as it had begun. I felt safe in Judy's flat, and I began to contact old business friends including Johnny Martin, Anthony Woodhead, and Jarvis. With their help, I managed to sell the Winnebago and procure the release of the few thousand pounds I had deposited in the Swiss Bank Corporation the year before. I wrote to Ernie giving him Judy's phone number. The telephone rang in the middle of the night.

'Albi, it's for you,' said Judy.

'How you doin'? I thought you'd disappeared on me for good. So what's been happening? What you been doing?'

'Sorry, Ernie. With all the reports in the press about me, I thought you wouldn't want to know.'

'I never saw any of that. You'd be small fry here. Look, my girl-friend, Patty, is coming over to see you. She'll explain what I've got together these days. You need some money for living? She'll have $10,000 for you.'

Anthony Woodhead had procured a London penthouse flat overlooking Regent's Park at an extremely low rental. I unofficially rented it from him, and Judy and I took up residence there. Patty arrived and gave me Ernie's particulars and the codes we should use when talking over the phone. Ernie had a connection in New York's John F. Kennedy Airport who could clear through US Customs any consignment from anywhere, provided it was smell-proof

and came in on Alitalia. The fee was 25% of the American
wholesale price. Ernie had an old Brotherhood of Eternal
Love associate, Robert Crimball, who was able to export
Thai sticks from Bangkok. His fee was 35% of the American
wholesale price. 40% was available for middlemen. A couple
of 1,000-kilo loads had already been successfully imported
and sold. Did I know anyone in any dope-producing country
other than Thailand who, for some money in advance and
lots more afterwards, could export dope by air freight? If so,
I could become extremely rich.

This was a once-in-a-lifetime offer, but I didn't know
anyone who could do what was required. I had completely
lost touch with Mohammed Durrani, Lebanese Sam, and
Lebanese Joe. No one had any ideas except Jarvis. One of his
friends had lived in Nepal for seven years. His name was
John Denbigh, and he was known as Old John. Jarvis
arranged a meeting for the three of us at his flat.

Old John was a very tall, mature, masculine version of Mick
Jagger. He was dressed like a Hell's Angel and adorned with
necklaces, chains, beads, amulets, and semi-precious stones.
He was a walking bust. But Old John had never smoked a
joint, and he bought and repaired stoves to make a living. His
words were full of wisdom, but if one stopped concentrating
on them for just one second, he seemed incoherent.
Otherwise, his wisdom would seem to profoundly by-pass all
forms of convention and platitude. Old John's street sense was
second to none; the streets of Fulham had given him that, as
well as his accent. He was a keen soccer player and cricketer.
His father had been educated at Oxford University. Old John
had absolute integrity and honesty. No one could wish for a
better, closer, or more trusted friend.

Jarvis rolled joints and made cups of tea. Old John smoked
Tom Thumb cigars and drank whisky. We discussed the
Welsh and English rugby teams. Wales had just slaughtered
England 20–4 at Cardiff Arms Park. After an hour, I
managed to bring up Nepal.

'You must have had an interesting time there, John.'

'Interesting, yes, and they are superb people, the Nepalese, I promise you.'

'Do you get many foreigners going there these days?'

'Well, the thing is there was this Englishman who told me he had nine talents. I told him I just had one: I could throw him out of the window. And he went and painted the outside of his house with religion, and then went to live outside the house. Madness.'

I just about followed that one and took it to mean that Old John had a certain contempt for expatriate communities in the East. I had to get more to the point.

'Did Customs here give you a hard time when you came back?'

'Hard? No, not hard. I heard one of them say, "Stop that cunt. I'm going to take him apart," and he came up to me and said "Excuse me, sir," and I said, "Sir? No. Don't call me sir. My name is Cunt. Please call me Cunt." That dealt with him. Then the other one said, "Can I see your passport?" and I said, "It's not my passport, it's yours," and gave it to him. He asked what I did in Nepal. I told him I was a barman. Vodka and lime. What would you like? He asked if I smoked any funny tobacco. I asked if he meant Kinabis, and he said it didn't matter. Then I caught a bus to Fulham.'

I had to come straight to the point.

'Can you send stuff out from Nepal by air, John?'

'Ooh! No. No. I can't do anything like that. No. No. No. Now, I know a man. He knows a man who might know.'

'How much would it cost?'

'Well, money is the thing, and they always do things for a fair and honest price, I promise you.'

'What's a fair price, John?'

'You will tell me, I'm quite sure.'

'What will you want out of it, John?'

'If I help you do business, I'm sure you will give me a drink.'

'A drink?'

'Yes. If a man does something for you, you give him a drink. Please, if everything goes well, give me a drink.'

'Can you check that the quality will be all right?'

'I only smoke Tom Thumb, but I know a man who has a knife.'

I took this as a yes.

'Can you make it smell-proof?'

'Not if God made it smell.'

'Do you know a man who can?'

'No. But if you do, let him come and do it, or give me instructions.'

'How much can they send?'

'I should think it depends on when you want to do it by.'

'Well, John, the Americans will want to do a ton as soon as possible.'

'Now I was in America once, and the thing is that Americans will always want more, and there is no end to their madness. Lovely people, for sure, but you have to keep them in line. When my visa ran out, the Immigration asked me why I wanted to extend it, and I said it was because I hadn't run out of money. He stamped it and said, "Have a nice day." So, if the Americans ask for a ton tomorrow, say you will do half a ton when Wales win the Triple Crown. That will deal with their madness, and everyone can get on with their lives. It saves all that tidding.'

'Tidding?'

'Talking Imaginary Deals.'

Accurately conveying the contents of my conversation with Old John to Ernie wasn't easy. I told Ernie hashish could be exported from Nepal for about the same price as Robert Crimball charged in Bangkok, but 500 kilos was the most they could do at one time, and someone would have to be sent out to ensure the consignment was smell-proof. Ernie sent his right-hand man, Tom Sunde, with money, instructions, and smell-proof know-how. Tom came to

London first before going to Kathmandu to meet Old John. He had been authorised by Ernie to keep nothing from me regarding the intricacies of the New York scam.

During the 1970s, the most powerful Mafia crime family in the United States was that of Carlo Gambino, the prototype for Vito Corleone in Mario Puzo's novel, *The Godfather*. Born in Sicily at the beginning of the century, Gambino was still of the old-school belief that the Mafia should steer away from involvement in drug-trafficking. Carmine Galante, the main contender for Gambino's position as the godfather of the New York Mob, had no such scruples. The Mafia should control everything, including dope. Carmine Galante's organisation used the services of Don Brown, an Irish-American who made his money dope-dealing in Queens, New York, and spent it in Los Angeles. Don Brown knew Richard Sherman, an extremely shrewd Californian defence attorney retained by Ernie Combs. Unwittingly, Sherman introduced Ernie to Don Brown. A scam was born.

Large quantities of missing goods provided strong evidence of the Gambino crime family's ability to remove items from John F. Kennedy Airport without going through the usual channels. Smuggling quickly followed. The preferred method was to send a cargo of legitimate goods from a New York company to the dope-producing country. The importing company in the dope country would ostensibly return the imported goods as faulty or different from ordered. In fact, a consignment of hashish would be sent and grabbed by the Mob.

As a prelude to the Nepalese scam, an air-conditioning company called Kool-Air had been formed in New York. It was ready to export real air-conditioning equipment. On separate flights, Old John and Tom Sunde, carrying a small suitcase full of Ernie's dollars, flew to Kathmandu to take care of business. First Old John had to form a Nepalese company capable of importing air-conditioning equipment and let me know its particulars. A week later, I received a telegram from Kathmandu. The message comprised one word, 'YETI.' I knew that yeti was the Nepalese name for the abominable snowman of the Himalayas, but this didn't help. Ernie was anxious for news. I didn't know what to tell him, so I cabled Old John in Kathmandu to call me.

'John, what's this message mean?'

'That's the name of the thing you wanted.'

I wasn't happy with calling an air-conditioning company The Abominable Snowman.

'That's really not a very relevant name, John.'

'It's very relevant, I promise you. They haven't caught one yet.'

I gave up.

'Okay, John, that's the name. Is everything else all right?'

'No. They don't eat spaghetti here; they like to use chopsticks or they eat wurst or smorgasbord. We can't get the thing to go for spaghetti.'

Each day I was finding Old John easier to understand. He was unable to ensure that the load would be transferred to Alitalia before it reached New York. He could only manage to ensure the consignment's New York arrival on other European or Far East airlines. I told Ernie. He said he'd work on it.

With the money Ernie had given me, I added some luxuries to the Regent's Park penthouse: a stereo system and records. Judy's father and his girl-friend had moved into the Brighton family flat, so Judy now had the use of her father's flat, which was quite near Regent's Park. At about four o'clock on a spring afternoon, I was alone in the penthouse, idly gazing at London's skyline and listening to *Ladies Love Outlaws* by Waylon Jennings. I looked down and saw four hefty men with overcoats rushing up the street towards the entrance to my block of flats. Something told me they were coming for me, but I didn't know who they were. The ground-floor entrance doorbell buzzed in the penthouse. I asked who it was, and a muffled voice said something incomprehensible. I released the downstairs door, put on my stoned glasses, walked out of the flat, and started descending the emergency stairs, reasoning that the men would be likely to take the lift. When I got to the bottom of the emergency stairs, I noticed that the four men were still outside the glass double-doored entrance. The caretaker was holding open one of the doors and talking to them. They all saw me, and the caretaker motioned his head in my direction. I walked slowly and brazenly to the door as if to leave the building. One of the men took a flash photograph of me.

Then another said, 'That's not him.'

'We're sorry, sir. Excuse us,' said another.

I flashed them a look of irritation, walked to the street, and took a cab to Soho.

It was obviously the *Daily Mirror*, with or without the police. How did they know? I had no idea, but I couldn't go back to the penthouse again and had to consider as lost the money and valuables left there. Anthony Woodhead, who was the penthouse's official occupant, might encounter a few problems, unless it was he who had tipped them off. I was meant to be masterminding the sending to the New York Mafia of the first-ever air-freighted hashish from Kathmandu, and I had nothing in the world but a few pounds in my pocket and a pair of stoned glasses. I telephoned Judy. She picked me up in her car, and we drove to Liverpool and checked into the Holiday Inn under a false name. The next morning, the *Daily Mirror* was slid under the room door. Again I dominated the front page, which was headlined THE FACE OF A FUGITIVE. Underneath was a large picture of me wearing my stoned glasses and moustache. I shaved, put Brylcreem on my hair, and combed it straight back. Judy went out to rent the cheapest possible bedsitter, £4 a week with shared bathroom and kitchen in an area called Sheill Park. I telephoned my parents to let them know I was okay, and telephoned Ernie to tell him what had happened. He was unperturbed. I didn't have the nerve to ask him for more money. He had some good news for Old John. The load could arrive on Japanese Air Lines (JAL); the Italians had been talking to the Japanese, and an arrangement had been made.

By far the largest organised crime network in the world is the Yakuza, with a membership of several hundred thousand. Originating in the early seventeenth century as a group of young Robin Hood-type rebels defying samurai overlords, the Yakuza emerged after World War II as a more typically Western collection of gangsters with dark suits and sunglasses. By the end of the 1960s, the Yakuza had forged important links with the Chinese Triads in Hong Kong, Malaysia, Taiwan, and Thailand; and an unprecedently powerful Chinese–Japanese syndicate was beginning to send large shipments of heroin to the United States. Some of these went through Kennedy Airport. Now the Yakuza and the Mafia were waiting for Old John's Yeti to do its stuff.

I gave Ernie the number of the telephone box at the end of the road and told him I would be there between 8 and 8.15 every Tuesday night. I cabled Old John in Kathmandu with the same information and the good news about JAL, and I began to live the life of a Liverpool dosser about to be a rich man. A few hundred pounds was scrounged from some long-suffering friends and family.

My lack of identity documents began to worry me. A 21-year-old policeman had been shot dead by the IRA, and the Birmingham Black Panther and the Cambridge hooded rapist were at large. One could be stopped by the police at any time, and it would be embarrassing for me to be unable to palm them off with a piece of paper showing some false identity. The Driver and Vehicle Licence Centre in Swansea required no proof of identity when applying for a provisional driving licence. I ordered one in the name of Albert Lane, and it was delivered to the Liverpool bedsit. I applied to sit a driving test and passed. A full licence was issued. I joined the local library and opened a Post Office Savings Account, using the name Albert Lane. A bone-shaker of a Bedford van was purchased for next to nothing, and Judy and I set off on week-long vacations to a variety of campsites. We loved this perpetual holiday lifestyle, but Judy would often complain about my insistence that the tent was pitched adjacent to the public telephone box, whose number had been handed out everywhere from Los Angeles to the Himalayas. I had to make and accept telephone calls at all hours and did not want to be traipsing across moonlit fields in my pyjamas. The telephone box was almost invariably next to the campsite's bathrooms and toilets. Ours would be the only tent in the vicinity. During the day, we would either take advantage of the campsite's recreation facilities or join a local library under a couple of silly names. During the evening, we would attempt innovative ways of acquiring further false identities.

Our favourite method was through fortune-telling. Judy dressed up as a sexy clairvoyant and sat alone in a pub. I sat some distance away. Sooner or later, a man of about my age would initiate a conversation with her and find out she was an astrologer, palmist, and numerologist, capable of telling his fortune. She needed a few details, of course: date and place of birth, mother's maiden name, and his travels or travel plans. Some of them had no intention of going abroad because they didn't trust foreign beer. We ended up with enough information to procure several birth certificates from St Catherine's House, London.

On Independence Day, July 4th, 1975, 500 kilos of hand-pressed Nepalese temple balls, some of the best hashish in the world, was flown from Kathmandu via Bangkok and Tokyo to New York. It was being smoked in Greenwich Village the next day. I was very rich again, and I was still in my twenties.

Ernie wanted to do another load right away, a bigger one. Old John wasn't keen. The suitcases of dollars that Tom Sunde had taken to Nepal had played havoc with the Kathmandu currency markets.

'This is the American madness. More, more, all the time. Next year the Nepalese won't plant rice, they'll plant the thing and all starve. They don't want money; they want medicine.'

I, however, agreed with Ernie and persuaded Old John to reluctantly commit himself to send a 750-kilo load. It worked. Other loads were sent from Nepal, but none were bigger. After one of the loads, Old John drove an ambulance to Kathmandu stuffed with antibiotics, bandages, and other medical supplies and left it there. He refused to do any more loads. 'Let Nepal be Nepal.'

Ernie generally sent one of his couriers over with my profit, and I had accumulated a stash of several hundred thousand dollars in cash. I rented flats and cottages in various parts of the country. My main preoccupation was still acquiring false documentation, and addresses were needed to send driving licences and other useful proofs of identity. I became a little silly and even successfully applied for provisional driving licences in the names of Waylon Jennings and Elvis Presley. The Swansea computer didn't bat an eyelid; it didn't remember the 1950s. I took the astrologically obtained birth certificates to Post Offices and obtained British Visitor's Passports.

Johnny Martin introduced me to Philip Sparrowhawk, a jack of all trades from Epsom who, for a price, could obtain bits and pieces of identification. His main source of income was importing textiles from the Far East, but he was also able to do useful things like get back-dated insurance; obtain new, second-hand, and rented cars with minimum formalities; and supply accommodation addresses and telephone lines for short-term use. Through this involvement, Philip and I became friendly, and it wasn't long before we joined forces and rented office premises at 38A, High Street, Ewell, Surrey. This quickly became the registered office of the Ewell Group of Companies, a cluster of £100 off-the-shelf companies staffed by falsely named directors and secretaries who never failed to give a suitable reference for an application for a passport or bank account. Some legitimate business transpired at Phil's insistence, but it was usually of the slightly shady kind: second-hand car dealing, mini-cabbing, backed by overtones of long-firming and insurance fraud.

Apart from the preoccupation with false identity, there was little to indicate I was Britain's most wanted fugitive from justice. I saw Rosie and Myfanwy frequently, as I did my parents. My social life extended. I re-established friendships with Oxford and Sussex associates, almost all of whom were happy to call me Albi, and made many new ones. They knew who I was, and I was fully aware that any one of them could turn me in to the authorities at any time. I just big-headedly assumed that anyone who knew me liked me and wouldn't do such a thing. I was too nice to be grassed.

Denys Irving, now fully retired from composing lewd lyrics and enthusiastically pursuing his new hobby of hang-gliding, was working with Mike Ratledge, another friend from Oxford. Mike was the sole surviving member of the Soft Machine, who were, along with Pink Floyd, the freaks' house band. He had been repeatedly voted *Melody Maker*'s best keyboard player in the world and featured on Mike Oldfield's smash hit, *Tubular Bells*. Now he and Denys were experimenting with integrated circuitry and electronic music. Both spent all day with soldering irons and circuit boards. My telephoning experiences on the campsites had led me to fantasise about an ideal telephone system. I wanted to be able to carry around a few pieces of change, rather than a bagful, go into any phone box, and phone a specific number, which would automatically divert me to whatever number I then dialled from the phone box. I would have to pay in coins at the phone box for the local connection and whoever rented the specific number would be charged by the telephone company for the onward call to wherever was dialled, be it domestic or international. Also, I wanted to be able to telephone this specific number from a phone box and 'give' it the telephone box number so that anyone else calling this or another specific number would be automatically diverted to the phone box. With such an invention, I could telephone wherever I wanted for pocket money and be reached by whomever I wanted to reach me without his knowing my precise whereabouts. Today, this would be a simple matter. Then, not so, but Denys and Mike, on hearing my fantasy, felt competent enough to be able to make such a machine. Mike devised the circuitry, and Denys did the rest. It worked, most of the time. I ordered the latest and best hang-glider from Ernie to give to Denys. He made me godfather to his and Merdelle's newly born son, Arthur. Denys went to Lagos, Nigeria, as an audio engineer. He met a marijuana grower and seller. I asked Denys to go back to Nigeria to determine whether marijuana could be airfreighted from there. He came back and said it couldn't. The hang-glider from Ernie arrived. Denys flew into the ground and died. I felt as if I'd killed him, one of my dearest friends.

Although I had been unable either to persuade Old John to restart operations in Nepal or to find an air-freighting hashish source in some other country, Ernie had allowed me to invest some profits in his Bangkok to New York Thai stick scams on the condition that Judy and I come to America to spend the pile of cash that was now accumulating in his Californian safe-deposit boxes. We were both dying to go, but one needed a full British passport and an American visa to visit the United States. I could have used one of the birth certificates I had and the batch of referees at the Ewell Group of Companies to get a full passport, but I was always worried that the person named in the passport would suddenly apply for a passport himself. Ideally, I needed someone who knew I was using his passport, would never apply for one, and would back me up in whatever way was needed. Judy thought of an old childhood friend of hers, Anthony Tunnicliffe. He lived near Birmingham and was a few years younger than I, but not too many. Judy was certain that for a reasonable sum of money he would forgo the ability to travel abroad. Judy also suggested that she take on her friend's wife's identity. That would make things doubly safe: Mr and Mrs Anthony Tunnicliffe. The real Tunnicliffes were overjoyed at the proposal. They truthfully filled in their passport application forms and took photographs of themselves. Their local doctor signed both photographs and forms as being authentic. The Tunnicliffes gave the signed forms and photographs back to me. Phil Sparrowhawk got a rubber stamp made which approximated that of the Tunnicliffes' doctor. Judy and I then filled out new passport application forms in our own handwriting. In appropriate handwriting, Phil filled out the doctor's bit on the form and on photographs of me and Judy and rubber-stamped them. We gave the forms back to the Tunnicliffes, who posted them to the Passport Office. The only check the Passport Office was likely to make was to telephone the doctor and ask if he'd countersigned the Tunnicliffes' application and photographs. No worries. Full passports bearing our photographs were delivered to the Tunnicliffes' Birmingham address within ten days. Now we needed American visas. To get them we had to show ourselves able to afford an American visit. We rented a flat in Birmingham in the name of Tunnicliffe. One of the phoney companies at Ewell, Insight Video, opened up a branch office in New Street, Birmingham, and employed a man named Anthony Tunnicliffe as the Midlands General Manager and a lady called Jill Tunnicliffe as secretary. A Tunnicliffe bank account was opened at the Midland Bank. We mailed our US visa application forms and passports to the United States Embassy in Grosvenor Square. They were sent back with visas valid for multiple entries not exceeding two months each visit.

In late 1976, with an over-abundance of caution, Judy and I flew as Mr and Mrs Tunnicliffe from Birmingham to

Denver, Colorado, via Brussels, Frankfurt, New York, and Chicago. A chauffeur-driven limousine took us from Denver to Vail, where Ernie, who had put on a tremendous amount of weight, Patty, and Tom Sunde shared a large and luxurious house. The snow was thick, and we were in time for Thanksgiving, with which I was totally unfamiliar. There was lots of mindless television. In freezing temperatures, I rode a horse over the Rockies and played with guns. I didn't like Colorado life.

Ernie also had a huge apartment in Coconut Grove, Florida, where he liked to spend the Christmas and New Year. The five of us flew from Denver via Dallas/Fort Worth to Miami. Judy and I checked into the Mutiny, a hotel immortalised by some Crosby, Stills, and Nash album, and were given a deluxe suite with a mirrored ceiling, sauna, Jacuzzi, bar, and four televisions. Lots of Colombian dope, dope dealers, gangsters, nubilia, and exotica flooded the streets. I liked Coconut Grove life. We took a year's rental of an apartment in a luxury condominium complex over-looking Key Biscayne and fitted it out with up-to-date everything, including a safe full of $100 bills. I bet $10,000, my first and last football bet, on the Oaklands Raiders to beat the Minnesota Vikings in the Superbowl. I won. I bought hot jewellery and a Cadillac Seville from a Mafia friend of Ernie's called Luis Ippolito, took a driving test, and got issued with a Florida Driver's License in the name of Anthony Tunnicliffe.

Our two months' permitted stay was running out, so Judy and I decided to visit Canada and then re-enter the United States. We went via New York, where we stayed at the Waldorf-Astoria and took a tourist helicopter ride through Manhattan's skyscrapers. New York had a kind of magical energy. We noticed its absence when we got to Toronto, where we were totally bored and took a Canadian Pacific flight to a slightly warmer Vancouver. We checked into the Seaporter Inn and watched the seaplanes taking off. The

next day we visited Stanley Park, and in the evening went to
the planetarium. We sat near the centre. At the circum-
ference of the almost deserted auditorium, peering at me
through the twinkling darkness, was Marty Langford's face,
agape with astonishment.

I suppose remarkable coincidences happen often enough,
but this was a bit much. The man who had been my closest
childhood friend for at least fifteen years and whom I had not
seen since 1973 and had no way of contacting was now a few
yards away. What is it about Vancouver planetariums that
attracts Welsh dope fugitives?

Marty and I talked. He had been living with McCann and
his Dutch wife Sylvia since he fled to Ireland three years
previously. Other members of the Tafia had gone their
separate ways. McCann, now using the name James
Kennedy and claiming he was a close relative of the late
President Kennedy, was doing very well for himself. He had
an office floor in the Guinness Tower in Vancouver, oil
interests in Venezuela, and had partially financed the film
Equus. He had a warm friendship with James Coburn and his
wife, Beverley. Marty declined comment on the source of
McCann's wealth. I gave Marty my new name and room
number in the Seaporter and told him to give it to McCann,
who rang the next morning.

'How's British Intelligence?'

'Slightly greater than that of the Irish, Jim.'

'You fucking Welsh arsehole. Still as smarmy as ever,
aren't you, H'ard? But I got to give it to you. You got out of
it and did it by yourself. I'll be over in half an hour.'

I quickly introduced McCann and Judy to each other
before Judy excused herself from our hotel room on the
pretext of needing to go to the hotel shopping centre.

'Are you still dope-dealing, H'ard?'

'When I can, yes.'

'Those days are fucking over, man. Dope dealers are
history. High finance is where it's at.'

'What's that?'

'Revolving letters of credit, shell companies and offshore banks. I'm spending money hand over fucking fist, and it's all other people's.'

'So, what's different?'

'What's different, you stupid Welsh prick, is that I'm living in the fast lane, and I'm legit.'

'I take it you're no longer a revolutionary.'

'I'm a fucking revolutionary until I die. Since when is selling dope on Brighton seafront a revolutionary act, for fuck's sake?'

'It's a bit closer than all this upwardly mobile corporate stuff you're into, Jim.'

'Is it fuck? H'ard, doing this business I meet the people who matter, the high rollers. You understand me, do you? There's only five hundred people in the world who control anything worth a fuck. And I've met them all, every fucking one of them.'

'Where's Graham, Jim?'

'He's become a poof. He's living in San Francisco or some other poof place. He's probably still dope-dealing, like you.'

'Did you do any more Shannon deals after I got busted?'

'I'm not telling you, H'ard. Graham never could control those idjits in Kabul. I found out who they are and their addresses in Kabul. I've got them when I want them. But those days are gone, H'ard. You need to wise up, but we'll keep in touch. If you ever get a real problem, you can ask for the Kid.'

Judy and I had arranged to meet Ernie, Patty, and Tom Sunde in San Francisco. A load of Thai sticks from Robert Crimball in Bangkok had just been cleared by Don Brown in New York, and the West Coast was considered the best market for top-quality Thai weed. This is where the money would be. After sales, Ernie was going to introduce me to his lawyer, Richard Sherman, and a friend of theirs who worked in the safe-deposit vaults in the Wells Fargo Bank. We flew there from Vancouver and stayed at the Mark Hopkins on Nob Hill. I didn't much like the views of Alcatraz, but I was interested to see, for the first time, the Haight-Ashbury district of San Francisco, one of the main candidates for the birthplace of the Sixties movements. It was disappointing and looked identical to every other area of San Francisco, which itself wasn't that different from most American cities. There wasn't a hippie in sight. Maybe they were all at home smoking Thai sticks. I filled up a safe-deposit box in the Wells Fargo Bank with the money I'd made by investing in this last Thai scam and took Judy to Las Vegas. When we weren't attending one of several dozen star-studded performances, we were gambling. I had bought a book on how to beat the system playing blackjack and studied it intensely. I gave Judy a $1,000 stake to play on whatever table she fancied. She chose Baccarat. I also allowed myself a $1,000 stake. After the first all-night session, I was ahead by $100 while Judy had won a total of $16,000. It was most humiliating.

Most of the upper-echelon marijuana dealers in America had apartments in both Miami and New York. I wanted the same. Judy and I flew from Las Vegas to New York and booked into the Plaza Hotel. Elvis Presley's death was announced while we were checking in. We found an apartment with huge rooms in the Pavilion Building on the corner of East 77th Street and York Avenue and filled it with the trappings of financial success. Ernie had a warehouse full of furniture to which we could help ourselves. Ernie also gave me the telephone number of his hashish and marijuana wholesaler in New York, Alan Schwarz, a charming multi-millionaire who was the darling of Manhattan's hip and cool. Alan had a whole network of dealers who worked for him in Manhattan and a team of drivers who were continually hauling Colombian marijuana from Florida coastal stashes to the streets of New York. He was very professional and efficient and the best guide possible to Manhattan social life. I first met Alan on his 21st birthday, which he gave at

Régine's. Guests included Margaux Hemingway and Bernie
Cornfield. The British residents of New York had not yet
acquired the label 'Eurotrash'. John Lennon and Mick
Jagger both lived in the Upper East Side, and they and their
entourages would sometimes grace our apartment with their
presence. The beautiful Guinness sisters, Sabrina, Miranda,
and Anita, often visited us, as did Jane Bonham-Carter and
Lady Antonia Fraser's daughter Rebecca. I hired a full-time
Black chauffeur called Harvey who took us everywhere in a
long black limousine.

McCann got in touch. He was coming to New York.

'I'm giving a dinner at Elaine's restaurant. Some really
fucking important people are coming. You and Judy can
come too. I'm opening the door for you, H'ard, the door to
high finance and the fast lane.'

Elaine's was a well-known actors' haunt at 88th Street.
McCann headed a table for ten, at which were seated various
people including Fakri Amadi, the head of Hertz in Dubai, Al
Malnik, the Wall Street whiz-kid who had married the
daughter of Meyer Lansky, and, to my utter astonishment,
Mohammed Durrani. McCann had obviously met him
through Graham and won him over. Durrani was introduced
as Michael, a name I knew he sometimes used, the Crown
Prince of Afghanistan. Durrani's very loud 'very pleased to
meet you' and his facial contortions clearly indicated that he
did not want me to reveal that I knew him. I was introduced
as Howard ap Owen, the leader of the Welsh Nationalist
Party. McCann insisted on drowning everyone in champagne
and kept pestering Peter Ustinov, who was sitting alone at an
adjacent table, to play him at backgammon. Durrani and I
arranged to meet the next day at my apartment. Judy cooked
him roast beef.

'Howard, please do not think I am doing business with
crazy Irishman. My cousin needs false passport for her
husband, who is European, and Irishman is only man I know
who can maybe get.'

'I can do that for you, Mohammed.'

'I am obliged, Howard.'

'It's no problem. I had to get one for myself. You heard about my problems, I suppose?'

'I hear some things, but I pay no attention. It does not affect you and me, Howard.'

'Do you still have the ability to air-freight merchandise from Karachi?'

'Of course. Raoul, he is doing every day. You have met Raoul, no?'

'Yes, but I don't know how to get hold of him or if he's prepared to do business with me.'

'Raoul is always prepared to do business under proper terms. I will speak with him and arrange meeting. Sam, too, is doing from Beirut. You should see him. Sam will be staying with me in my house in French Riviera in few weeks' time. You and your wonderful wife are most welcome to come.'

I telephoned Ernie and related to him the new possibilities now presenting themselves. He caught the next flight to New York.

'That's fantastic. When can they send it?'

'In about a month or so, Ernie. I should think.'

'Hmm! That long, huh? Okay. I'll get started and set up the companies. We'll do it like the Nepal one. By the way, can you help me out on the next Bangkok deals? My guys are pissed with flying over to Bangkok and back with messages and money. They always get hassled by US Customs for having Thai stamps in their passport. Do you have any guys we could use?'

I called Philip Sparrowhawk. In two days he was in Bangkok giving Richard Crimball a bag of money he had picked up from Tom Sunde in Hong Kong. Phil based himself in Bangkok for the next couple of years and developed his own personal relationship with Richard Crimball and others working in the business of exporting Thai marijuana.

Judy and I took Concorde from Washington to Paris and
after a few days flew to Nice. We checked into the Carlton in
Cannes. I rang Durrani.

'You have heard what has happened to crazy Irishman few
days ago?'

'No, Mohammed, I haven't.'

'I will explain you.'

Durrani related how McCann had left New York for his
wood and glass mansion in Brunswick Beach, Vancouver.
The Royal Canadian Mounted Police came to his residence
and took him away. Apparently, they had proof he wasn't
James Kennedy of the Massachusetts dynasty and reason to
believe he was James McCann, a fugitive from British justice
since his escape from Crumlin Road prison, Belfast, several
years ago. Bail had been refused. The grounds given by the
Canadian authorities were that 'the protection of the public
demands the detention of the applicant. He has escaped
custody twice, he has enormous financial backing and is an
international fugitive. He is a public menace whose threats
to public officials cannot be treated lightly.'

Over at Durrani's house in the Alpes-Maritimes, I sat down
with Lebanese Sam. He found the proposal of being paid 35%
of the wholesale price in America for all the hashish he could
send from Beirut very attractive. We set up communication
methods. There was time to kill before Sam was ready to export
the Lebanese hashish and before a meeting with Raoul
concerning export of Pakistani hashish could take place. Judy
and I rented a Mercedes, and we toured France, ending up in
the Dordogne Valley at the converted mill of her brother
Patrick Lane. He had given up snail farming (the snails had run
away one night) and was eager to restart one of his more
lucrative past activities. I had always enjoyed Patrick's company
and knew that Graham had high regard for his accountancy
abilities. I thought it might be sensible to use Patrick to open up
some foreign bank accounts. Keeping all that cash in safes and
safe-deposit boxes in America was limiting its use.

'Patrick, what do you know about offshore banking?'

'Absolutely nothing outside Switzerland, which everybody knows about.'

'If I paid all expenses and gave you a few grand, would you study offshore banking and tax havens and fly around the world to test things out personally? Perhaps you could open up a few company and personal accounts.'

'When do I leave?'

Judy and I left the Dordogne, drove south, and couldn't resist visiting Albi. At the centre of the city was the cathedral, a vast fortress-like edifice containing a statue dedicated to St Judith. We took this as the ultimate confirmation that we were meant to be with each other. We went over the Alps to Milano, and, after a wonderful night at the Villa d'Este in Cernobbio just outside Como, we drove across the Italian–Swiss border at Chiasso and along the shores of Lake Lugano. We stayed at the Hotel Splendide in Lugano, Europe's Rio de Janeiro, and had breakfast overlooking the lake.

'Albi, I have to tell you something.'

'Go ahead, love.'

'I'm pregnant.'

We both burst into smiles.

'But I'm not going to have the baby in America as Mrs Tunnicliffe. I want him or her to be born in England, Albi. They don't let women fly if they're very pregnant, so I'll have to live a train ride away from London.'

'You know I'll have to go to America sometimes, Judy, and maybe even Lebanon and Pakistan.'

'I know, Albi, but I have no choice.'

The sun's rays glistened off the lake's surface. On the opposite shore, framed by magnificent mountains, lay a little village.

'That place looks so beautiful, Albi. I'd love to go there.'

'Okay, love, we'll drive there for lunch and celebrate.'

It was a ten-minute drive. On the bridge over the lake we

passed a restaurant called La Romantica, drove through a village called Bissone, and came across an unmanned border post. There was a sign stating Campione d'Italia, and the Italian flag was flying. Cars were speeding through the border in both directions, so I carried on driving. The village was an exquisite mixture of old and modern architecture, and everyone seemed extremely wealthy. There was a large casino. We drove through the village, and after about a mile of country, the road split into two. We drove down the left-hand fork and were stopped by four Japanese guards. We tried the right fork. It terminated in a tennis stadium. This place was wild. We were in Italy but couldn't get to anywhere else in Italy. We must still be in Switzerland. In the centre of the village was a restaurant called La Taverna. Impeccably clad waiters ushered us to an alfresco table covered with gleaming glass, cutlery, and porcelain. Our waiter spoke perfect English.

'Are we in Italy or Switzerland?' I asked.

'We accept both currencies, sir. We accept all currencies and all credit cards. May I suggest you help yourselves to the antipasto table?'

'But which country are we actually in?' I persisted.

'Italy.'

'Do you live here?' I asked.

'Now, yes, but I am from Sicily.'

A London taxi drew up outside the restaurant. A handsome, bespectacled fifty-year-old German came in accompanied by a garishly dressed Rastafarian, a rich cockney businessman, a Sophia Loren look-alike, and a blonde Teutonic beauty. The place filled up with eminently watchable personalities.

I had read somewhere that Mafia chieftains drank Brunello di Montalcino with their meat dishes. It was on the menu, and I ordered it. We ate and drank to our hearts' content.

'This is an amazing place, Judy. The telephones are Swiss. That policeman is Italian, but the licence plates on his car are Swiss. What is going on?'

Although one couldn't drive from Campione d'Italia to anywhere else in Italy, there once existed a cable car connecting the village to the nearest Italian mountain, and boats plied between Campione and harbours on the truly Italian side of Lake Lugano. Benito Mussolini built a casino in the village. A secret tunnel, known by everyone, connected the casino to the priest's house. I loved Campione.

Judy and I toured around Switzerland and opened a few bank accounts and safe-deposit boxes, she in her real name, I in the name of Tunnicliffe. In one of her safe-deposit boxes, Judy stowed away her Mrs Tunnicliffe passport. Lebanese Sam was back in Durrani's house in the Alpes-Maritimes. Judy went to Campione to look for a flat to rent while I drove from Geneva to Cannes. Sam had arranged everything in Beirut and was ready to send a 1,000-kilo load of hashish to Kennedy Airport. Tom Sunde flew to Zurich with money from Ernie, which I took and gave to Lebanese Sam in Geneva for him to take to Beirut. Two weeks later, Judy and I were sitting in a newly rented flat in Via Totone, Campione d'Italia, overlooking Lake Lugano with breathtaking views of Lugano town and the towering peaks of San Salvatore and Monte Bre. I had just made another $300,000. Lebanese Sam went back to Beirut to repeat the successful scam.

Meanwhile McCann was making spirited attempts to be released from his Canadian captors. Using an intrigued Vancouver media, he declared, 'I'm offering you a deal. I'll leave. That's the deal. If you keep me arrested, the effect will be like a stone dropped into an Irish brine of violence. The ripple will peel you like an apple.'

McCann addressed Canadian Immigration spokesman Jack Betteridge with the words: 'Mr Betteridge, you are an enemy of the Irish people and will be tried in front of an Irish tribunal. You are also a fucking fascist pig, and justice will be served on you.'

Fascinated British Columbian television audiences heard

McCann repeatedly explain that his arrest was engineered by
MI6 as a result of his unearthing an Ulster Protestant gun-
running organisation in Vancouver. He claimed he was a
member of the Official IRA and had represented Sinn Fein
in Vietnam and Cambodia in the 1960s. He had a birth
certificate in the name of Joseph Kennedy, and he carefully
explained how 'Jim' was an old Gaelic abbreviation for
'Joseph'. Various bomb threats were made to Canadian
embassies in Ireland and South America. The Canadian
Mounties weakened, gave Jim back his false passport, and
put him on a plane for Paris, where he was seen escorting Aki
Lehmann, wife of the prominent New York banker Robin
Lehmann, at the fashionable Paris night-club Castell's.

At the beginning of October 1977, Judy and I locked up the
Campione flat and travelled by train and ferry to Victoria
Station. We checked into Blake's Hotel in Roland Gardens
and began searching for a suitable London flat. Judy was
nervous about using a phoney identity to rent the flat in case
there were any complications during the birth which might
reveal the falsity and get me into trouble. In her own name,
she had no bank account, other than a few Swiss ones. We
had to find someone prepared to rent a flat for us. Nik
Douglas and Penny Slinger were two friends whose slight
acquaintance we had made before leaving for America a year
earlier. They were living together in Chelsea. Both were
extraordinarily talented individuals. Educated in the
sciences, Nik produced records and managed pop groups in
the early 1960s; moved to Spain and developed new
techniques for utilising solar energy in the mid-1960s;
studied Sanskrit, Tibetan, Buddhism, Hinduism, and
Tantric Yoga in India, Tibet, and Nepal in the late 1960s;
and studied homeopathy, Indian medicine, and Eastern
alchemy in the early 1970s. He had published many books
on Eastern culture and religion and had directed a film,
Tantra, which had been produced by Mick Jagger. Penny

held a first-class honours degree in Fine Arts. Her surrealist art had been published and exhibited on several occasions. When I met them, they were working together on a number of art and literary projects. I was excited and inspired by them and their work and decided to help them out in whatever way I could. They had never asked me to give them any significant money, but I knew they could use it.

At the end of October, at St Theresa's Hospital, Wimbledon, I watched Judy give birth to our daughter, who was too beautiful to be called by any of the names we had experimented with over the last few weeks. For days she remained magically unnamed and mysterious. Then Penny, who visited Judy's bedside with Nik, said, 'She told me her name was Amber.'

It was, and Judy and I went to register her birth at the registry office. We put down the father's name as Albert Waylon Jennings, a singer for the group Laughing Grass. Years later, when I was in prison, Amber discovered her birth certificate. She was right in the middle of an adolescent identity crisis. It couldn't have helped much.

While in London, I ran into Sally Minford, the sister of John Minford, my Balliol Dramatic Society friend. She was now living with Michael O'Connel, a talented musician and recording engineer. They wanted to open up a recording studio and needed capital. Without disclosing the source, I provided some money, and a Pimlico recording studio called Archipelago was formed. In a short period, artists such as Elvis Costello were using the facilities, and Island Records were subletting them.

At a social function in Islington, I ran into Anthony Woodhead. He had not been suspected of foul play after the investigation into my disappearance from the Regent's Park penthouse. This he had achieved by putting the blame on his Czechoslovakian girl-friend and getting her to admit she had sublet me the penthouse without his knowledge. I had never seen anyone so relieved to see me. He had spent a year in San

Francisco and had befriended a bent US Customs Officer who could clear air-freight at San Francisco Airport provided it arrived on a Pan American flight. Woodhead asked if I knew anyone who could export hashish. I said I knew someone who could do it in Lebanon, and another person who could do it from Thailand. We agreed straightforward terms: he and his friend would pay half the costs in Lebanon (or Thailand); my source and I would get half the money from the sales in San Francisco.

Lebanese Sam's second deal to Don Brown in New York didn't make it. Sam got busted in Beirut just before another 1,000 kilos of hashish were about to be exported. There were inquiries made in New York, but Don Brown and the Mob were not questioned. Business could continue, but not for some time, and the method would have to be considerably refined. On arrival in New York the consignment would have to appear as if it had been exported from a non-dope-producing country. The air waybill could no longer show Bangkok or Beirut as the airport of the consignment's loading. If it did, it would certainly be busted by US Customs. Phil Sparrowhawk flew in and out of Bangkok with message after message and idea after idea. Changing the origin was difficult. There would be no air-freight scams from Thailand to New York for a while, but there might be one to San Francisco from somewhere else.

Durrani came to London to discuss the implications of Lebanese Sam's bust. He stayed at his house in Dulwich, and I visited him there.

'Howard, thank you for British passport you sent. It is perfect. Unfortunately, I think you should get new one for you, too. Sam knows you use Tunnicliffe passport. Maybe he wrote down detail which police now have. Maybe not. I don't know.'

'I'll get another one, Mohammed. Thanks for the advice.'

'I need one more favour from you. I want my son to go to the Oxford University. You can arrange?'

'It's not like that, Mohammed, I assure you.'

'I will pay handsome price.'

'That's what it's not like. You can't buy your way into Oxford.'

'But I meet many rich people here in London. They all say their children go to the Oxford University.'

'That's because rich people can afford to send their children to expensive schools, and it's easier to get into Oxford from an expensive school, partly because the teachers and facilities are better and partly because expensive schools have closed scholarships to Oxford and Cambridge.'

'What is closed scholarship?'

'Some places in Oxford can only be given to those who have attended a particular school.'

'You know names of these schools?'

'Some, yes. Eton, Harrow, Winchester . . .'

'Please help me get my son into one these schools so he can go to the Oxford University.'

'I'll try my best.'

'I am obliged, Howard.'

'Mohammed, is it possible to send merchandise from Karachi in such a way that it appears to come from some other place? Also, another question. Is it possible to load merchandise on a Pan Am flight in Karachi?'

'Raoul is coming to London this week. We are buying hotel in Knightsbridge, and he has agreed with me to meet you as you requested some time ago. You can ask him. If it is possible, he will do.'

Raoul had no doubts.

'Pan American flight to San Francisco is no problem. For the one to New York, we can do the needful in many ways. Two I can tell you now. We can take merchandise from Karachi to Dubai in dhow, then send from Dubai airport. You can choose any airline. We have to pay men in dhow. Otherwise, same price. There is other way. We put merchandise on PIA flight from Karachi, but we arrange different air waybill to say merchandise only tranship in Karachi; it come from some other place in Far East where PIA do service to and from Karachi.'

'What sort of place, Raoul?'

'I am thinking Singapore or Hong Kong. I am back in Karachi very soon. Durrani will let me know your decision.'

Don Brown was still not ready to accept any freight at New York, but Anthony Woodhead's San Francisco connection was, and he had paid Woodhead the agreed $100,000 deposit. I took the money to Mohammed Durrani in Dulwich and gave him the address to which the hashish, placed in boxes described as containing surgical instruments, should be sent. Less than two weeks later, Woodhead rang me at the Richmond flat and said it had gone through perfectly. Would I please come to San Francisco to pick up my and Raoul's cut and to meet his bent US Customs friend? I said I would once I obtained a new passport.

I badly needed a false passport of the same calibre as the Tunnicliffe one, which could no longer be safely used in the light of Lebanese Sam's bust. I spoke of my problem to Nik Douglas, who thought he knew of someone in Norfolk who would be prepared to sell the privilege of being a passport holder.

On an early spring morning in 1978, Nik and I drove to Norwich, where I obtained a passport in the name of Donald Nice. By the end of March, I had become Mr Nice (my real name is Donald, but please call me Albi) and had all sorts of documentation to prove it. Patrick Lane had returned from his global investigation into the banking of hot money and related matters. Apart from opening five current accounts in Montreal for reasons he could not properly articulate, he hadn't actually done anything other than collect a sun-tan and a massive library of books on tax havens. But he had read most of the books and felt competent to do whatever I asked. I was spending more time with Nik Douglas and Penny

Slinger and getting very interested in the work they were doing in esoteric Eastern practices. I met some fascinating people, including the renowned psychiatrist R. D. Laing and best-selling authors Lyall Watson and Robin Wilson. The financial aspects of Nik and Penny's work were becoming increasingly complex with the royalties from the sales of her pictures and his various media productions and the buying, exhibiting, and selling of oriental antiques. I introduced them to Patrick, who had now taken occupancy of our flat in Campione with his wife and young daughter to set up a tax consultancy business called Overseas United Investors. Coincidentally, Campione happened to be one of the best tax havens in the world. Nik and Penny were suitably impressed with Patrick, who formed three offshore companies: Sceptre Holdings, Cayman Islands, to hold all Nik's antiques; Buckingham Holdings, British Virgin Islands, to receive all royalties; and World-wide Entertainments, Monrovia, Liberia, to handle all audio/video media business. All the companies had bank accounts at the Foreign Commerz Bank, Zurich. Donald (Albi) Nice was appointed managing director of World-wide Entertainments and a consultant to the other two companies.

Mr Nice had reasons to do legitimate business just about anywhere in the world. I was beginning to feel dangerously invulnerable, and I felt not a trace of nerves when I walked into the United States Embassy, Grosvenor Square, presented my Mr Nice passport and company documents, and asked if I could be issued with a multiple indefinite entry visa as soon as possible. I got one the same day.

Leaving Amber and Judy in Richmond, I flew to New York and transferred the apartment on East 77th to the name of World-wide Entertainments. The next day, I was at the Mark Hopkins Hotel on Nob Hill, San Francisco, waiting for Woodhead to bring me just over $1,000,000, 25% of which was mine, the rest belonging to Durrani and Raoul. Woodhead didn't show up. I waited a week and

called every person I knew who might be able to locate him.
He had vanished.

There is a general rule in most hashish-smuggling
ventures: if the scam gets busted by the authorities, the scam
shareholders lose their investment, pay any costs, and no one
else is held responsible for the loss. There is another general
rule: if there is any kind of rip-off, the shareholders do not
lose their investment, get paid their profit, and the person
who was ripped off is held responsible. The logic is sound:
bonding together against the enemy during troubled times
but paying the penalty for trusting the wrong person during
untroubled times. Most criminal organisations abide by
these principles. Many, however, particularly the Sicilian
Mafia and the tightly-knit gangs of South and East London,
modify the rule by eliminating the responsibility of the
person ripped off if he kills the person who did the rip-off.
This principle has become clichéd as 'Either a body on the
floor or a body in court.' Only these actions can excuse non-
payment. This chilling modification can serve as an effective
deterrent because the identity of the rip-off perpetrator is
usually known. In normal society, most deterrent measures
fail because the detection rate is so low. According to the
rules, I owed $750,000 to Raoul and Durrani. I could pay it,
but it would set me back a bit. I returned to London a
miserable and vulnerable Mr Nice.

'Okay, we're ready. Here's what you do . . .'

It was Ernie. Don Brown and the Mob were ready again
to receive in Kennedy Airport, New York, and Ernie was
giving me the details to put on the airway bill. He favoured
the dhow to Dubai and then air-freight to New York
method. What the hell could I do? I went to see Durrani at
Dulwich and told him exactly what had happened. He said
as far as he was concerned, he would wait for his cut until I
contacted Woodhead, however long it took. Durrani would
talk to Raoul that evening and conjectured that although
Raoul would have to be paid some money, he would

undoubtedly be understanding. I called Durrani again the next day. A tearful female voice answered. Durrani was in Westminster Hospital recovering from a heart attack. I went to the hospital. Durrani was ghostly pale, his voice was almost inaudible. A man with strong Afghan features sat at his bedside.

'Howard, Raoul's numbers are on this paper,' whispered Durrani, 'and if you have any problems, this gentleman, Salim Malik, is also from Karachi and in our business. Please send my commission to my Amsterdam bank account, also written on paper.' Not a muscle moved on Malik's face as he pulled out his business card and gave it to me.

'Do you like London, Mr Malik?' I asked.

'I have been coming here since 1965. I like the Hyde Park. London is a good place. British peoples are good peoples. I am here visiting my friend tomorrow, then back to Pakistan.'

'I'll see you both tomorrow, then. Get better, Mohammed. Very pleased to have met you, Mr Malik.'

The next day at the hospital, the staff nurse told me Durrani had suffered a massive heart attack overnight and had not survived it. He was forty-two years old.

Raoul was waiting for me in the lobby while I was checking into the Intercontinental Hotel, Karachi, looking forward to my first visit to a hashish-producing country.

'So, you are now Mr Nice,' said a grinning Raoul, 'and you are most welcome in Pakistan. Let us go to your room.'

In my room, Raoul pulled out from his pocket two enormous bundles of Pakistan rupees and a piece of Pakistani hashish.

'For spending and enjoying, you will need. So, how things are?'

Sheepishly, I explained the position.

'Mr Nice, I am always reasonable man, but I have already paid my people their profit. Simple reason being: you told me merchandise had arrived in San Francisco. I am bit short of money. I need $500,000 to settle account. Please do the needful, and I will get dhow ready to take merchandise to Dubai for New York.'

I had to pay him. Patrick Lane, now producing a weekly newsletter called *The Offshore Banking Report* and handling a large chunk of my money, arranged for Raoul's account in Geneva to be credited with $500,000. I gave Raoul the air waybill details and stayed in the Intercontinental Hotel for days waiting for the telephone to ring. Raoul called and came round with the air waybill as soon as the load was ready to leave Dubai airport. I checked the details, wrote down a coded version of the air waybill number, and flew to Zurich, from where I telephoned Ernie. A few days later, Ernie called me in London.

'It worked. I guess you want Judy's brother Patrick to take care of the money, yeah? Let's do it again in two weeks.'

I saw Nik and Penny in London, and they introduced me to Peter Whitehead, the film director who had reached fame in the Sixties with his film of the 1965 Beat Poetry Conference at the Royal Albert Hall, Wholly Communion, and his film *Let's All Make Love in London*. He was the leaseholder of the two upper floors above the Pizza Express at the corner of Carlisle Street and Dean Street in Soho and wanted to sell the lease. I thought the premises would make excellent headquarters for Mr Nice's World-wide Entertainments. The flat was right in the trendy middle of London's entertainment industry, a few yards from Paul McCartney's office in Soho Square, a few yards from where Karl Marx had lived, and a few yards from Lulu's place. The top floor was speedily converted to living quarters, that below to offices. Judy, Amber, and I moved in, then I flew back to Pakistan to repeat the successful scam.

This time I stayed at the Intercontinental Hotel in Lahore's fortress city waiting for the telephone to ring. My duty was to ensure I remained in the room all the time. Ernie would telephone if the deal had to be called off. A few minutes could be vital. However, I sneaked out to have a

look at the famous starving Buddha sculpture in the local
museum and at Rudyard Kipling's 'Kim's Gun'. Again there
were no problems, and in a couple of weeks I found myself
back in London being told by Ernie that the scam had
worked. The year was beginning to show a healthy profit.

We did it again. The Holiday Inn, Islamabad, provided
me with a phone. This time my sojourn in Pakistan was
longer than a few days. Delays had been occasioned by
political, civilian, and military unrest. Zulfikar Ali Bhutto,
the Prime Minister of Pakistan, had been accused of rigging
elections in favour of his People's Party, and violent riots had
become commonplace. Bhutto imposed martial law but had
been arrested by his appointee General Zia ul-Haq, the
Chief of Staff of the Pakistan army, on charges of murder. A
Lahore court sentenced him to death, and he was being held
in Rawalpindi, the twin city of Islamabad.

I had plenty of hashish to smoke, plenty of Pakistani
rupees, and a few days to myself. I had been advised by
Raoul to visit Murray Hill Station on the borders of
Kashmir, a few hours' drive from Islamabad. Foreigners
were not allowed to rent cars, so I made a private
arrangement with a local taxi-driver who spoke a little
English. We were driving on poor roads through the foothills
of the Himalayas. I saw and smelt fields of marijuana. A
large, five-foot-long, prehistoric-looking lizard ambled
across the road in front of us and disappeared into a
marijuana bush. The taxi screamed to a halt, and the driver
pointed and yelled, 'Krow! Krow!'

'What is it?' I asked.

'It is Krow, Mr Nice, burglar best friend.'

'I don't understand.'

'You want to come to my brother cousin, Mr Nice? I will
show you.'

'Yes, please,' I said, well in the mood for arbitrary
adventures with burglars' friends and brother cousins.

We took a track off the road, drove for miles, and stopped

outside an old, meandering group of dusty yellow buildings. An old man dressed in colourful rags came out through a hole in the wall and grunted at the taxi-driver.

'This is Mohammed, Mr Nice. He is pleased to meet you, Mr Nice.'

The two babbled away in some unknown tongue and beckoned me into a walled courtyard full of Krows of all sizes. At a signal from Mohammed, one of the Pakistani workers caught hold of a large Krow by its tail, body-slammed it against the high wall, and let go. The Krow stuck to the wall. The Pakistani climbed up the vertical Krow as if it was a ladder. I could see why the Krow was the burglar's best friend but still found it hard to imagine housebreaking with a giant lizard. I needed a joint.

We continued to Murray Hill Station and had lunch at the Cecil Hotel, which was run by a Pakistani who spoke perfect English. Murray resembled an old-fashioned ski resort, complete with primitive cable-car lifts, but there was no snow and it seemed unlikely that there ever would be. There was a brewery which produced a bottled drink named London Lager. It was the best bottled beer I had tasted in my life, owing its quality to a strict adherence to a hundred-year-old recipe imported from the British when they knew how to make beer.

Back at the Holiday Inn, Islamabad, Raoul came round. He confirmed the existence and uses of the Krow. He also gave me the air waybill for the new shipment of hashish ready to leave Dubai. I flew to Paris and stayed overnight at L'Hôtel d'Alsace in Rue des Beaux Arts, where Oscar Wilde spent his last days. I called Ernie. He was in poor health as a result of a persistent thyroid problem and asked if I would handle things in New York on this occasion. Handling things meant collecting a couple of million dollars from Alan Schwarz once he'd sold the hashish and giving Don Brown 25% of it.

I caught an Air France flight to New York, freshened up

at the East 77th Street apartment, and met Don Brown at
Mortimer's, an Upper East Side restaurant run by an
Englishman, John Beamish, and popular with free-spending
culture-vultures and cocaine dealers. Don was a portly, red-
headed man with thick glasses. He was jovial and liked corny
wisecracks. He seemed an unlikely candidate to be running
the criminal side of Kennedy Airport. I met Don again the
next day for dinner. This time he brought one of his friends,
an Italian called Willy. We were eating at Nicola's, a
restaurant popular with gangsters, actors, and CIA refugees.
On the wall, next to covers of recently released books about
the Mafia, were notices that cash was the only form of
payment allowed in the restaurant.

'So you're called Don, too, huh?' said Don Brown in a
classic attempt to promote unease, trying to make me
wonder whether he was having me followed and checked
out. Ernie had probably told him I was trotting around the
world as Mr Donald Nice and getting a kick out of it. We
weren't supposed to divulge these details to each other, but
we did. Likewise, Ernie had told me Don's surname was
Brown. I wasn't supposed to know, of course.

'I would rather be Nice than Brown, Don.'

Don roared with laughter.

'Mr Nice, we've done our shit, and the Jewish kid, Alan,
has got it. When you give me and Don the money, we don't
want to have to count the motherfucking shit, and we don't
like small bills. Your shit from Dubai weighed exactly 2,308
pounds, which means you owe me $577,000. I get that
$577,000 before any other cocksucker gets a dime. Are we
straight on that?'

'If that's what Ernie did, that's what I'll do, Willy.'

'Yeah, I guess that is what Ernie did, so you do it. Give the
money to Don.'

Don was still laughing at my, not that funny, comment.

'So how do you get a name like Nice, for Jesus Christ's
sake?'

'I chose it, Don. I bet you didn't choose Brown, did you?'

'You got that right. Okay, time to go. I'll be in the Pierre Hotel until you bring me the money.'

'What room number, Don?'

'I don't know. I'll be using the name Nasty.'

Don Brown was true to his word, and after receiving cardboard boxes of dirty dollars from Alan Schwarz, Mr Nice took $577,000 to Mr Nasty.

Thai sticks were piling up in Bangkok, and Ernie wanted to do the next air-freight scam from there. I was a mere investor. Phil Sparrowhawk was also now given the privilege of investing. A ton of Thai sticks left Bangkok, and disappeared. None of Don Brown's crowd or those who worked for Richard Crimball in Bangkok could trace it. Eventually it was found lying in a freight shed in Charles de Gaulle airport, Paris. The load of 'sewing machines returning under warranty' had not attracted any undue attention, but there didn't seem any way of getting it to New York on Alitalia or Japanese Air Lines, the only two 'friendly' airlines. I thought of a solution. The New York company would send a large consignment of real sewing machines, this time to a newly formed company in Rome. The Rome company would find the sewing machines unacceptable and decide to return them under warranty. The New York company would instruct Alitalia to consolidate both the Paris and Rome shipments at Rome and forward them to New York. It was complicated, but it should work. It did.

I stayed in New York. Ernie decided to do another Bangkok scam. This one didn't work. The DEA busted it in New York and arrested sixteen New Yorkers alleged to be at the centre of the Donald Brown organisation. I took the next flight out of New York.

Luckily Donald Brown himself had not been arrested. Neither had Willy the Italian. It was still safe for me to be Nice. But there would be no more air-freight scams to New York. They had come to an end. Between 1975 and 1978, twenty-four loads totalling 55,000 pounds of marijuana and hashish had been successfully imported through John F. Kennedy Airport, New York. They had involved the Mafia, the Yakuza, the Brotherhood of Eternal Love, the Thai army, the Palestine Liberation Organisation, the Pakistani Armed Forces, Nepalese monks, and other individuals from all walks of life. The total profit made by all concerned was $48,000,000. They'd had a good run.

Judy's sister, Natasha, visited Judy and me in London. She had spent several months sailing in the Mediterranean, and had met a hashish-smuggling Californian sailor called Stuart Prentiss. They exchanged confidences, and Stuart expressed a keen desire to meet Natasha's hashish-supplying brother-in-law. Stuart had a boat and he wanted to use it to smuggle hashish into Scotland. He owned a yacht-chartering business based on Kerrera, a small island a few miles from Oban, and was confident of his ability to import hashish safely without attracting attention from the authorities. He didn't have a source of supply in the Mediterranean. Lebanese Sam was still in prison, so I tracked down Eric to see if he still had any of his Lebanese connections. He didn't. There had been all sorts of problems in Beirut: people had been killed in the war, others had emigrated, the quality of commercial hashish had greatly deteriorated, and heroin had become the export of choice. However, Eric had cultivated a connection in Morocco, Sharif, whom he had yet to use. For a reasonable price, Sharif claimed he could deliver a ton of hashish to a boat anchored offshore close to Al Hociema. We went ahead.

It proved to be a trouble-free scam. At the end of 1978, Stuart's boat delivered a ton of Moroccan hashish to his remote Scottish island. Every day for a week, 300 pounds of the load would be taken to the mainland, driven to London, and sold.

Nothing got busted; everyone got paid. I brought up the subject of a repeat performance. Stuart said he wanted to do just one scam a year. I said I could wait. With the profits, Judy bought a flat in Cathcart Road, Chelsea. We started doing it up.

The time had come for World-wide Entertainments to waste some of its money on legitimate businesses. In an attempt to compensate for my lack of talent in rock music, I thought I should manage and finance someone else's. At a Christmas party I met P. J. Proby and Tom Baker. Proby had sung demo discs for Elvis, toured with the Beatles in the Sixties, and had a few British hit records and West End performances to his credit. Tom Baker, a friend of Proby's, used to act in *The Virginian* and was now a film director. He was looking for a suitable manager for Proby, someone with money and recording facilities. I, as Mr Nice, took on the job.

There had not been any significant mention of me by the media for over four years. But in July 1979, it was discovered that Chief Superintendent Philip Fairweather's confidential report into my disappearance while on bail during 1974 had been leaked to the press. Britain's top crime reporter, Duncan Campbell, wrote about it in the *New Statesman*, explaining that Fairweather had been summoned by MI6's legal adviser, Bernard Shelton, and told that 'a former Balliol College fellow undergraduate of Marks, who is now an MI6 officer, contacted Marks with a view to using his company AnnaBelinda, which also had a shop in Amsterdam, as a cover for his activities. He later realised that Marks was engaged in certain activities and requested him to obtain information concerning the Provisional IRA.'

I didn't pay the article much attention at the time, but this was the first admission by any British government authority that I had worked for MI6 and had been asked to spy on the IRA.

Jim McCann, after his media-inspired face-off with the Canadian Immigration authorities, had not been in France long before he was arrested in the club-house of a villa estate

on the Riviera by a squad of French and German police.
They locked him up in Marseille's notorious Les Baumettes
jail and began the process of extraditing him to Germany to
face charges of bombing the British Army base at
Mönchengladbach in 1973. Luckily for McCann, there was
grass-roots concern in France about the country's failure to
behave as a proper asylum for political refugees and its
tendency to cave in to other countries' extradition demands.
The French Government had not long ago acceded to
German demands for the surrender of Klaus Croissant, a
lawyer to the Baader-Meinhof organisation. There were
protests, and subsequent attempts by the Italians, who
wanted a French-residing supporter of the Red Brigade, and
the Spanish, who wanted back a member of the Basque
guerrilla group, ETA, were thwarted by determined
champions of political asylum. McCann's defence was taken
on by the same Marseilles lawyers who had successfully dealt
with the ETA case. To his lawyers, McCann told one story:
he was not James Kennedy, he was James McCann, a fund
raiser for the IRA. To the Communist paper *Libération*, he
told another: his name was Peter Joseph (Jim) Kennedy, and
he was a harmless underground journalist. The Organisation
Communiste Internationale, a Trotskyist trade union group,
rallied to McCann's cause, referring to it as '*un scandale
judiciaire et politique*'. McCann was overjoyed and made the
following pronouncement:

> *Camarades. Je suis très touché par votre solidarité . . . mes
> circonstances personelles sont le resultat d'une conspiration
> entre les services secrets anglais et allemands de l'Ouest,
> tumeur fasciste au coeur de l'Europe democratique.*
> Yours in Combat,
> James Kennedy (McCann)

The French followed the Canadian strategy and gave up.
They refused to extradite McCann to Germany because his

blowing-up of a British Army base was a political act, and they gave him political asylum. We met at La Coupole in Montparnasse, Paris.

'The Kid's a fucking legend, H'ard, a fucking legend. I've got these Trotskyite fucking snail-eaters in the palm of my hand. No one can touch me. I've got political asylum. But I need some fucking bread, man. Those Marseilles lawyers cleaned me out. Are you still dope-dealing, H'ard?'

'No, Jim. I took your advice. Now I'm into high finance.'

'Fuck off, will you? I know you're still dope-dealing. I need you to send me some nordle from Kabul.'

'How much? A couple of ounces okay?'

'I need half a fucking ton, at least, you Welsh cunt.'

'Are you saying you've got Paris airport straightened?'

'I can straighten anywhere I fucking want to, H'ard. You know that. But I need you to send the nordle to Ireland.'

'What? Shannon again?'

'Dublin. It's nearer that fucking Welsh ferry of yours. You know people in Kabul, do you?'

'Only the same ones you know. Why don't you ask them yourself?'

'Well, Durrani's fucking dead, and that cunt Raoul thinks I ripped him off.'

'Did you?'

'Of course I fucking did. I had problems, man. It's better you ask him, H'ard.'

'If I ask Raoul to send dope to Ireland, he'll know it's for you. He's not going to go for it. But I do have someone in Bangkok.'

'Where the fuck's that?'

'It's the capital of Thailand.'

'I've never fucking heard of it.'

'It used to be called Siam.'

'What fucking use is that? I need nordle, not cats.'

'Jim, the nordle from Thailand, Thai sticks, is some of the best in the world.'

'I know what fucking Thai sticks are, you stupid Welsh fucker. I was smoking them last night.'

'Well, I'll send you some of those.'

'Okay, H'ard, but it's got to be done quickly, and no fuck-ups.'

Phil Sparrowhawk was still living in Bangkok. I flew there to see him and checked into the Hyatt Rama Hotel as Mr Nice. Phil introduced me to Robert Crimball, Ernie's Brotherhood of Eternal Love associate. There would be no difficulty air-freighting Thai sticks to Ireland from Bangkok airport. The marijuana had already been harvested and dried. But there was one problem: the marijuana had not yet been tied on to sticks, and this would take some time. Robert felt there would be market resistance to Thai marijuana not presented in the traditional form, entwined around a six-inch stick. I said that might be true in America, but in England, if the dope got you stoned, there would be little market resistance. London heads would be quite likely to return the bare sticks complaining that they didn't get you high.

I stayed in Bangkok for just one night, then went to Hong Kong to pick up money that Patrick Lane had arranged to be collected by Mr Nice from the Hong Kong & Shanghai Bank. Phil came with me, and I gave him the money. I flew from Hong Kong to Zurich and then took a train to Lugano to meet Judy and Amber. We were now resettling in Campione d'Italia. A few months earlier, Patrick Lane had moved his home and tax haven consultancy business from Campione to Ireland. The business had not made a single penny. Still, his presence in the Emerald Isle might prove useful.

McCann had rented a smart executive home near Fitzpatrick's Castle in Killiney, the Beverly Hills of the Dublin area. Judy, Amber, and I moved into it for a week. The scam worked fine, and McCann brought round a large van full of tins of Thai marijuana. There was a total of 750 kilos. As in the old Shannon days, I used a few friends for driving the marijuana from Ireland to England or Wales. I had also agreed to use two friends of Phil. He had promised them some work.

There were a total of fifteen cross-Channel runs. Thai marijuana was much bulkier than hashish, and each car could only take 50 kilos. Phil's two friends, who included English international soccer star Eddie Clamp, did the last run. They got busted by Her Majesty's Customs and Excise at Liverpool. This was the first-ever proof to the authorities that large quantities of dope were being smuggled through Ireland. It had been happening for over eight years. The method of entry remained unknown.

'We'll do another one, H'ard, but none of your fucking burglars, Third-Division Scottish footballers, and academics on that fucking Welsh ferry. This time the Kid will bring it over. You understand me, do you?'

'How are you going to bring it over!'

'As bananas.'

'Bananas?'

'Our Gerard's got a fruit company. They take fruit from Southern to Northern Ireland every fucking day. And they take it from Northern Ireland to Scotland.'

'Don't they get stopped and searched, Jim?'

'According to you Brits, Northern Ireland is the same fucking country as Scotland. So how can there be any Customs? I thought you were a fucking dope smuggler. You should know these things, man.'

'I'm talking about the land border between Southern and Northern Ireland, Jim.'

'That's no fucking border.'

'I know, but they still have Customs and searches, don't they? Like the Welsh ferry.'

'Fuck the Welsh ferry. And no fucker searches the Kid. If the boys can take guns over every day for the struggle, and farmers can take their pigs over to get bigger subsidies, I'm fucking sure I can take over some fucking bananas.'

Phil sent another load from Bangkok to Dublin. On a late summer's morning, I sat in a rented car just outside the ferry terminal at Stranraer on the west coast of Scotland waiting for the arrival of the ferry from Larne. McCann's fruit lorry was meant to be on it. Jarvis sat in a large van in a car park a mile away. I watched every vehicle drive off. There was no fruit lorry. There was no answer from Jim's telephone in Killiney. I gave up waiting and set off for London, listening to the car radio. The lunchtime news described how a big articulated truck running north from the docks at Cork with a load of South American bananas had pulled into a lay-by on the main road just south of Dublin. A rented van was parked in the darkness. Men from both vehicles emerged and began to talk. By chance, a courting couple at the other end of the lay-by were watching the proceedings. A man with a strong Belfast accent spotted the couple and screamed, 'Fuck off out of here.'

The couple left and called the police. A patrol car arrived at the lay-by. McCann confronted it with a pistol. A policeman got out and kicked the gun out of McCann's hand. McCann dived into a car and drove it into a hedge. He was overpowered, yelling, 'I did it for Ireland.'

The Irish Army bomb disposal team blew open the truck doors. There was no bomb. Instead, there were twenty-one tea chests full of Thai marijuana: the largest bust in Ireland.

Seven

MR NICE

During the late 1970s, most of the twenty-eight tons of marijuana that Americans smoked every day came from Colombia. Hundreds of tons a month were loaded on to large freighter ships in Colombian ports. These mother ships would anchor miles away from the South Florida coastline and offload, several tons at a time, to a fleet of smaller craft that would land their cargoes at private moorings and deserted beaches. Some of the imported marijuana would be sold in Florida, while the rest would be distributed to other dope-smoking populations. The first of these operations was the brainchild of Santo Trafficante, Jr., the chief of the Florida Mafia. Trafficante had inherited this position from his father, a partner of New York Mafia boss Salvatore 'Lucky' Luciano. Trafficante had set up casinos in Cuba in 1946 but was jailed when Fidel Castro took control in 1959 and ousted the Mafia. For some reason, Castro allowed Trafficante to leave Cuba with all his money. On his return to America, the CIA paid him to assassinate Castro. Trafficante took the money and tipped off Castro. According to Chicago Mafia leader Sam Giancana, Trafficante was then asked to assassinate President Kennedy. The rest is

uncertain, but Trafficante was certainly efficient, and
Colombian marijuana was flowing in at such a rate that its
wholesale price began to plummet. Consumers wanted
something different. Eventually, ton loads were being sold on
the streets of Miami and Fort Lauderdale at the rock-bottom
price of $200 a pound, while hashish and Thai sticks were
fetching $1,000 a pound. In London, the situation was very
different. Moroccan and Pakistani hashish was plentiful and
affordable at £300 a pound, and any decent marijuana would
be similarly priced. It had always been possible to make a
profit by smuggling hashish from London to America, as I
had done with the rock-group scams, but now the low price
of Colombian marijuana in America had made it equally
possible to profit by smuggling marijuana from America to
London. A few small consignments had made their way over,
and Trafficante and his underlings were pleased to make
some foreign-exchange earnings. They thought of the
possibility of smuggling large quantities to Europe, not from
America, but directly from Colombia. Trafficante, Louis
Ippolito, and Ernie explored the thought. Ernie was happy to
do any amount. Trafficante wanted to do a minimum of fifty
tons. He thought anything less wouldn't be economically
feasible.

England's consumption of marijuana and hashish was
about three tons a day, considerably less than America's
twenty-eight tons. One to two tons was, and still is,
consumed in London every night. But to sell that amount
took longer. It would be difficult to sell more than a ton of
Colombian marijuana a week, every week. Fifty tons would
last a year.

Stuart Prentiss was ready to do another scam into
Scotland, but he wasn't able to handle fifty tons. He could
get away with importing fifteen tons, but he would need
money in advance to buy another boat. He could store five
tons for as long as was necessary, but that was it. The other
ten tons would have to be quickly taken from Kerrera,

preferably by boat, and stored elsewhere. Another landing place and some suitable storage facilities were needed. The Florida gangsters grudgingly accepted these terms.

Peter Whitehead, the person from whom I had obtained World-wide Entertainments' office in Soho, bred falcons for the Saudi Arabian royal family in the tiny village of Pytchley in Northamptonshire. The building looked completely innocuous from the outside, but inside, fierce falcons occupied a complex of enormous purpose-built cages. It was ideal for storing marijuana.

Peter Whitehead also continued his profession of producing and directing films. He would sometimes have to rent locations in strange places. In Scotland, one can rent stately homes with land down to the sea. Whitehead could make a film at a location rented for the purpose of landing and storing marijuana. It was an excellent front.

The following letter was written on stationery headed 'World-wide Entertainments Inc., European Head Office, 18, Carlisle Street, London', to the Lochaber Estate Agents, Fort William, Inverness-shire:

Dear Sirs,
    During the winter period, our company will be producing a semi-documentary film located in the Western Isles, and set in the latter half of the last century. We intend to rent a large lochside property capable both of accommodating the staff (about 6 to 10 people) and of featuring in certain parts of the set.
    We would wish to assume tenancy by about December 1st of this year and stay for a minimum of three months. Adequate funds are available for the right property. If you have anything which you might consider suitable for our purposes, would you please let me know as soon as possible?
Yours faithfully,
Donald Nice.

Conaglen House, a baronial mansion on the coast just by the entrance to the Caledonian Ship Canal at Fort William, was available for £1,000 a week.

James Goldsack, after a brief spell of being in prison and a long spell of being a junkie, was now back to perfecting his business of wholesaling marijuana and hashish. Jarvis, Johnny Martin, and Old John were also keeping body and soul together in similar fashion. The three of them should be able to sell a ton a week.

Patrick Lane was now in a position to move almost unlimited quantities of money from one part of the world to another. If given cash in London, he could credit it to any account in the world. Patrick and his family moved from Limerick into an expensive mansion overlooking Hyde Park.

Karob was a deep-sea salvage tug, an ideal craft for smuggling large quantities of contraband. Salvagers could be found anywhere on the ocean without attracting suspicion. If questioned, the captain could claim to be acting on a tip-off of a boat in distress. Communications between salvage tugs were often covert and coded. Loading and unloading equipment was in abundance on the decks. In December 1979, *Karob* picked up fifteen tons of Colombian marijuana and steered through the hot Caribbean towards the chilly and stormy waters of the Irish Sea. Stuart Prentiss's two 40-foot yachts, *Bagheera* and *Salammbo*, slipped north from the island of Kerrera into the maze of deep-sea lochs round the Inner Hebrides. *Salammbo* returned to Kerrera with five tons of Colombian marijuana. Prentiss's family and friends unloaded the cargo. *Bagheera* took ten tons to Conaglen House, where four large three-ton box-vans were waiting. Tom Sunde, Ernie's number one, was there to help unload. By his side were eight vegetarian New Yorkers, friends of Alan Schwarz, who had been flown in for the occasion. They had no idea where they were. Jarvis took five tons to the falconry in Pytchley. James Goldsack took five tons to a stash he had in Essex. On New Year's Day, 1980, fifteen tons of

the highest quality Colombian marijuana lay poised to hit
the streets of England. It was the largest amount of dope ever
to have been imported into Europe, enough for every
inhabitant of the British Isles to get simultaneously stoned.

While the builders were fixing the bathroom at Cathcart
Road, Judy, Amber, and I moved into a £500-a-week flat at
Hans Court, Knightsbridge, directly opposite Harrods. We
would have breakfast of caviare omelettes at the Caviare
House. Judy became pregnant again. I asked her to marry
me. She refused. She would marry me only in my real name.
No Mrs Nice for her. But she did approve of our getting
engaged. We threw a disgustingly lavish party at Hans
Court. The food was limited to caviare and foie gras, the
drink to Stolichnaya and Dom Perignon, the décor to swans
carved out of ice, and the sounds to the Pretenders. Peter
Whitehead married Dido Goldsmith, daughter of Teddy
and niece of Sir James. I was Peter's best man. Bianca Jagger
was Dido's best lady. Our daughters met. Jade played with
Amber.

Every head in England was stoned. The streets were
awash with Colombian marijuana, and everyone knew it,
including the police and Her Majesty's Customs and Excise,
but they couldn't bust any. It was selling at the predicted rate
of a ton a week, but the Florida gangsters couldn't believe
sales were so slow. Something had to be wrong. Were they
being ripped off? They thought so and strong-armed Ernie
to agree that they send some representatives to England to
make an inventory of unsold marijuana. The Florida
representatives were Joel Magazine, a Miami defence lawyer,
and a Sicilian with the unlikely name of Walter Nath. They
stayed at the Dorchester Hotel. While checking the
quantities of unsold marijuana, Nath also made private
enquiries with his own London friends to determine whether
they could sell the Colombian marijuana at a faster rate.
Nath's friends unwittingly introduced him to an undercover
officer of Her Majesty's Customs and Excise, who followed

him to Scotland, where he was with Stuart Prentiss checking
the marijuana stored there. Stuart Prentiss noticed they were
being followed, lost his pursuer, and threw a few tons of
marijuana into the sea. For the next few weeks, large bales
of Colombian marijuana were being washed ashore on the
Scottish coast, smoked, handed in to the police, and eaten by
sheep and deer. The news media were amused. The Florida
gangsters were not. But sales carried on.

Marty Langford helped out by occasionally driving
marijuana to London from Pytchley, where Jarvis's friend,
Robert Kenningale, was keeping an eye on the stash while
feeding dead rats to the falcons. Marty also kept in touch
with McCann's wife, Sylvia. While British Customs Officers
were closely watching London dealers and Scottish beach-
combers making fortunes out of Colombian marijuana,
McCann's trial for the importation of Thai marijuana into
Ireland began in Dublin. McCann had been beaten up by
the IRA while awaiting trial but had recovered sufficient
poise to mount an inspired defence: he was tracking down an
enemy of Ireland, an agent of MI6, who was poisoning Irish
youth by importing marijuana. The name of the agent was
Howard Marks, who used the alias Mr Nice. McCann was
acquitted.

I sent Jarvis out to Campione, where I had stored my Mr
Nice passport and other Nice documentation, instructing
him to bury the passport in the public gardens in Campione.
There it remains. I kept noticing strange things: clicks on
telephone lines, the same unfriendly faces wherever I went. I
was being followed. But if they knew who I was, why didn't
they bust me?

I was sitting at the bar of the Swan Hotel, Lavenham. I had
become very paranoid at Hans Court and had booked a
weekend break in the name of John Hayes. Judy was settling
Amber into bed. The hotel provided a baby-listening service,
and she was going to join me at the bar before we had dinner.

Two men about my age came up to the bar and ordered their drinks. I had ordered a Tio Pepe sherry, and I took it to a vacant table. Suddenly, one of the two men grabbed my arm.

'Can I see your watch?' he asked, and firmly put a pair of handcuffs on his and my wrists.

I recovered quickly enough. It was fairly obvious I was being nicked.

'We are Customs Officers and we are arresting you.'

'Why am I being arrested?'

'You are being arrested on suspicion of being involved in a cannabis drugs offence. Do you understand?'

'Yes.'

'What is your name?' asked one of the officers.

Maybe they didn't know who I was and thought I was a regular dope dealer.

'I'm not saying.'

'Why not?'

'No comment.'

'Are you staying in this hotel?'

'No comment.'

'Are you staying here alone?'

'No comment.'

'Turn out your pockets.'

I emptied out my pockets: a driving licence, a book containing up-to-date accounts of the Colombian scam, and a key to the falconry in Pytchley that gave me access to the several tons of dope there.

'This driving licence is in the name John Hayes. Is that your name?'

'Yes.'

'Is this your address?'

'No comment.'

'What do you do for a living, Mr Hayes?'

'I'm training to be a Customs Officer.'

He didn't even smile. A couple of other Customs Officers came up to our table.

'This has been found in Room 52, your room. It is clearly hashish. Is it yours?'

'No, of course not.'

'This hashish was in your jacket pocket. Are you suggesting we put it there?'

'I don't know, do I?'

'Does it belong to your girl-friend in your room?'

'No, it's mine. Could I see Judy and our daughter?'

'Of course. You must regard us as your friends. I'm Nick Baker, and this is my colleague Terry Byrne. We can go up to your room before we all go to our London office in New Fetter Lane.'

I hugged and kissed Judy and Amber. I knew they wouldn't mess with Judy, just question her a bit and let her go. I also knew, more certainly than I have ever known anything in my life, that no matter how much she was questioned she wouldn't tell them a thing.

'Be strong, love,' we both said.

At London the questioning continued.

'What do you do for a living, Mr Hayes?'

'My work is of a secret nature. Look, what's all this about?'

'Have you got a passport?'

'No.'

'You've never been abroad at all?'

'No.'

'What do you do for a living?'

'I can't answer these questions. My work is secret.'

'What time did you arrive at Lavenham?'

'No comment.'

'Do you know Martin Langford?'

'No comment.'

'Do you know Stuart Prentiss?'

'No comment.'

'Do you know James Goldsack?'

This went on for ages. I asked after a while if I could

merely raise my finger rather than having to say 'no comment' all the time. Baker wouldn't oblige.

'Mr Hayes, I am making a contemporaneous note of this interview. I won't see your finger being raised. Would you make an audible reply, please? Do you understand?'

'Bleep.'

'Is John Hayes your real name?'

'Bleep.'

'Would you object to giving us your fingerprints?'

'Bleep, bleep.'

'Is that because your real name is Howard Marks?'

A wave of relief came over me. I was me again for the first time in six and a half years.

'So, Howard, how have you been earning a living these last few years?'

'No comment.'

And so it went on through the night until Baker and Byrne took me to Snowhill Police Station. Judy came to see me the next morning and asked me to marry her. I said yes.

After thirty-six hours in the cells, I was hauled in front of Judge Miskin at the Old Bailey. Represented again by Bernard Simons, I was being remanded back into custody at Brixton Prison for the 1973 speaker scam. The next morning, the Guildhall magistrates also remanded me into custody for conspiring to import several tons of Colombian weed and having a bunch of false passports. Also with me were Marty Langford and Bob Kenningale, who had both been arrested at Whitehead's falconry; James Goldsack and his worker, Nick Cole, both of whom had been arrested in London; Californian yachtsman Stuart Prentiss and his worker, Alan Grey; and Patrick Lane's assistant, Hedley Morgan. Patrick Lane somehow escaped the net and fled to the security of Ernie in California. Customs Officer Baker told the magistrates that the Customs had just busted us with more dope, £15 million worth, than the grand total of dope they'd ever busted up to that point. I felt proud, completely forgetting the consequences of being accused of such severe illegality. Newspaper headlines proclaimed that I had just been severely grilled by the British Secret Service, that I had joined the IRA, and that I had been protected by the Mafia.

Back at Brixton, these bulletins, coupled with radio news reports, had assured that I would be accorded a notorious criminal's welcome. I was separated from my co-defendants and put in a two-man, toilet-less, water-less cell in A Wing. My cellmate was a shifty young Jewish fraudster named Jonathan Kern. A Wing comprised a ground floor and three upper floors of cells and accommodated about 200 prisoners. There were some notable legends from London's gangland: Ronnie Knight, husband of actress Barbara Windsor; Duke and Dennis of the feared and respected Arif family, Turkish Cypriots who became London's most heavily investigated crime family since the Krays; Tommy Wisbey, the Great Train Robber; and Mickey Williams, a half-Irish and half-Jamaican Londoner whose behaviour even Her Majesty's Prison, Durham's infamous control units could not inhibit. One morning, Mickey was next to me and Jonathan Kern as we were 'slopping out' plastic buckets of our night's excrement.

'Watch him, H. He's a wrong 'un, a real wrong 'un. He'd grass up 'is own muvver.'

Kern heard him and walked away.

'Thanks, Mick.'

'It ain't nuffink, H. He ain't in your business, is he?'

'No, Mick. I didn't know him before.'

'Coz there is a few wrong 'uns in your business, H. You know what I mean? I thought he might have been one of 'em. And it's such a good business, H. But someone ought to shut a few mouths up. I heard your co-defendants talked a bit?'

'Yeah, they said more than they should, more than they wanted to, but they're not really criminals, Mick.'

'Then why are they doing crime, H? Tell me that. If they

can't do the time, they shouldn't do the crime. That's simple. Am I wrong? I know I ain't. I know what I'm doing when I get out. No more jumping over bank counters with a gun. I'm doing drugs. But there'll be no grasses in my firm. No live ones, anyway. Let's keep in touch when we're on the out, H. I got loads of geezers who work in the airport and docks in London. Might be able to 'elp each other.'

This was typical of many conversations I and other dope dealers had with more traditional criminals in British prisons at the end of the 1970s and beginning of the 1980s. The money we had made in our profession tended to dwarf that made by robbers, fraudsters, and thieves. Prisons are excellent forums for the combining of criminal talents. If a dope smuggler is locked up twenty-four hours a day with a forger, a counterfeit air waybill or bill of lading will come up in the conversation. Accordingly, many heavy criminals had begun to deal dope, all kinds from anywhere. Some of the results were predictable. A lot more ruthlessness and violence was injected into dope-trading activity. Rip-offs and guns became more common. Inevitably, a Customs Officer was shot and killed while busting a container of Moroccan cannabis. The perpetrator was a London villain. Instead of seeing this tragedy as an obvious consequence of the folly of drug prohibition (high profits attracting criminal organisations), the authorities seized upon it as proof of a congenital association between drugs and violence. Marijuana smokers and dealers, despite being generally law-abiding and peace-loving, were in bed with ruthless assassins and should be treated as such. Give them long and stiff sentences.

I made several appearances in Guildhall Magistrates Court, mostly for administrative reasons and for futile bail applications. I would hardly be given another chance to abscond. Returning to prison from one of these court appearances, I looked into a prison interview room I was walking past and observed Jonathan Kern talking to Her

Majesty's Customs Officer Baker. They didn't see me. Later
on in our cell, Kern began asking questions about my case. I
hadn't yet seen any of the evidence against me, but Kern's
link to Baker could provide a valuable avenue of misin-
formation. I could give no end of false leads as to what my
defence was. I wove a fantastic tale for Kern's ears and told
him that the marijuana had been provided by Peruvian
terrorists, who were now anchored off Ireland with a further
sixty tons. Unfortunately, Kern was again seen talking to
Baker, this time by a heavy East Ender, who gave Kern a
thumping as soon as he had the chance. Kern was transferred to another prison. I was given another cell to occupy.
This time I shared with a man called Jim Hobbs. He had
been arrested for having sexual relations with a man under
the age of twenty-one, but he kept the nature of his offence
fairly quiet. Sex offenders (nonces), like convicted policemen and grasses, get a rough time in British prisons. They
are considered fair game for a bit of physical torture. It
wasn't much use Hobbs's explaining that the under-age
victim was actually eighteen. At best he was a poof, an iron.
And he might be lying. Hit him anyway. Despite his strange
leanings, I liked Hobbs and appreciated his disdain for
authority and his generosity to prisoners without funds.

The prison authorities had no objection to my getting
married and even went so far as to let me out, escorted by
two prison guards, to a Welsh Congregational Chapel in
South London to perform the deed. The wedding was most
definitely shotgun: Judy was five months pregnant, and my
daughters Myfanwy and Amber were the bridesmaids.
Johnny Martin was best man. After the wedding, I begged
the two guards to allow me to attend the reception. They
would be very welcome guests, and I promised not to escape.
In a chauffeur-driven Cadillac, Judy, a guard, and I were
driven to the Basil Hotel. Champagne and congratulations
flowed. Judy and I were allowed to spend some time alone in
a hotel bedroom. The guards and I got drunk.

I got on with most of the guards at Brixton and encountered little or nothing in the way of sadism or cruelty. The coveted position of A Wing tea-boy was offered me, and I took it. There were lots of perks. I was allowed out of my cell for most of the day. The screws brought me little presents of harmless contraband: Danish blue cheese and dirty magazines. I was given social visits of a couple of hours rather than the few minutes allotted by prison rules. Remand prison regulations were less stringent than they are now. A prisoner was allowed a meal and some alcohol to be delivered to him from outside on a daily basis. It was easy to smuggle in dope with the food. I still had quite a lot of cash that the authorities hadn't confiscated. Almost all the wholesale dealers who had owed money for Colombian marijuana I had given them on credit paid up in full. Johnny Martin, who had been interviewed by HM Customs, but not arrested, looked after the cash stash.

Ernie felt guilty for having allowed uncool American gangsters access to the British stores of Colombian weed. If he had controlled them, there would have been no bust. Ernie offered to pay all my defence costs, however high. He told Judy she would never have to worry for money. All his connections and wealth were at her disposal.

Judy had to take up Ernie's offer sooner than we thought. Her sister, Natasha, had been busted attempting, without our knowledge, to do a scam on her own. She and her boy-friend were caught off the Mexican coast with a small boat-load of marijuana. They were languishing in filthy Mexican jails. Ernie got on the case and got her released. It did take a while, but during that time, Natasha and her boy-friend were imprisoned together in a luxury apartment with a balcony and all modern conveniences. While inside, Natasha conceived and gave birth to a baby boy. She called him Albi. Ernie definitely had excellent connections in Mexico.

On November 23rd, 1980, my adorable daughter Francesca was born. I had petitioned the Home Office to allow me to attend her birth, but they refused.

She was the only child of mine who was welcomed into
this world in my absence. It made me angry not to be there,
but her birth gave me the strength I needed to face the
future. Tough times and a long period in prison seemed at
hand. Then one of my heroes, John Lennon, was gunned
down in New York, killed either by a lunatic or by the CIA.
His death echoed his profound definition of life: 'that which
happens when you are making other plans'. The tragedy
saddened me but also increased my fighting spirit. Judy sent
me a book on yoga, and I began a discipline to which I've
always adhered when incarcerated: half an hour a day of
yoga positions and ten minutes of meditation.

Gradually, Bernard Simons brought in the written
depositions of evidence against me. There was quite a bit. A
key found in my pocket on the day of my arrest opened a
door at the falconry in Pytchley behind which lay a few tons
of Colombian weed. Accounts of whom had been paid what
throughout the entire deal were in my own handwriting.
There were sightings of me meeting co-defendants in
London and Scotland. A suitcase of money had been found
under my bed. These were difficult to explain away, but
explained away they had to be.

As any lawyer and any acquitted crook will endorse, guilt
has nothing to do with whether one actually committed the
offence in question. Guilt is a technical relationship between
charge and evidence and must be established beyond doubt
by the prosecution, who have to persuade a jury that the
evidence is consistent with only the prosecution version of
events and not any other. A great deal of the evidence against
me was consistent with my having organised an importation
of fifteen tons of dope. With what else was it consistent?

Dreams become of enormous importance in prison.
McCann came to me one night in the middle of a nightmare.

'Use the Kid, you stupid Welsh cunt. I fucking used you.'

My barrister was Lord Hutchinson of Lullington, QC,
a socialist with a record of defending spies and anti-

establishment trouble-makers. Russian espionage agents George Blake and Vassall had benefited from his advocacy, as had Penguin Books when they were prosecuted for publishing D. H. Lawrence's *Lady Chatterley's Lover*. I explained to him my defence: In 1972, I had been recruited by MI6 to catch IRA arms dealer James McCann by sucking him into dope deals. I was doing very well until Her Majesty's Customs and Excise messed up the British Secret Service's plans by busting me in 1973. Bail was arranged. I skipped as arranged. The media, however, had somehow procured confidential information that I was an MI6 agent and this had blown my cover. Knowing no other life than that of a spy, I was instructed by MI6 to work for the Mexican Secret Service, who, strangely enough, were also interested in catching McCann due to their belief that he was aiding the Mexican terrorist group, the September 23rd League, in arms acquisition and fund-raising through dope deals. The Mexican Secret Service supplied me with a passport in the name of Anthony Tunnicliffe and all manner of front documentation. Against all odds, I managed to track down McCann in Vancouver, thereby continuing to do my bit for Queen and Country, as well as keep Mexico stable. I informed the Canadian authorities, but McCann wriggled out of their grasp. I found McCann again, this time in France. He again wriggled out of the authorities' grasp, but not before I had found out that he was now working with Colombian narco-terrorists in South America as well as with heroin drug lords from the Golden Triangle area of Laos, Thailand, and Burma. I was given a complicated brief, answerable to both British and Mexican governments. I had to infiltrate the Colombian drug hierarchy and find out where the bosses were banking their money and how it was getting into the accounts of known members of the September 23rd League. Also, I had to ensure that McCann was caught red-handed, preferably in Ireland or Europe. All my espionage activity was done under the guise of my being a hippie marijuana-only dealer and smuggler. In order to fulfil my dangerous brief, I involved myself with two separate dope deals: Colombian weed to Scotland and Thai weed to Ireland. The Irish deal was done first. When the dope landed in Ireland, I informed MI6 how to catch McCann red-handed. McCann again outwitted the authorities and got freed by a Dublin court. Meanwhile, infiltration of the Colombian drug hierarchy was proceeding very well. I had even got my brother-in-law, Patrick Lane, to bank all their money. Soon, I'd know the whole picture, and the Mexican Secret Service would make me their hero. Then, as in 1973, HM Customs stepped in and busted me. They probably had something against MI6. Who knows?

'That is your defence, Howard?' gasped an astonished Lord Hutchinson of Lullington, QC.

'Yes. Why? What's wrong?'

'It is, absolutely without doubt, the most ridiculous defence I have ever heard in my life.'

'You mean you don't believe it?'

'Belief is not a factor, Howard. I am obliged to be your voice in court, even if your defence is idiotic.'

'Almost all of it can be backed up with evidence, Lord Hutchinson. There's plenty of newspaper reports to show I was an MI6 agent tracking McCann.'

'And where might this Tunnicliffe passport be now? The one given you by this South American Secret Service. Mexican, was it?'

'The Tunnicliffe passport is British, Lord Hutchinson. I expect MI6 provided it to the Mexican Secret Service for my use. It's covered with Mexican entry and exit stamps, some of which prove I wasn't even in Scotland when the marijuana was imported. Any suggestion that I was actually on the beach supervising the importation and transport of the dope is ridiculous.'

'It's a pity, dear boy, that no one from the Mexican Secret Service is prepared to come to London to testify that you did work for them.'

'Lord Hutchinson, my immediate superior, Jorge del Rio, a member of the Mexican Government, is only too happy to come and testify on my behalf.'

'Hmm! Interesting. I am looking forward to working at the Old Bailey again.'

Most books were allowed into Brixton prison, but those on terrorism weren't. Solicitors could bring in photocopies of anything they wanted. Day after day, an embarrassed Bernard Simons brought me books on South American and South East Asian revolutionary groups to, as he put it, 'refresh my memory'. The prison authorities had no objection to guide books being read by prisoners.

'What are you doing with all these travel guides to Mexico, Marks?'

'I'm going there on my holidays once I get acquitted, Governor. They can't keep an innocent man locked up for too long.'

'I'm glad to see you're keeping your sense of humour, Marks. Enjoy your reading.'

'Thanks, Governor.'

There was one really awkward bit. Despite my maintaining in my defence a position of never having met any of the Florida gangsters, HM Customs Officer Michael Stephenson was claiming that late one night he observed me leaving one of the gangsters' rooms at the Dorchester Hotel. This observation had to be neutralised. I had a friend who, for a short time, was a boy-friend of Rosie's. He was Welsh, went by the name of Leaf, and kept a pub, the Oranges and Lemons, at St Clement's, Oxford. Leaf came to visit me in Brixton prison.

'Leaf, do you remember I stayed with you once in Oxford, last year?'

'Aye, of course I do. I wasn't that drunk. I remember it well.'

'Can you remember the date?'

'Hell, no. I wasn't that sober, either.'

'It was a Friday night, right?'

'It might have been, Howard.'

'It was. Because after we all got up on Saturday, we watched the rugby match. Now do you remember? Wales lost to Ireland.'

'That's right. Will I ever forget it? We lost by 21 to 7 at Lansdowne Road in bloody Dublin. Jeff Squire was captain. Mind you, we beat them this year at Cardiff Arms Park, but only by 9 points to 8.'

'Last year's match was on March 15th.'

'Could well have been. I can easily check it. I've got all the Welsh rugby matches on video.'

'I've already checked it, Leaf. Would you be prepared to testify on my behalf at the Old Bailey about where I was that night?'

'I'd bloody love to.'

The trial started on September 28th, 1981, the same day, many years previously, that marijuana had first been rendered illegal under British law. I was facing a maximum of 18 years in prison (14 for marijuana and 4 for false passports). Patrick Lane wrote me a poem:

Dear Brother: Five hundred days stand between us, and
All the distance I have managed to create.
No word has passed, no smile exchanged, no touch of hand,
And yet, as Dawn intrudes, we still relate.
I cannot sleep whilst you, awake across the Globe, await
The turn of Fortune's wheel, and take her dare,
To chance your luck against the odds as they rotate
And play for both of us and all the precious 'ours' we share.
In Time and Space and Circumstance we're Night and Day
Upon the circle, although the axis is the same.
But all around your friends and family hope that they
May share with you and help you play, and win, this game.
In one brief span, as the world turns, the sun's warm kiss
Touches many loving hearts that beat with yours: you will
  get this.

Only three of us pleaded not guilty. Prentiss's defence was that he had committed the offence under duress. This defence works if the jury believe that a more serious offence was avoided by the commission of the offence charged. Prentiss was going to say that he imported fifteen tons of Colombian marijuana because if he didn't, the Mafia would kill him. Hedley Morgan would maintain that he didn't know the money he handled derived from sales of dope. I was a spy whose theatre of operations was dope deals.

The Crown took six weeks to present the prosecution before Judge 'Penal Pete' Mason. John Rogers, QC, was the Director of Public Prosecutions' counsel. Hiding behind bags of weed, address books, passports, files, witness statements, and telephone gadgetry, he humourlessly laid out the case: 'This was crime on the grand scale . . . It is no surprise that a man of the defendant's background and intelligence set up the UK side of the organisation just like a high-powered business . . . He warmed to his work . . . Mind-boggling quantities of cannabis and money. The whole of this smuggling operation was like a military operation . . . An intricate web of bluff and counterbluff and false names . . . Marks had so many identities one wonders how on earth he remembers who he was . . . The organisation had to be very slick, very smooth and carefully planned to succeed, and it will not surprise you to learn that those involved are extremely intelligent people.'

This led to the *Daily Mail* and *Daily Telegraph* heading their stories: OXFORD MASTERMIND IN A £20M DRUGS RING and THE GRADUATE CONNECTION.

Peter Whitehead was the Crown's key witness. He had been put into a most difficult position. His ethics were such that he would not wish to be responsible for putting anyone in prison. But he didn't want to end up in the nick himself. He saw a way out without directly incriminating me and took it. The price he paid was to be a prosecution witness. Peter behaved most honourably when he testified but he had left

some question-marks about what I had done. Lord
Hutchinson tore into Peter and eliminated most of those.
Although Lord Hutchinson's cross-examinations were
brilliant and although my junior barrister, Stephen Solley,
had analysed the prosecution evidence in the most
thoroughly competent and conscientious fashion imaginable,
we had achieved only one victory: casting doubt on the
observation made by HM Customs Officer Michael
Stephenson of me in the Dorchester Hotel. By the time Lord
Hutchinson had finished with him, Stephenson wasn't sure
he'd ever been to the Dorchester. He's never forgiven me.
The rest of HM Customs were already prematurely cele-
brating their victory. I was going down.

Lord Hutchinson thought so too and had a word with
Penal Pete. Plea-bargaining does not happen in British
justice, but indications of the judge's likely course of action
can sometimes be obtained. Lord Hutchinson went to
determine whether Penal Pete would be likely to give a
maximum of seven years' imprisonment if I pleaded guilty. I
could handle it. I'd get parole. Penal Pete refused. He
wanted to give a much longer sentence.

For a whole week, I gave my evidence after first promising
to tell the truth, the whole truth, and nothing but the truth.
I had plenty of documentation establishing I was a Mexican
spy, but confirmation of my MI6 activities was then only to
be found in old newspaper headlines. Through perfect legal
manipulation, Lord Hutchinson managed to get the
newspapers read by an enthralled and sympathetic jury. I
was a spy all right. All the newspapers were unanimous in
that opinion. One even quoted MI6's lawyer as confirming I
was an agent. John Rogers rose to cross-examine. His lack of
effort astonished me. He had no idea which questions to ask
and merely mouthed empty rhetoric about what a bad but
brilliant person I was. At one point, he was definitely on my
side, saying: 'It is conceded that you worked for the Secret
Service until March 1973 . . .'

Now the jury definitely knew I was a spy. Occasionally, Rogers went for me: 'You are using a little bit of the truth and then glossing it . . . You fanned your legend, didn't you? You encouraged the Marks religion to grow, that you were a secret agent on the run from the police, and made as many smokescreens as you could, while indulging in very high-level drug trafficking . . . Let me challenge you to name this MI6 controller you say recruited you for the Mexicans.'

I had no problem answering that one and gave the name of Anthony Woodhead, the husband of Anna of AnnaBelinda, the man who had ripped me off for a million dollars. I don't know what repercussions he experienced, but I expect he could afford them. My cross-examination was at an end.

Leaf was the first defence witness. He was so obviously telling the truth that the jury were left in no doubt that HM Customs Officer Michael Stephenson was wrong when he testified that he saw me at the Dorchester Hotel. The last defence witness was Jorge del Rio, a bona fide senior Mexican Government law-enforcement officer. Because of the sensitivity of his testimony, the Old Bailey court was cleared and the Mexican's evidence was given in camera. The Mexican confirmed that he knew me as Anthony Tunnicliffe, that he was introduced to me by Anthony Woodhead, that I was employed by the Mexican Secret Service, and that I had been paid large amounts of cash to infiltrate Colombian drug organisations. The jury loved it. Officers of HM Customs and Excise were beginning to look a bit worried.

In his closing speech, John Rogers, QC, launched into an attack: 'Marks is the biggest-ever trafficker apprehended with a single consignment. His claims of being a secret agent are utter rubbish. It is conceded that Marks was recruited for three months in 1973 by someone who was indiscreet enough to ask for his assistance. The rest is a myth mounted by Marks in order to conceal his real activities. His cover story is that he was an Intelligence agent. I invite you to treat that as a load of rubbish.'

Lord Hutchinson was far more convincing: 'Howard Marks was used by MI6 to infiltrate the IRA. Three times he traced James McCann, but three times he managed to slip away. But British Intelligence would not come into this court and admit, as the prosecution did, that Howard Marks was working for them. They just sit up in the public gallery here. You can see them, members of the jury, I'm sure. Howard Marks was left as the "spy out in the cold". It is the code of the Intelligence services. They say, "You are on your own, old boy." You may remember the cases of those Russian spies, not only Kim Philby, but also Anthony Blunt. It appears that British Intelligence can grant immunity from prosecution to spies who have acted against this country. But not so, it would seem, when they have actually been acting on behalf of this country.'

Judge 'Penal Pete' Mason summed up: 'You have seen Mr Marks, ladies and gentlemen of the jury. He has extra-ordinary charisma and an encyclopaedic knowledge of the evidence, enabling him to come up with an answer to every question. As with the other defendants, you must decide whether he participated in this conspiracy or not. Either he had nothing to do with it, or he was into it up to his neck.'

The jury returned verdicts of not guilty on each of us. I don't think for one minute they believed the defences presented to them. They just didn't want us nice guys to spend countless years in prison for transporting beneficial herbs from one part of the world to another. A juror can acquit a defendant for any reasons he or she wishes: a fact that is infrequently broadcast. Enough acquittals, and the law will change. Stuart Prentiss and Hedley Morgan walked free from the Old Bailey. I received a two-year sentence for false passports. With remission, I had five days to do. I looked up at the public gallery and saw Judy. I would be with her, Amber, and little Francesca for Christmas. All her love and relief came forth in the most beautiful smile I had ever seen. I had beaten the system. I had triumphed and would walk the streets within a week.

Not everyone shared my jubilation. HM Customs had other ideas in mind than my immediate freedom. I had completely forgotten about the 1973 rock-group scam. HM Customs hadn't. The trial was set for the middle of February. Bail was refused.

Two weeks after my acquittal, Chief Superintendent Philip Fairweather of Thames Valley Police took an eight-inch kitchen knife into his garden and plunged it into his stomach. He had recently confessed to having leaked to the press the MI6 report documenting my work for the Intelligence services, and he knew that I had obtained my unjust acquittal partly on the basis of this leak. Rather than face charges under the Official Secrets Act, this 58-year-old World War II veteran and distinguished police detective committed hara-kiri in his home. No one was meant to die in all this nonsense.

Bernard Simons had discovered that after my arrest and deportation from Amsterdam, the Dutch authorities proceeded to try me in my absence. For reasons best known to themselves, they found me not guilty of exporting from Holland the Lebanese hashish that had got busted in Las Vegas in 1973. British law embodies the doctrine of *autrefois acquit*, whereby a previous acquittal in a foreign court may, in certain circumstances, serve as a bar for prosecution of a similar offence in a British court. A jury is empanelled to decide if the offences are similar enough for *autrefois acquit* to apply. It seemed to us that exporting a certain quantity of hashish from Amsterdam to Las Vegas was a similar charge to knowingly assisting precisely the same export. Beating the 1973 charge was going to be easy. It wouldn't even get to trial.

At the Old Bailey, in front of the Recorder, Sir James Miskin, I entered a plea of *autrefois acquit*. The judge explained to a bewildered jury the nuances of dissimilarity of

offences. He asked them if they thought the Dutch offence
could be considered the same as the British one. The jurors
stared in baffled silence. Judge Miskin said that 'No' would
be an appropriate answer. The foreman said 'No.' Lord
Hutchinson jumped up and objected. Judge Miskin told him
to take it up at the Court of Appeal and dismissed the jury.
The case was going to trial.

I won the first round. Gary Lickert, the friend of Ernie's
who had brought all the dollars to Amsterdam and driven to
pick up the speakers in Las Vegas, had been flown over to
pick me out in an identity parade. He didn't really want to
be British justice's first American supergrass, and at
Snowhill Police Station he looked closely at everyone except
me. He couldn't identify anyone. The prosecution case was
considerably weakened. Despite this advantage, Lord
Hutchinson felt I would be unlikely to get acquitted again,
and on the day of trial went to the judge's chambers to plea-
bargain. He came back with an offer of three years
maximum. I took it. I got three years. What the judge and
HM Customs did not realise, but I did, was that due to my
being arrested first for the 1973 rock-group scam, all the
time I had done in custody would count as credit for that
offence, even though it also counted for credit against my
two-year sentence for false passports. With remission, I
would be free in less than three months. I felt as if I'd beaten
the system again, almost. However, I did have a criminal
record. I was a convicted marijuana dealer who used false
names. Could I live with the shame?

Eight

HOWARD MARKS

Her Majesty's Prison, Heathfield Road, Wandsworth, is a good place to be released from. At 8 a.m., May 6th, 1982, I was standing outside clutching a plastic bag containing a picnic lunch and a few books. In my pocket was about fifteen pounds and a travel warrant to Brighton. A few others being released at the same time were waiting at the bus stop. I was lucky: Judy was picking me up. I wouldn't need the travel warrant. I'd frame it as a souvenir.

The two years had gone by quickly enough, and I'd beaten the real charge. A daily dose of yoga and a vegan diet had made me feel fitter than ever. I was going to play tennis, run, meditate, stand on my head, have inner peace, and join yuppie health clubs. Johnny Martin was holding a large stash of my cash in Brighton. Ernie had paid for the purchase of the ground floor above Judy's Chelsea basement in Cathcart Road and for the costs of converting the two floors to a maisonette. Furthermore, he'd promised to give me a load of dollars once I became a free man (he still felt responsible for my being busted for the Colombian load). Judy had booked tickets to Corfu for me, her, her sister Masha, and my three daughters Myfanwy, Amber, and Francesca. I was looking forward to jogging on Greek beaches, imprinting footprints at the edge of the tide. But now it was raining, heavily. Why was Judy taking so long? Maybe there were traffic jams on the Brighton road.

'You want me to let you back in, Marks?' joked a key-jangling screw turning up for work.

'Not yet, chief. I need just a bit more freedom,' I said with a feeble attempt at humour.

'Well, when you do, just knock on door.'

Then hundreds of screws started turning up for work.

'She's not turning up, Marks. She's shagging the taxi-driver around the corner. And she was with me last night. Come in and have some porridge.'

It was almost 9 a.m. I couldn't handle it any longer and splashed away from the jeering contingent of uniformed Geordies. There were no phone boxes. I hailed a cab.

'Where to, guv?'

'Victoria Station,' I said.

It seemed as good a place as any. There were trains to Brighton, and phone boxes.

It was a very wet rush-hour. The journey took an hour and cost me a tenner. I got out of the cab and became mesmerised by the mass of humanity speedily leaving the station. An ingrained prison habit made me automatically start waiting until everyone else had passed. I realised where I was. I went to a phone box. There was no answer from our Brighton number. Where was Judy? I had a coffee. I rang again.

'She was very late. She's awfully sorry. She's gone to the Chelsea flat,' said Masha.

I took a Tube, the wrong one, got lost, and took another cab to the flat. I was already out of money.

The flat was a building site. The rain had stopped, but there was no one there. I stood outside feeling sheepish.

Then the car drew up and Judy emerged. I'd seen her in Wandsworth visiting-room only yesterday, but now she

looked even more amazing. I knew I could touch her. We
hugged, got into the car, and began a dreamlike drive to
Brighton, the sun strengthening after each mile and
illuminating one magnificent view after another. We stopped
at the Gatwick Airport Hilton for sausage, bacon, eggs, and
champagne. I needed a joint. We resumed the drive to our
Brighton home, where I was welcomed and hugged by
Amber and Francesca. The air was charged with emotion,
champagne, and the scent of hashish.

'You won't go back to dealing, will you?' said Judy. 'I
couldn't stand another two years on my own.'

'Of course not.' I think I might have meant what I said.
Life was good. There was no pressure.

The Passport Office had told Judy that I would have to
present myself in person at Petty France in order to get a
renewed passport. Just a formality, I assumed. It was strange
thinking of travelling again under my own name. I hadn't
done so for nine years. On arrival at Petty France, I was
ushered down a series of corridors to an office labelled
simply 'Special'.

'Mr Appleton will be along in a minute,' a very bashful
secretary said as she motioned me towards a seat. 'You may
smoke if you wish,' she added, looking distastefully at my
Old Holborn roll-up.

Appleton marched in and looked puzzled as I stretched
out my hand. But he shook it.

'How do you do, Mr Marks? I must say I really ought to
congratulate you on the high quality of your false passport
applications. They were far superior to what we usually get.
Most people must think we're idiots. You should see some
of the insulting rubbish sent us.'

'I'd like to,' I said, genuinely curious.

Appleton ignored the remark and affected a stern and
formal voice.

'We are in principle prepared to give you a passport in

your own name, Mr Marks, but we must have the false ones returned to this office. Immediately. We know Her Majesty's Customs have confiscated passports bearing your likeness in the names of Cox, Goddard, Green, and McKenna, all of which we issued from this office. But our records show you have obtained at least two more passports from us in the names of Tunnicliffe and Nice. We must have those back, and we must have any others that perhaps we don't yet know about.'

The Tunnicliffe passport had been kept by the Old Bailey clerical staff after I had produced it in my own defence. The Nice passport had been buried in a small park on the Swiss–Italian border at Campione d'Italia. I explained this to Appleton, though I modified the location of the burial to Milan's Monumental Cemetery. I might need the Nice passport one day. Strange things happen.

'Are you ever going to apply for a false passport again, Mr Marks?'

'Oh, no! Those days are over. It's so good not to be a fugitive any more,' I said, sincerely.

'Well, Mr Marks, I've decided to enable you to take your family holiday in Corfu by issuing you a passport valid for two months. If your account of the Nice and Tunnicliffe passports is shown by us to be correct, we will extend your passport's validity.'

I didn't argue. There is no obligation for the British Passport Office to issue a passport to anyone; and although there is no law requiring an individual to have a passport to travel, its absence can be one hell of an inconvenience.

'Thank you very much indeed, Mr Appleton.'

I again put out my hand and again got the puzzled look.

'It's waiting for you downstairs, Mr Marks. Have a good holiday.'

A few weeks before my release I had begun reading about Corfu. Its history was the usual two-thousand-year Mediterranean mish-mash of domination by Corinthians,

Illyrians, Romans, Goths, Lombards, Saracens, Normans, Sicilians, Genovese, Venetians, French, Turks, Russians, and British. Most accounts of the island's history and geography were boring, but Lawrence Durrell's *Prospero's Cell* made it fascinating. It seemed as if it was impossible to go anywhere in Corfu without treading in the footprints of Ulysses. Durrell extolled the virtues of a daily seductive siesta sandwiched between sun and sea and drenched with wine and olives. I couldn't wait. Although he didn't specifically mention it, the beaches looked good for jogging.

The first morning in Corfu began to fulfil Durrell's promises. The house we shared was perched on a cliff near Kassiopi and surrounded by sandy beaches and lush vegetation. It was very early, and I was the only one awake. I put on my track suit and started jogging down the path to the beach. Long before I reached the sand, I ran out of breath. This wasn't supposed to happen. Then my right knee gave in. All the prison nights spent dreaming of beach and wave jogging seemed more wasted than ever. I thought yoga made you fit. It clearly wasn't good for stamina or knees and was no preparation for jogging. I hobbled back to the house and looked forward to resuming a life of complete debauchery, devoid of inner peace and physical fitness.

Through exhaustion, knee damage, and retsina hangover, I stayed bedridden for most of the next few days. Then sunbathing, sea swimming, and more retsina combined to remove the jailbird pallor from my skin and the smell of the nick from my nostrils. I played with my three daughters and fell deeper in love with each of them. We explored the island in our rented car. Sometimes Masha would baby-sit, so Judy and I could enjoy ourselves like never before.

Our immediate neighbours were long-time residents of Corfu and significant figures on the island. Through them we met the former British Consul in Corfu, John Fort, and a selection of retired English gentry. They were typical expatriates: former Foreign Office employees, news correspondents, and arms dealers. They were riveted to coverage of the Falklands war, then in full swing. As long as the war kept going until Wimbledon fortnight and the cricket Test matches, the summer would not be boring. Any lull in the reporting was filled by a round of golf followed by a plate of fried eggs washed down by large glasses of cheap Greek gin at a modest local taverna known as the 'nineteenth hole'. Judy and I were frequently invited to play golf, but after a few painful lessons, I realised the game was not for me. However, the fried eggs and gin were not to be missed, and I enjoyed these 'après-golf' sessions immensely.

'What's your line of country, dear boy?' asked John Fort.

'Borderline,' I said without really thinking but recalling days of crossing frontiers. What the hell! I'll level with them.

'Well, to tell you the truth, John, I'm a convicted marijuana smuggler that's just come out of the nick.'

The 'nineteenth hole' was suitably silenced. Judy raised her disapproving eyes to the ceiling.

'How absolutely fascinating!' burst out a gin-and-egg-yolk-saturated ex-arms dealer called Ronnie. 'Do tell us the whole story.'

I gave a censored version, leaving out the IRA and MI6 stuff, and was the hero of the hour.

'I say, but aren't you that spy chappie the papers talk about,' asked Ronnie, 'from Oxford? Balliol, wasn't it?'

This had gone far enough. Judy went to the ladies'.

'Yeah, but none of that is very interesting any more,' I mumbled with contrived bashfulness. 'It's not like the old days.'

'You're right,' agreed Ronnie. 'You're right. Precious little is. Look at that awful business in Goose Green, for example . . .'

To my relief the conversation moved on to the Falklands conflict. Just a few minutes later, Ronnie gripped my arm and guided me to a quiet corner of the room.

'Do you miss it, Howard?'

'What?' Was he referring to Oxford or prison?

'Smuggling, old boy. It must have been thrilling stuff. What on earth can you do now without getting bored?'

'Maybe I'll start smuggling again,' I said.

'Could do worse,' encouraged Ronnie, 'a lot worse. Here's my card. Although we all have to have a home on a Mediterranean island, you can't beat travelling for my money. I still keep my hand in – a few irons in the fire. Must hold on to our talents, whatever they are.'

Back in England, I devoted several weeks to the family. We drove to Kenfig Hill to stay with my parents, my first visit back there for almost ten years. Although I was easily the locality's most notorious wandering boy, reactions to me from people in the streets and pubs suggested I'd never been away. We talked about the weather and the Welsh rugby team. No one mentioned my boyhood friend Marty. It was complicated. I was free, he was still in prison. He'd been convicted of working for me, and I'd been found not guilty of employing him. With Judy and the children I walked over Kenfig dunes to Sker Beach and thought of boats unloading hashish on to the sand, guarded and protected by R. D. Blackmore's mermaid, immortalised in his *The Maid of Sker*. The shore was deserted. Anchored in the distance were the massive hundred-thousand-ton iron-ore ships that my father used to discharge after he left the sea and came to work ashore. The blast furnaces and chimney stacks of Port Talbot's giant steelworks still made most of the sky invisible. On the walk back we noticed the turrets of the buried city's castle just poking eerily through the sandy ground. Where the dunes meet the road lies The Prince of Wales, old Kenfig's medieval town hall and home of the finest draught Worthington in the world.

'Howard, what do you think about the talking wall by here?' a fellow drinker enquired. 'Bloody amazing, really, when you think about it.'

'What talking wall?' I asked.

'The one upstairs by here, mun,' he emphasised. 'You know, it's in what used to be the old council room. On some nights the wall starts talking in very old Welsh. They've had the professors from the University here loads of times. Hard to explain, mind, isn't it? Walls talking, like, you know.'

'Were the lads who heard it drunk?' I asked.

'Oh aye, but no more than normal, like.'

Sure enough, there was a talking wall upstairs. Drunk and sober people from all sorts of different places had made a special journey to Kenfig to hear it. Various audio experts from the BBC had recorded and analysed the wall's spooky emissions. Welsh-language experts from the University of Wales had identified masses of medieval Welsh vocabulary whispering away in nooks and crannies. Specialists in solid-state physics and integrated-circuit theory suggested complicated theories to explain the phenomena. I couldn't find out much more. I kept being told it was 'something to do with the silicon in the sand'. The wall still hasn't talked to me, but I've yet to give it a proper opportunity.

Judy, the two girls, and I also spent a few days in Upper Cwm Twrch at my father's smallholding, stuck in the middle of nowhere with a view of everywhere. An almost completely overgrown path meandered from the dwelling, through the Black Mountains, to an otherwise inaccessible lake, Llyn Fan. Many Welshmen (including all the locals) believe this lake to be the one featured in Arthurian legend. It certainly looks the part. Sheer cliffs form the banks. There are no fish. There are no waves, even when the wind is blowing. Weird and large birds hover over it.

The weather was unusually sunny, and we took many walks, picking berries and mushrooms. The surrounding area was littered with everything from ruined Roman castles to disused coal mines. The native sheep were friendly. Some even belonged to us and had large M's branded on their sides. Most of the sheep-shit trails ended in little pubs that served delicious beer and enormous portions of disgusting deep-frozen food. I'd brought my own hashish, and some of the mushrooms had psychedelic properties. Life was good, but the money stash was dwindling. And Ernie hadn't got in touch.

Back in Brighton there were messages to call Bernie Simons, my solicitor. Since my release, a number of authors had contacted him expressing an interest in writing my biography with my co-operation. They included Piers Paul Reid, author of *Alive* and the latest book on the great train robbers. Bernie said there could be good money involved, but I would have to be careful. There could be legal complications.

The Inland Revenue had also been in touch with Bernie. I hadn't paid any tax since 1973. The Revenue said I'd made lots of money from dope, whatever the Old Bailey jury thought, and they wanted their cut. Bernie said I needed an excellent accountant, both to sort out my taxes and to ensure me a proper income from any book written about me.

I kept wondering about the thirty thousand pounds Her Majesty's Customs and Excise had seized from the Hans Court flat when I was arrested. I had 'proved' that the money had been given me by the Mexican Secret Service.

'Bernie, can't we sue the Customs for that thirty grand they nicked?'

'Howard, you were astonishingly lucky to get acquitted. This would be pushing your luck a bit, don't you think?'

'But, Bernie, not suing them would be like admitting it was dope money. An innocent person would do exactly as I suggest.'

'Are you instructing me to sue them?' asked Bernie.

'Yes. Yes.'

Bernie initiated proceedings for the return of the money. The Customs went berserk. They assured Bernie I'd never get a single penny, even if I won the court case. Bernie's reluctance disappeared. We'd go for them. We'd get them.

Bernie took me to meet Stanley Rosenthal, a brilliantly astute accountant working in a nondescript office off Marble Arch. He suggested that a company be formed to receive money from publishers of any book about me. It was called Stepside Limited. Stanley said he would inform the Inland Revenue he was representing me. I told him about suing Her Majesty's Customs and Excise. He laughed.

The Revenue called a meeting for June 30th, 1982. I turned up at the Inland Revenue's Special Office (A10) with Stanley and Bernie. We were greeted by an extremely amiable Welshman named Price and an English prick named Spencer. When Bernie introduced himself, Spencer said that solicitors were worth respect only when their clients pleaded guilty. This was a bad start. We should have walked out. Price and Spencer questioned me. My lines were easy: I had no money. I'd never made a single penny out of cannabis dealing. I tried to once in 1973, but the load was busted, and I got a conviction. Any evidence of my ever having money was either due to the kindness of other people giving me loans or to large advances from the Mexican Secret Services. Price and Spencer didn't believe it. Despite my being cleared by the highest court in the land of any cannabis dealing, they felt I'd made some income over the last nine years. They'd be in touch.

To ensure against arrest, Old John had spent the last couple of years in Kathmandu. We wanted to see each other for old times' sake and celebrate August 13th, my birthday and that of Old John's lady, Liz. Appleton had extended my passport for another two months, so with our wives and children we met in Lyons, a good place for Leos. It didn't take long to adjust to hotel room service and French restaurants. We went to the Beaujolais vineyards and drank a lot of Fleurie.

'The thing is, what we should do, is bring this in and forget all the other kinds of madness, for now.'

Old John was still a little obscure, but he clearly wanted us to become wine merchants and importers, at least until things cooled off.

'That's not a bad idea, John. We could both put in a bit of money, re-rent the top floor of Carlisle Street and use it as our central office. But we don't know much about wine.'

'Yeah, but there's the Mad Major, isn't there?' said Old John. 'We sold him a stove, and the thing is, we then saw him in Greece. A complete lunatic, but the man is a total gentleman. Knows everything about wine.'

The Mad Major, whom I'd yet to meet, was Major Michael Pocock, a military alcoholic who had spent some years in the past exporting wine from France to England.

'Okay, John, let's do it. Judy will be pleased to see me doing something straight.'

Judy, the children, and I went back to England via Ticino, Switzerland. We wanted to see Campione d'Italia while it was still summer, relive some good times, enjoy the views, and eat in the Taverna. During our first evening we were given a warm welcome by our ex-neighbours, bar-keepers, and restaurateurs, who seemed not to know of my recent incarceration. Aware that, unlike last time here, we didn't have unlimited money, we checked into a modest hotel just outside Lugano. The next morning, we took a lakeside stroll and sat down in a café in Piazza Reforma, the main square. Every building there is either a bank or a café. We were sipping *cappuccinos* and watching the children play when Judy suddenly sat bolt upright, caught hold of my arm, and pointed towards the Union Bank of Switzerland.

'Howard, I'm sure I opened an account there. I think it was quite a bit of money you gave me to put in.'

It was possible, I suppose. Money was a bit like snow in Switzerland. It came in avalanches, and I often lost track of it. It was, after all, over two years ago, and there'd been some water under the bridge.

'Was it a lot?' I asked.

'I can't remember.'

'Is the account in your name?'

'I think so.'

I watched Judy disappear into the bank. She was there a long time. I began to worry. She'd probably opened the account with her Mrs Tunnicliffe passport and forgotten. Maybe she was being grilled by the police. After half an hour, she emerged with an extremely broad smile.

'Over twenty thousand pounds.'

We checked out of the Ticinese doss-house and into Lugano's Hotel Splendide. The mini-bar was emptied in about twenty minutes. Room service brought up several bottles of champagne. We got roaring drunk and had our first furious quarrel since my release. The next day, neither of us could remember what it was about.

On our return to England, feeling considerably richer and furiously scratching my head to think of any more banks that might be holding my money, I re-took possession of 18, Carlisle Street, that small part of Soho that the prosecution had alleged I used as my dope-dealing headquarters. The electricity bills were still in the name of Mr Nice. I met Old John's Mad Major. He was a pleasant man, and knew his wine. He would do as our connoisseur, but it was a pity he drank so much.

The Soho Square area had a few secretarial/business services. I had spent a fortune on them in the past, each new identity requiring an address, a phone number, and headed notepaper. Now I was trading as myself, perhaps I should open my own business service and charge other people for taking telephone messages, making photocopies, and holding mail. It might even make money as well as being a good front. It wouldn't be my package that arrived from Karachi, it would belong to one of my clients. I could start with just one secretary. I found one called Kathy.

I went to see Stanley Rosenthal again. Two more companies were formed: Moontape (trading as West End Secretarial Services) for the business service and Drinkbridge for the wine importation. Each would operate from 18, Carlisle Street, Soho.

Piers Paul Reid backed out of writing my biography. He'd been ruthlessly conned by the train robbers into writing a load of bullshit and had now read enough about me to feel fearful of a similar embarrassment. Bernie suggested David Leigh, the head of the *Observer*'s investigative team and author of books on government secrecy and high-profile trials. He had his own literary agent, Hilary Rubinstein, who could get the best advance. In fact, he managed to obtain only fifteen thousand pounds (less than Judy had found in her Swiss bank account). It was from Heinemann, and was to be split between me and David. But I'd agreed. It looked like fun. The money was super-straight, so I would be able to spend it quite openly. There'd be lots I couldn't tell David, of course, like Ernie's involvement in the Colombian scam, but I'd deal with that later. I could always be creative.

David and I went up to Scotland, where I showed him the offloading and storage points in Kerera, Conaglen, and Oban. We visited the falcons in Pytchley. He needed somewhere quiet to interview me and write. I took him to the smallholding in Upper Cwm Twrch and, after a couple of days, left him there. I phoned him a few times. He was spending most days collecting colourful fungi. He could have written *The Observer's Book of Mushrooms*. It would have been better for both of us if he had.

The hearing for our attempt to retrieve the thirty thousand pounds held by Customs took place at the Royal Courts of Justice in the Strand in the autumn of 1982 before Master Bickstall-Smith. Both parties to the dispute were represented by the same legal counsel that had appeared at the 1981 Old Bailey trial. A bit of a re-run. The Crown's QC maintained that despite my acquittal, the money resulted from some kind of dope-dealing. I was a notorious drug smuggler and had made no money in any other way. The good Master would have none of it. He summed up with an extraordinary speech: 'Mr Marks might be the biggest smug druggler [sic] in the world, but money is money, and we have to stop somewhere. He has been acquitted. The money is his. But before I finish, I want to say a few words about kif. Last summer, my wife and I went to Morocco, to the Kasbah and the Rif. We were driving through the kif plantations when we came across a man sitting in the road blocking our course. My wife told him in no uncertain terms to move. She threatened him with our gun. Do you know he just stayed there! He wouldn't budge. He was stoned. That's how strong that stuff is. Well, good luck, Mr Marks. The money is yours.'

Her Majesty's Customs and Excise appealed against the decision, threatening to take it to the House of Lords if necessary. Eventually, HM Customs relented and agreed the money was mine but they would pay only on the understanding that the money be used to clear my debt to the Inland Revenue. They would not pay me directly. I wasn't going to get a cheque signed by HM Customs payable to me. But I regarded the decision as some kind of victory.

Ernie still hadn't been in touch since my release. Then Patrick Lane, who had been financially cared for by Ernie since my 1980 arrest, telephoned me saying that Ernie wanted to meet me in Vancouver. Would I go over? My passport had now been extended for a full year. Of course I would go to Vancouver. I checked into the Seaporter, the same hotel where I'd re-met Jim McCann six years ago. I lay on the bed and waited for Ernie to call. The phone rang. It was Patrick calling from the lobby. He came to the room. It was great to see him. He was already drunk, and I soon joined him in alcoholic reverie.

'How's Ernie?' I asked.

'Well, it's a bit embarrassing,' replied Patrick, 'but he's become a hopeless junkie.'

'What! That's impossible! Ernie taking smack!'

'It's not smack, Howard, it's Demerol, but it's just as bad. He's going to phone here. You'll see what I mean.'

Ernie did phone. He was rather incoherent, but from what I could understand, he had been advised by Tom Sunde that it was too dangerous for him to travel to meet me. Things would quieten down, and he would see me then. I was disappointed.

'What's Tom Sunde doing these days?' I asked Patrick. 'Is he still at Ernie's beck and call?'

'Far from it. He's now a full-time CIA agent.'

This was incredible. Ernie a junkie and Tom a government spook.

'But how?' I asked, finding this very hard to take. 'I mean, is Tom working for the opposition, or does Ernie have all kinds of spooks on his payroll?'

'I really can't say any more,' said Patrick. 'I'm sworn to secrecy. Don't forget, Tom might have been responsible for your acquittal. You'll find out everything in due course, I'm sure. The only thing to remember now is not to trust Tom or believe anything he says.'

This was getting too bizarre for words.

'Pat, I'm going back to England to do my own thing. Tell Ernie to call me whenever he feels it's safe to do so.'

'That's definitely the best strategy,' said Patrick, just a little patronisingly.

I returned to Heathrow, empty-handed and confused about Ernie, Tom, and Patrick. It seemed as if I would have to go straight, whether I wanted to or not.

I did go very straight for several months, and by mid-1983 18, Carlisle Street had become a hive of legitimate business activity. There were several telephone lines, a ten-thousand-pound word processor, a large photocopying machine, and a telex. West End Secretarial Services had over fifty clients who paid good money for message-taking and mail-holding. Office accommodation was let out at extortionate hourly rates, the telex constantly chattered out incomprehensible gibberish from remote parts of the world, and people would queue to use the photocopying machine.

Following visits to Paris and Dieppe undertaken by the Mad Major and me, Drinkbridge imported thousands of bottles of wines and spirits. The Mad Major stored them in a cellar in Twickenham, and a selection of Jarvis's and Old John's friends distributed them to diverse quarters. Our clients included the British Shipbuilders Association and Margaret Thatcher's throat specialist, Dr Punt.

Kathy word-processed away at wine lists and at letters from strangers to other strangers. She also dealt with David Leigh's rough drafts for the biography. Heinemann had paid the advance. I'd bought a Mercedes. The Chelsea maisonette had been completed, and we'd moved there from Brighton. Meticulous accounts were maintained, and national insurance, income tax, graduated pensions, corporation tax, and value-added tax were most conscientiously paid. I was very busy and very straight.

I was also very bored. None of this was exciting and none of it was making any real money. Although the cash stash was dwindling more slowly, it was still dwindling. Accordingly, I wasn't that unhappy to get a phone call from Jim McCann in his absurd Belfast accent.

'I want to see you in Paris. Right away. Got something for you, kid. Check into the George V. You'll be safe. My boys will be covering you. We've called an amnesty.'

'Can you send me the air-fare, Jim? I'm skint.'

'Fuck off!'

Twenty-four hours later, I was working my way through the mini-bar. I wondered what insanity Jim had in store. At my Old Bailey trial, I had publicly accused him of being the world's biggest narco-terrorist and arms smuggler. He owed me for that bit of PR. The phone rang.

'Get out of the room, take the lift downstairs, and walk slowly out through the hotel's main doors,' whispered a soft Dublin brogue. 'Your man will be outside.'

I did as instructed. Jim was parked outside in a big Mercedes, bigger than mine. I got into the passenger seat, and he drove off. He burst out laughing and handed me a very strong joint. I burst out laughing and smoked it.

'I've got everything under control, kid, from the fucking Khyber Pass camel jockeys to the decadent fascists that run this poxy pisshole,' he boasted, for some reason pointing to the Louvre. 'I can get what I want, where I want, when I want. I'm back in the fast lane.'

'That's great, Jim. You know I still owe people for those Thai sticks you lost in a lorry-load of bananas outside Dublin.'

'I owe you nothing, you Welsh scumbag. You owe me your freedom and your life.'

'Oh yeah,' I protested. 'What would you have done if you hadn't met me? Probably carried on mugging old ladies in Andytown and setting fire to school libraries in the name of the cause. You Irish prick. You owe me a drink at least.'

We had several drinks in Castell's and Régine's. By now, Jim was well known at each. His front had progressed, buying and selling art. We moved to Elysée Matignon, a club patronised and rumoured to be owned by Jean-Paul Belmondo, who greeted Jim as a long-lost friend.

'Jean-Paul, let me introduce you to Mark Thatcher, just back from Saudi Arabia. Mark Thatcher, this is Jean-Paul Belmondo.'

I hated Jim when he did this. Why did people believe him? I pretended to be Mark Thatcher. It wouldn't last long. We got drunk. We smoked more joints. Roman Polanski walked in. McCann introduced me to him as Andrew Lloyd Webber. I left. Jim followed. We got back into his Mercedes.

'Can you still sell dope? I mean lots.'

'Of course, Jim. You know I'm the best.'

'Can you pick it up in Amsterdam, take it over to England, and sell it?'

'I'll get someone to do that, Jim, for sure. It'll have to be on credit, mind.'

'I know. I know. You Welsh arsehole. I'll have 250 kilos ready for you next Wednesday. Leave a car in the Marriot Hotel park. Leave a copy of *Playboy* on the passenger seat. Leave the keys in the exhaust pipe. I'll load the car up, and somewhere in the country you'll have to transfer the dope to a truck or caravan or whatever you're using to carry it over the Channel. Here's a sample of the dope and a book for you to read. I'm taking you back to your hotel now. Let me know when you've sold the gear. And no rip-offs.'

The dope was half a kilo of excellent Afghanistan/Pakistan border hashish. The book was an internal DEA publication instructing dope-busting agents what to look for in commercial shipments. There were hundreds of pages of examples of busted dope shipments and what had caused them to look suspicious in the first place. This was fascinating. Where had Jim got it from? Throwing caution to the wind, I smuggled both sample and book into England.

Who could I use to pick up the 250 kilos? Selling it once it was in England would be no problem. I still knew plenty of dealers, but they didn't have trucks. Only London villains tended to have those at their disposal. I wondered if Mick Williams was out of the nick yet. He'd be able to handle it. I called his number.

'H, you don't know, old son, how glad I am to hear yer. Let's 'ave a meet, shall we?'

We met at Richaux, opposite Harrods. Mick listened to my proposal.

'I'm over the moon to do it, H. I need a quick trade. My mate's got a truck. Goes over all the time. Sweet as a nut. My other mate's got a BMW. He just done a ten stretch. Did every day. One of your own, H. Straight up. It's all sorted.'

The truck went to Rotterdam. The BMW was taken from the Marriot Hotel, Amsterdam, by one of McCann's henchmen, loaded to saturation with well over 250 kilos of hashish, and reparked in the Marriot. Mick Williams went to pick it up and was descended upon by the Dutch drug squad. Mick's sister told me about it. Mick was 'gutted'.

I was pretty 'gutted' myself. Mick was in prison. I'd lost money I'd put up as expenses for Mick and his mates. I'd have to take care of Mick's defence costs. I'd almost got busted. I might get busted. McCann would figure I owed him a million pounds.

'Don't ever fucking see me again, you Welsh piss-artist, unless your act is completely together. You hear me?'

'Okay, Jim. Thanks for the shit.'

Shortly afterwards, McCann was arrested in Amsterdam by Dutch police, not for hashish but on the basis of a German extradition warrant relating to the 1973 charge of blowing up a British Army post in Mönchengladbach. Still furious over France's previous refusal to hand over McCann, the Germans were going to strong-arm the Dutch into doing just that.

Mickey's bust was a bit of a lesson. Maybe I really should go straight: concentrate on my little straight business empire in Soho and normalise my tax affairs.

However, the Inland Revenue made it clear that whatever settlement might be reached, they'd be on my back for ever. Stanley Rosenthal explained the advantages of non-residency. If I could live outside the United Kingdom and spend only two months a year physically doing business in the country, I would incur no British tax liability, and the Revenue would have no business being on my back in the future. Judy did not wish to live too far away from Britain. Switzerland was out of the question, much too cold and expensive. We wanted somewhere new and warm. Our time in Corfu had been enjoyable enough, but the island's telephone technology was still prehistoric, and who needed Greek as a second language? We narrowed down the choice to Italy or Spain.

Italy began as the clear favourite. I'd spent that six months as a fugitive in Genova in 1974. Judy and I had maintained a place in Campione d'Italia for three years. We felt fairly familiar with the Italian language and traditions. The Mafia still fascinated me despite my familiarity with some of their operations. We decided to do some exploration, starting with Tuscany. We flew to Pisa and rented a house outside nearby Lucca. We visited Florence, Siena, and Livorno. We saw an open-air opera at Puccini's house and drank some Brunello di Montalcino. The sensuality of the country and people captivated us again, but we were getting increasingly irritated by such quaint Italian customs as paying exorbitant fees to sit on a beach and frowning on foreigners not sporting Gianni Versace socks. Nevertheless, there were always the addictive autostradas, so one morning we rose early and drove south.

At Castellamare di Stabia, the eight-lane autostrada from Rome suddenly turns into a horse-and-cart track. The visitor has four conventional choices: see Naples and die from mugging, go to Capri and die from poverty, trudge through Vesuvius's volcanic ash in Pompeii, or die from exhaust fumes crawling around the Malfi coastline. We ignored these distractions, parked the car at Naples airport, and caught an Itavia flight to Palermo, Sicily. My suitcase flopped onto the carousel, pursued by three large, snarling Alsatians. Judy looked horrified.

'What have you got in that case, Howard?'

'Nothing, love. Don't worry. This is a domestic flight. They can't search our bags. We haven't come in here from any foreign country.'

'But, Howard, you swore you would never carry dope when we travelled with the children. Those were your precise words.'

I had faithfully promised not to bring out any hash with me from England, and, as a supreme sacrifice, I had stuck to that promise. Something weird was happening.

'Who are you meeting here? I knew something was going on when you suggested coming here.'

Judy knew nothing of the 250-kilo bust involving me,
Mickey Williams, and McCann. But my agitated behaviour
over the last couple of weeks had ignited her suspicions.

'I'm not meeting anyone here. I promise. I've no idea
what this is about.'

It was true. I didn't.

Four armed policemen grabbed me and escorted me and
my suitcase to an empty room. Judy was told to *aspetti, per
favore*. The Sicilian cops tore my baggage apart, looked in
every crease and pocket, and took away each item of
paperwork. The words of the Dutch chief prosecutor ran
through my mind: 'For this charge, Mr Marks, you can be
prosecuted and serve consecutive sentences in England,
America, Holland, Austria, France, Ireland, and Italy.'

I had already been done for it in England and Holland.
Were they going to do me in Italy now, for the same charge?
During the 1970s, I'd entered and exited Italy with a variety
of different passports and broken the country's stringent
currency regulations on countless occasions. Did they know
this?

One of the Sicilian cops came back, clutching my paperwork and brandishing a computer print-out. Grinning
broadly, he extended his hand.

'Ah! Signore Marks. *Il capo di contrabando. Il spione.
Benvenuto a Sicilia.*'

This was unexpected. Judy and the children were politely
ushered in. We were all taken to a furnished room.

'*Dove restare in Palermo?*'

I explained we had booked rooms at the Villa Igiea (the
old haunt of Lucky Luciano and Palermo's finest luxury
hotel). The policeman called the hotel and summoned its
chauffeur.

Palermo is a seriously criminal city. The city's centre is
dominated by its prison. The mega Mafia trial involving
several hundred defendants was in full swing. A newly-dug
tunnel connected the prison to the courthouse. Tanks

guarded the gates. The heavily armed guards allowed no photographs. Around the corner, olive-skinned kids played Sicilian hopscotch within the white-chalked outlines of recent murder victims. Photographs were not encouraged. None of the taxi-drivers used their meters. All the clothes boutiques and hairdressers were men's. Bodyguards were everywhere. Telephonic communications, particularly by Italy's standards, were excellent. The cuisine was among Europe's finest. The solitary international flight was a weekly non-stop to New York, packed with hit men and currency-regulation violators posing as olive-oil exporters. I wasn't bored for a moment, but I had to agree with Judy that it was no place to develop my legitimate business empire. We left, but not before I had opened an account at the Banca di Sicilia. Asking people to pay into an obvious Mafia account might increase the speed of settlement.

A day or so later, we were at the departure lounge of Pisa's international airport. Poking around the duty-free shelves, I ran into Neil Kinnock. He was smoking a cigarette. I liked what I knew about Kinnock. Would he turn out to be the long-awaited (at least in Wales) combination of King Arthur, Owain Glendower, and Nye Bevan that would oust the iron lady Thatcher and become our new Prime Minister?

'You're Mr Kinnock, aren't you?'

'Yes. What part of Wales are you from?'

We launched into an enjoyable discussion of South Wales geography and weather. We lamented the recent performances of the Welsh rugby team.

'Howard. Come here,' Judy's voice boomed from nowhere.

'Wait a minute, love, I'm talking to Mr Kin . . .'

'Please, Howard, come here at once.'

She was angry. Why?

I excused myself from Neil Kinnock's presence. Judy started walking away, very briskly.

'What's the matter, Judy? What is it?'

'What on earth do you think you're up to talking to that evil screw from Brixton prison? You're meant to be glad to have seen the back of people like that. Was he the one you were secretly meeting in Palermo?'

It was a fact. Neil Kinnock looked remarkably like a Brixton screw whom Judy had frequently encountered while visiting me in prison.

'Judy, that was Neil Kinnock. He would have been a good straight man to know. You just blew it.'

Judy went a deep shade of red and buried her head in my chest. We broke into laughter.

After we boarded the plane, the children saved our faces a little by going up to Kinnock and getting his autograph.

The Dutch system of justice is extremely civilised. Mickey was released after serving a few months, and the authorities did not appear to want to find anyone else to arrest. We met again at Richaux, opposite Harrods.

'Them Dutch nicks ain't 'arf good, H. Blinding food, screws you can 'ave a laugh with. You could do a ten standing on your head. So what you been up to, H?'

I explained my intention to live abroad.

'Ever been to Palma, H?'

'Not really, Mick.' I had, in fact, once visited Palma when doing the Morocco to Scotland scam, but it was only for one night, and I'd stayed on a boat.

'Give it a whirl, H. I got a gaff there. You can use it anytime.'

Mickey's kind offer was accepted. We flew to Palma de Mallorca and stayed at Mickey's flat in Magaluf. The immediate vicinity fulfilled all one's nightmares about package holidays. The streets were packed with screaming British soccer hooligans. Pubs with names such as London Pride, Rovers' Return, Benny Hill, and Princess Di emptied lager louts into a bewildering array of discothèques, souvenir stalls, and fish and chip shops. Strangely enough, there were

very few street fights. A similar alcoholic and boisterous
mass thronging an English street would very quickly turn
into a riot. The holidaymakers looked happy. Even paradise
couldn't compete with guaranteed sunshine, ubiquitous
promiscuity, and non-stop drinking. A lot of money was
being spent. It would be easy to make some with minimum
investment. But could one bear to live here?

'It can't all be like this,' said Judy. 'Let's rent a car and
have a look around the island.'

She was right. Within minutes, the stench of booze and
vomit was replaced by sweet perfumes of cherry and almond
blossoms. Most of Mallorca is deserted and beautifully
tranquil. The highest mountain is taller than any in the
British Isles. At its foot live people who have never seen
the sea, thirty miles away. Small villages hang off hills and
provide accommodation for some of the world's greatest
artists, musicians, and writers. The city of Palma is a delightful mixture of medieval Italian and Moorish architecture.
Non-vandalised telephone boxes are in abundance, and
people smoke hash in the street. The airport is one of the
busiest in the world. The weather is perfect. We figured we
could live here. We looked around for a home, found a few
possibilities, and went back to London to decide.

Nine

MARKS

Ernie had left several messages on my private answering machine asking me to call. I rang the number he'd left and spoke to him in the same code we'd used for a decade. Through other well-rehearsed codes, he asked if I still knew hash exporters in Pakistan and, in particular, did I know one able to air-freight five tons of the best hash to New York? Ernie was very definitely back in business. I said I'd get on to it right away. Ernie was the one person Judy could not object to my dealing with. He'd done so much for us. I mentioned to Ernie the DEA manual McCann had given me. Ernie told me they were selling them in dime stores. Concentrate on Pakistan.

I thought of Salim Malik, whom I'd met at Mohammed Durrani's deathbed. He might not even remember me. He'd only spent two minutes in my company and thought my name was Mr Nice. I called the number from a London phone box. He answered. He didn't remember me from Adam but agreed to meet me on neutral territory. He suggested Hong Kong or Damascus. I chose Hong Kong.

It had been four years since I'd last visited the Far East. I was looking forward to it. I thumbed through *Time Out* in search of a cheap air fare. A company called Hong Kong

International Travel Centre appeared to have the best
prices, so I went to its offices in Beak Street. All the
company's considerable business was run by just one
Chinese couple, a heavily birthmarked young male called
Chi Chuen (Balendo) Lo and his beautiful and older girl-
friend, Orca Liew. He was from Hong Kong, she from
Malaysia. I was impressed by the way they operated and took
an immediate liking to them. I promised to visit them on my
return from Hong Kong. They promised to buy their
Christmas and New Year refreshment from Drinkbridge.

British Caledonian took me from Gatwick to Dubai and
from Dubai to Kai Tak, arriving mid-morning, the day
before my arranged meeting with Salim Malik. I checked
into the Park Hotel on Chatham Road, Kowloon side, and
decided to be a tourist for a day.

During my few years' absence, Hong Kong had changed; or
maybe there was just an awful lot more of it and twice the
population. Vast stretches of development land had been
reclaimed from the sea. Monstrous high-rise buildings
wrapped in bamboo scaffolding cages were hastily replacing
not-so-high-rise buildings. Due to a respect for plant life far
exceeding that of most Western environmentalists, Hong
Kong's civil engineers and planners had ensured that no trees
would be damaged by construction work. The result was a
series of incongruous juxtapositions of gnarled woodwork and
neon. The trees looked pitifully small, like bonsai trees in
Kensington Gardens.

I walked along Kowloon's new promenade and gazed at
the mind-blowing skyline of Hong Kong Island. I took the
Star Ferry, still plying between Hong Kong and Kowloon,
still as cheap as ever and still plastered with instructions for
the Chinese not to spit. I did the Hong Kong Island tourist
routine: took the tram up the Peak, ate a tiger's prick at the
Jumbo floating restaurant in Aberdeen, took the world's
longest escalator to Ocean Park, sipped snake's blood in
Jervois Street, and drank in a hooker bar in Wan Chai.

Newspapers were full of reports bemoaning the promises London was making to Peking regarding the return of Hong Kong to Chinese rule. British Government supporters excused the apparent cowardice by maintaining that it was simply a case of a 100-year lease running out. But this was blatantly misleading. In fact, the lease applied to just a part of the Kowloon peninsula and the so-called New Territories. The rest, a main chunk of the Kowloon peninsula (Tsim Sha Tsui), Hong Kong Island, and a few hundred other islands, the British had simply ripped off and appended to the Empire. The Chinese had no internationally recognisable claim of ownership. But this caused Peking little concern. After all, at any time since the Sixties, the Chinese could have grabbed the lot by making one phone call to Westminster. Margaret Thatcher would not be able to do what she did in the Falklands. When Portugal turned left in the mid-Seventies and tried to give up Macao, its colony in China, Peking refused. Not yet. The Chinese would take everything back when it wanted to. It wants to in 1997. It will. Who runs the place, anyway? Five million Chinese, twenty thousand Americans, and seventeen thousand British. Who's kidding whom? The Chinese are long-term planners. It took them over 150 years to build their Great Wall. It took them only 100 years to be given on a silver platter the largest shopping, banking, and shipping centre in the world. They know what they're doing.

Malik and I had agreed to meet in the lobby of the Peninsula for morning coffee. It would be full, and strangers would be sitting next to each other having idle conversation and complaining about the newly built planetarium blocking the view of the sea. We wouldn't stick out. Malik was sitting alone at a table staring intently at the entrance. He nodded recognition. This was a relief. But he did not smile.

'Do you mind if I join you?' I asked in a voice clear and loud enough to be heard by nearby customers totally absorbed in their own affairs.

'Why not? It's a free country.'

'Well, I don't know about that,' I said. I sat down.

'Did you think you were free before 1947, when you were part of British India?' I whispered.

Malik almost smiled.

'How have you been, Malik, since we met on that sad day?'

'I am in good health. How well did you know my friend?' he asked.

'I know he was a policeman here for eleven years. I know he had a textile business in Dubai. I know he was a grandson of the former King of Afghanistan. He drank Johnnie Walker Black Label and smoked Benson & Hedges. I visited him many times at his house just outside Cannes. In my pocket I have a photograph of him standing next to me and my daughter, Amber.'

Suddenly, Malik's eyes dug right into me. He turned away; then he looked alarmed. 'Give me your hotel phone number. I'll call you later.'

I gave him a Park Hotel card and scrawled my room number on it.

As I walked to the lobby doors, I was aware of being watched. I was going to be followed. I wondered by whom: Her Majesty's Customs and Excise, the Inland Revenue, people working for Malik, McCann's henchmen, or the DEA trying to catch Ernie? It didn't much matter. Hong Kong is one of the easiest places to lose a tail. I ran out of the hotel, turned left, crossed Nathan Road, and ran up to Chungking Mansions, a 1960s high-rise that had been converted to a warren of Middle Eastern-run emporia and cafés. No business licences were issued for premises on the upper floors. Each door there displayed a sign stating: 'Do Not Knock. Private Residence.' If one should knock, the door was immediately opened, revealing a small, illegal restaurant. Within a few minutes of leaving the Peninsula, I was eating a vegetable curry prepared by Bombay Muslims.

There didn't appear to be any tail when I left Chungking
Mansions, but just in case, I took a speedy walk through a
maze of alleyways and dived into the Tsim Sha Tsui underground station. This was my first sight of Hong Kong's new
Mass Transit Railway. To familiarise myself, I took a train to
another station a few stops down. I bought a Railcard. Next
time, I would be able to do it much quicker. I emerged from
the underground and went to the Park Hotel for a lie-down.

Malik called in a few hours.

'Same place at eleven,' he suggested.

I didn't like the idea of giving the tail a second chance, but
I agreed. The Peninsula lobby was a lot quieter, but Malik
seemed infinitely more relaxed. His eyes twinkled, and he
smiled broadly.

'So, you are not the Mr Nice. You are D. H. Marks.
According to hotel.'

'You can call me Mr Nice if you want, Malik.'

'No. I shall call you D. H. Marks. In Pakistan, we know
your good reputation.'

'Thank you, Malik. Are you happy to do business with
me? Because if so, I have a proposition to discuss with you,
at your convenience.'

'D. H. Marks, I am always happy if, by the grace of Allah,
I am doing business with honest people.'

'Are you able to get the product?' I asked.

'Yes, *inshallah*, but I will not deal with the devil product.'

I presumed he couldn't possibly have meant hashish and
was referring to either heroin from the Golden Crescent area
of Iran, Pakistan, and Afghanistan or black-market Stinger
missiles. These latter had been donated by the Americans to
the Afghan rebels for use in their struggle against the former
Soviet Union, but an alarming number found their way to
the weapon shops of Peshawar and were sold to a variety of
terrorist groups.

'Malik, the product I'm talking about is the one you used
to sell in Hyde Park in 1965.'

His smile was broader than ever. He held out his hand.

'D. H. Marks, this is the mother-business. I have got the best. And, *inshallah*, it can be got out of my country many ways. But no Americans. Already I have seen one DEA here in hotel this morning.'

'Well, they're everywhere, Malik. But the product might well end up in America.'

'Where product end up and with who it end up is not my concern. I meet only you, D. H. Marks. How I give product, you say. How you give money, I say.'

'Okay.'

We shook hands on it.

Malik had to leave that night. We discussed how we would communicate with each other in future and agreed that our next meeting should be in Hong Kong, and that its purpose would be for me to give him a reasonable deposit of cash, together with instructions for exporting a load of hashish. We looked forward to it.

The next day I opened up a bank account. You never know when you'll need one. I chose Crédit Suisse. It was situated on the thirty-second floor of an enormous gold-coloured skyscraper called the Far East Trading Centre, situated in the Admiralty area of Hong Kong Island. I was told a Mr Stephen Ng would be my contact there on the bank staff. I deposited one thousand Hong Kong dollars.

The scamming bug was now well and truly back. Bangkok was less than three hours away. Phil Sparrowhawk came to mind. Although we'd parted on less than perfect terms following the loss of 750 kilos of Thai sticks in McCann's banana truck during 1979, Phil had written me a welcome-home card on hearing of my release from Wandsworth prison. He'd given me his Bangkok telephone numbers. I didn't want them on my hotel bill, so I went to the Cable and Wireless building in Middle Road, which had facilities for making long-distance calls anonymously.

'You're joking, surely. Oh! No! It can't be, can it?'

Phil still had his neutral accent, with just a trace of cockney.

'I was thinking of coming to see you, Phil.'

'Oh, yeah. When?'

'Right now. I'm in Hong Kong.'

'Fantastic! I'll book you into the Oriental Hotel. It's still the best in the world. Tell me which flight, and I'll meet you at the airport.'

After I checked out of the Park Hotel, Cathay Pacific took me to Bangkok. I'd forgotten how good Asian airlines were compared to those of Europe and America. The air hostesses were smiling, happy beauty queens, as opposed to dowdy Pan American frumps. The in-flight entertainment was provided free of charge through electronic headphones rather than through farcical toy stethoscopes rented out to passengers by other airlines. The food was hot and spicy, and the drink endless.

Immigration and Customs officials at Bangkok's Don Muang International Airport were friendly and welcoming. Phil stood just beyond them. He looked as nondescript as ever. One couldn't tell if he was down to his last penny or if he'd just made a million. We started towards the airport car park.

'Well, Albi, I . . . I suppose I call you Howard now. What's it to be first, a massage, a drink, check-in at the Oriental?'

'The hotel, I guess, but I tell you what I need, Phil, and that's a few very strong joints of Thai weed. It's murder trying to get any in Hong Kong.'

'I thought you might say that. There's some already rolled in the car.'

'Great! You haven't started smoking yet, though, have you?' I asked.

'No, but it's easy for anybody to get any quantity. I mean any quantity.'

We got into Phil's car. It, too, must have been non-descript. I can't remember. But it was clean and had three tightly rolled joints in the virgin ashtray.

I was halfway through the second before I became very stoned. Like every other Bangkok driver, we were stopped at permanently red traffic-lights, listening to high-pitched Thai pop, and yelling and swearing at droves of persistent, windscreen-hammering kids trying to sell flower chains. We were sweating streams, and choking on black clouds of exhaust fumes. An elephant trundled past. Orange-robed monks held out saucepans for food. Oversized billboards depicted cartoon characters speaking in Sanskrit. Monsoon clouds gathered as we approached the Oriental. Phil dropped me off outside and went to park his car. Red-eyed and legless, I went to the reception desk.

'Long flight, sir?' queried the clerk, mistaking my stoned state for one of tiredness and jet-lag.

I smiled, vacantly.

'You have been given VIP accommodation, Mr Marks, in the Joseph Conrad Suite. This way, please.'

Joseph Conrad had been instrumental in the founding of the Oriental Hotel. Other authors, such as Somerset Maugham and Evelyn Waugh, also wrote and lived there. Suites are named after them. White cane furniture, period photographs, bamboo, and leafy tropical flora abound.

A few minutes after I had been shown to my room, Phil arrived. We both said how glad we were to see each other and how stupid we'd been to let McCann's banana madness split our partnership. Phil regretted not having stayed in England to benefit from the Colombian scam, but he'd done all right. Robert Crimball, Ernie's original Bangkok supplier, had been badly busted and was serving a horrific 45-year sentence, but Phil was regularly visiting him in prison and was working on a way of buying his freedom. Robert had given Phil his contacts, enabling him to maintain good relations with suppliers of Thai weed. Moreover, Phil was still in touch with Jack 'The Fibber' Warren in Australia.

A few of Phil's loads had worked, and he was all right for money, very all right. Some of his hard-earned dope money

had been invested in a host of legitimate businesses. He had
a Chinese partner with whom he operated a food export
company, and he also partnered an American named Dennis
in a manpower company. Both ventures had expanded their
operations to encompass the Philippines, where Phil, through
some Australian friends, had made the acquaintance of a
British aristocrat and scammer named Lord Moynihan. Phil
was glad I'd sent him to Bangkok all those years ago. He'd
married a Thai who'd just given birth to his daughter.

Once the monsoon was over, the new marijuana crop
would be almost ready. He was going to buy several tons. He
could get any amount exported by air or sea. He could
arrange to supply private boats, sitting and waiting 200 miles
away in the South China Sea, with unlimited amounts of the
finest Thai weed. His connections outside of Thailand,
however, were limited to those who could smuggle into
Australia. He needed others, particularly in America and
Britain. Did I still know any?

I brought Phil up to date with my activities, carefully
leaving out any mention of Pakistan. He was pleased that
Ernie was raring to do business and was impressed with what
I was running in Soho. He asked if West End Secretarial
Services could serve as his London office. I agreed. It would
make a good front for our future illegal activities. There
clearly would be some.

Business over, we went out on the town to Patpong, two
parallel streets containing over a hundred bars and noodle
stalls and several thousand prostitutes, busily go-go dancing,
stripping, and sticking Coca-Cola bottles, razor blades, and
table-tennis balls up their vaginas. We bought lots of girls
lots of drinks of non-alcoholic cordial. We were popular.

The hookers attempted to find out if we were naïve and
rich.

'Butterfly. You no like me. *Fahlang,* buy me one more
drink. You velly handsome man. How many times you been
Bangkok, *fahlang*? You like my body? Which hotel you stay?'

Howard Marks,
Oxford, 1965

Kenfig Hill,
Wales, 1967

Daily Mirror

EUROPE'S BIGGEST DAILY SALE

5p   Saturday, April 19, 1975   No. 22,154

MIRROR PICTURE EXCLUSIVE ON Mr MYSTERY

THE FACE OF A FUGITIVE

DISGUISED: Mystery man Howard Marks on the run in London last week.

By EDWARD LAXTON and TOM MERRIN

THIS is the new face of Howard Marks, the mystery man who has been on the run a year today.

Marks, disguised with a moustache and tinted glasses, was photographed in London last week. The smaller picture, right, shows how he looked when he disappeared.

In London Marks has been living in a luxury rented flat in Park Road, Regent's Park. Neither the other residents nor the caretaker knew the identity of the quiet man in Flat 92.

Yesterday senior Customs investigators raided the block and found the flat empty. Marks had left last Friday.

Now detectives from three forces have been alerted to step up the search for Marks, who is alleged to have worked for

Swoop on London hide-out

three separate bosses: the Mafia, the IRA and the British Secret Service.

Marks, a 29-year-old Oxford graduate, was arrested in Holland in November 1973. He and five other people were accused of a multi-million pound drug smuggling plot.

Marks, who claimed that he had been pressed by the Secret Service into informing on the IRA, was allowed bail of £50,000.

But on the eve of his Old Bailey trial he vanished with a man who called at the flat in Leckford Road, Oxford, where he lived with 26-year-old Mrs. Rosemary Lewis and their two-year-old daughter Myfanwy.

Last October Marks turned up in Padua, Italy. The Mafia had agreed to protect him in exchange for his silence about the drug traffic.

About two months ago he returned to Britain on a false passport. A friend said he came back because he could not endure his existence abroad.

For the mysterious Howard Marks the price of freedom has been a life of fear as a fugitive.

With Judy, Las Vegas, 1976

Campione, 1977

With Judy, Bunratty Castle,
Ennis, Ireland, 1979

The four tons of cannabis taken from Alan Athur Grey's bungalow at Glengarry, Invernessshire.

Oxford graduate cleared of £20m drugs link

By Stewart Tendler, Crime Reporter

Howard Marks, the Oxford graduate charged with being the British mainstay of a £20m cannabis smuggling ring, was acquitted yesterday at the Central Criminal Court of involvement with the drug organisation.

In his defence Mr Marks, aged 36, told the court during an eight-week trial that at had worked for MI6 to infiltrate an IRA arms and drug smuggling business, and later for Mexican agents against South American terrorists financed by drugs.

Yesterday the jury, which had been deliberating since Thursday morning, also acquitted a Briton and an American of charges connected with the smuggling ring which brought 15 tons of cannabis from Colombia to Britain. But they found Mr Marks guilty of two offences involving false passports.

Mr Marks may also face proceedings alleging that he absconded from bail in 1974 while awaiting trial on a separate drug charge. Judge

Mason, QC, was told yesterday that the Director of Public Prosecutions is considering the earlier charge.

While the jury was out the court began to hear pleas in mitigation by five men who had earlier pleaded guilty to charges connected with the cannabis in Britain. After the verdicts on Mr Marks, Morgan Stewart Prentiss, aged 41, the American of no settled address, and Hedley Morgan, aged 34, of Potters Bar, Hertfordshire, the judge was asked to make an application preventing details of some of the mitigation pleas for the five from being reported by journalists.

Lord Hutchinson of Lullington, QC, for Mr Marks, of Cadogan Crescent, Chelsea, London, nothing should be reported from the pleas of mitigation which might be prejudicial to Mr Marks if the 1974 case to trial. The judge refused to grant the application.

Mr John Rogers, QC, opening the case against the men,

had earlier told the court that James Goldsack, aged 32, an Oxford graduate from London, had acted as accountant for the cannabis in Britain, was stocktaker, and had driven one load down from Scotland to a warehouse at Laindon, Essex.

Martin George Langford, an artist, aged 36, of no settled address, took messages at a flat in London and collected 180lb of cannabis from a warehouse at Pytchley, Northamptonshire.

Mr Rogers said Alan Arthur Grey, a farmer, aged 47 of Glengarry, Inverness-shire, took no part in the import of the cannabis to a place on the coast of West Scotland, but he stored

Daniel Farm, Laindon. Mr Cole ran a furniture business and stored more cannabis. Customs men found 2.75 tons stored at the farm.

Mr Richard Du Cann, QC, defending Mr Goldsack, said his client had been a drug addict. He had had no direct contact with his colleagues in the ring because that was the way Mr Marks ran the organisation.

During the course of Mr Marks's trial Mr Marks told the court that he had been recruited in 1972 by MI6 to spy on Mr James McCann, a leading Provisional IRA activist who used the finances from drug smuggling to finance arms purchases

.................Mr McCann three

Mr Marks said he was introduced to the Mexicans by MI6 and infiltrated a cannabis smuggling ring to get information for them.

[] Sir Michael Havers, the Attorney General, is to consider allegations that a journalist may have committed contempt of court in talking to a juror after Mr Marks had been acquitted.

The possible contempt, by David Pallister, of The Guardian, was reported to Judge Mason. Mr Pallister was placed in custody, but was released after Mr Geoffrey Shaw, appearing for the reporter, told the court that the question of contempt might be dismissed. He said the Contempt Act, 1981, did not prohibit conversation with jurors.

....................the matter

With the family,
Brighton, 1982

Villa Igeia, Palermo, 1983

With Amber, Hong Kong, 1984

With Amber and Francesca,
Hong Kong, 1985

nfig Hill-born Howard Marks
s made and lost millions,
twitted police and customs
icials in 14 countries and was
quitted after a trial at the Old
iley. In the second of a two-
rt series based on a book on
arks's life, PAUL REES looks at
arks's recruitment into MI6, his
rest, life on the run and re-
rest after a headline-making
pe smuggle in the Scottish
ghlands.

C McMILLAN joined MI6 in 1969. By
2, Ted Heath had ordered the outfit
· Northern Ireland. It was not long
are Jim McCann came to their notice.
now, Marks and Plinston, who were
ding for a route from Montreal, had
ted to act as independent distributors
he provinces as well as London. They
ited another big deal with McCann.
They met him in Amsterdam. When Marks
ed back to Oxford, McMillan turned up at
shop. They talked about Secret Service
· Later, McMillan asked him if he would be
rested in helping. Yes, he said, before catch-
a plane for a prolonged burst of Irish
ity. "Listen, Howard," said McCann. "The
os have found out about me selling dope in
lin. They are putting a lot of pressure on me
nip them arms from Amsterdam. Can you
se have the services of some of your drivers
ny product?" No.
McCann led on the image of himself as a
runner, His fertile imagination worked
retime — he would blab about 'end-user'
dicates, RPG-7 rocket launchers and the
sipid arms factory, but no one ever saw him
h a consignment of weapons. Though the
were not fooled, the Dutch police were. Re-
gly went about asking for guns and lit his
as with 100 guilder notes in restaurants.
an intelligence believed him, too.

KGB spies

While the Mediterranean, California and
rock music industry came into the smug-
g equation, McMillan again popped into
abelinda. Marks was thinking about his
are — Asia, the Middle East, the Med, the
, Zurich bankers, Italy, Amsterdam and

"Something has come up over which you
ht be able to assist." KGB spies, and a
ect woman at the same Embassy Marks
invited to a party there, with his penchant
"dames," MI6 hoped he might loosen her
gue. She never showed. "Don't ——
rard. We will find ——

Buccaneer or public benefactor?

Mrs Judy Marks, wife, off ... whose husband was cleared of drug smuggling. Right, Kenfig-born Howard Marks.

was to become his second wife, he went
Brighton. Christmas Day, 1974, saw him lat
a slap-up meal in the Dorchester Hotel in P.
Lane.

He was soon in the money when a boat fr
Morocco docked and £1,000 a month comm
sion flowed from the sales. The Mirror were
the scent again. Marks ended up in a Livery
shim before fleeing across the Atlantic, w
Judy Lane, on false passports, via Zurich. O
anony ..evening in Vancouver in 1973
bumped into McCann whose imagination
been stimulated by the Canadian winter
had an office door in the Guinness Tow
bragged about his oil interests in Venezu
claimed to be putting finance into the I
Equus and spoke of his friendship with Jac
Coburn. He was known as Mr Kennedy.
Marks claimed he was so rich he did
know how to spend his money. He said he w
working with New York dealers, had a Mia
condo and that he was getting fitness c
scious. He had a wall safe "stuffed with dolla
Marks had been welcomed in Amer
because a 400lb shipment from Damascu
Ecuador had been accidentally routed
London and discovered. Marks could help
find a new route. He could, says David Leig
High Time (Heinemann; £9.95), a book
Marks's life, be seen driving around New Y
in an enormous limousine with a chauf
called Harvey — he was frequently seen
Studio 54 and Nicola's restaurant
The Canadian Mounties caught hold
McCann, but he was bailed and shot out of
country. Marks carried on in the followin
months, he visited eight countries, changed
address six times and his identity three tin
He put together nine different smuggling op
tions, made a million dollars and lost a mil
dollars.
"Had he been under surveillance," s
Leigh, "he could have been spotted in Frar
Switzerland, New York, Italy, Wimbled
where he attended the birth of his daugh
Amber, before going back to Paris and N
York. Then he could have been seen swann
up the Himalayas, then Karachi, Zurich, dir
banking hours, and Italy. From there, he w
have been sighted in Germany, then Cadiz
Madrid, Frankfurt, New York again and
Francisco."

Popular sympathy

Two deals remained — one through Irela
with McCann, which took first when an Iri
Army bomb-disposal team blew open the tr
doors to discover, to their surprise, 15
chests full of dope. The last one was the big
Just after Mrs Thatcher came into po
Marks, via Scotland, smuggled enough d
into Britain to make 30 million joints.
moved into a luxury flat, near Harrods a
feasted himself — he announced his enga
ment to Judy and just as he was enst
himself was arrested ———

have a front end, and unwittingly, Mac the ——
would provide Ma ———

DAILY MIRROR, Tuesday, July 26, 1988

English toff's power rivalled Mafia barons
DRUGS KING OF THE WORLD IS TRAPPED AT LAST

HELD IN SPAIN: Briton Howard Marks

MILLIONAIRE Howard Marks, arrested yesterday as the king of the
drugs world, vanished from Britain after a sensational Old Bailey
trial.

He was cleared of masterminding a
£20 million drug smuggling ring.

Now he stand accused of heading a
MULTI-BILLION POUND international
empire.

By SYLVIA JONES

Police who have tracked him around
the world describe him as one of the
most sophisticated drug barons of all
time with a ruthless organisation matching anything operated by the Mafia or
the feared Colombians.

Marks, arrogant and handsome, lives
the life of an English gentleman.

Receiving GED from Richard Webster, Terry Haute Penitentiary, 1991

With T. Bone Taylor, Terre Haute Penitentiary, 1993

With Laurent
Fiocconi
(bottom left),
Terre Haute
Penitentiary
Recreation
Ground, 1994

With Dan
Topolski,
Terre Haute
Penitentiary,
1994

With Big Jim
Nolan of the
Outlaws,
Terre Haute
Penitentiary,
1994

With James
'T. Bone'
Taylor,
Veronza
'Daoud'
Bower,
'Boomerak'
and other
friends, Terre
Haute
Penitentiary,
1995

With the
Super Furry Animals,
DeJa, 1995

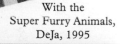

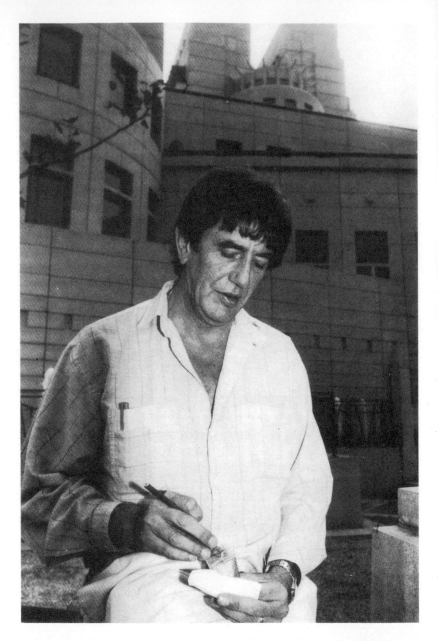

Outside MI6, London, 1996

After about ten bars, the thrill wore off. We hailed a *samlor*, a three-wheeled motor scooter with a covered seat on its back axle. There are tens of thousands careering round the streets of Bangkok twenty-four hours a day. They are better known as *tuktuks* and sound like epileptic power saws. With an unexpected mastery of Thai, Phil asked the *tuktuk* driver in which direction he was heading. The *tuktuk* driver said he was going to have a late-night meal in Pratunam market where all *tuktuk* drivers ate. This sounded good. We agreed to pay for the *tuktuk* driver's meal if he took us there. He couldn't believe his luck, and we tore off at breakneck speed.

Pratunam market is a vast expanse of rustic kitchens and well-worn tables competing with each other for space and custom. Some tables and kitchens are under tents, others under corrugated tin roofs. The whole area is bathed in blinding fluorescent light. Everyone wears shades. Hundreds of hookers, some puzzlingly wearing fake Thai Air stewardess uniforms, focused intently on their food. There would be no potential clients here. *Tuktuk* drivers had no money. There were no menus. A few giant crabs and frogs had escaped from a kitchen and were scraping and hopping between tables and chairs. No one took a blind bit of notice, except us. I wanted to smoke a strong Thai joint. This was too good not to witness completely stoned. Phil had none left, and his house was too far away. The *tuktuk* driver was called Sompop. He could get ready-rolled ganja cigarettes in just half a minute at rock-bottom prices. I was beginning to like Sompop. We ate some unidentifiable reptiles. I got stoned. Phil got bored. We agreed to meet each other the next morning. Phil caught another *tuktuk*. Sompop took me to the Oriental Hotel. I asked him if I would be able to see him on my next visit to Bangkok. He said he would like that very much, but he had no address or phone number. I asked if there was anywhere other than the hopelessly chaotic Pratunam market where he regularly spent time. He said he went every Friday evening to the Erawan Buddha next to the Erawan Hotel. That would do fine.

I had breakfast with Phil. We went over everything again and talked vaguely about smell-proofing marijuana shipments and their cost. Phil took me to the airport. He'd brought some more Thai weed, which I chain-smoked all the way to the airport car park.

It had been a productive twenty-four hours, and I felt invigorated as I climbed aboard the Thai Air flight to Hong Kong. The hostesses smiled seductively. These were real ones, not the phoneys in Pratunam. I accepted a copy of the *Bangkok Post* and was intrigued to read a headline: 'Wales Hopes To Export Its Water'. The article explained how the Welsh Water Authority was attempting to sell some of its vast and never-ending supply of fresh water. Storage tanks and facilities would be provided in South Wales at Milford Haven, Britain's largest natural harbour and oil-importing port. Oil tankers would be bulk-loaded with fresh water piped from the harbour's storage tanks. Many countries were short of water, and this proposal, the article concluded, made a lot more sense than the recently aborted attempt to tow icebergs from the Arctic.

I had a strong urge to get involved in this business. I don't know why, and I didn't know how. Drinkbridge, the name of our wine company, would be a remarkably appropriate name for such a business. One of the keys to business success is to pretend to be doing what one ultimately wants to do. The Thai weed was still revving-up my brain. I decided to present myself to the Welsh Water Authority as the man who could buy their billions of gallons of surplus water. First I would need to learn all I could about the subject. That wouldn't be hard: I'd read books, talk to my father, and employ a researcher. I would also need some credentials: namecards and Drinkbridge company notepaper that didn't have grapes and bottles of wine all over it. Hong Kong would be a good place to begin getting that together.

There was no problem with Customs at Kai Tak airport. The small plastic bag of Thai marijuana in my sock remained undiscovered. I checked into the Park Hotel and walked down to Cable and Wireless to telephone Ernie and tell him supplies could be arranged from both Pakistan and Thailand. He told me that while in Hong Kong I should present myself to a friend of Patrick Lane's, Bruce Aitken, who ran a finance company called First Financial Services. Investment money for the forthcoming Pakistan scam and generous expenses for me would probably be sent through him and given to me in Hong Kong sometime in the New Year. He would get Patrick to call him immediately.

Bruce was a likeable American who convincingly played the part of an investment broker. Patrick had already advised him about the investment money. I asked if he knew a reliable accountant for company formation. He suggested Armando Chung and made an appointment for me to see him the next morning.

It was the end of the business day, and Bruce offered to take me out before he went home. He left me in the basement of the New World Centre in Tsim Sha Tsui East, at a place called Bar City, a complex of several bars having different themes. I chose the Country Bar, where sixty Chinese were jiving, square-dancing, and singing along to a Filipino band playing Waylon Jennings.

I drank a lot, went to a few more bars, and found myself in Bottoms Up, Hong Kong's notorious yuppie titty joint, which had recently been over-glamorised in the James Bond film *The Man with the Golden Gun*. It was about 2 a.m., and members of the Western and Japanese banking, business, and diplomatic communities were passing out, vomiting, quarrelling with their wives, and unashamedly leering at anything that was topless. There were several categories of African and Asian hostesses: noisy, rude ones who shoved their tits in the faces of men who bought them gallons of expensive coloured water, quiet ones who were prepared to be shagged in the nearest doss-house, and beautiful rich geisha types who flattered and flirted in the hope of either changing or cementing their fate.

I sat alone for about ten seconds. Two Hong Kong geishas with the unlikely names of April and Selena joined me. They were terrified of the prospect of Hong Kong being governed by Chinese Communists.

I couldn't fully sympathise with their fears, for as far as I could determine, China had been ferociously capitalist for about eight thousand years and had set up thriving business communities in every country in the world. It had been Communist for less than a century. They'd get over it. Already, the mainland Chinese had surrounded Hong Kong with fourteen gigantic skyscraper developments called Special Economic Zones. Each was a mini-Hong Kong. The worst that could happen to Hong Kong, the end product of combined Western and Chinese ruthlessness and the paradigm of Keynesian economic success, was that it would expand.

April and Selena thought these views of mine to be rather naïve. They wanted out. Ideally, they wanted to marry yuppie millionaires from London and become British, but they would settle for less. They would even go so far as to pay good money for documentation that enabled them to become British residents. I thought of my Mr Nice passport lying dormant in Campione d'Italia. Would one of these geishas like to be Mrs Nice? I could get a load of false passports and marry twenty exotic Far East hookers and get handsomely paid.

April, Selena, and I went to an all-night Japanese sushi bar. After many cups of steaming sake, we exchanged phone numbers and addresses. I promised to get them and their friends some husbands. They assured me that anything I wanted in Hong Kong was mine: places to stay, the best business connections, admission to all clubs, and hookers. I asked if they could get me some marijuana, just to smoke. 'Marks, I'll get you anything under the sun, no problem,' laughed April, pulling out a joint as we left the Japanese restaurant and asking a cab-driver to take us to a club called Nineteen Ninety-Seven.

Armando Chung, the accountant, saw me at his office in the Wing On building the next morning. I left him some money and instructed him to incorporate a company named Drinkbridge Hong Kong Limited and open up a bank account. I'd be back in the New Year. I spent the rest of the day and the rest of my money buying Christmas presents in the Kowloon arcades.

I couldn't sleep on the plane back to London. I kept thinking of tankers full of water, plane-loads of hashish, suitcases of money, and honeymoon suites full of Chinese hookers.

'You've been away a long time,' said Judy as I fell through the door. 'You said you wouldn't be long.'

'I've been gone only a few days. It's a long way. And I've done a lot. I've been busy.'

'You're always busy, Howard. You don't change. Another friend of yours from prison has been calling here. Jim Hobbs. I suppose you'll be seeing him now.'

She was right on all counts. I promised myself I'd take her and Amber and Francesca to Hong Kong when I next went. They'd love it. Hobbs would be useful. He was a trustworthy and hard-working guy. Maybe he'd like to marry a Chinese hooker and earn his keep.

We visited my parents' home in Wales over Christmas. The offices of the Welsh Water Authority were nearby. I had spent about a week reading all there was to know about the bulk transport of water and had made an appointment to see Roy Webborn, the Authority's Assistant Director of Finance. I told him I represented a syndicate of Far Eastern businessmen who were interested in purchasing giant tanker-loads of water and taking it to Saudi Arabia. Webborn explained that Welsh water wasn't yet available for bulk export, but there was plenty of it in the hills, and oil tankers were leaving Milford Haven carrying nothing but sea-water ballast. If any business interest was prepared to pay for the installation of bulk fresh-water loading facilities at Milford Haven, the Welsh Water Authority would pay for the pipes to take the water there from the hills and sell it cheaply. I said I'd see what I could do. He gave me a stack of laboratory test reports and impressive multilingual, multicoloured brochures.

January 1984 was cold. The British public were still listening to last year's big hits: *Karma Chameleon*, *Red Red Wine*, and *Uptown Girl*. Little was happening, so I was delighted to get a call from Ernie Combs.

'Hi. How you doing? I got good news for you. Frank's in Frankfurt with the contract. Can you see him right away?'

'Frank' was our code for money. 'Frankfurt' was code for Hong Kong. The contract was the instructions for whatever deal Ernie had decided to go for.

'Sure. Shall I call you when I get there?'

'I have a new number for you. It will answer "LAPD", but it's not the Los Angeles Police Department, it's a friend of mine called Flash. He's an electronic genius. Ask for me, and he'll put you through to whichever hotel I'm staying in. I live in hotels these days.'

This time I flew British Airways, again booking my ticket through Hong Kong International Travel Centre. Arriving in the early morning, I took a cab from Kai Tak airport to the Park Hotel, checked in and walked to Cable and Wireless to phone Ernie. He told me to contact his friend Bill, who was staying in the five-star luxury Mandarin Hotel on Hong Kong Island. I travelled over on the Star Ferry.

Bill was a heavily set US military type. He had been in the Special Forces in Vietnam and spoke fluent Russian. Ernie knew some strange people.

'There's exactly $1,250,000 in that suitcase. I counted it myself. My orders are to give it to you.'

'What am I meant to do with it?' I asked.

'I don't know. You mean you don't know? You guys are something else. It ain't like working for the Government, I can tell you.'

'Ernie give you any instructions for me, Bill?'

'Who is Ernie?'

'The guy who gave you the suitcase of money to give to me.'

'He was no Ernie. He was some gook who works in a bank a couple of blocks away. But you are for sure the guy I gotta give this money to. You're British, right? And I want you to take it right now. I'm fixing on getting me a couple of Chinese broads tonight, and I don't want all that cash cramping my style. It's heavy. I'll carry it downstairs for you. I'm on my way out anyway. You can get a cab.'

I stood outside the foyer of the Mandarin Hotel. There wasn't a cab in sight. Then suddenly an endless snake of red and white Hong Kong cabs came driving past at a snail's pace. The cab-drivers were yelling out of the windows, and their hands were continuously pressing the horns. It was a taxi strike, and the strikers had decided to block up Hong Kong's streets as part of their protest. No road traffic was moving. I was stuck. I could hardly lift the suitcase, let alone carry it to the Star Ferry. Luckily a Mass Transit Railway underground station, Central, was just on the corner. Sweating and heaving, I dragged the suitcase down the thronged steps to the lengthy ticket-machine queues. I couldn't get it over or through the turnstiles. My trousers got ripped in the attempt. A couple of Chinese schoolboys helped me carry it to the densely packed Tube train. I pulled the suitcase out at Tsim Sha Tsui station, and, on the point of collapse, reached the top of the station steps.

The strike had turned into a riot. Swarms of screaming Chinese were tearing around throwing missiles through shop windows and looting the wares. Piles of electronic machinery and cheap jewellery littered the pavements and disappeared in armfuls. People were robbing whatever they could. The contents of my suitcase were more valuable than the sum total of all the stolen goods I could see. I began panicking. My heart was racing, and I was so weak I simply could not budge the suitcase. I sat on it and watched the riot. Eventually, I found the strength to lift it and stumbled into the Park Hotel.

'I take your bag, Mr Marks,' said a diminutive Chinese porter, picking up the immense weight, putting it on his shoulders, and running down the corridor to the elevator. I went running after him. He put down the suitcase, smiled broadly as I gave him a 100-Hong-Kong-dollar tip, and ran away.

I collapsed on the bed, jet-lagged and exhausted. I'd smuggled in a few ready-rolled joints from London. One of them put me to sleep.

A couple of hours later, I woke surrounded by three room attendants.

'Ah! Mr Marks, you must close door. Maybe robber come. Today crazy day in Hong Kong.'

This was most irresponsible. I'd gone to sleep leaving a suitcase containing well over a million dollars in the middle of the floor with the door wide open while I fell unconscious puffing away at a large joint. I couldn't risk leaving the room, not even to go downstairs. I couldn't telephone Ernie from the hotel room. That would be uncool. It was still morning in London. Hobbs should be at the Soho office. I'd given him some odd jobs to do for Drinkbridge. It would be all right to phone there from the hotel.

'Jim, can you get the next flight to Hong Kong? Ask Balendo at Hong Kong International to give you a ticket on my account.'

'Nothing would give me greater pleasure, Howard.'

'Bring your birth certificate, Jim. You might be getting married.'

The Park Hotel was not Hong Kong's best-equipped

hotel. There was a black-and-white television and some piped muzak. I had enough hash for only three joints. I put the suitcase in the wardrobe and smoked three joints. I telephoned April.

'Ahh, Marks, you back in Hong Kong. Me and Selena think you never come back. You go Bottoms Up tonight?'

'No, I have to stay in my room to receive telephone calls.'

'You want me and Selena come see you. No problem. Where you stay?'

'Park Hotel.'

'Where?'

'It's on Chatham Road. April, can you bring some . . .?'

'I bring everything, Marks. See you.'

'Ahh, Marks, why you stay in this hotel, and in Room 526? This number bad luck for you,' said Selena.

'*Fenshui* all fucked up,' agreed April.

'What's *fenshui*?' I asked.

'It's what *gwailu* professor call "geometric omen",' said April. 'What you get depend on what you look at.'

'What's *gwailu*?'

'You are *gwailu*, Marks. It mean White devil.'

'So if the view sucks, you say the *fenshui* is not up to standard.'

'Not just view, Marks, orientation, too. This hotel very bad. Why you don't stay Shangri-La? It's very good hotel. My friend works there as assistant manager. I get you good deal. Cost same money as here. I arrange for you.'

'Okay. I just have to wait here until my friend comes from London tomorrow. Then I'll check into the Shangri-La.'

'Who is your friend, Marks?' asked Selena.

'He's called Jim Hobbs. He is coming to Hong Kong to get married.'

'Is he marrying *gwailu* or banana?'

'What's a banana?'

'Yellow outside, White inside. Like ABC, American Born Chinese.'

'Jim's not marrying a *gwailu* or a banana. He's marrying a real Chinese.'

'Who?' asked Selena.

'You tell me. Maybe you or maybe April.'

'Ah, Marks, you good man; you bring us husbands,' said April.

'Well, so far, only one, and he hasn't got here yet. But there'll be more.'

'Is Hobbs handsome?' Selena enquired.

'No.'

'Is he rich?'

'No.'

'Is he young?'

'No.'

'Is he sexy?'

'I don't know. He's gay.'

'I'll marry him. How much will he cost?'

The million-odd dollars in the wardrobe had put me in a magnanimous mood.

'Selena, I won't charge you. And soon, I will bring you a husband, April, and I won't charge you either. This is to show good faith. I would like the three of us to start a business. You find the wives and charge them. I'll find the husbands and pay them. We three split the profits between us.'

'This is good business, Marks,' agreed Selena, 'but to save face with you, I must pay for Hobbs. What do you want?'

'No money. Just help me when I'm in Hong Kong. Show me around. Take me to places where no other *gwailus* go. Let me know all the secrets.'

'Are you a spy, Marks?' asked Selena.

'No. I'm a hashish smuggler.'

'I told you,' shrieked April. 'I knew it. Marks, like I say before, we can get you whatever you want, anything under the sun. You want apartment, car, sex, dope, or go to private club, no problem. We can do. But each time you must pay us what it cost and some commission. Same for you. Charge me and Selena for husband. Make commission. This Hong Kong business style. Between friends, too.'

'Okay, then pay me 100,000 Hong Kong dollars for a husband for each of you, but keep the money yourselves, and take out of it your charges for whatever I ask you to do for me. Then I can telephone you from abroad and still ask you for help.'

'Yes, Marks, this is good plan. I've made some joints. No tobacco. Cambodian grass. We smoke?'

A few joints and a few hours went by. Selena and April divulged details of their private lives. Selena was the mistress of a number of Japanese tycoons. April was the mistress of a senior British diplomat. They were high-class hookers who only had sex when paid to do so.

Dawn came. The girls left. I fell asleep.

Sometime in the evening, Hobbs arrived. I explained the problem with the money. I told him to whom he was getting married and why. He thought the idea amusing and was convinced he could recruit for the cause some more men of his orientation. I asked him to stay in the room and look after the money while I dashed around to sort things out.

First I went to Cable and Wireless to telephone the LAPD number.

'LAPD. Can I help you?'

'Is that you, Flash?'

'Sure is, buddy. You want our friend?'

Flash put me through. Ernie had been worried and was glad I called. There was more money for me to pick up in Hong Kong. Bill was still at the Mandarin. He had $250,000 ready for me. Richard Shurman's son Steve was in the Peninsula Hotel. He was holding about $150,000. Bruce Aitken was holding about the same amount in his office in Edinburgh Towers. Steve had the full and detailed instructions for the scam, but Ernie, indiscreetly lapsing a bit into a worrying junkie-like slur, made it clear that with the money he was wishing to do two scams: two tons by sea from Bangkok and five tons by air from Karachi. Ernie might be a bit incoherent, but he was still capable of getting it on.

With no baggage, I checked into the Shangri-La Hotel on the waterfront in Tsim Tsa Shui East. April had done the business. The management were expecting me and had upgraded my room to a penthouse suite. The sights of Hong Kong harbour were spellbinding. I guess the *fenshui* was up to par.

The hotel had safe-deposit boxes for the use of clients. None was big enough to accommodate all the money being guarded by Hobbs in the Park Hotel, let alone that to come, but the largest would take about half. I rented it.

From a phone box I called Bill at the Mandarin and said I'd see him there late the next morning. I called Steve at the Peninsula and arranged to meet him in the lobby at midnight.

A young, blond-haired, Californian surfer type was waiting for me when I arrived. Next to him was a Panosonic videorecorder cardboard box.

'Hi, man. I guess you must be Howard. The money is in this box. This letter's for you. By the way, I think we're hot.'

'What do you mean, Steve?'

'The Customs searched me at Hong Kong airport. They found the money and asked a bunch of dumb questions. I just said the money was mine, all $150,000 of it. All mine. I've come to do some big spending. My dad said it was completely legal to bring money into here.'

'Money is legal enough here, but for sure the Hong Kong Customs will let the DEA know about it. And it's kind of dumb bringing videorecorders from the US to here. Did the Customs find this letter?'

'No. They didn't search my pockets. And I bought this videorecorder here this morning.'

'You left the money in the room unattended?'

'Yeah. I kinda hid it. And I put the "Do Not Disturb" notice on the door.'

'From where did you make the booking for this hotel, Steve?'

'From Los Angeles.'

'So we can assume that your telephone is now tapped, there's a bug in your room, and at least one of the guys watching us in this lobby is a DEA agent. Thanks, Steve.'

'Hey, I'm sorry, man. What else could I do?'

'Don't worry. It's not your fault. When you finish your drink, take the box back up to your room. Empty the money into a suitcase. Put the videorecorder back into its box. Stay in your room. Sometime tomorrow morning, a girl called Suzy Wong will come to your room.'

'Great!'

'What make is your suitcase, Steve?'

'It's a Louis Vuitton. It's real neat.'

'Suzy Wong will bring you a new one and take away yours with all the money. A few minutes after that, I'll call you from the lobby here. Then bring the videorecorder in its box, and give it to me. You won't see it again.'

'Hey, man, that cost me $400.'

'I'll give you $500 tomorrow morning.'

'Sounds good to me.'

Steve went back up to his room. There were now just three people in the lobby: an expensive hooker, an Indian, and a crew-cutted occidental, who to my mind was clearly a DEA agent. I stared at the heavily waxed floor. A huge cockroach ran out from under a seat.

'My goodness. Would you believe it? A cockroach in the Peninsula! This would never have happened a few years ago. We'll see more of this sort of thing when Hong Kong goes back to China. May I join you? I am Sam Tailor.'

I stood up and shook his hand. I had heard of this man. He was Hong Kong's best-known tailor. His clients included Dennis Thatcher and David Bowie.

We talked. Sam explained how his family had lived in Hong Kong for several generations. They were brought over

by the British. The Empire's divide-and-rule strategy had
not worked: Chinese wouldn't bust other Chinese, so
Indians were imported to police the unruly Hong Kong
natives. They had stayed on. Those who weren't police or
security guards tended to have thriving businesses. He was
worried about 1997. Communist China would not be too
kind to the Indians. He gave me his business card. I said I'd
visit him next day and order some clothes.

It was almost 2 a.m. I left the Peninsula. I didn't appear to
be followed, but I ducked through some alleyways just in
case, and I went to Bottoms Up.

Selena and April were both still on duty. We made
arrangements for Hobbs and Selena to meet tomorrow
afternoon at the Hong Kong Registry Office and for April
(using the name Suzy Wong) to pick up the money from
Steve at 11 a.m. and take it to her apartment in Tai Koo
Shing on Hong Kong Island.

After a few drinks, I called in the Park Hotel, explained the
arrangement to Hobbs, picked up everything of mine except
the huge suitcase of money, and returned to the Shangri-La.

I read the letter from Ernie. The instructions for Pakistan
were to get five tons of the finest commercial hashish and air-
freight it to John F. Kennedy Airport, New York. The
consignment must be labelled as 'telephone components',
the consignor's name must be KAA, the Japanese national
telephone company, and the consignee's name must be
AT&T, the huge American telephone company. The air
waybill must show the origin to be Tokyo.

The instructions for Thailand were to get two tons of the
finest commercial marijuana and send it by container sea-
freight to Long Beach, California. The consignment must be
labelled 'oil exploration gear' and addressed to 'Long Beach
Petroil'. Any sensible Indonesian consignor could be used.
The origin had to be Jakarta.

More money was coming, another $450,000. I had to
keep the Pakistani up-front costs down to $1.5 million, the

Thai up-front costs down to $500,000. I had to ensure that at the end of the day Ernie was due 60% of the gross returns. If I could do all this, then $250,000 of the $2,250,000 Ernie was now sending could be regarded as an advance against the scams' successes. Should the scams both fail, I should regard the $250,000 as my overdue coming-out-of-prison, thanks-for-not-snitching money.

If all went well, I would make a couple of million dollars. If it didn't, I still had $250,000. I felt rich. I was looking forward to a busy day.

Early the next morning, I caught the Star Ferry and went to the Wing On building to see Armando Chung. Drinkbridge Hong Kong Limited had been incorporated. Address, telephone, telex, and secretarial services could be provided by Armando's office staff. Suitable notepaper and business cards were immediately available for use. An account had been opened at Hong Kong & Shanghai Bank. I should present myself to them. After completing some formalities, I rented the biggest safe they had, and I took the Star Ferry back to Tsim Sha Tsui.

Just outside the Star Ferry is the best fresh fruit-juice bar in the world. Sipping a concoction of guava juice and yoghurt, I could see the entrance of the Peninsula Hotel. April emerged with a Louis Vuitton bag. She wasn't followed. I went into the lobby and telephoned Steve's room. He came down with the videorecorder and joined me for a quick cup of coffee.

Sam Tailor's establishment is in Burlington Arcade, about half a mile from the Peninsula. Carrying the videorecorder, I took a cab there, hoping and believing I was being followed. The shop was full of Europeans being measured up for clothes. Sam was at the back and singled me out for his special attention. I paid for several suits and shirts, and asked if I could leave the videorecorder there while I did some more shopping, I walked swiftly out of the arcade and down the steps of Tsim Sha Tsui underground station.

Jumping on and off trains, I took a circuitous route to
Central Station to see Bill at the Mandarin. If the DEA were
following the videorecorder box, they'd be completely
confused. If they were following me, I'd lost them.

Bill gave me a large red leather briefcase containing
$250,000. I took it by cab to the Shangri-La and emptied the
contents into my safe-deposit box. I rented a hotel
limousine, went to the Park Hotel, and in three journeys
took a million dollars to the Hong Kong & Shanghai Bank
and placed it in the safe I'd just rented. On the third return
journey, I called in to pick up the $150,000 from Bruce
Aitken in Edinburgh Towers and took it to the Shangri-La
safe-deposit before getting to the Park Hotel. I picked up
Hobbs and the remainder of the money, $250,000 from the
big suitcase. After leaving Hobbs with some generous
expenses and a description of Selena, I dropped him off at
the Hong Kong Registry Office and went back to the
Shangri-La. After locking the money securely away, I walked
to Cable and Wireless and called Malik. He'd come to Hong
Kong the next day. He would stay in the Miramar Hotel. I
rang Phil in Bangkok and told him I'd visit him there in
seven to ten days. I rang the LAPD number. Flash put me
through to Ernie, who wanted to send the remaining
$450,000 as a wire transfer to a bank account. It would be
sent from an impeccable source. I gave him the details of my
account in Crédit Suisse at the Far East Financial Centre in
Admiralty, Hong Kong. I walked back to the Shangri-La and
telexed Roy Webborn of the Welsh Water Authority saying
that the initial reaction to his proposal was favourable. Got
to keep the front going. I rang up April and told her to bring
round the Louis Vuitton bag. There was enough room in the
Shangri-La safe-deposit box for another $150,000. I rang up
Sam Tailor and asked him to please deliver the
videorecorder and clothes to the room I'd still kept on in my
name for Hobbs at the Park Hotel. I lay down on the bed,
and had a joint. Everything was under control.

I thought of Judy and the children. Now I could easily afford to fly them out here. I rang the Chelsea flat and asked if they wanted to come for a Far East holiday. They didn't have to think about it for too long. Judy got the tickets from Balendo, who was happy to put them all on my account. He was proving a good man. Maybe I'd even invest in Hong Kong International Travel Centre. Or better still, buy a partnership and become a travel agent. It would be a fantastic front. One would have an excuse for travelling anywhere.

April rang. She, Selena, and Hobbs were downstairs in the lobby. I went down. Hobbs and Selena were giggling. The actual marriage would take place in a month or so. April gave me the Louis Vuitton bag. I put it into the safe-deposit box.

'You look tired, Marks, or maybe just stoned.'

'Maybe both, April.'

'You need some gall-bladder blood.'

'What for?'

'Very good you drink snake's gall-bladder blood. Make you fuck all night, ahhhh! I'm joking, Marks, but it will wake you up.'

'I've had snake's blood before.'

'Maybe, Marks, but not from gall-bladder. *Gwailu* never take this.'

'Okay. Let's get some.'

At the corner of Jervois Street and Hillier Street on Hong Kong Island is a shop stuffed with bags, cages, and baskets of writhing snakes. The four of us walked in. Within seconds, April, Selena, and the snake-merchant were screaming in Cantonese at the tops of their voices. I thought they were about to attack each other, but it turned out they were arguing which snake would be most likely to wake up a *gwailu*. Three different snakes were pulled out of their baskets. The snake-merchant squeezed each hissing snake along its length until he reached the gall-bladder. Then he took a knife and surgically removed the gall-bladder. The three gall-bladderless snakes were tied up in a bag. The three gall-bladders were slit open, and thick, dark green blood oozed out into a waiting brandy glass. Hobbs had seen enough and left the shop. The snake-merchant then poured a large measure of expensive brandy over the green blood and shook the glass.

'Drink, *gwailu*.'

I drank. It tasted like cheap brandy. It cost 3,000 Hong Kong dollars.

The snake-merchant sent the bag of mutilated snakes to the snake restaurant next door. Hobbs steadfastly refused to go inside and eat snake soup. We went somewhere else. I had a plate of larks' tongues followed by a bowl of cockerels' testicles. We took a cab to some anonymous club in Wan Chai and got drunk. April and Selena left for Bottoms Up. Hobbs and I went to the Country Bar in Bar City.

'Jim, how would you like a three-week stag night in Bangkok?'

'When do I go? Is this for another marriage?'

'No. I want you to take a bag of money there. You can leave tomorrow. Book the ticket through Balendo in London; it looks better. Check into a Bangkok hotel that has safe-deposit facilities and have a good time until I get there. Don't spend too much.'

'What shall I do there, Howard?'

'It's up to you. Crawl the gutters. Get to know the place.'

Jim went back to the Park Hotel. The snakes' blood was keeping me awake. I walked for hours along the Kowloon waterfront. Large red signs blared Kung Hei Fat Choy. It would soon be the Chinese New Year, the Year of the Rat. A variety of red dawns battled victoriously against Hong Kong's neon chandelier, allowing skyscrapers to sprout on the surrounding hills. At Ocean Terminal, massive ocean liners dwarfed newspaper stands a few feet away. Weirdly shaped Chinese junks drifted noiselessly by, narrowly missing schools of clattering sampans. Groups of old men and women practised very early morning Tai Chi in concrete public gardens. Illegal street vendors with large, sheet-covered wheelbarrows were selling steaming, mouth-watering delicacies. Maybe Hong Kong would be a good place to live. I wondered how Judy would like it.

Inviting as the king-size bed was, there was no point my trying to sleep in it. My mind was too active. I had two breakfasts, watched some television, and read the newspapers before taking Jim the Louis Vuitton bag of money. He was very excited to be going to Bangkok. We travelled to the airport together. Balendo had arranged for Hobbs's ticket to be waiting for him at the Cathay Pacific desk. That guy was getting better and better.

Malik had checked into the Miramar. We met in his room. He foresaw no problem in arranging the five-ton air-freight export.

'D. H. Marks, this we can do, *inshallah*.'

'Can you change the origin to Tokyo?'

'Why not? PIA fly from Tokyo to Karachi and from Karachi to New York. We can put on in Karachi and adjust paperwork.'

'What about all the other information that has to go on the air waybill?'

'Whatever is on a typewriter, we can type on air waybill. In Pakistan, this happens in all businesses, not just our mother-business.'

'Can you make sure it's really smell-proof? I once lost a load in New York because of a sniffer dog.'

'I know. I know a great deal about your past. Raoul has talked to me. He is not your friend. He is not mine either. I know you have been to the Oxford University. I would like my son Yasser to go there. Maybe you can arrange? Do not worry, D. H. Marks. I have the smell-proof technique with grease and tin. Also, and this you will not believe, the Sind Narcotics Control dog handler is my good friend. Before we send shipment, we will bring him and his dogs to smell. If they don't smell, shipment is safe, *inshallah*.'

'Can you do it for $300 a kilo up-front and a return of 30% of the gross?'

'I will need a little more up-front. The price of everything is going up. Pakistan is not Third World any more.'

'Malik, you must know I don't bargain in the mother-business. I know what it costs you: nothing. You'll have responsibilities if things go wrong, and $1.5 million will easily cover them.'

'You are right. I will do it. When will you pay deposit?'

'Where do you want it?'

'Most of it, say $1 million, can come here to Hong Kong. My friend works here in BCCI bank. You can give to him. At the time the shipment leaves, I need to have the rest in cash in Karachi.'

I thought for a few seconds.

'I'll give you $500,000 here in Hong Kong before we leave. In about ten days, I'll come to Karachi to test the product and check how things are going. If everything's okay, I'll come back to Hong Kong and give your BCCI friend another $500,000. When the shipment is ready to leave, I'll give you $500,000 cash in Karachi.'

'This is good plan, D. H. Marks. But let me know if you or one of your people is flying into Karachi with large amount of money. I will arrange to make sure there is no bothering on arrival. Otherwise, Customs might confiscate. I will be very glad to see you in my country. You should stay in Sheraton Hotel.'

'Karachi has a Sheraton now? It used to have only the Intercontinental.'

'Intercontinental is now called Pearl. Pakistan has Sheraton, Hilton, and Holiday Inn. It is good place to invest. Zia has been good for the country. When you come I will show you many money-making possibilities.'

'I look forward to it, Malik. Shall we go somewhere to eat now?'

'I would prefer to stay in room and order takeaway from

Gaylord Pakistani restaurant. Please to join me, D. H. Marks.'

The lack of sleep was taking its toll. A telex was waiting for me back at the Shangri-La. It was from Balendo. Hobbs was in the Montien Hotel, Bangkok. Judy and the children were arriving in Hong Kong tomorrow. Exhausted and looking forward to their visit, I fell asleep.

The next morning, I explained to the hotel management that my wife and children were arriving. The penthouse suite was plenty big enough, and they were glad to arrange appropriate beds. I asked if they could arrange flowers, food, champagne, and little toys for the kids to be ready in the room. I rented a chauffeur-driven limousine and headed for the airport.

The Cathay Pacific flight arrived on time. Judy looked happy and tired. Amber and Francesca looked both exhausted and excited. The chauffeur issued ice-cold face-cloths from the limousine's glove-compartment fridge as he drove to the Shangri-La. The faces of Judy and the little girls broke into rapturous and wondrous smiles as they walked into the penthouse suite and beheld the Hong Kong harbour view and the spread that awaited them. Soon a jet-lagged sleep overcame them. I sat gazing at the faces I loved.

Malik and I went to the Hong Kong & Shanghai Bank, where I gave him $500,000 dollars. He took it to BCCI, then caught a plane back to Karachi. He had things to do. I telephoned Stephen Ng at Crédit Suisse, gave him the number of the Shangri-La, and told him to expect an overseas remittance. I went to the Park Hotel. The video-recorder box and clothes from Sam Tailor had arrived. I untidied the bed in the room and had a coffee in the lobby before going to Burlington Arcade to pay Sam.

Judy and the children were wide awake when I got back. We took an evening boat ride around Hong Kong harbour.

The following day we took a hydrofoil to Macao. After getting used to the sight of Chinese selling Dim Sum on the steps of a Portuguese cathedral, we took a bus into the

People's Republic of China. Mainland China had not long opened its doors, and the people seemed to be either tilling the soil or making and selling electronic goods. We were curiosities to each other.

We did another three days of sightseeing and shopping before I had a call from Stephen Ng.

'Mr Marks, we have received a remittance of $450,000 credited to your account. Your instructions, please.'

'Hold on to it until I need it.'

'Mr Marks, will you need to access the funds at extremely short notice?'

'Maybe. I don't know yet.'

'How about I place the money in a fiduciary time-deposit with bank-guaranteed minimum yield of 6%?'

'That's fine.'

I had no idea what he was talking about. I would need to study all this banking stuff.

There was no longer any reason to stay in Hong Kong. 'Who wants to come to Thailand?' I asked.

'I do,' cried Amber and Francesca in unison. 'I do. I want to go to Thailand.' Judy smiled. I called Balendo.

After stashing all the money in the Hong Kong & Shanghai Bank, checking out of both the Park and Shangri-La Hotels, and consigning the videorecorder, clothes, and other shopping to be air-freighted home to London, we flew Thai International Airlines, first-class, to Bangkok. Balendo had arranged a VIP suite at the Oriental Hotel, and one of the hotel's limousines took us there.

'*Sawabdee kap*. Welcome back, Khun Marks, and a special welcome to Thailand to your wife and your beautiful children. You have the VIP suite at the top of the new building. Fruit baskets, oysters on ice, and drinks have been prepared. Enjoy your stay.'

'I have to go out, love. Make some phone calls. See if I can get hold of Phil. I don't want to ring him from the hotel.'

'Howard, for God's sake, you've only just got here.'

'I came here to see Phil.'

'I thought you were bringing us here on holiday.'

'Well, that too. I won't be long.'

'I've heard that before. I know what it's like when you and Phil get together. I'll see you tomorrow.'

First I dropped in on Hobbs at the Montien Hotel.

'Howard, I can never thank you enough for sending me here. Bangkok is the closest to Heaven I ever want to be.'

'What do you like about it, Jim?'

'The clubs, the food, the people. Everyone is so happy here. I love it.'

'Is the money safe?'

'Oh yes. It's downstairs. I've hardly spent a penny. It's so cheap here. This is like a luxury hotel, and it's cheaper than a Paddington doss-house. I can't believe it.'

'Get to know any good places?'

'Well, not many that you'd be interested in, Howard, but I did find one that I know you'll want to visit. It's called the Superstar, just up the street here in Patpong, and is full of European and American dope dealers doing business, all very openly. I'm sure you'd know some of them.'

We walked down Patpong past the Superstar. *One Night in Bangkok* was blaring out. I couldn't resist the temptation to enter. Beauties from Chiang Mai and transvestites from round the corner were on the bar counters, shagging the customers' minds as the volume of Murray Head's hit reached a deafening pitch:

> One night in Bangkok and the world's your oyster
> The bars are temples but the pearls ain't free
> You'll find a god in every golden cloister
> And if you're lucky then the god's a she
> I can feel an angel sliding up to me.

'Ah, *fahlang*. You look so handsome. You like Superstar? How many times you been Bangkok?'

Several girls writhed over us and between us as we sat down at a table. Jim stared gleefully at the transvestites, and I stared at the Chiang Mai beauties. In the distance I saw Mickey Williams at a table with five young bikini-clad girls. His smile showed evidence of a permanent orgasm. I walked to his table.

'H, me old son. I had a feeling I'd run into you here. On my life I did. Sit down here with me lovely darlings.'

'Good to see you, Mick. I haven't thanked you properly for the loan of your flat in Palma. We had a great time. It looks like we'll move to Mallorca to live.'

'My pleasure, H. My pleasure. Missus all right, is she?'

'Yes, thanks. She and the kids are here with me.'

'It's none of my business, H, but if I had a wife and kids, I wouldn't bring them to Bangkok. I don't think they'd like massage parlours.' He looked across the room. 'Hey, H. There's that fucking nonce that was in Brixton with us on that table over there. What's his name? Hobbs, that's it. Hobbs. The dirty bastard.'

'He's with me, Mick.'

'What! What are you doing hanging around with a nonce, H? Ain't like you a bit.'

'I'm sure he's not a nonce, Mick. He's just a gay who prefers teenagers to geriatrics. He doesn't go after young kids. I mean, how old do you think that girl is, the one trying to give you a blowjob?'

'Yeah, but it's different here in Bangkok, H. You know that. It's a different culture. It's gotta be. And even if, like you say, he's not a nonce, he's just an iron, a poof, I wouldn't trust him an inch. If he can't keep his arse shut, how can he keep his trap shut? I don't like him seeing me with you. Who's he going to tell?'

'Mick, he's far less a danger than the two DEA guys sitting at the end of the bar. Besides that, you and I aren't doing any business together at the moment, are we?'

'You think they are Old Bill, those two? I'd been

wondering myself, as it goes. And I did want to talk a bit of business with you, H, as it happens. I got this geezer . . .'

'Let's go outside, Mick, and get a bite to eat.'

'Shall we take these little darlings?'

'No, you leave them, and I'll leave Hobbs.'

'I don't like the idea of him leering at them when we've gone, H. The dirty bastard.'

'He won't, Mick. I just told you he's gay.'

> One night in Bangkok makes a hard man humble
> Not much between despair and ecstasy
> One night in Bangkok and the tough guys tumble
> I can feel the devil walking next to me.

Mickey Williams and I walked outside.

'I'm sorry I didn't tell you this when I saw you last, H, but I was trying to get a little touch together on me own. I met this geezer in the slammer in Amsterdam. He got Schiphol together there. A mate of his works for a freight consolidation company actually in the bleeding airport. If we send him a box of gear, he can make it come up clean as a whistle in London, Holland, or Canada. It's a blinding coup, H, I'm telling you. Well, this same geezer, who's still in the slammer, had a connection out here for sending gear. He gave me his phone number and some kind of address, but no one seems to have heard of him. So if you know someone in Bangkok who can send us 500 kilos, and I know you do, H, you've got yourself a nice little trade. I got all the details with me here. I'll put £50,000 of me own money into it. Fifty-five, H. Half what we get through is yours, half mine. I got the money sitting in London. That's how much I know it'll work. I can't do no more, H.'

'Can I sell it once it gets through?'

'If it pops up in London or Canada, I'd want you to, H, but if he brings it out in Amsterdam, I said he could sell it.'

'We can do it, Mick. Give me the details.'

'Another thing, H. I need to change up some money. A few thousand quid. I don't want to do it at me hotel: they ripped me off once already. The banks are shut, and I'm a bit lairy of banks if I'm not robbing them.'

I flagged a *tuktuk*, and we both took it to the money-lending area of Bangkok's Chinatown, the largest Chinese settlement outside China. Sitting in the *tuktuk* made me think of Sompop. I would try to see him this Friday at the Erawan Buddha.

Mick and I walked down the narrow, shambolic streets. Doorways led to opium dens and businesses of all kinds. Noodle stalls cluttered the doorsteps. Although it was late, several dozen money-changers were still open selling local currency at prices far cheaper than the banks. They also operated as illegal bookmakers, taking bets for just about anything. We walked into one. Mick's eyes were darting in all directions. We asked how many baht they would give for English sterling. It was an excellent rate. Mick changed £3,000. We walked out.

'H, did you get a butcher's at that peter they got?'

'At what, Mick?' I was beginning to forget my cockney slang.

'The peter, H, the bleeding safe. They might as well stash their loot in a fucking jam jar. That bank or betting shop, whatever it is, got no security, no alarms, nothing. I blagged harder ones than that when I was a nipper. It's got to be worth going back there, H, one night after they shut. Like taking sweets from little kids.'

'Be careful, Mick. This city has strange ways.'

Phil was at home when I telephoned. We arranged to meet in the lobby of the Dusithani Hotel.

'Phil, can you send two tons of Thai by container to the West Coast?'

'Is the Pope a Catholic? Why do you ask? Of course I can.'

'Can you change the origin of the consignment and make it look like it came from Jakarta, Indonesia?'

'Naturally.'

'How do you do it?'

'Bangkok is not really much of an international seaport. It's too far up-river. A couple of local Thai shipping lines use it, but no foreign ones. Everything for the US transits through Singapore. Freight from Indonesia also transits through Singapore. We bung this Chinese freight agent in Singapore a bag of money, and he'll adjust the paperwork.'

'Will it be good-quality grass?'

'The best. The new crop has just been harvested. There's a sample in that envelope.'

'Can you make it smell-proof?'

'No problem there. We vacuum-pack and nitrogen-flush the lot.'

'Can you do it all on credit?'

'Say that again. I don't think I heard you right.'

'Can you do it all on credit?'

'No way. Those days are gone, Howard.'

'They haven't. I can still get credit in Pakistan, Phil. As much as I want.'

'Then send two tons of Pakistani hash to Manila. I've got a connection there who can re-route it to Australia, where I can get three times the money I can get in America.'

'Sure. I'll do that. Just as soon as you've sent the Thai.'

'It's not that I don't trust you, Howard, but I did learn from you, don't forget. Why don't you just pay for the Thai you want, and I'll pay for the Pakistani I want?'

'Okay. You want to do the Pakistani one first?'

'You must be joking. You started this.'

Phil clearly wasn't going to budge. He was a tight old sod. I knew he got the Thai grass on 100% credit. His only expenses would be transportation and giving the Singaporean freight agent enough money for a night's whoring in Patpong. But he would never admit it. I'd have to let him get something for nothing.

'Phil, I know what it costs here. You know I know. Forty

dollars a kilo is the absolute maximum. The rest of the expenses are cheaper than a night out in London. So $100,000 will cover the lot. If you don't want to give me that on credit, I'll pay you.'

'When?'

Phil went into a different gear when he thought he might receive some money.

'I'll pay you now, Phil.'

'What do you mean by now?'

'Soon. Whenever you want.'

'What do I get at the end? Credit is one thing, but it costs me loads just to keep my show on the road. There are all sorts of expenses. So many people depend on me to keep them in the luxury they've just started getting used to. If I let them down, I'm a dead man. I'm talking about paying off Thai army generals, police chiefs, and Bangkok gangsters, as well as the farmers in Khon Khaen. You know how many deals get busted or never make it. The Thais don't understand this. They want paying anyway.'

'I'll pay you 25% of the gross return. There is absolutely no chance of getting any more.'

'You aren't giving much away, Howard, that's for sure. But I can probably live with it. Tell you what. Give me $100,000 now. When the two tons is on its way from Singapore to the West Coast and I've given you the bill of lading and all the other paperwork, give me another $100,000.'

'Okay. A friend of mine from the nick, Jim Hobbs, is over here with the money. Meet him for breakfast at 10 tomorrow morning in the lobby of the Montien. By the way, I've got another proposition for you.'

'What's that?' asked Phil. 'How much is this one going to cost me?'

'The same. Nothing. How much to air-freight 100 kilos to Amsterdam?'

'Now, that really is seriously expensive these days. They're building a new airport at Don Muang, and security is really tight. I have to pay the cops, the army, the Customs, the freight agents, and the airline. Credit with those people is impossible.'

I knew full well Phil was lying. Credit was much easier to get for air-freight than for sea-freight because the whole process was so much quicker: hours instead of weeks. There was less time for things to go wrong. But that was Phil. In any event, this deal had come to me purely by chance. I didn't know how likely it was to succeed. I'd simply go for a 10% kickback and make some more money selling the grass in London, Amsterdam, or wherever Mickey's guy would clear it to.

'You must be slipping, Phil. But tell me how much.'

'I must get paid 50% of the gross when it's over. And that's something I can't be moved on. I'll need $100,000 upfront.'

'I don't bargain, Phil, as you know, but . . .'

'You do bargain; you just don't call it that.'

'Phil, there's no way I can give you more than about $75,000, £50,000 actually, upfront, and you'd have to settle for 40% of the gross.'

'When would I get the £50,000?'

'In about seven to ten days. It's sitting in London.'

'It's no good to me there, Howard. I need it here, or in Hong Kong.'

'I'll get it to Hong Kong.'

'Okay.'

I gave Phil the instructions for both scams. We talked about other matters. I told him about my progress in researching the tanker transport of water. He said he was financing research into making paper from rice husks and currently submitting the proposal to a joint Saudi/Thai business consortium headed by Sheikh Abdularaman A. Alraji, who, according to the *Guinness Book of Records*, was the richest man in the world. If the committee liked the proposal, the Saudis would build a rice-husk paper mill in

Thailand, and Phil would become legitimately rich. He offered to submit the Welsh water proposal for similar consideration if I could get it together immediately.

I liked the idea. I had all the documents with me in Bangkok. They were in my briefcase ready to impress any official who wanted to open it. With some concentrated effort, I could type up a feasibility report. I was familiar enough with the material. I'd get back early to the Oriental Hotel and make a start. It was, after all, a writer's hotel.

While Judy took the children to the Floating Market the next day, Hobbs gave Phil $100,000, and I set about writing the feasibility report for the richest man in the world. It was pretty much a re-write of the Welsh Water Authority's bumf coupled with some bits and pieces and pasted on to Drinkbridge Hong Kong Limited notepaper. The secretarial services at the Oriental Hotel made the report presentable. Two days later it was completed and officially submitted alongside Phil's rice-husk project.

It was Friday evening. I went to the Erawan Hotel to the site of the Erawan Buddha. The hotel is small and gracious and was once popular with foreign diplomats. It is said that many Thai labourers died during the course of its construction. A small Buddha was placed in the corner of the construction site, the right prayers were said, the deaths ceased, and good luck was bestowed upon the labourers. They made lots of money and became rich.

The Buddha is still there. It has become a shrine for those praying for upward mobility. Strangely shaped instruments blow sacred discords and traditional Thai dancers swirl erotically around the Buddha while the want-to-be-rich make and promise whatever sacrifices they can. Hawkers crowd around selling gold leaf to daub on the Buddha and caged birds to set free when making a wish.

Sompop was on his knees, burning joysticks and chanting. He saw me when he'd finished his prayers. He looked as if I'd answered them.

'You come back to Bangkok. You want *ganja*? I pray for money and good luck. I see you. I'm very happy man.'

'I'm leaving Bangkok tomorrow, Sompop. Here's some money for you. I'll see you in about a week.'

I had given him the baht equivalent of about $1,000, many months' wages. I left him on his knees, head buried in the pavement, hands trembling as they clutched the money.

Ten

MR DENNIS

Leaving Judy and the children in Bangkok, I took Air India to Bombay, then Pakistan International Airlines to Karachi. I checked into the Sheraton, spent hours looking for a phone box, failed, walked into the Pearl Hotel, and asked to use their hotel phone. I called Malik. He was on his way to the Sheraton.

Malik was in traditional Pakistani garb. With him was a similarly dressed but much younger man.

'D. H. Marks, welcome to Pakistan. This is my nephew Aftab. His job is to steal duty-free goods from airport and sell them in Bhoti bazaar. He is my business partner.'

'Welcome to Pakistan, D. H. Marks,' said Aftab.

'First, D. H. Marks, the mother-business. The product is ready for your inspection. It is safely in my control at a warehouse in Baluchistan. We can go there any time. Right this minute if you wish. We have a car outside at our disposal. Here is a small sample. Here also is PIA timetable. You will see that a few flights are possibilities. We will need to book space for this quite large consignment at least forty-eight hours in advance.'

I took hold of the soft, sticky slab of black hash and put my lighter flame to one of its corners. The flame jumped to the hash. That was always a good sign. Wisps of blue smoke accompanied my favourite aroma. I sucked at the smoke, the taste making me want to fill my lungs. The bridge of my nose throbbed. This hash was excellent, the best Pakistani I'd ever tried.

The dope supplies in neighbouring Afghanistan had almost dried up when the Russians took their tanks to Kabul in 1980. The invasion forced over five million Afghanis to flee from their country and become refugees in Pakistan. The Pakistani province bordering Afghanistan was the lawless North West Frontier Province (NWFP). The population both sides of the border is mainly made up of Pathan tribesmen. The NWFP countryside was officially and totally under the control of Pathan tribal chieftains. Pakistan's military and police had to abide by statutes not allowing them to stray off the main roads between towns, not even in pursuit of a murderer, kidnapper, or rapist. They could negotiate with the tribal representative. Nothing else.

The NWFP became the headquarters, strategy-planning centre, and battle-training ground of the *mujaheddin*, the freedom fighters who have no understanding of the concept of surrender. Either Russia would be defeated and leave Afghanistan or the *mujaheddin* would all die. There could be no compromise.

Arms and supplies, many sent from the governments of countries sympathetic to the *mujaheddin*'s struggle against the Communists, were amassed in settlements in NWFP. To no one's great surprise, much found its way to the bazaars in NWFP's main trading city of Peshawar at the foot of the Khyber Pass.

Traditionally, the area now known as NWFP had always been an ideal cannabis-growing region. The Himalayan heights and crystalline pure air enable the life-giving tropical sun to have almost direct contact with the plant, which responds by massaging itself with hashish, its home-made resin. Afghanistan, on the other side of the Himalayas, was equally ideal, and the holy city of Maza-al-sharif had become famed as the centre of the best hashish in the world. Some of the refugees to NWFP were experienced cannabis cultivators and harvesters. They needed money to live. The *mujaheddin* needed money. For centuries, the Afghan techniques of hashish production had remained within the country's borders. Now they had been established and expanded in Pakistan and produced limitless quantities of high-grade commercial hashish, known in the Western hemisphere as 'border hash'.

'You want to see whole consignment now, D. H. Marks?' asked Malik.

The jaunt to Baluchistan might have been a laugh but would have achieved nothing. If Malik was going to do a rip-off, he could do it just as well after I'd seen the load as before. I felt there was more to gain by displaying total trust.

'Malik, if you tell me you have five tons of this, I believe you. There is no need for me to test you.'

'As you wish. We will now bring consignment to Karachi for packaging and smell-proofing.'

'Do you know anything about paper-mill business, D. H. Marks? I am wanting to buy second-hand paper-mill machinery from closed-down factories in Great Britain. Paper-mill business will be really wonderful business here in Pakistan.'

'I'll have a look when I get back to London. Let me know exactly what you want. Do you need anything else from England?'

'Yes, information about good schools in Great Britain for my children.'

'I'd be glad to, Malik. I'm not staying here long. I need to get to Hong Kong. I'll give your BCCI man $500,000. I'll find out which date is preferable for air-freighting the consignment. A few days before the date, I'll come back here to Karachi from Hong Kong with $500,000 cash. You give me the air waybill. I'll give you the money.'

'All right. This is good. But don't forget to let me know which flight you are on. Oh, that reminds me, D. H. Marks. Phones in Pakistan are not safe to use. I have own operator, my cousin. When he is on duty, I know phone is not tapped. Otherwise, might be tapped. When you call, maybe he is not on duty. Do you have legitimate business with telex machine in London?'

'Yes, of course. You want me to communicate with you by telex in future?'

'I prefer. I have big travel agency here in central Karachi, next to American Express building. I will give you the telex number. Always put telex message in terms of legitimate business. And think carefully, D. H. Marks, about legitimate business, like paper-mill, here in Pakistan. We should have some legitimate business between us.'

'Malik, can your travel agency get PIA airline tickets cheaper than anyone else?'

'Of course. All Customs Officers and government peoples use my agency, Travel International. My cousin is in very senior position in PIA. It is under-counter price, not official. But PIA does not fly to Hong Kong. I will get you complimentary first-class return ticket to Hong Kong on Lufthansa. This is only airline that flies directly between Karachi and Hong Kong.'

'Thank you very much, Malik. The reason I ask, though, is that I have a Chinese friend who runs a travel agency in London. Most of his business is with people travelling to the Far East. As PIA fly from Pakistan to both England and China, I thought maybe he could provide a cheaper service from London to Peking than his competitors do by routing passengers through here. I don't know. It was just a passing thought.'

'I think it is excellent idea, D. H. Marks. Chinese peoples are good peoples. Relations between Pakistan and China are

first-class. We are very best of neighbours. Did you know
that PIA was first-ever foreign airline to go to Communist
China? It is no secret that China is testing our atomic
bombs. To promote travel to China via Pakistan should be
easy matter. I will talk to my family about this.'

Three days later, I was back in Hong Kong, staying at the
Shangri-La. From Cable and Wireless, I telephoned Ernie
through Flash at LAPD and reported the position. He said
to send the consignment from Karachi as soon as possible.
Any day was okay.

I booked the next day's Lufthansa flight to Karachi. From
a public telex service I sent a telex to Malik: 'Arriving
tomorrow with German company – UK paper-mill representative.' I took $500,000 in cash from the Hong Kong &
Shanghai Bank to Malik's friend in BCCI and then another
$500,000 to my room in the Shangri-La. It was a large
amount to hide in baggage when flying. There was no real
worry. I would simply check it in at Hong Kong airport,
and Malik was ensuring I wouldn't get searched or embarrassed on arrival at Karachi airport. Nevertheless, the plane
could be diverted from Karachi for some reason, and I might
find myself somewhere with some explaining to do. I ought
to make some effort to conceal it.

I phoned April and asked her to buy three large and
expensive matching suitcases, books on education and schools
in England, and books on the paper industry, and arrange for
them to be delivered to the Shangri-La Hotel. I rang up Sam
Tailor, told him I was delighted with the clothes, said I was
on my way back to London, and offered to promote his
business as best I could through my connections in London.
Did he have any promotional material I could take back?
Sam sent over a cardboard box full of cloth samples,
brochures, patterns, and sales literature. I rang up April
again and asked her to get some lengths of different materials
sent round to the hotel.

Wrapping bundles of money in a selection of voiles and

silks, I arranged each suitcase so that the top layer, occasionally allowing glimpses of clothing and textile samples, was crammed with innocuous paperwork and sales promotional trivia. I stayed in.

Twenty-four hours later I was standing next to the carousel in Karachi arrivals hall. I rarely did this. When travelling alone, I would almost invariably take just hand luggage. I didn't like checking-in suitcases. I could stand neither the wait nor the weight. The three matching suit-cases came up first. The advantages of first-class travel: one's luggage was susceptible to no ridiculous weight restrictions and was the first to get unloaded. I'd already grabbed a porter and given him a handful of Pakistani rupees. We trundled over to Customs. There is no green channel in Karachi airport.

'Why are you visiting my country? Is it business, pleasure, or official?'

'Business.'

'May I see your passport?'

I expected this question. How else would he know not to search me? Malik would have had to give him my name. I gave the Customs Officer my passport.

'I see you visited my country a few days ago. What is your business, sir?'

This question was a surprise. Malik had assured me there would be no confrontation of this kind.

'I have a few business interests. This visit to your country concerns the paper-mill business.'

'Who will you be seeing in this country?'

'Prospective purchasers of second-hand paper-mill machinery. I represent a British firm who dismantle closed-down paper-mills and sell the equipment.'

'Do you have a business name-card, sir?'

'Yes, I do.'

To say no would have guaranteed a search. My wallet contained three separate business name-cards: I was either a

manager of West End Secretarial Services, London; a
company director of Drinkbridge Hong Kong Limited, who
from other documentation could be deduced to be a bulk
carrier of water; or a researcher for Drinkbridge (UK)
Limited, a wine importation company. None was an obvious
choice for a would-be second-hand paper-mill machinery
salesman. I picked out one at random.

'According to this, you are in alcohol business. Do you
know alcohol is illegal in Pakistan? What is this to do with
paper-mill business? Please open this suitcase, sir.'

Bloody Malik! Why was he letting me go through all this?
I opened the suitcase the Customs official was touching. A
few books on English public schools tumbled out.

'Are you in book-selling business, too? Please, sir, open
this suitcase also.'

It was getting difficult.

'Drinkbridge has been a British family company for
generations. The company has several businesses, including
bulk haulage, real estate, and heavy plant machinery. We
have wine distribution networks throughout the world. A
large percentage of our overseas profits is reinvested in the
country concerned and channelled into education and
cultural promotion. We have plans to finance both paper-
mills and schools in Pakistan.'

I opened the second case. Revealed was a variety of literature related to paper manufacturing.

'Please pass, Mr Marks. Welcome to Pakistan.'

That was close. And he still had my business card. Where
was Malik?

The porter wheeled my suitcases outside. Still no sign of
Malik or his sidekick, Aftab. Malik had not only failed to
protect me against a possible bust, he was also leaving me
stranded with $500,000 not knowing where to go.

The airport is one of the few places in Pakistan to have a
public telephone box. I called Malik's number. Aftab
answered.

'D. H. Marks, how are you? Uncle is not here at the moment. He has been in Baluchistan for a couple of days. He is expected back at any moment. When are you coming to Pakistan?'

'I'm already here. Didn't you get my telex yesterday?'

'No. I have been at the telex machine since Uncle left. There has been nothing from you.'

'I sent a telex saying I'd be arriving today with the German company. You didn't get it? That's impossible. I got an answerback from your telex.'

'No, I did get that telex, but how am I to know that it's from you? It was not signed D. H. Marks; it was from Hong Kong, not London; and we are not doing business with any German company.'

'Aftab, the German company meant Lufthansa, the airline on which I was arriving. Never mind. I'll take a cab to the Sheraton. Tell Uncle Malik to come and see me when he gets back.'

I put the phone down.

'Mr Marks. Mr Marks.'

Someone in uniform was running towards me. I thought I was going to be grabbed and properly searched. I wondered about Pakistani prisons.

'Mr Marks, I am the steward of the Lufthansa aircraft cleaning crew. You left your duty-free perfume on the plane. Here it is.'

I climbed into the Sheraton courtesy bus. It felt safer than a taxi.

'D. H. Marks, I am so sorry. Please believe me. I am so sorry. I am so cross with that stupid Aftab for not under-standing simple telex. What is matter with him, I don't know. I assure you it won't happen again, *inshallah*.'

'I'm not going to try it again, Malik. But don't worry. I'm safe and the money's safe. The only bad thing is that the Customs Officer obviously suspected me and he has my business card.'

We were in my room at the Karachi Sheraton. Malik had

come over to the hotel as soon as he had arrived in Karachi
and heard about the cock-up.

'Is everything okay with the consignment?'

'Of course, D. H. Marks. It is now all in my warehouse in
the city. Packaging and smell-proofing is now beginning. It
will not take long. By tomorrow we are finished. Do you
have date to send?'

'Yes. As soon as possible. Any day is fine with us.
$500,000 has been given to your man in BCCI.'

'I know, D. H. Marks. I have been given notification.'

'And, Malik, I'm sure you know I also have $500,000 cash
with me.'

'I do not want this until you have seen consignment and
paperwork. I am sure we can send on Monday, February
6th, in three days' time. The day after tomorrow, please
come to make your inspection. Please, D. H. Marks, stay in
this hotel room until then. Karachi is dangerous place.
Unforeseen may happen. We must always bear in mind
unforeseen. American and European Embassies all have
drug investigators on their staff. They wander around city
trying to work things out.'

'Are there any DEA agents based here, Malik?'

'Only one. Harlan Lee Bowe.'

I remembered his name from the prosecution papers
relating to the 1973 rock-group scam.

'Any British Customs Officers?'

'Again, only one. Michael John Stephenson.'

Stephenson! I'd badly embarrassed him at my Old Bailey
trial. God, he'd love to bust me out here.

'I'll stay in, Malik. I'll watch TV and read. Just come and
get me for the inspection. I'll be all right. Here's some books
on English schools and universities for you.'

'Here is small piece of your hashish for you, D. H. Marks.
I know you would like to smoke. I, too, smoke sometimes.'

I read about the paper industry. It wasn't very exciting,
but I filled my head with the jargon. There was a video

channel on the hotel television. It showed Western films with Urdu subtitles. Any kissing or exposure of the female body had been brutally censored. For good measure, a few minutes each side of any offending footage had also been removed, and it was impossible to work out what was going on. I smoked my way through the piece of hashish Malik had left. That made following the plot a lot easier.

After an uneventful forty-eight hours, Malik and Aftab turned up at my room. Their car was outside. Aftab carried my suitcase of money, and we drove off into Karachi's slums. We drove to a large stone warehouse, and the double doors were opened by two grim-faced guards. Inside was a central area circled by several separate rooms. This was a hive of quiet activity. About twenty people, each looking like a cross between Yasser Arafat and Genghis Khan, were carting around large metal containers, buckets of grease, cans of petrol, and welding equipment. A few just sat and stared. In the corner were four large piles of cardboard boxes. Each box had been professionally banded and stencilled with AT&T's address in New York. Each had a label, in both Japanese and English, proclaiming its origin to be Tokyo. Malik had done an excellent job. He went through the process with me.

Each 500-gram rectangular slab of hashish was put into a sealed plastic bag. The plastic bags were taken to a separate room, washed with petrol, and left for several hours. A new set of workers whose hands had not touched hashish took the plastic bags into another room and placed them into metal tins. Lids were welded on to the tins, which were taken to another room and washed with petrol. Waiting in yet another room were slightly larger tins containing a few inches of warm fat. The smaller sealed tins were put into the larger tins and more fat poured in to the brim. The larger tin was welded tight and placed into the cardboard box. The consignment was now ready to take to the airport storage, where its smellproofness would be given the final test by Malik's cop with the dogs.

'D. H. Marks, here is your copy of the air waybill.'

'This is fantastic, Malik. Thank you.'

'It was my duty.'

Back at the Sheraton, I memorised the air waybill number and destroyed the air waybill. Malik had given me a first-class ticket for a Swissair flight to Zurich. After the PIA flight carrying our hash to New York, it was the next flight to leave Karachi for Europe. Once Malik telephoned me with the news that our consignment had left, I would check out and go to the airport. I would telephone Ernie via LAPD from Zurich. Once I knew the consignment was in Ernie's hands, I would telex Malik stating that good second-hand paper-mill equipment was available.

Karachi and Zurich airports provided no worrying incidents. At the hotel information desk I booked a room at the Carlton-Elite hotel just off Bahnhofstrasse. From the PTT office in the arrivals hall, I telephoned Ernie and gave him the air waybill number and the phone number of the Carlton-Elite. I telephoned Phil at Bangkok. He told me that Judy and the children had just left him for London, and that the sea-freight would take about a month to organise.

I checked into the hotel. Again there was a video channel, this time without censorship. I watched some films. I walked around the streets of Zurich, calling back at the hotel at least every two hours. I was restless and impatient for news of whether or not the five-ton Pakistani air-freight scam had worked. I waited and waited for Ernie's call. Finally, he rang.

'Get the champagne out. We've got it. It's all ours.'

I lay on the bed and went to sleep. I felt very relaxed. The scam had worked. I had made a lot of money.

Or so I thought.

I flew back to London late the next day after telexing Malik the good news. Judy had been back a night.

'Well, we're rich again, love,' I said.

'I think there's been a problem, Howard. Ernie called. He didn't sound too good.'

I went out to the telephone box in Fulham Road and called LAPD.

'That you, buddy?' It was Flash.

'Yeah, Flash. Can I talk to our friend?'

'Rather you than me, buddy. Putting you through right now.'

Ernie sounded as if he was dead. His voice was an almost inaudible whisper.

'It didn't make it.'

'What do you mean! You told me you got it. I've told everyone it's got through.'

'Well, it didn't. Tom said it could never have been sent.'

'This was Tom's thing, Ernie?'

'Well, it was Carl's connection, really.'

'Who is Carl?'

'Tom's boss.'

'I thought you were Tom's boss, Ernie.'

'Yeah, me too. I'm kinda tired. Here's Carl.'

A cold Germanic voice came down the line.

'Howard, you've never met me, but I did you one hell of a favour when you were in prison in London. I got you your freedom. You owe me.'

'Thank you, Carl. You got paid, I presume.'

'That's irrelevant. Howard, did you see this put on the plane yourself? Did you see the plane being loaded?'

'No. Did you see it being unloaded?'

'That's irrelevant. My people are 100%. Your guy in Pakistan owes us $1,500,000. And we've had some expenses. Give me the guy's name and address. I'll get the money back.'

'Carl, put Ernie back on.'

'He's asleep.'

'I'll call later.'

What the hell could I tell Malik? There was no doubt in my mind that whatever had gone wrong was not Malik's fault. The load had been ripped off in New York. Either Carl was ripping it off, or he had been ripped off by his 100% people.

I had to let Malik know immediately. The last thing I wanted to do was talk to him, but the paper-mill jargon wouldn't convey this news by telex. I thought of Aftab quizzically staring at a telex message stating 'second-hand equipment disappeared'. I would have to telephone. This was an emergency.

'Malik, give me a good time to call you back. I have to talk to you.'

'Now is good time.'

'The consignment has been lost.'

'So be it. These matters are in the hands of Allah. We can only do our best.'

'The Americans say you never sent it.'

'D. H. Marks, I do not care what American pigs say. If you think there is monkey business on my side, make your own investigation. If you conclude I am at fault, I will pay you back money and give you gun with bullet to shoot me. You are still my guest here in Pakistan whenever you want.'

Telling Malik the bad news had turned out to be a lot easier than I had thought.

Ernie rang. He sounded slightly stronger. I called him back from a cardphone box.

'You know what you do when you fall off your bike?'

'No, I've never ridden one,' I answered.

'You get right back on it. Let's go with Malik again.'

'You don't think he ripped you off?'

'I'm pretty sure he didn't. I can't figure out whether Tom and Carl did or not, but they won't be involved with this one. This one involves Bill, you know, the guy you met in the Mandarin.'

Ernie explained that his next scam would be a simple one. The instructions and money for execution of the scam would be brought personally by Bill to Karachi in a month's time, provided Malik could ensure he wouldn't be stopped on entry.

There were affairs to attend to in England. I met Mickey Williams. He gave me £50,000. I kept it. I needed cash in London. I'd pay Phil what he needed for the Dutch air-freight scam out of my own money in Hong Kong. John Denbigh, Jarvis, and the mad Major Pocock were keeping Drinkbridge's wine business flourishing, and West End Secretarial Services was attracting more and more clients. I laundered chunks of cash through each of the businesses to bring them up to scratch and paid professional researchers to build up a library of information on paper-mills, second-hand equipment, Pakistan, water, and tankers.

I went to see Balendo and Orca at Hong Kong International Travel Centre and paid them the several thousand pounds I owed. I told them about the availability of cheap PIA tickets and support, generally, in Pakistan. I offered to promote their travel agency as much as possible in my travels and look for deals such as this one with PIA. I would try to get as many people as possible to book through them. Balendo said he would like to make me Hong Kong International's official Far East representative and give me commission for any airline ticket sales I put his way. I could get as many tickets as I wanted on credit for me or anyone I nominated. He would print me an appropriate business name-card. I had the front I wanted.

David Leigh had almost finished writing the book about me. I read what he'd written. It was obvious he was running out of steam as well as out of time and space. The first thirty years of my life had been accorded far too much detail, and patently faked dialogues jarred and annoyed me. The last, and what I thought the most interesting, part of my life was getting hurriedly skimmed over. I wanted the title to be

Thank You for Smoking. David wouldn't go for it. It would be called *High Time*.

Partly to promote the book and partly because I fancied the publicity anyway, I gave my first-ever press interview. It was conducted by my old Oxford friend David Jenkins and formed the basis of a piece he wrote about me in the March 1984 issue of *Tatler*. David and I, both equally devoted to Welsh rugby, the Rolling Stones, and getting totally out of it on good hashish, had enjoyed each other's company on many occasions. The article portrayed me as a nice, wicked stoner with brains and bottle. It mentioned my intentions to export Welsh water by the tanker-load and the Inland Revenue's current assessment of my tax debt to them, £1,500,000.

Although Stanley Rosenthal was skilfully keeping the Inland Revenue at bay, the Treasury's debt collectors were still convinced that I was far from skint and had loads of money stashed away. They were obviously prepared to come down from demanding £1,500,000 but were certainly not going to settle for just a cut of the £30,000 I'd managed to screw out of Her Majesty's Customs and Excise. In the end they accepted that I hadn't made any money smuggling dope and settled for a final payment of a further £40,000, payable by the end of the year. I would not be able to pay them with cash or hash. I would have to mortgage the Chelsea flat.

March saw me back in Hong Kong attending Hobbs's wedding with Selena. I was the best man. One of Hobbs's friends was ready to marry April. Hobbs went back to Bangkok for his honeymoon. His wife spent hers on the game in Bottoms Up.

Phil arrived with the paperwork for the sea-freight scam to Long Beach. The container had left Singapore. Withdrawing what was needed from Crédit Suisse and the Hong Kong & Shanghai Bank, I gave him the promised $100,000 and a further $75,000 for Mickey's air-freight scam. This would leave in a week. I would come to Bangkok to pick up the air waybill.

Bill would be in Karachi in two days. I had to get there before him.

There were the inevitable post-mortems on the missing five-ton PIA load when I arrived in Karachi from Hong Kong, but Malik remained understanding. I gave him lists of second-hand paper-mill equipment that was available for sale in Britain. I gave him Bill's flight particulars. Malik would arrange a trouble-free arrival.

In a Sheraton chauffeur-driven car, I went to the airport to meet Bill.

'I gotta hand it to you, buddy. You got this place straightened out. I was the only guy Customs didn't tear apart. Now listen to this. In this bag is . . .'

'Wait till we're alone, Bill,' I whispered.

'You mean this rag-head understands English?'

'Most Pakistanis do, Bill.'

'That's a new one. I thought they spoke some kinda Indian. I guess we're going to the Sheraton.'

'I'm booked in there, Bill, so perhaps you'd prefer to stay at the Hilton.'

'No, I can only stay in the Sheraton while I'm here doing the kind of work I'm doing. I'll explain later.'

At his room in the Sheraton, Bill took out a bottle of smuggled Jack Daniels. He continued what he was saying in the car.

'In this bag is $300,000. How much dope will that buy me?'

'It depends what you want done with it, Bill – sent by sea-freight, put in suitcases, whatever.'

'I don't want anyone to send it out. I'm sending it out via the United States Embassy in Islamabad. This is US Government business.'

'You mean you just want a pile of dope? You'll take it over from there on?'

'Well, I'll need a bit of help because I won't actually be here to do everything. But I'll set the whole deal up.'

'What exactly will you want done, Bill?'

'The dope has to be put into specially constructed wooden crates. I have the dimensions here. Then the crates have to be taken to the American President Line in Karachi docks. The United States Government will then ship the whole works to the United States naval base in Alameda, California. The crates have to be delivered to the American President Line by you personally. We can't let these dope-dealing rag-heads know what's going on.'

'Okay.'

'Howard, you know I'm a CIA agent, right?'

'The possibility had occurred to me.'

'The US Government has a number of secret bases, spy networks, and equipment scattered throughout Pakistan. Occasionally, we have to send equipment back in such a way that no one knows what the fuck we are doing. I have clearance to send spy-helicopter parts back from here by ship on the American President Line. I'm given a lot of room to manoeuvre. No one can open this in Alameda except me. I cheat a bit. Like now I'm going to send some dope. I have friends in Washington who are sympathetic to whichever of these rag-heads over here are anti-Communist. They ain't gonna mind if I do a dope deal and get the rag-heads some money. The CIA own the American President Line. Once the dope is on there, it's mine.'

'So I drop a couple of wooden crates at the American President Line, let you know, and you take it from there.'

'Well, kinda, but I won't be here on the spot. Here's what you do. Even though everyone calls you Howard, your first name is Dennis, right?'

'Yes.'

'What I've noticed with these rag-heads is they use their last name like we use our first. So for security's sake, when you ring up the US Embassy in Islamabad, say you're Mr Dennis from Special Missions.'

'I've got to ring up the US Embassy?'

'Sure. Call them from here. The CIA owns the Sheraton. That's why I stay here. The Embassy will be expecting your call. Once you've packed the dope, call them. Tell them you have Fred Hilliard's consignment ready and ask what date they want it at American President Line. Take it there on the date they tell you to. That's it. So how much dope can you get for $300,000?'

'There are going to be other costs like transportation within Karachi and packaging. These guys have to be paid good money when they handle dope in this town. I'll let you know tomorrow. Are you Fred Hilliard?'

'No, he's my buddy in Washington. He sorts things out in the naval station in Alameda. He's done this kinda shit lots of times before.'

'Did Ernie tell you who's getting what out of this?'

'You get 15%, Howard, and Malik gets 25%. We pay all upfront costs out of that $300,000. Take this money to your room.'

'This is easy job, D. H. Marks. We will do, *inshallah*. But what is this spy plane bullshit? These Americans are crazy peoples.'

'How much can you send for this money, Malik?' I asked.

'*Inshallah*, I will send two thousand kilos. Give me specifications of crates. We will have whole thing ready in few days.'

'Okay. I have to make a quick trip to Bangkok in the meantime.'

'I will get you first-class return ticket on Thai International Airlines.'

Leaving Bill in Karachi, I went to Bangkok to pick up the air waybill for the load to Mickey Williams's friends in Holland. Mickey needed the whole document, not just its number. I gave it to Hobbs to take back to London and give to Mickey. I wondered how he'd react to picking up such a vital piece of information from a so-called nonce.

Back in Karachi, Bill had suddenly left without explanation. Malik had packed two thousand kilos of the same good Pakistani hash into the weirdly shaped crates. A Mazda pick-up truck had been purchased. The crates were sitting on the truck. It was ready to go.

I called the United States Embassy in Islamabad. They were not expecting a call from Mr Dennis of Special Missions. They had not heard of Fred Hilliard. They had no idea what I was talking about. I tried again the next day with the same result.

I was stuck. Ernie and I never called each other if I was in places like Karachi or Bangkok. It was a golden rule. I had to get out of town.

Instructing Malik to hold everything until I got back, I took the next flight out. It was Alitalia, and it went to Rome. I called Ernie. He had no idea what had happened to Bill. He would try to find out. There was no answer from Mickey Williams's number. I rang some other numbers. Judy and the children were in Mallorca house-hunting. I caught an Iberia flight from Rome to Palma.

Judy had found a cheap, beautiful old house in La Vileta, a village almost swallowed up by Palma. It needed a lot of attention, but we decided to buy it. In the meantime, Judy had rented a small furnished flat in the Bonanova area of Palma. There was no phone. One would be installed soon. I called Mickey Williams.

'Sweet as a nut, H, me old son. We got it all. In a couple of days you can have it to sell in London.'

At long last, a drug scam had actually worked!

I flew Air Europe to Gatwick and met Mickey Williams at the Warwick Castle in Maida Vale.

'Half of it is in the car outside, H. Here's the keys. The car's down to no one. If you get pulled, it's on you. When you've done with the car, park it back near where it is now. Give me a call when you've got my money, and I'll give you the other half of the gear.'

I called Jarvis. He came round and took the car away.

I telephoned Phil in Bangkok and gave him the good news.

Two days later Jarvis brought the money from the sales of the Thai grass. I gave most of it to Mickey to pay him off and took delivery from him of the rest of the Thai.

I telephoned Ernie. Bill was back in Karachi. Everything had been sorted out. I was to go back there immediately.

I had gone through passport control at Heathrow's Terminal 3 and was about to enter the pre-boarding room for PIA's flight to Karachi when I was stopped by a plain-clothes policeman.

'We're just having a word with people going out East, sir. Is Karachi your destination or somewhere else in Pakistan?'

'I'm meeting someone in Karachi.'

'A business meeting, sir?'

'Yes.'

'May I ask what is your business, sir?'

'I sell water.'

'Water?'

'Yes, water. Welsh water, actually.'

'Big demand for that in Pakistan, is there, sir?'

'Not that I'm aware of. But there's a demand for it in nearby Saudi Arabia, and I am meeting Sheikh Abdularaman A. Alraji in the Karachi Sheraton. The Sheikh has several businesses in Pakistan. I usually meet him there.'

'May I see your passport, sir? Mr Marks, I see you have visited Karachi quite a few times in recent weeks. Bangkok, too. The Sheikh likes to meet you there as well?'

'The company I work for is based in Hong Kong. Flights from Hong Kong to Karachi usually transit through Bangkok. I often take advantage of the opportunity to stay a couple of days in Thailand.'

'Thank you, Mr Marks. Enjoy your flight. Sell plenty of water.'

I didn't know it at the time, but I had been recognised and questioned by one of Her Majesty's Customs and Excise Investigative Branch Officers. He got on to their man in Pakistan, Michael Stephenson. Stephenson told Harlan Lee Bowe, the DEA's man in Pakistan, that a big-time British dope smuggler was about to arrive in Karachi. Bowe remembered my name from the 1973 rock-group scam. Unknown to me, they were watching me arrive at Karachi airport. Stephenson wanted my blood. Bowe didn't mind helping him.

I checked into the Karachi Sheraton. Bill had disappeared again. I called up the US Embassy in Islamabad.

'Good morning. This is Mr Dennis from Special Missions,' I said, convincingly.

'Good day, Mr Dennis. We've been told to expect your call. I'll put you through to the department concerned.'

Good. Bill had got things together.

A gravelly voice came on the line.

'Mr Dennis, we are still in the process of paperwork preparation. I don't have to tell you it's a delicate matter. Would you please call us on a weekly basis until we are ready?'

'Sure.'

The money in London from the sales of the Thai grass was beckoning me. I might as well head right on back. Malik gave me a small grey suitcase full of information about paper production in Pakistan and a first-class Pan American Airlines ticket to London. On the plane, I sat next to Elizabeth Taylor. We talked about Wales. She got off at Frankfurt.

My suitcase did not show up on the carousel at Heathrow. Pan Am personnel apologised and said they would deliver it to my address as soon as they found it. Although ignorant of Bowe and Stephenson's surveillance at Karachi, I now knew

I was under investigation. The questioning on departure coupled with the missing suitcase on arrival could mean nothing else. First-class passengers' suitcases do not disappear on direct flights. There was nothing embarrassing in the suitcase, just paper-mill bullshit, but still, the enemy was definitely on to me. I'd have to be careful.

If a scam works, it is rational to do a repeat. Mickey Williams, Phil, and I repeated the Bangkok to Amsterdam air-freight scam and carried on doing so until Mickey's contact in Amsterdam figured he didn't need us any more. He'd either made enough or was getting dope air-freighted to him cheaper from someone else. Serious money poured into my European coffers. During the repeats, I flew a couple of times to Bangkok and Hong Kong to take care of air waybills and money transactions. Hobbs had found a few more husbands. April and Selena had found a few more wives. Pocket money flowed into my Hong Kong coffers.

The sea-freight load from Bangkok to Long Beach made it. Hefty wire transfers arrived at my account in Crédit Suisse, Hong Kong. Some of Ernie's Californian couriers brought cash to give to me in Switzerland and Hong Kong. I opened up a bank account and safe-deposit box in Geneva. Unfortunately, the sea-freight scam could not be repeated. One of the guys in Long Beach had got busted doing another load.

Once a week I telephoned the US Embassy in Islamabad. Finally, the Embassy official said that the consignment should be delivered to Karachi docks to the offices of Forbes, Forbes & Campbell, the freight agents for the American President Line, on Sunday, June 10th.

I arrived in Karachi on June 6th. I would have to drive the Mazda truck about two miles from Malik's city warehouse to the docks. Malik would lead the way in his car but not stop at Forbes, Forbes & Campbell. He'd go straight back to the warehouse. Bill wouldn't approve of Malik's knowing about the American President Line, but I certainly had no reason to distrust Malik. After the truck was unloaded, I would park it somewhere near the docks. I did the journey a few times in Malik's car.

Driving in Karachi is not easy. Most of the streets look like livened-up junkyards. Cars resemble large-scale Meccano models but function much worse. Trucks are decorated with bizarre multi-coloured portraits and landscapes. Camels commonly head mile-long traffic jams. Hand carts, mechanised rickshaw-type vehicles, scooters, motorbikes, and pushbikes weave insanely through the jams. Pedestrians babble and throng around the almost stationary vehicles. Beggars without legs push themselves from car to car on low trolleys. The only highway code is to get to the front as quickly as possible by whatever means are available. Accidents are sorted out on the spot by either a fight or a cash payment. A Westerner once got lynched for running over a Pakistani schoolgirl. I'd be glad when this bit was over.

I called the US Embassy on the morning of June 10th to ensure there was no change to the plan. There was. Delivery had to be postponed until June 22nd.

My temporary passport had to be handed in to the Passport Office in London by June 15th and exchanged for a new one. I had to leave Karachi almost immediately to have any chance of being back in time.

I was back in London within twenty-four hours. The Passport Office had decided that I was now worthy of being issued a full ten-year passport. It would take three weeks. Jarvis agreed to go to Pakistan and be Mr Dennis in my stead. He was back a week later and explained that when he took the Mazda truck to the American President Line, he was told that they knew nothing about it. No booking had been made. Jarvis felt he had no choice but to leave the Mazda and crates outside the office and leave the keys with the freight agent, telling him the US Embassy would soon be in touch. Jarvis, as Mr Dennis, then phoned the US Embassy explaining the position. They promised to get on to it. Malik had seen Jarvis just before he left for London and agreed he had done the right thing.

I reported to Ernie through LAPD. He groaned.

The brand-new Mazda truck, with its precious cargo of hashish masquerading as illicit spying equipment, sat outside the offices of Forbes, Forbes & Campbell for three whole months. According to Malik, it became a well-known landmark in Karachi, the strange-shaped crates attracting the curiosity of visitors to the port. Then suddenly, without warning, the truck and boxes disappeared. Ernie called. The load was on its way to Alameda. We should be drinking champagne within a few weeks.

The pace slowed right down for a while. Judy and I walked around our new, but far from habitable, house in Spain.

In the fifteenth century, a little Mallorquian settlement named Es Vinyet was famous for its density of vines. A plague destroyed them, and Es Vinyet disappeared for a few hundred years until it was renamed and repopulated by a few farmers at the beginning of the last century. Its new name was La Vileta. Because of the impossibility of building any closer to Palma's city walls, La Vileta attracted Mallorquians who were seeking jobs in the city. It changed from a rural area to a dormitory for Palma's carpenters and stonemasons. These craftsmen utilised their considerable skills in customising their own homes and communal buildings. La Vileta's architecture is far from uniform, and it has many peculiar buildings. Judy and I had bought one of them, a three-floored, 150-year-old house with stone walls a few feet thick and five enormous palm trees struggling to share a small garden. La Vileta has plenty of bars, and these, like most bars in Spain, serve perfectly adequate food. There is, however, only one actual restaurant in La Vileta. It is called, appropriately enough, Restaurante La Vileta and is owned and successfully run by Bob Edwardes, a Welshman hailing from just outside my birthplace in Kenfig Hill. Naturally, we became very good friends.

Life was very relaxed and Spanish as Judy and I attempted to restore the house to its former glory, taking a lot of time off to explore the island.

More than three weeks passed by. I regularly called LAPD. Flash kept saying Ernie had no message for me. Then one day he put me through to Ernie's hotel room.

'You ain't gonna fucking believe this.'

'I think I might have to, Ernie. What is it?'

'Did Bill ever mention to you a guy called Fred?'

'Yes, he did.'

'Well, Fred is dead, and so's our load.'

Fred Hilliard had died of a heart attack while the wooden crates of dope were heading to Alameda on the American President Line. Only Fred had been capable of clearing the load, which was now about to be discovered and cause one almighty scandal. The United States Navy was not meant to be smuggling top-quality hash through its shipyards. Questions would be asked. Governments might topple. Bill had fled on hearing the news of Fred's death. He was in some Brazilian jungle. Ernie had sent guys out to look for him. If Bill could not be found, Ernie was going to put Tom and Carl on the case. He was running out of reliable government agents. When this was over, he was going to have a long vacation.

Again, Malik was incredibly understanding. He suggested we give the mother-business a rest and concentrate on paper-mills and other legitimate businesses in Pakistan.

Malik's advice was on my mind when Judy and I attended the wedding of her brother George to Assumpta O'Brien. The wedding took place in Belfast and was attended by crowds of people all sounding like Jim McCann. I wondered how he was doing. It had been a while since I'd heard any news of him.

George and Assumpta had spent the last few years teaching English for the British Council in Beirut. 1984 had been an eventful year in the Lebanon. The US Marines had finally given up and left the country to its own devices. The ensuing battle for control of Beirut was bloody and complicated. Buildings exploded and people were kidnapped and murdered. Befuddled newspaper readers in the West tried to distinguish Shi'ite, PLO, Druze, and Maronite from each other, as those who could afford to left Beirut in droves. George and Assumpta had been sad to leave. They loved the Middle East and loved teaching English. They were at a loose end. If I paid for them to set up a school in Pakistan, would they do it? Of course they would.

And so began the International Language Centre, Karachi (ILCK). Within weeks, an impressive start had been made. The old American consulate in Karachi was available for rent. We turned it into a school. Hobbs was given a break from his marriage-counselling activities in Hong Kong and flown to Karachi to be the school caretaker. English teachers were interviewed in London, and a few were given the honour of a post in Karachi.

Real English taught by real British teachers went down well in Pakistan. Success beckoned. Malik was very pleased. I made him a director of ILCK. He made me a director of Mehar Paper Mills, a business he owned in Lahore.

Japan and all things Japanese had fascinated me since my childhood. I had played its national game, Go, for decades; I loved raw fish; and I was constantly buying Japanese electronic and optical products for my amusement. I found stories of samurai intriguing and was particularly impressed with the philosophy of doing away with oneself when one had reached one's prime. I wasn't suicidal: I had passed my prime, so it didn't apply to me. But the idea of a constantly improving life with none of the worries of old age had a curious appeal. Constantly visiting Hong Kong, a few hours from Japan, and never seeming to have the time to catch a flight to Tokyo was frustrating me.

'You fancy coming to Tokyo, love?'

Judy smiled.

'You know I'd love to. The kids will adore it. There's a Disneyland there.'

There are several night-life areas in Tokyo. One of them is called Roppongi. It's a city of discothèques. At 6 p.m., hordes of immaculately dressed middle-aged businessmen pour from their offices, check their briefcases into the discothèque's cloakroom, and rave on the dance floor, studying their gesticulations in the mirrors on the wall. Judy and I were making a tour of the clubs. We came across a twelve-foot high-rise with a discothèque on each floor. Each discothèque had a different theme. Reggae, Country and Western, Doo-wop, and other themes were advertised. On the fifth floor was a club called the Cavern. There was a picture of John and Yoko. We paid our admission fees.

The rooms had been done up to look like those of the original Cavern in Liverpool, a club I had actually visited over twenty years ago. On the stage four Japanese were dressed in Beatle suits. They looked identical to the Beatles. Each either had the appropriate high-tech skin mask or had undergone plastic surgery to achieve the total resemblance. They played exclusively Beatle songs, word-perfect and note-perfect. They *were* the Beatles. It was uncanny.

When we got back to our hotel, the Keo Plaza, there was a message to call Stanley Rosenthal. *High Time* had been published. Reviews were awful. The Inland Revenue had read it and freaked out. They could not be seen to be treating me as someone who wasn't a dope smuggler if I was publicly confessing to actually being one. They had withdrawn their offer of settlement and wanted to see me as soon as possible. I flew back to London. Stanley and I went to the Inland Revenue. The English prick Spencer had been taken off the case. We saw Price, the polite Welshman. I explained that much of what I'd told Leigh was mere empty bragging with no basis in fact. These lies and exaggerations had been included in the book just to enhance its commercial potential. I had been aware of possible repercussions, I said, which was why I had recorded my interviews with David Leigh. Mr Price, I offered, was welcome to listen to the actual cassette recordings, if David Leigh and Heinemann had no objections. Mr Price did not call the bluff and reiterated the original offer of paying £40,000 by the end of the year. The Chelsea flat was mortgaged, and he was paid.

Although I enjoyed being a smuggler most of all, I was enjoying being a travel agent's sales representative far more than being a wine importer, second-hand paper-mill salesman, bulk water transporter, or manager of a secretarial service. My hotel accommodation was often luxuriously upgraded, and airline personnel were more than polite to me.

A careful scrutiny of my businesses revealed that they were actually losing money rather than making it. As a result of my money-laundering, the businesses' accounts looked good, and they had from time to time provided some sort of cover; but I longed for a front that would actually make money rather than merely deplete my marijuana profits. The only legitimate profits I made these days were the commissions Balendo gave me for the airline tickets he sold to the odd customer I put his way.

The chaotic regulations governing prices of scheduled flight tickets and the systematic breaching of those regulations enabled London travel agents to make their money in a variety of ways. A regular scheduled airline was required to sell its tickets at fixed minimum prices to a regular travel agent, i.e., one registered with IATA, the International Airline Transport Association, who would add a fixed percentage, about 10%, to the minimum price.

An airline would much prefer to sell tickets at below minimum prices rather than fly a plane-load of empty seats. Consequently, illicit deals were set up between non-IATA-registered travel agents and the airlines, allowing cheap tickets to hit the streets and enabling travel agents to make a

25–30% mark-up, depending on their relationships with the airlines.

An airline would often extend considerable credit to a productive travel agent, perhaps up to three months. The travel agent would tend to get its money from the customer long before it had to pay the airline. Accordingly, capital became available for short-term investment, yielding ancillary profits to the travel agent.

Hong Kong International Travel Centre, through the painstaking hard work of Balendo and Orca, had established first-class relationships with several Far East airlines. Good mark-ups were being made on ticket sales. The turnover, however, was nothing special, primarily because of the back-street location of its offices. The business was unable to really take advantage of the credit available to them from the airlines.

Balendo and Orca had often mentioned that once they had accumulated enough capital, their intentions were to open up a big office more centrally located and corner the Far East travel market by providing airline tickets cheaper than anyone else could. The positive cash flow generated would then be invested on the Hong Kong stock market, where Balendo's Hong Kong family had the right connections.

I offered to invest £100,000 if I could be appointed a co-director of the company. I wanted to take an active part in the running of the business, but I promised not to get in the way.

The offer was not refused. I closed down the businesses operating from 18, Carlisle Street, Soho. I moved out. Hong Kong International rented a massive shop-front and office in Denman Street, just off Piccadilly Circus. I moved in. Whenever I happened to be in London, which was getting less and less often as Palma was taking its hold, I would spend most of the working day there.

Hong Kong International occasionally bought airline tickets from CAAC, the Chinese national airline. Balendo was convinced that a personal visit to Beijing would secure a better deal. He asked if I would come along.

In the spring of 1985, Westerners in China were still thin on the ground, even in Beijing. Other than open her doors, China had done little to accommodate visitors from other lands. Beijing was a really weird place. It swarmed with bicycles. There were no birds in the air or dogs in the streets. There were no taxis for hire. Foreigners were segregated from Chinese at every conceivable opportunity. They had to use different shops and spend special Monopoly money called Foreign Exchange Certificates that were not available to the Chinese. Not surprisingly, black-market currency exchange flourished.

As guests of CAAC, Balendo and I visited the Forbidden City and Tianamen Square. As guests of the China Railway Service, we were taken to the Ming tombs and clambered over the Great Wall into Outer Mongolia.

Several meetings in incomprehensible tongues took place at the offices of CAAC. I understood very little, but Balendo emerged from the final meeting with a broad smile. CAAC agreed to sell us tickets at rock-bottom prices. They had also agreed to give us the exclusive authority in Britain to issue and charge for Chinese visas and to be the first foreign agency allowed to sell outside of China tickets for purely domestic flights within China. Balendo was evasive about how he'd achieved this. Was this some heavy Chinese gangster stuff? I hoped so. But it was far more likely that some money, presumably part of my £100,000, either had been or was about to be paid.

On the way back from Beijing, I stopped off at Bangkok. Phil presented me with a new business proposition. He wanted us to open up a massage parlour. This was hardly an innovation in Bangkok. The city was flooded with them: on street corners, in hotels, and next to public car parks. Some specialised in blow-job orgies. Others actually provided a massage. The most popular ones administered body massages, in which the client is placed on a lilo, smothered with hot oil or soapy water, and scrubbed clean with a pussy instead of a scouring pad. Further interaction was optional. First-class hotels provided only straight, or almost straight, massages. They were losing a lot of money by failing to offer body massages.

The largest hotel/shopping complex in Asia is that housing the Hyatt Central Plaza, midway between Bangkok city centre and Don Muang International Airport. The Hyatt is a five-star luxury hotel, the first one encountered between the airport and Bangkok. Its clientele comprised mainly airline pilots relaxing between flights and business-men on short stays. There was little reason for a hotel guest to make the sometimes inordinately long journey to the city centre. The hotel had first-class restaurants and sports facilities. Endless brand-new shopping malls, all mirrors, escalators, and water fountains, were adjacent. One could get whatever one wanted. Except body massages. The Hyatt had agreed to let Phil open up a body-massage parlour in its basement. To keep up appearances it would also provide straight massages, haircutting, and manicures. About thirty body-massage professionals were to be employed full-time. Customers could charge all services to their hotel bill. The hotel would then pay Phil. The word 'body massage' would never appear on the customer's hotel bill, of course. And it would be 'blow-dry' rather than 'blow-job'. Some wives and expense-footing company bosses might eventually raise their eyebrows at the frequency of grooming and toenail-cutting charges, but much would pass through unnoticed. The customer would even be able to bring his masseuse to his bedroom. The Hyatt would be the first luxury hotel in Bangkok to have a brothel on its premises and hookers on room service. Phil wanted me to come in with him fifty-fifty.

I never really had any desire to be a glorified pimp, but I couldn't resist it. Telling people I was a travel agent was useful and safe. Telling them I owned a Bangkok massage parlour was a lot more fun. I could offer a free body-massage membership card to anyone I needed to impress.

'I'm in. How did you swing it, Phil?'

'Through that guy I told you about, Lord Moynihan. He owns massage parlours in loads of hotels in the Philippines, including all the Hyatts. I wouldn't trust him further than I could chuck him, but he's useful and has got some amazing contacts. He knows everyone in the Philippines, from Marcos down. And he can do what he likes in the airport in Manila.'

'How did you meet him?'

'Through Jack the Fibber, Jack Warren. Remember his son Barrie, the one who died in 1979?'

'Is Moynihan a real lord?'

'Definitely. I checked him out. He's Lord Moynihan of Leeds. His half-brother is Colin Moynihan, the Minister for Sport in the British Government. He was a pretty controversial member of the House of Lords, taking Spain's side over the Gibraltar issue. He got busted for some petty fraud, with overtones of murder, and scarpered to Spain. Franco took care of him and made him a Spanish knight or something. Then he set up in the Philippines. He's as bent as arseholes. Went to the same university you did, Oxford, but he's a good bit older than you. I told him about you, just said that I knew another crook from Oxford. He wants to meet you. We should go to Manila some day. You'd like it.'

Phil and I caught a Philippine Airlines flight from Bangkok to Manila. The plane doors opened, and Jack the Fibber and Lord Moynihan walked on to the plane. I was impressed. Jack and I hugged each other.

'Sorry to hear about Barrie, Jack.'

'Ain't a day goes by I don't think about it, Howard. You're looking good.'

Phil introduced me to Moynihan.

'Call me Tony. Delighted to meet you, old boy. We'd better get off this plane. Much baggage?'

'None, Tony, just what we're carrying.'

'Oh! I needn't have brought my porter. Never mind. Shall I take your passports?'

Marching off the plane and in front of long queues of arriving passengers, Moynihan gave our passports to an Immigration Officer, who smiled and stamped them. Immediately outside, surrounded by a small ring of armed police, was Moynihan's Cadillac stretch-limousine. We all climbed in.

'You're welcome to stay with us, of course, but we do have slightly more than our usual quota of house guests. I've taken the precaution of booking you into VIP accommodation at the Manila Mandarin in Makati. Phil and Howard, please be my guests for Sunday lunch tomorrow. I'll send this car round to pick you up at 1 p.m. Jack, I know you have other things to do tomorrow.'

Jack was not one of Moynihan's house guests. He was also staying in the Manila Mandarin. Phil went off to see his Manila girl-friend. Jack and I went out drinking.

Although Jack was in his late sixties and had suffered the appalling tragedy of his son dying in a Bangkok gutter from a heroin overdose, he had not lost his ability to make anyone weep with laughter with his Australian wit and his incessant mischief. He had tales to tell. He had shared a cell with Mick Jagger when they busted him in the 1960s. He had thieved from most of the world's top jewellery stores. First we went to Del Pilar, the main night-life area. It was much the same as Bangkok's Patpong – lots of bikini-clad girls dancing on bars and tabletops – but it was considerably cheaper, and the music was a lot better. The dancing girls' company could be bought for a pittance paid to the, usually American or Australian, bar owner. The hotels never objected to extra overnight guests. Some of the bars were quite outrageous, in particular one named Blow Job on the Rocks, where, if so minded, one could stick one's dick into a mouthful of crushed ice.

Wherever he went, Jack would accumulate a gathering of beggar children. He gave them loads of money. Five young beggars were hanging on to us when Jack suggested going somewhere a bit more off the wall. We all piled into a jeepney, the Philippines' most popular means of transport for short journeys. Jeepneys are reconstructed from Jeeps left in the Philippines by the US Army after World War II. Their outsides are covered with multicoloured paintwork, hundreds of mirrors, and statuettes of horses. Their insides are Aladdin's caves of Roman Catholic bric-à-brac and blaring sound equipment.

Our jeepney stopped outside a bar called The Pearly Gates, whose main difference from any other bar in Manila was in the service: it was performed wholly and exclusively by nuns. Nuns showed customers to their tables, took their orders, and served the drinks. Nuns introduced the raunchy entertainment. Jack and I drank beer. The beggars drank Coca-Cola.

The nuns introduced a ladies' excuse me. Various couples took the floor. A few nuns barged between couples, excused themselves and danced with the bemused male partners. Jack went up to a dancing American couple, tapped the lady on the shoulder, said 'Excuse me', and began trying to dance with her partner, who did not find it amusing. A scuffle broke out. A few of the beggars pulled out knives. If they'd kill for anyone, they'd kill for Jack. The scuffle died down.

'Are these real nuns, Jack?'

'Often wondered the same myself. There's one sure way to find out.'

'What's that, Jack?'

'Try to buy a couple of them out for the evening. I'll go and ask the Mother Superior there behind the bar.'

Jack and the senior nun had a discussion at the bar. Jack paid her some money and returned, all smiles.

'We got two of them until midnight.'

Back in the jeepney, they certainly seemed like nuns and answered all questions as if they were nuns. They were not the least bit shy and did not bat an eyelid when I lit up a Thai grass joint I'd smuggled in from Bangkok.

We stopped at a bar named The Hobbit House. Nine of us poured down the miniature stairway. We were warmly greeted by a roomful of midgets. None of the bar staff or entertainers was over five feet high.

'You going to buy a couple of these out, Jack?' I said as a joke.

'That's an idea. I'll buy seven of them out. Seven fucking dwarves. I'll grab me a Snow White before the night's out.'

After several more drinks in bizarre bars, five Manila street beggars, seven dwarves, two nuns, Jack the Fibber, and I fell out of the jeepney outside the Manila Mandarin. Jack walked to Reception and asked for a table for sixteen to be prepared in the hotel's gourmet restaurant.

The hotel staff were used to being surprised by requests from Jack. He tipped them fortunes, so they always accommodated his every demand. They weren't exactly keen on this freaky entourage traipsing through the plush lobby, but they'd put up with it.

Jack ordered too much of everything: lobsters, oysters, roast meats and poultry, and the entire dessert trolley. The nuns and dwarves ate handsomely. The beggar children ate nothing, but put all the uneaten food into plastic bags to take away. Jack paid the huge bill, gave all the waiters enormous tips, escorted the nuns, dwarves, and beggars to the still waiting jeepney, and bid them all goodnight.

Lord Moynihan's limousine was outside the Manila Mandarin at 1 p.m. the next day. The chauffeur took Phil and me beyond the city limits of Metro Manila to a plush and expansive residential area. We pulled into the driveway of a large house, once the residence of the Peruvian Ambassador. Moynihan greeted us and introduced me to his beautiful Filipina wife, Editha, and their three house guests: Jimmy Newton, a London solicitor; his Australian wife, Helen; and an Australian named Joe Smith. Joe looked like a cross between

Crocodile Dundee and Kirk Douglas. His arms were tattooed, and his eyes laughed. Several servants brought us Pimm's cocktails. Moynihan took me to his office. We sat at his desk.

'Howard, what we say in this room remains private, you understand. I know Phil is your good friend, at least, he claims to be, no? But I prefer him not to know the details of all conversations we might have. Understood? I understand a book has been written about you. I would be absolutely thrilled to read it. Do you have a copy?'

I usually carried a few copies with me to flash at impressionable strangers.

'Yes, Tony, I do,' I replied. 'It's at the Manila Mandarin. I'll give it to you. Who told you about it?'

'Your friend, Phil. You see why I'm hesitant to trust him. I find him a little indiscreet. But you'll give me a copy?'

'Sure.'

'Signed?'

'If you wish.'

'Excellent. Now Jimmy, whom you just met, is my very best friend. We were at both Stowe and Oxford together. By the way, which school did you attend? Phil was a bit vague when I asked him. He said you went to Oxford but did not know anything else.'

'I went to a mixed grammar school in South Wales.'

'In that case, Howard, I presume I'm safe in saying you went on to Jesus College, Oxford, the home of brilliant Welsh minds, no?'

'No. I went to Balliol.'

'Really! It's some considerable time since I've had the honour of a Balliol man for lunch. Well, anyway, back to my point. Howard, I won't beat about the bush. I know you are a man of great charm, intelligence, wealth, and abilities in, shall we say, certain unorthodox trading techniques. I have the strongest intuition we should be able to help each other. Forgive me being blunt, but you have the occasional need for a false passport, no?'

I smiled.

'Well, Jimmy gets the very best passports. British, naturally. One wouldn't want to be anything else these days. If you wanted one, it would be very easy to arrange. Would you like me to suggest to him you might like to be his client?'

I hadn't used a false passport since I was Mr Nice and didn't feel I actually needed one these days. Still, it could come in handy.

'Yes, please, Tony. Thanks. Does Joe sell false passports too?'

Moynihan gave one of his characteristic and loud forced laughs.

'No, no, no. I thought you might be about to ask me about him. Joe Smith was actually the first person ever to smuggle marijuana into Australia. You see, I do know some interesting characters, what! I suspect Joe still smuggles marijuana into Australia. He is also growing it here in the Philippines, using, I think, seeds from Thailand. Would that make some sort of sense?'

It made perfect sense to me. Joe sounded interesting.

'Now, Howard, he's been wanting to meet you for some time. We were both delighted when Phil told us he had persuaded you to come here. You have now been introduced to each other. Please feel free to do business with each other. I would be grateful for some sort of commission, of course, but how much, I leave to you.

'Howard, again I'll be blunt. I've lived here for seventeen years and know everyone who matters in the Philippines. Elizabeth Marcos is a very close friend of mine, as are quite a number of those in power. Whatever you want done here, and I think I do mean whatever, you can rest assured that I am more likely to be able to facilitate it than anyone else. For example, I was able to secure for Joe a large area of land in Mountain Province for his agricultural activities. He says it's ideal for his purposes. It was easy for me, actually, because my summer residence is in Baguio, right at the edge of Mountain Province. Manila is far too hot in the summer. If there's anything I can do for you, please don't hesitate.'

'Tony, do you have any pull with Philippine Airlines?'

'Of course. Why?'

'Well from time to time I'm a travel agent. My company specialises in China. I've just come back from Beijing. I came here on Philippine Airlines from Bangkok and noticed that they had just started a service between Manila and Beijing. As Philippine Airlines also fly from Manila to London, we could offer our customers an alternative airline to fly from London to China, with perhaps a couple of days' stopover in the Philippines.'

'Well, Howard, I must say it wasn't the sort of thing I had in mind from you. But, yes, Ramón Cruz, who runs Philippine Airlines, has been a friend of mine for years. I could easily have had him here for lunch today. He'd have come at the drop of a hat. Let me know when you want to see him. Shall I send Joe in to see you? I'll see how lunch is getting on. We're having lamb.'

Moynihan left me alone in his office. I gazed at the books on his shelves: *Burke's Peerage*, *Who's Who*, *The Oxford Dictionary of Quotations*, and *History of the English-Speaking People*. I noticed among them, sticking out like a sore thumb, a copy of David Leigh's *High Time*. Moynihan was a careless liar. But why that question about Jesus College? Maybe he'd never read the book; maybe he collected signed copies of all books.

Joe Smith walked in.

'Good to know you at last, mate. It's like telling a granny not to suck eggs, but don't trust this cunt Moynihan. I bet the cunt told you all about me.'

I nodded and smiled. I liked Joe.

'Well, we may as well take advantage of it, mate. What I'm after is a good contact in Pakistan. I got my own guy in Bangkok that gives me great gear. Phil knows him. I got what

I want here. I've been bringing dope into Australia all my life. I need someone reliable to get shit out of Pakistan. There's a huge demand for it back home. I don't need credit. I'll pay upfront. I ain't ready yet. I just want to know if I can call on you when the time's right. Come down and see what I've got in Sydney first.'

'Call me whenever you want, Joe.'

We shook hands and exchanged phone numbers. We joined the table for lunch. Moynihan was holding forth.

'The Philippines is an extraordinary country: eight thousand islands covering an absolutely vast expanse of the Pacific Ocean. Did you know there are over eighty-five separate tribes and languages, none bearing the remotest resemblance to each other? King Philip of Spain just drew a circle around the whole bloody lot and gave it his name. The Spanish ruled their primitive subjects from Mexico, gave them all Spanish names, and made them into Catholics. The priests said, "Yes, it's all right to dance and chant in the streets, but do remember it's called St Stephen's Day, not Pisangpisang," or some such name. Then the priests gave them the gory stuff about the crucifixion, all those nails and blood and whatnot, and, of course, the savages absolutely adored it. They lapped it up. After a few centuries of that, America marched in and made it their one and only colony. There was never an American colony before the Spanish-American War, and there has never been another one since.'

Jimmy Newton spoke up.

'This outburst of imperialism must have amused the British, Tony, especially at that time, at the height of Empire.'

'Oh, it did, Jimmy, it did. You must know Kipling's *The White Man's Burden*.'

'Remind me, Tony.'

Moynihan launched into an over-dramatic rendition of Kipling's poem:

'Take up the White Man's burden –
Send forth the best ye breed –
Go, bind your sons to exile
To serve your captives' need;
To wait in heavy harness
On fluttered folk and wild –
Your new-caught, sullen peoples,
Half-devil and half-child.'

'One can see what they mean when they speak of the Philippines having spent two hundred years in a convent, then fifty years in Hollywood,' commented Jimmy Newton.

Moynihan got his second wind.

'Indeed one can, and now, as a result, all the Filipinos want to go to either Heaven or Los Angeles. They seem to prefer the latter, I might add. Other than this insane desire to go to the United States, there is nothing else that appears to unite them: no common culture or national pride. In fact, the Philippines is the only country I know of where being a half-caste is considered as a step-up from being indigenous. Extraordinary! Yet they are such lovely people. I love Kipling's description of them: "Half-devil and half-child".'

Lady Editha laid out the caviare.

'Are these the fish eggs you nicked from Philippine Airlines, Tony?' asked Joe.

'Well, the first-class cabin crew did facilitate the means, yes, but I think "nicked" is the wrong word. I think they feel themselves handsomely rewarded. My biggest complaint about the Philippines has always been the food. Judging from what's available, even at expensive restaurants, the local cuisine seems to have blended the worst elements of Spanish and Chinese fare into an inedible gruel. Accordingly, I have to make my own arrangements to get such basic necessities as foie gras and caviare. Even decent Christmas puddings and Colman's mustard have to be specially imported.'

'Must be rough on you, Tony,' said Joe.

'Well, quite frankly, it is. I merely wish to eat what I'm accustomed to. I'll gladly pay for it, and if I have to buy it from Philippine Airlines' chief steward, I'll do so.'

'Do you not like any Philippine food, Tony?' I asked.

'They do have one delicacy to which I'm partial, and that's a specially prepared jawbone of a tuna fish. They serve it at only one restaurant in the world, and it's just outside Davao in Mindinao. I've just come back from there. We could go there some time, Howard. I'm sure you'll be back in the Philippines in the not too distant future.'

Beluga caviare and Stolichnaya vodka were followed by roast lamb. There was plenty of Château Palmer to wash it down. *Crème brûlée* with Château d'Yquem made for a good dessert. The men spread out for coffee. Phil sat with Moynihan and Joe. I sat next to Jimmy Newton.

'Jimmy, I'd be interested in buying one of your books. What are your terms?'

'Delighted. I'll need two photographs and a £500 deposit. If you're happy with the passport when completed, I'd want another £2,000.'

'Are they real ones, actually issued by the Office?'

'Oh, I only use real people who for some reason will not travel, usually London tramps. I get their birth certificates and take it from there.'

'That's fine. You're on.'

'Excellent. If, Howard, you know of others who may be interested, I'll gladly pay a commission.'

I thought of Hobbs and his friends of dubious persuasions. If they could be armed with false passports, they could marry a bunch more Hong Kong girls and make me some more money. The idea had potential.

'I'll let you know, Jimmy.'

Jimmy Newton gave me his Knightsbridge address and telephone number.

Phil and I flew back to Bangkok the next day. Moynihan

had told him about my request for assistance in doing business with Philippine Airlines. I explained in detail what had happened with respect to Hong Kong International Travel Centre and its expansion into China. Phil listened intently and offered to open and finance a Bangkok branch of Hong Kong International Travel. I accepted.

After staying just one night in Bangkok, I flew to Palma, where Judy was organising the conversion of our new home. I phoned LAPD. Flash answered. 'Is that you, buddy? I'm sure glad you called. There's bad news. They busted Ernie. He's been in the can for over a week.'

Ernie wasn't supposed to get busted. On his payroll were top lawyers, police, politicians, CIA agents, senior Mafia figures, and Hell's Angels, to name but a few. He had been a fugitive for twelve years. What had gone wrong?

When I next called LAPD, Ernie was out of jail. The cops had discovered his true identity, busted him for the 1973 rock-group scam, and let him out on bail. He didn't want to risk talking to me on the phone just yet, but if Judy and the children came out to California, he'd give them a good time and some messages for me. He'd correctly assumed that I couldn't get an American visa.

Joe Smith rang. He didn't realise I was a travel agent until Moynihan told him after I'd left Manila. Joe was a travel agent, too. His agency had offices in several Australian cities. Would I come to Sydney within a month?

Phil rang. The Bangkok office of Hong Kong International Travel Centre was about to open. I was needed at the opening. Work on the body-massage parlour was making good progress. I should go over and have a look at it.

Moynihan rang. He had spoken to Ramón Cruz of Philippine Airlines. It looked promising. I should fly over soon to meet him.

Balendo rang. The Chinese Ambassador to Great Britain had agreed to officially open Hong Kong International

Travel Centre's new offices in Piccadilly. I would have to be in London to attend the opening.

There was a telex from Malik. Mehar Paper Mills, the company of which I was a director, had been successful in negotiating a several-million-dollar loan from the Pakistan Government. Very important business meetings were about to take place in Karachi. I should try to attend.

Legitimate business was beginning to get as hectic as the mother-business.

Patrick Lane rang and suggested to me that Judy and the children stay with him while they were visiting Ernie in California.

'Judy, you want to travel again, love?'

'Where to?'

'To California, to Patrick's.'

'Of course. The children would love to see their cousins. I suppose you'll be going to Bangkok to check on your massage parlour.'

'Well, I might call in there, but I've got to go to Australia for the travel business.'

'You lucky thing. I've always wanted to go there.'

'Why don't you meet me there after you see Patrick?'

'I think that's a wonderful idea, Howard.'

We flew from Palma to London. Judy and the children were given round-the-world flights via the United States and Australia. I stayed in London at the travel agency. After a week or so, I booked a flight to Australia. I went to Australia House to get an Australian visa. I had to leave my passport overnight. The next day when I went to collect it, I was told I could not have an Australian visa because I had been convicted of a serious charge. A hundred years ago that would have guaranteed a trip to Australia; now it was enough to prevent it.

I rang Joe and told him I couldn't come to Sydney. I'd see him in the Philippines some time. I made arrangements to meet Judy and the children in Hong Kong.

I flew to Bangkok. The body-massage parlour was almost finished. It was called Panache. A number of extraordinarily beautiful girls had already been signed up. The downtown Bangkok travel agency was finished. A lavish party was thrown. Representatives from all the important airlines and tour operators attended.

I flew to Manila and met Ramón Cruz of Philippine Airlines. He said that Philippine Airlines were about to open their own office in London and was delighted to meet the director of a non-IATA-registered travel agency with which his company could liaise. He was sure we would be able to do business in the future.

President Marcos was originally from a village near Laog, the main city of Ilocos Norte. After his rise to power, he arranged for his son Bombol to be appointed Governor of Ilocos Norte. Moynihan had been invited to Bombol's birthday party and had extended the invitation to include me.

Early on a Saturday morning, Moynihan and I were flown at Philippine Government expense from Manila to Laog in a small private plane. Bollinger champagne and smoked salmon sandwiches had been pre-packed for consumption on the plane. A chauffeur-driven limousine took us from the runway to the Governor's mansion. There was a huge barbecue in the garden.

The party was a very grand affair with an open-air orchestra. Several Government ministers were present. I was introduced to Bombol, who grinned and said nothing. I made the acquaintance of some Filipino dignitaries and took the opportunity to collect lots of business cards and give away many of my own. I was getting hooked on this business-card thing. Several Filipinos came with us to Laog airport to see us off on our return flight to Manila. I was welcome to go back there anytime.

After another day or so in Manila, I flew to Hong Kong, arriving just before Judy and the children. We checked into

the Shangri-La. Ernie had given her new telephone numbers
for me to use. LAPD had become compromised. Ernie
stressed the need for greater security precautions,
particularly in communications. A friend of Ernie's was
arriving in Hong Kong the next day to meet me. He would
book into the Regal Meridien. His name was Gerry Wills.

Eleven

D. H. MARKS

Gerry was blond, large, and amiable. With him was his vivacious wife, Wyvonna, who let me into their hotel room, excused herself, and left. Gerry seemed embarrassed to be caught in the act of smoking a tiny splif of some excellent-smelling grass. He put out the splif and held out his hand.

'Hi. How you doing? Man, am I glad to meet you. From what Flash and Ernie told me you might be the answer to all my prayers.'

'How are you, Gerry? You can answer one of my prayers right now by relighting that splif.'

'Hey, you like this stuff, Howard? It's the best Californian skunk weed I've ever had in my life. But it stinks. I get paranoid about the smell in the hotel room.'

'They are a bit funny about dope here, Gerry,' I said. 'It's not that they dish out huge terms of prison or anything like that if you deal the stuff, but even rolling a joint can put you in jail for a few weeks.'

'That's trippy. With us in the States, it's the exact opposite. No one cares if you smoke a joint, but if you bring in a few kilos, they lock you away forever.'

'But people do smoke dope here, Gerry, usually Cambodian weed.'

'Whaw! Cambodian weed! I bet that's good. Howard, is it safe to talk in these hotel rooms?'

'Probably not, but I usually do.'

'Well, no one knows I'm here. I'm positive of that. And I don't really want to leave the room. I've got a bunch of money under the bed. Ernie told me it was okay to bring any amount of money into Hong Kong. I was really surprised.'

'Were you searched at the airport?'

'Hell, no. We didn't even see a Customs Officer. I figured they didn't have any. I mean if everything here is duty-free, they don't need any.'

'Oh, there's Customs Officers here all right, Gerry. They notice things even if they got nothing to bust you for. They'll never stop you bringing in money, though. They like to see you do that.'

'What if they know or suspect it's dope money?' asked Gerry.

'That wouldn't matter. Hong Kong was set up on dope money during the Opium Wars. If the Chinese hadn't liked getting hooked on opium and if the British hadn't been ruthless exploiters, Hong Kong would have remained a small fishing harbour. Old habits die hard. The colony is glad to see all types of money flow in and enrich the economy.'

'That's smart. Real smart. So what I wanted to ask you was would you help me get a load together in Pakistan? Let me explain. Me and my buddies got $3 million we want to invest in bringing ten tons of the best hash to Los Angeles. I'm going to buy a boat, do it up, take it to Pakistan, buy ten tons of the best dope, and take it across the Pacific. The boat and equipment's going to cost me about $1 million upfront. Will $2 million get me ten tons of the best in Pakistan?'

'In principle, yes it would. It depends on how much you are prepared to pay the Pakistanis if the scam is successful and where and how you want the dope delivered. Do you want it piled up on a remote Pakistani beach or delivered a long way offshore?'

'We figure we could sell the hash for at least $2,500 a kilo. That's $25 million to spread around. I think your end of it, the Pakistani end, is worth $10 million. I don't know yet whether picking up on a beach or delivery offshore will be the way to go. It depends on the boat I get. But it has to be the very best dope. I want to put my own stamp on it, literally. I'm serious. Can you do that?'

'You want to stamp "Gerry" on each slab?'

'Well, no, that would be kinda corny. But I want the stamp to be distinctive and to show that the hash came from the Afghan Freedom Fighters and that the money from its sales would be going to the fight against the Communists.'

'That's pretty much exactly what does happen,' I said.

'Yeah, but the average guy in the States doesn't realise that. If they see it on a stamp, they'll believe it.'

'Do you have a particular stamp in mind?'

'I've been thinking a lot about it. What I want is a picture of Communist Kalashnikov A47 guns disappearing in a cloud of hash smoke and a logo saying "Free Afghanistan – Smoke Russia away." You reckon you could do that?'

'I'm sure we could. When do you want to start?'

'I thought I had started. I've got $400,000 deposit to give you right now. It's all in one big suitcase. All in small bills, which is a drag. In a week, I'll get some more brought here. I'm responsible to my people, so I have to see the whole load in Pakistan. Once I do that, I'll pay you the balance left from $2 million.'

I had no desire to repeat the experience of carrying a heavy suitcase full of money through the streets of Hong Kong. Nor did I wish to make countless trips with smaller bags of cash to safe-deposit boxes in hotels and banks. It was time to make fuller use of Stephen Ng at Crédit Suisse. So far, all the money through that account had been moved through interbank transfers. I had not yet asked Stephen Ng to deal with any significant cash amounts. I called Crédit Suisse early the next morning.

'Hello, Mr Marks. What can I do for you?'

'Stephen, I'm about to receive a significant cash payment. I'm a bit nervous about carrying it to the bank, even in a taxi. What's the safest way of getting this to you?'

'How much cash are you expecting, Mr Marks?'

'Four hundred thousand dollars.'

'United States or Hong Kong dollars?'

'United States.'

'Mmm, a considerable amount. When you are in possession of the cash, call me and I will send two security couriers to meet you and pick it up. I will credit it to your account. There will be a bank charge of 1%.'

'Thanks, Stephen.'

'You are welcome, Mr Marks.'

Keeping on our room at the Shangri-La, I checked into the Regal Meridien. Gerry brought the suitcase down, and I asked him to stay. I called Stephen Ng. Half an hour later, two Chinese gentlemen arrived. Without checking the contents, they picked up the suitcase, gave me a postage-stamp-sized piece of paper with a Chinese character written on it, and left.

'Those guys friends of yours?' asked Gerry.

'I've never seen them before in my life.'

'Whaw, man, you're something else, buddy. You let two gooks you don't know take away all my money without counting it in exchange for a scrap of paper with a hieroglyph on it. Ernie said you operated kinda unconventional, but this is too much.'

I showed Gerry round the night-spots of Hong Kong. He fell in love with the place and with every hooker he met. Judy showed Wyvonna round the shopping malls. They left for Los Angeles. Judy, the children, and I went to Karachi. We were met by George and Assumpta. They were driving a yellow car sporting a bright red, white, and blue logo for the

International Language School, Karachi. We stayed in a house they'd rented. I met Malik.

'D. H. Marks, why are you bothering again with Americans? They are crazy peoples. We can be millionaires in paper-mill business, *inshallah*. The Pakistan Government has already agreed to finance Mehar Paper Mills. There is also possibility that Hyundai from Korea will be involved. We can make handsome kickback. If we do mother-business, let us do with British or this Australian man you speak of, not with crazy peoples with spy-planes that have heart attack.'

'I suppose you think the stamp is a crazy idea.'

'No, D. H. Marks, I like stamp idea. It is good for Afghanistan and good for mother-business. And private boat is child play here in Pakistan. Every day they are doing.'

'So, will you do it?'

'If this is your wish, D. H. Marks, I will, *inshallah*.'

'You don't mind if an American comes here to inspect the load before it leaves?'

'That is up to you. My commitment is to you, not to any American. You are most welcome to accompany me to NWFP to my tribe's hashish factory near Peshawar in Khyber Pass. You can choose quality. You can make inspection. But no American can go there. Even you will have to pretend to be Pakistani. I will arrange. If you are satisfied, I will bring hashish to Karachi and put in warehouse. Then, if you want, you can show to American. That is your affair.'

'Can you make sure it's absolutely the best quality?'

'D. H. Marks, the very best quality is too expensive, even in Khyber Pass. And you will never see outside of NWFP. I will explain you. When plant first flowers, top is cut and chopped and put into white goatskin in ground. This is first quality, but amount is very small. Second flower is cut and put into brown goatskin. This is second quality, and amount is much bigger. Third flower is cut and put into black goatskin. This is third quality, and amount is very big. When we make hashish we use many bags third quality, some second, and one or two first. Price of first quality is maybe one hundred times that of third quality. For $2 million payment for ten tons, we can maybe have 5% first quality, 20% second quality, and 75% third quality. Usually it is only 3% first quality, so you will have excellent product. But you will try it; you will know.

'And, D. H. Marks, Americans must not bring boat into the Pakistan. They will do crazy things and get busted. My peoples will take to them. They must wait offshore. It will be easy matter for them.'

'When do we go to the Khyber Pass?'

'I will go immediately. We will be honoured to receive your visit in one or two weeks. Please give some money to my friend in BCCI. It is up to you how much. And before you leave, please give me passport photograph. Just wear open-neck casual shirt. No jacket or tie. You will now be member of my tribe, the Afridi. That's what passport will say.'

Hobbs hated Karachi and loathed being a school caretaker. Although his eyes perked up at my idea of getting him and his friends some false passports to marry some more Hong Kong hookers, he was more keen on getting back to Europe.

I had been impressed with Ernie's LAPD telephone set-up. A pity it had been compromised. I wanted a similar set-up. It didn't matter where in the world it was based as long as the country had a reasonably efficient telephone service. I could give out one phone number to all my contacts. It would be permanently manned by someone trustworthy like Hobbs who, if instructed by me, could transfer the call to wherever I happened to be. Anyone could get hold of me if I wanted him or her to, but no one other than Hobbs would know where I was. I had more control over who talked to me, and I was less likely to get busted.

I asked Hobbs where in the world he'd most like to be. He said Amsterdam. Within a week Hobbs had obtained a flat with two separate telephone lines and the requisite telephonic gadgetry. Within two weeks the Dutch police had installed a telephone tap, but we didn't know that. I've learned with hindsight that it is really dumb to allow all covert calls to be routed through any one location. If the cops are on to it, they get a lot of information.

After flying to Hong Kong, picking up some money from Gerry's wife, Wyvonna, and giving it to Malik's friend in BCCI, I returned to Karachi. Malik gave me a Pakistani passport bearing some unpronounceable name and my photograph. Malik and I flew PIA to Islamabad. A car met us and took us to Flashman's Hotel in Rawalpindi. In the cloakroom I changed into typical Afridi tribesman's garb and smoked a quick, but powerful, joint. The people of the NWFP are of all shapes, sizes, and colours. Neither blond hair nor blue eyes are that unusual. Wear the right clothes and appear a little weather-beaten and stoned, don't say a word, and you'll pass as a native. Another driver in another car came and picked us up. We drove for several hours through the NWFP until we came to Peshawar, where we stopped for a cup of tea in the middle of an arms bazaar, which also specialised in the repair of ghetto-blasters and air-conditioning units. A couple of traders came up and shook Malik's hand. Driving north-west toward the Khyber Pass, we passed through Landi Khotal and took a small road off the so-called highway. A Pakistani policeman stopped us at a primitive border post and examined our passports. No words were exchanged. A hundred yards later we came across another border post. This was manned by fierce, heavily armed Afridi. Each one of them knew Malik. We were transferred to a jeep and tore off up a mountain track.

'Are we in Afghanistan now?' I asked Malik.

'If you look at atlas in London bookshop, D. H. Marks, it will say you are in Afghanistan. But really there is no border.

Only in Western mind is border. These Afridi peoples have
lived in mountains here for centuries. The mountains are
theirs. They know nothing of countries and borders. They
have been called many different names by West: Indians,
Afghans, Pakistanis, and even British. But this is bullshit to
them. They have always been Afridi. We are Afridi, both
sides of mountains which you call Afghanistan–Pakistan
border.'

Eventually we came to a large wooden fort, the inside of
which was devoted to the manufacture of hashish. Goatskins
were piled up everywhere. I wondered which quality went
into skins that were both black and white. At the centre of
the fort was a line of what appeared to be wooden scaffolds.
A very old white-bearded man had walked beside us as we
drove in. We stopped by the scaffolds. The old man
embraced Malik. Both men cried openly.

The scaffolds were in fact very basic six-feet-high
cantilevers. On one end of the see-saw was a large, almost
perfectly spherical boulder, which was held up about ten feet
above ground by the weight of two Afridi tribesmen holding
down the sea-saw's other end. Directly underneath the
threatening boulder was a large hole in which a fire raged.
Almost covering the hole was an enormous cooking pan, like
that used to prepare a giant paella. The pan was filled with
the contents of the goatskins. Every ten seconds, the two
Afridi tribesmen would release their end of the cantilever.
The boulder came crashing down on the paella pan,
pulverising the resinous chopped plant tops, and was then
quickly returned to its mid-air vantage position. Slowly, but
noticeably, the pan became full of a piping hot, dark brown
goo. This change in the molecular structure enabled the
plant's full psychoactive potential to be realised. Smoking
the stuff straight out of a goatskin didn't work. When the goo
became thin enough, it was placed in wooden moulds, each
shaped to hold approximately half a kilo. Gerry's designer
stamp was embossed on each slab as the goo was hardening.

The slab contracted as it cooled and almost jumped out of the mould. Eight thousand slabs had been prepared. There were twelve thousand more to go.

Workers' living quarters bordered the inside of the fort's walls. The old man took us to his hut. It was a very humble abode. The only evidence of the twentieth century was a noisy air-conditioning unit with generator. In the smaller of two rooms, eight thousand slabs gave off their beautiful, warm aroma. They were chilling. A sample had been placed in a hookah pipe, which was now ceremoniously offered to me.

It was rather a pointless exercise. Between the joint in Rawalpindi, the majesty of the mountains, the high altitude, the culture shock, and the reverse Clinton phenomenon of inhaling without smoking the paella-pan emissions, I was going to be stoned whatever I smoked. Still, maybe I could get more stoned, and one can tell a lot from the taste. I sucked in a couple of lungfuls. I got more stoned and I liked the taste. All eyes were on me. Should I say it's fantastic or say it's not bad? Say it's worth every penny of $2 million, or say it's camel shit and they'd better come up with better? I took out a packet of Rizlas and asked if I could have a little to roll a joint. I explained that I was more used to smoking it that way and could make a more accurate quality assessment. I smoked the joint and held out my hand to Malik.

'You are satisfied, D. H. Marks?'

'Very.'

A lamb had been slaughtered in my honour. There were three courses. The first was lamb kidney chunks wrapped in crispy fat. The second was roast lamb. The third was a plate of lamb fat. Pakistani Coca-Cola washed it down.

On the drive back to Landi Khotal, I asked Malik whether or not the people in the hash factory knew that hashish was illegal in the West.

'They would not know meaning of question. They are doing honourable business. The only law here is law of nature, not law of rich men. By law of nature, I do not mean law of jungle, I mean like your Ten Commandments.'

'What if Philip Morris or John Player came here and said you had to sell to them from now on?'

'They would not get past gate with policeman. Believe me, D. H. Marks, you are first man who is not Afridi to come to this hashish factory. Afridi only deal with people they know. It is D. H. Marks, not John Player or Philip Morris, they will sell to.'

I had a quiet reverie of fantasy and megalomania.

Judy had seen enough of Karachi. The place was filthy, Francesca had been very ill indeed, and there was little to do. They left for London. I stayed in Karachi a week or so attending to the affairs of the language school and turning up for the odd paper-mill meeting, at which I was totally redundant. The school was doing really well, attracting not only local Pakistanis but also staff from foreign Embassies and their families. In Karachi it wasn't just the American and British Embassies that had a 'drug man' on their staff. The Dutch Embassy was another. The wife of their 'drug man' was being taught English by George and Assumpta. This amused me. The expatriate community here would clearly be quite small. I asked Assumpta if she'd come across Michael Stephenson. She'd seen him once or twice but knew his wife far better. They met on a regular basis. I asked if she'd come across Harlan Lee Bowe.

Apparently he could be found most nights in the American Club, one of the very few places in Pakistan allowed to serve alcohol, sitting alone at a corner table, drinking and scowling. She and George had often seen him. They went there quite often as the manager's son attended the school.

The three of us entered the American Club. All the tables were empty. The barman made a fuss of us and gave us complimentary drinks. DEA Agent Harlan Lee Bowe walked in, sat at his corner table, took a sip from his drink, and scowled at us. He had the stamp of a DEA agent: overweight with large moustache. We started making loud anti-American comments. He called the waiter to his table, and they muttered to each other. The waiter came to us. Bowe had complained we weren't even American, let alone members. The waiter explained we were guests of the management. We burst out laughing. Bowe left, fuming.

I had to go back to Hong Kong to pick up some money being sent over by Gerry. I would have to overnight in Bangkok. There are worse fates. Phil was out of the country, so I checked into the Bangkok Peninsula, which is walking distance from the Erawan Buddha. It was a Friday. Sompop was there.

'*Sawabdee*, Kuhn Marks, *sawabdee*, Kuhn Marks. I have Buddha for you. Please wear always.'

He gave me what looked like an antique bronze coin, but it clearly wasn't currency.

'Wear always, Kuhn Marks, except when with woman or when in toilet or when in bath, *mai dee*. Wear in sea or lake is okay, *dee mak mak*. No harm come to you, Kuhn Marks. You have good luck. Buddha look after you. Tomorrow you buy gold chain for Buddha. Wear always, Kuhn Marks.'

'*Ka poon kap*, Sompop, thank you. How is the *tuktuk* going?'

'Ah, Kuhn Marks, Sompop no more have *tuktuk*. You give money. I buy flower-seller business. You number one, Kuhn Marks.'

Sompop now had a gang of flower sellers hawking their wares to free-spending businessmen having a night of drinking and fucking in Patpong. As a means of intelligence-gathering, these would be second to none. I tried him out.

'Sompop, have you seen my friend, the one I was with when I first met you?'

'You mean Kuhn Phil. I know him but he no recognise me. Two night ago, him drink in Kings Castle with big black *fahlang* and *fahlang* from Amsterdam. Last night he leave for Australia.'

So Mickey Williams had somehow got hold of Phil, and the Dutch air-freight scam had, presumably, been resurrected, this time without me. I couldn't really complain. I didn't own Phil, and it wasn't I who had introduced him to Mickey. But I was glad to know what was going on. Sompop was proving most useful.

At a Bangkok's jeweller's I bought a gold chain and also set the Buddha into a gold frame. I put it round my neck. I would abide by its rules.

At Hong Kong I met Daniel, Gerry's powerfully built boat skipper. An Alaskan crab boat had been bought. It was being prepared for its duties. Daniel gave me a few hundred thousand dollars. I gave it to Malik's friend in BCCI. Daniel also gave me a ghetto-blaster which had been modified into a short-wave radio transmitter/receiver. One could sit on a beach with it and communicate to the boat without attracting attention. Daniel wanted me to take it to Karachi. He said Gerry was on his way to London to see me.

A night in Hong Kong, drinking in Bottoms Up, was followed by another night in Bangkok, and then a day in Karachi. I put Dan's ghetto-blaster into a room in George and Assumpta's house that had been set aside for my own use.

I flew to Zurich to meet Hobbs. I was still too nervous to go to Amsterdam. I owed them seven months of my life. Hobbs said he thought the Amsterdam telephone-switching system, through which the previous few months' travel, meeting, and banking arrangements had all been made, had been compromised. He couldn't put his finger on the problem. It was just a feeling he had. He looked extremely worried. I told him to close down the Amsterdam operation, give me a bunch of passport photographs, and have a holiday in Bangkok. I told him how to contact Sompop.

In London, Gerry Wills, together with a friend of his, Ron Allen, had arrived before me. They'd brought some money. I'd asked John Denbigh and Jarvis to relieve them of the cash and take care of them until I got back. John and Jarvis both thought they had been observed during their meetings with Gerry and Ron. Another worry.

Ron Allen was from Chicago and was a major distributor of marijuana in the Midwest and Canada. Gerry wanted Ron to check the quality of the dope in Karachi. I couldn't see that as presenting any problem.

Jimmy Newton gave me a false passport in the name of William Tetley. I gave him some money, orders for three false passports, and six photographs of Hobbs.

Hong Kong International Travel Centre's Piccadilly office was officially opened by His Excellency Hu Ding-Yi, the Ambassador for the People's Republic of China, and Madame Xie Heng, the Ambassador's wife. His Excellency was introduced by Peter Brooke, the Member of Parliament for the area. Other guests included the Right Honourable Lord Bethell, MEP, senior members of foreign Embassies, and Hong Kong Government officials. Over a hundred people from the travel industry were present. I had invited all my family and friends. They would be impressed and comforted by my legitimate business success. We were the tenth largest travel agency in Great Britain, and we were doing most of the ticketing to Hong Kong and China. My daughter Francesca presented the Ambassador's wife with a bouquet of flowers.

Balendo had become very keen on exploiting Malik's relationship with Pakistan International Airlines to offer a cheap deal to China. He wanted to go to Pakistan and do some of his own travel research. I suggested he go immediately. I could use his company over there to lend credibility to my travel-agent cover. Visiting Karachi with two well-known American dope dealers, one needs all the front one can get.

Balendo, Gerry, Ron, and I flew separately to Karachi. I went first. I got drunk on the flight and reeled through

Karachi airport looking for George and Assumpta, whom I'd asked to meet me. They were nowhere to be seen. I thought they might be waiting in their car outside. I walked out into the open car park. I could see the yellow ILCK car about twenty yards away. George and Assumpta were standing by its side, waving. To my left was a white car with three Caucasians inside. The driver looked like Harlan Lee Bowe. I drunkenly staggered up to the car. It was Bowe.

'You waiting for me?' I slurred.

The three stared at me in embarrassed silence.

'Come on, admit it. You're waiting for me, aren't you?'

'Why do you think we are waiting for you?' one of the others said in a pronounced Dutch accent. I guessed him to be Holland's 'drug man' in Pakistan.

'I'm expecting to be met. You're obviously waiting for someone, aren't you? Are you sure it's not me? Who are you waiting for? What are you doing here?'

'Look,' drawled Bowe, 'we are not here to meet you, okay. Who were you expecting to see?'

'Someone who fits your description.'

'His name?' asked Bowe.

What the hell was I doing? It was definitely not cool to be having this drunken banter with the DEA and Dutch CRI while I was in the middle of the biggest deal I'd ever done from Pakistan. I wriggled out.

'Ah, there's the guy I'm meeting. Sorry.'

I walked over to the ILCK car and got inside.

Balendo was arriving the next day. At the arrivals hall, I was peculiarly pleased to catch sight of Her Majesty's Customs and Excise Officer Michael Stephenson furtively creeping around and whispering to Pakistani Immigration Officers. Let him see me meet Balendo. Let him see my impenetrable straight front. This would be fun.

Balendo did not emerge. Stephenson had disappeared. I gave it another hour, then asked an Immigration Officer if any more passengers from London were still to come

through. I was told there were always some delays. I called
Malik. Aftab and Malik arrived within about forty minutes.
Malik had checked the passenger list. Balendo was on it.
Malik had rung up the Immigration Department. Balendo
was being detained. No further information.

I found this hard to take. Why would Balendo get held? If
this happened to my straightest contact, what would happen
when Gerry and Ron arrived tomorrow? Should I stop them?

Malik went to the airport Immigration Office. He would
have a friend or cousin who worked there. After a while he
reappeared with three Pakistani Immigration Officers and
Balendo. Immigration were maintaining there was some
irregularity in Balendo's passport. It was a British Hong
Kong passport, which as such did not entitle the bearer to
quite the same range of privileges as a normal British
passport. However, as Malik had offered to sponsor
Balendo, it would be all right for Balendo to spend his
intended few days in Pakistan. Malik seemed content with
the explanation. I wasn't. Perhaps simply because I'd
noticed Stephenson.

George and Assumpta had employed a secretary for the
school. She was one of the very few Chinese living in
Pakistan. Her mother, Ellie, ran an illegal Chinese restaurant which was very popular with the Europeans, almost a
home from home.

We thought it would be a good idea to take Balendo, who
was staying with us in George's house, for a meal. Some
Cantonese noodles might help him recover from his immigration ordeal. Armed with a few bottles of wine, the four of
us turned up at Ellie's. Sitting at a table were Bowe, the
Dutch cop, and a few others. On the wall above them was a
large poster advertising the International Language Centre,
Karachi. They looked astonished to see Balendo. They got
up and left. We had a good meal.

Malik and Aftab were waiting for us at George's house.
The Immigration Department had just called Malik.

Balendo had to go back in detention. Malik had arranged that Balendo be 'detained' at the Karachi airport hotel, but that was the best he could do. We drove Balendo to the hotel. Balendo apparently fitted the description of a wanted Chinese heroin trafficker and could not be officially let into the country until extensive enquiries had been made.

Something was clearly adrift. Balendo has an enormous raspberry birthmark covering the side of his face. There isn't another birthmark like it in the world.

The hotel was comfortable enough, but Balendo had seen enough of Karachi. He didn't feel he could recommend it as a stopover to China. He wanted to go home. Malik fixed it.

George and Assumpta had made a number of friends in Karachi. One of them was Eddie, an American who was a medical consultant at the Aga Khan Hospital. He was away for a week and had garaged his car for safe-keeping at George's house. The afternoon after Balendo's arrival, I dressed up in my Afridi costume and drove Eddie's car to the airport. Gerry and Ron were arriving from London. They had flown via Amsterdam. I hung about in a crowd of Pakistanis waiting for their friends and families to arrive. Bowe and Stephenson, each wearing dark glasses, drove up in the same white car I'd seen previously and ran into the airport. They quickly returned, got into another car, a dark blue one, and drove off.

Gerry and Ron came through Customs and Immigration. They laughed at my outfit as we climbed into Eddie's car. I gave each of us a ready-rolled joint of our freshly made hashish. Blue fumes filled the car. I drove off in the direction of the city centre.

It wasn't long before the dark blue car appeared in the rear mirror. As a pedestrian I have no difficulty losing a tail. As a driver I do, particularly when I'm stoned. I couldn't think where to go. Bowe and Stephenson did not know I was driving this car. They were following Gerry and Ron, not me. There was no pressing reason to think they knew we were fellow scammers. I shouldn't go anywhere where I was known. But I only knew how to get to places where I was known. God, I was stoned.

I mustn't let Bowe and Stephenson get any information they don't already know. That's the key. I drove Eddie's car to the Aga Khan Hospital and parked in the car park. Ron turned down the radio.

'Whaw, this is some hash you got us, buddy. What do you think of it, Ron? You gotta sell it,' said Gerry.

'I'm stoned all right, guys, but I'd like to smoke some without tobacco, and without that fucking music. Man, is this place primitive. It's like Mexico. Howard, why are we parked in this hospital? You got an appointment or a sudden medical problem? Don't tell me this is where the dope's stashed.'

'Hey, that's real cool,' said Gerry, 'stashing it in a hospital. I told you, Ron, this Howard is something else. Do you have another joint, buddy? This one's kinda had it. Man, this is good gear.'

'The DEA were waiting for you at the airport here.'

'So fucking what?' said Ron. 'Those bastards wait for us everywhere. They were always on our backs in Mexico. They don't know what we're doing here. They don't even know where we are right this minute.'

'Yeah, it would be a drag if they knew where our stash was,' commented Gerry.

'They followed us here from the airport. They're probably parked outside waiting for us to leave. The stash is nowhere near here.'

'Then why the fuck are we here?' asked Ron. 'Let's drive off, lose the tail, and go to the stash.'

'This car belongs to someone who works at this hospital. That's why we're here.'

'Oh, you're returning his car,' deduced Gerry.

'No, he's away for the week.'

'Then why the fuck are we here?' asked Ron, again. 'Gerry, turn that fucking music off.'

'Hey, man, some of it's really far out. They can get it on. What's the night-life scene like here, Howard? As good as Hong Kong? I thought Amsterdam was kinda neat with them hookers in the windows and cafés selling joints. I bet there's loads of them here.'

'Gerry, there's nothing here: no bars, no hookers, no night-spots, nowhere you can smoke hash in public. Everything is illegal.'

'You're kidding. I thought this was where it all happened. Don't you have a massage parlour here or something?'

'That's in Bangkok. We could go there if you like.'

'Bangkok. That's it. That's full of hookers, right? Yeah, let's go there when Ron's seen the load. What kind of girls are they in Bangkok?'

'Quit it, you guys, let's get on with what we're meant to be doing. Howard, you still haven't told me why the fuck we're parked at this hospital. Can we please get out of here?'

My security precautions were clearly lost on Ron. Luckily, it was getting dark. I passed out a few more joints, started the car, and drove like the clappers. I definitely wasn't being followed.

We arrived at George's house. Gerry and Ron were offered a drink. Gerry requested Jack Daniels on the rocks; Ron asked for a Heineken. They made do with home-made vodka and a bottle of London Lager, brewed and bottled in Murray Hill Station, Pakistan.

Malik turned up and took Gerry, Ron, and me to his warehouse, which now contained the entire load of twenty thousand kilos. Ron was happy. We went to Bangkok and checked into the Hyatt. The Panache body-massage parlour was in full swing. Phil came round. He quickly realised Gerry and Ron were smugglers and displayed his most hospitable side. They were given the best Thai weed available and shagged themselves stupid. They wanted to live in Bangkok. Once this Pakistan load had landed safely, they'd turn right around and pick up a load of Thai, a really big one. They were deadly serious.

Hobbs was still in Bangkok. He'd found about a dozen European gays prepared, for a small consideration, to make lifetime marital commitments to unknown Hong Kong hookers. He had their passport photographs. I explained to him that I needed to set up more telephone-switching stations as we were going to be very busy doing a load from Pakistan. I still favoured switching stations, but resolved to use each one only for a few specific calls. He would set one up in Hong Kong with his new wife's assistance. He also had a friend in the Philippines, Ronnie Robb, who would be prepared to set one up in his house.

Gerry wanted to know if there was anywhere else like Bangkok in the Far East. Leaving Ron in a Bangkok massage parlour with the newly found love of his life, we flew to Manila on separate flights and checked into the Manila Mandarin. Gerry tramped around the brothels and fell in love with a Filipina hooker. For a small fee, she was delighted to make her telephone available. I saw Ronnie Robb and made an arrangement with him for the use of his phone. I had a couple of dinners with Moynihan and apologised for not having enough time to fly down to Davao and eat a tuna's jawbone. Joe Smith and Jack the Fibber were both away in Australia. Gerry and I ran out of the personal dope we'd smuggled from Bangkok, found it impossible to score in Manila, and flew to Hong Kong.

April got us some dope, agreed to set up a phone station, and supplied Gerry with a stream of hookers. More of Gerry's couriers arrived with bags of money, which I passed on to Malik's man in BCCI. The total had reached $2 million.

Another phone station was set up in Singapore by Daniel and another of Gerry's crew, and two more in London by Jarvis and John Denbigh. Flash had set up a few more, masquerading as AIDS hot lines, in the United States.

By mid-December 1985, Gerry's boat was in the Arabian Sea ready to be loaded. To Malik's never-ceasing amazement,

Gerry and a friend of his, Brian, stayed in the garden of George's house and maintained continual contact with the boat via the modified ghetto-blaster. The time came to load. At a quiet little dock near the main port of Karachi, a well-crewed dhow lay laden with our hash. Brian got on board. The dhow disappeared into the cool night. Two Pakistani Customs motor launches escorted it for a while, then silently returned. Gerry maintained radio silence. After what seemed like forever, but was probably about eight hours, the Customs motor launches set off again into the Arabian Sea. As dawn broke they returned escorting the dhow. A dour-looking Pakistani got out, carrying a crate of champagne as if it was filthy offal. He gave it to Gerry. Gerry gave it to me.

'Ernie told me "champagne" was your code for success. We did it, buddy.'

Gerry and I flew to Bangkok for a quick celebration. Gerry stayed there. I went on to Hong Kong, bought a couple of suitcases full of Christmas presents and flew back to London.

'So you've decided to be home for Christmas, have you? We are honoured.'

'Sorry, love, it got complicated out there for a while, but it's all okay now. I can take it easy for a few months.'

Christmas 1985 was fairly free from major business interruptions. I picked up a couple of false passports from Jimmy Newton to facilitate Hobbs's bigamy and mailed them to Hong Kong. I ordered several more with the passport photographs of Hobbs's Bangkok cronies.

The house in Mallorca was now eminently habitable, with swimming pool and various other luxuries/necessities such as three telephone lines, a radio-telephone, satellite tele-vision. Early in the New Year, we flew out to begin making it our main residence. We settled down into expatriate life and enrolled the children into Queen's College, a nearby English-speaking school. Through parents' meetings and other school functions we made friends with a few other

English residents, in particular David Embley, a retired Birmingham businessman, and Geoffrey Kenion, a retired film and theatre actor who had starred in Agatha Christie's *The Mousetrap*.

I attended classes to learn Spanish. I played tennis. I drove the children to school every morning. I pottered around the house fiddling with electricity, hi-fi, and video. I took advantage of the exploding CD phenomenon and began a long-overdue study of classical music. There was very little about my behaviour to occasion comment. I was a straight Brit who'd made enough money to live in the sun. I patronised the local bars.

Judy became pregnant again. Would we have a son this time?

The Marcos government in the Philippines was overthrown in a bloodless coup. Marcos fled to Hawaii. Cory Aquino was in charge. She vowed to clean the place up. Moynihan rang a couple of times to assure me that he was still able to operate under the Aquino regime. He said that Joe Smith had resurfaced. He had successfully grown some more excellent-quality marijuana from Thai seeds and was anxious to do some business.

'Champagne in Mozambique.'

It was Ernie. Our hash was in Mexico. Rather than take the load directly from Pakistan to California, it had been decided to unload in Mexico, where Ron Allen had excellent connections. Mozambique had been our code for Mexico since my Old Bailey trial. From Mexico, manageable amounts of about a ton or so would be taken as needed by private planes over the border to Texas. Road transport would then deliver the hash to Ernie's stashes in California, from where it would be sold to wholesalers. There was still a while to go, but an important phase, the Pacific crossing, had been safely accomplished. The Philippine telephone station, which had only had to take one call, was shut down.

After marrying a couple more Hong Kong hookers, Jim

Hobbs moved to Portugal to set up a new telephone station. Before it became operational, he was busted in a Lisbon back street with his arms around a young homosexual prostitute. A few Hong Kong harlots now had grounds for divorce. I gave some money to a friend of Hobbs to get him a lawyer and help him through.

'Champagne in my room.'

The hash had hit Los Angeles. Ernie was going to take his time selling it to get a good price. I should carry on my life as normal. It would still take some time before I'd be paid. Traditionally, the boat crew are the first to get paid. After that it's a bit of a mad scramble, but Ernie had always ensured that I'd got my share pretty quickly.

Weeks of normality fused with expectation drifted enjoyably by. Ernie called once a week with a progress report. I maintained a life of blissful domesticity. Then one day Gerry Wills called with the appalling news that Ernie and his girlfriend Patty had been arrested at their room in Los Angeles. They were registered under a false name. Gerry didn't know how serious the bust was, but there was talk of dope and money being found in the room. Ernie had violated his conditions of probation, but as the majority of the load was still safely in Mexico, there couldn't be any serious financial loss. It would be best to let things cool down a little and not try to sell any more hash until we knew the facts.

That was fine with me. I had plenty of money. I had more time to enjoy my family life. Ernie's bust sounded minor. He'd get out soon. He did last time.

It wasn't, however, fine with everybody. Daniel, who had now taken the boat to Australia, was under pressure to pay the crew. Malik claimed to have most of the *mujaheddin* pestering him every day, demanding their share. People wanted paying.

Patty was released on bail. According to her, the DEA did not seem to know of the existence of a ten-ton load. They were busting her and Ernie for a pound of hash, boldly displaying Gerry's logo, and $50,000 found in their hotel room. Nothing else. Nevertheless, Ernie had strenuously suggested that there should be no more sales carried out until he was free.

The dealers to whom Ernie had advanced the hash before his arrest began to take advantage of Patty. Hundreds of thousands of dollars disappeared in various rip-offs. Gerry couldn't hold off his creditors any longer. I agreed to his taking control of the sales that were left. Gerry explained that, unlike Ernie, he was unable to transfer large amounts of money out of the United States via banks. His workers were too tied up with sales to courier money over. I would have to take the responsibility for transferring the money due to me and Malik.

I rang up Patrick Lane, who had now moved to Miami, to get him to renew his connections with the New York money launderers he'd used during the 1980 Colombian marijuana scam. He would also ask Bruce Aitken in Hong Kong. He'd be happy to be back in business.

John Denbigh agreed to go over to the United States, physically collect all the money due from Gerry, look after it, and give suitable amounts to Patrick for transfer to my account in Crédit Suisse, Hong Kong.

Quite a number of the new friends I'd made in Mallorca learned of my nefarious past. I made no secret of it. I had a feeling Geoffrey Kenion, who was just embarking upon a new business venture, would welcome the prospect of earning a little extra cash. I asked if he would be prepared to carry some money from the United States for a fee of 10%. He jumped at it.

I had a feeling David Embley would be equally keen. I was wrong. He was a Name at Lloyd's. He wasn't particularly short of money and didn't want to take that kind of risk, but if there was anything else he could do to help, please let him know.

John Denbigh had not long left for the United States when I received a very unwelcome call from him.

'Your dog is sick.'

Cockney slang is not my strong point, but this statement had only one possible interpretation: my telephone at home was tapped, and now whoever was tapping it knew that I knew. There didn't seem much point in asking 'Do you mean Bonzo or Rover?'

John went on to explain that during Ernie's arraignment and pre-trial court proceedings, the prosecution had inadvertently let it be known that the DEA and Spanish police had installed wire interceptions on my phone lines in Palma the previous December.

International dope smugglers have to make thousands of phone calls. There are many who say they never use the phone because it's too insecure. They are either lying or not doing any business. Dope smuggling is fraught with unexpected obstacles. Problems have to be solved quickly. The multinational and multicultural nature of the personnel involved severely limits the possibility of utilising any workable encryption of the intended content of the phone call. All dealers and smugglers use simple and fairly transparent codes. Any attempt at sophisticated coding quickly leads to disastrous misunderstandings. I have never heard or made a dope-smuggling call which isn't obviously just that. The precautions taken to code calls are largely a waste of time. But these precautions become habits, and they're a lot of fun. Furthermore, they do most definitely serve to confuse whoever is listening. Names used for people and places change and evolve at high speed. Different people use different nicknames for each other. Without an intimate knowledge of the callers' lives together, an on-the-spot deciphering by a third person can prove impossible. It is more effective than modern technology. Attempts to use state-of-the-art scramblers result in hunks of useless and unworkable gadgetry littering

Himalayan mountain tops and bottom drawers of dope dealers' offices in the West.

So telephone calls had to continue, some to and from my home made in the certain knowledge that the DEA were listening to them. But the name of the game was not to convince the DEA that John Denbigh, Gerry Wills, and I were really a gang of travel agents. The name of the game was to ensure they didn't bust us or any more of our dope or money. Half a kilo of hash was not much out of ten thousand kilos, and $50,000 not much out of $25,000,000 but it had been an ill omen.

Crucial calls, i.e. those pinpointing locations of dope or money, would, of course, have to be made between locations that were not subject to known wire-taps. Telephone boxes are best, but some countries' public telephones do not allow calls to be received. Spain is such a country. For that reason alone, it's a silly place for a dope dealer to live. One has to make complicated arrangements. With the increase of participation occasioned by Ernie's demise and with a wire-tap on my home phone, I would be needing some virgin telephone numbers. I asked David Embley if he would unofficially rent a flat and telephone for me to use. He agreed.

The conversion of our home in La Vileta had been done by a Mallorquian named Justo. We enjoyed a good business relationship and sometimes would socialise together. He also had a travel agency in Palma. I told Justo that I occasionally needed to receive telephone calls at locations not directly connected with me. He very kindly allowed me to use his travel agency for that purpose whenever I wished. He also introduced me to some friendly Mallorquian bar owners who were perfectly happy for me to receive phone calls at their establishments.

Restaurant owners whom Judy and I had come to know through our regular custom were most accommodating about letting me receive calls while sampling their wares. Pavan's, a Thai restaurant in Santa Ponsa, would be ideal for incoming calls from Bangkok. The Taj Mahal in Magaluf was perfect for calls from Pakistan.

I could receive calls at the tennis club. I could receive calls at Bob's Restaurante La Vileta. I could receive calls at numerous people's houses. It was all just a matter of timing: being there when the phone rang.

It worked fine. Geoffrey Kenion brought over a couple of hundred thousand dollars. His commission helped him to open Wellies, a waterfront restaurant and bar in Puerto Portals. Patrick sent several hundred thousand dollars to my account in Crédit Suisse, Hong Kong. John Denbigh also knew someone in New York who could transfer cash outside of the United States. The dollars piled up in Hong Kong.

Malik needed paying, and he needed to see me. He deserved a full explanation. I would soon have to go to Hong Kong to visit my bank. Moynihan and Joe Smith wanted to see me in Manila. Phil wanted to see me in Bangkok. I made plans to leave. David Embley, who had often salivated when I referred to my Bangkok massage parlour, asked if he could pay the place a visit at his own expense. I gladly said yes. I wanted to create as much confusion as possible. My travelling with David would puzzle those on my tail.

First I flew to Zurich, where I had no money, and wandered into a couple of banks, where I had no accounts. Leaving Zurich airport for Bangkok, where I had no dope, I had my briefcase thoroughly searched by the security guards. This had never happened to me before at Zurich.

I saw Phil in Bangkok. He was nervous. He admitted to me his involvement in the resurrected Dutch air-freight scam. It had involved Air Canada and one of the loads had just got busted in Heathrow. There had been several arrests. I saw Sompop.

'*Sawabdee*, Kuhn Marks. I have two more for you. You must wear three now for good luck.'

He gave me two more Buddhas. I put my hand in my pocket to bring out some money.

'No, no, Kuhn Marks. No money for Sompop. Please give to poor children.'

'Okay, Sompop. Tell me where to give.'

Sompop took me to Rajavithi Road to Bangkok's Foundation for the Welfare of the Crippled. I gave them a donation of $3,000. They put my name on a marble board.

I went to a Bangkok jeweller, encrusted the two new Buddhas in gold, and fixed all three Buddhas on a large gold chain.

I flew from Bangkok to Manila, checked into the Mandarin, and went out drinking. The Firehouse Bar in Del Pilar was known for its music and dancing. Females outnumbered males by ten to one. The place was packed, throbbing and simmering in Manila's tropical night heat. I went to the bathroom and splashed coolish water on my face. My shirt was wide open exposing chunks of magical Buddhist gold. The bathroom door opened. In walked a strong young Filipino. He stared at the riches hanging around my neck, looked around, and took out a knife. A grin crossed his face as he turned into one of the characters I had read about in children's pirate stories. He was going for me. I started getting scared.

And then an earthquake happened. The ground trembled violently, objects fell off walls, and people were tearing madly through the bathroom seeking the emergency exit. I was carried out into the safety of the street by the crowd. These Buddhas were powerful stuff.

Apparently earthquakes happen quite often in the Philippines, and life was back to normal within a few hours. I stayed in my hotel until David Embley arrived. We went out drinking.

Malik arrived in Manila. As I had expected, he was very understanding about all the problems that had occurred in the United States. Although he was pressed for money, he would be patient and wait for the will of Allah. There was no doubt that Malik and I were under observation. We kept seeing the same shifty American characters lurking around us wherever we went. It didn't bother me. It certainly didn't bother Malik.

'Let American pigs follow. They don't matter any more in East. Early this year they lose Marcos from Philippines and Baby Doc from Haiti. These were two very big friends of America. Last month American pigs bomb Libya and kill Gaddafi family, using your country, D. H. Marks, as aircraft carrier. For many years Americans destroy Beirut and Arab world for sake of Jewish peoples. In the East, they are devil. Let them stew in their own juice and eat their own meat. In two days, I am going to Damascus to see political friend. After that, I go to Islamabad to meet Pakistan Government financier for paper-mill business. Let American pigs follow.'

'Why do you tolerate people like Harlan Lee Bowe in your country, though, Malik?'

'Harlan Lee Bowe and all DEA are in Pakistan under cover of diplomatic status. Until now, Pakistan has allowed American diplomats in Pakistan. Don't forget, D. H. Marks, America and Pakistan are on same side against India in Kashmir dispute and on same side against Russian invasion of Afghanistan. But because of Libya slaughter, Pakistan might expel American diplomats. Then there will be no DEA.'

'But Bowe seems completely off the wall, Malik, much worse than the average DEA agent.'

'They are same. All DEA are same. They come to Pakistan. Government gives them big house with servants. DEA very pleased with this luxury: man to open garage door, two bearers to bring in food, many cooks and cleaners, chauffeur, and many more. DEA do not know that all their servants every day give report to people in mother-business. Afridi friend of mine cleans up the desk of Harlan Lee Bowe every morning. In afternoon Afridi come to me with full account. If we want, it is simple matter to get rid of Harlan Lee Bowe. But why? He will be replaced by same type

American pig, who maybe doesn't want Pakistani servant. It is better to keep the Harlan Lee Bowe. We know him. We know this devil.'

The next day was another Sunday lunch at Lord Moynihan's. Joe Smith was there. I took Malik along to impress him. Moynihan was a senior Freemason. So was David Embley. I took David along to confuse Moynihan.

Marcos's expulsion seemed to have given Moynihan more power rather than less. Joining us for lunch were three of the new Aquino Government's Sequestering Department. They toured the country looking for land belonging to Marcos's cronies. They had just grabbed Imelda Marcos's extravagant summer palace in Leite. Moynihan maintained that he was thinking of turning it into a hotel. He addressed us all.

'Well, gentlemen, I trust you enjoyed lunch. Mr Malik, I feel I should apologise for entertaining you in what must appear to be, given the recent bloodless coup, a rather spineless country. I can't imagine the Pakistani Army being brought to a standstill by a gathering of flag-waving nuns.'

'That was the Marcos regime,' said one of the sequestrators. 'The army was demoralised. Under Aquino, the morale will quickly return.'

'I must say I am behind you all the way. One needs a strong army. And I must say I do approve of the way you are creatively dealing with the previous regime's ill-gotten gains. My foreign guests here are investors of the shrewdest kind, and they see good possibilities now in the Philippines.'

'Would your honoured guests be interested to see the one-time summer palace of Mrs Marcos in Leite? Her collection of shoes is still there.'

Moynihan looked at us expectantly. The three of us nodded vague enthusiasm. Moynihan went on. 'Then I suggest the following. Joe has his private plane in Manila airport. Let's all fly down to Davao, stay a night, eat some tuna jawbone for lunch the next day, fly up to Leite, look at the summer palace of Lady Imelda, I mean Mrs Marcos, and fly on back. I think that would be a lot of fun. Howard and I could play Trivial Pursuit on the plane. Shall we do it?'

'You mean you want me to fuel my plane, rent some pilots, and fly across the country just to eat some fucking fish heads and look at women's shoes?'

'It's rather more than that, Joe, really,' protested Moynihan.

'Oh, I'll do it,' said Joe. 'I'll go down to the airport now to see to it.'

He walked out, tossing me a small bag of his home-grown Thai/Philippine grass.

The next morning, Moynihan, Joe, Embley, and I were flown to Davao by two pilots in Joe's private turbo-prop. Malik had to return to Pakistan and could not join us. I clutched my Buddhas as we almost hit a dog on landing. A short way from the landing strip, squeezed between the jungle and the ocean, was a hotel called the Intercontinental. It didn't look like an Intercontinental. The mail was delivered by a windsurfer. People from anthropology documentaries ran up and down palm trees and emerged from the sea clutching enormous lobsters. The bar played Noël Coward. Joe and I walked into the jungle and smoked some of his stuff. Pretty girls pretending to be savages danced around us.

After a drunken night, we drove quite a long way through the rebel strongholds of Mindanao. Kidnaps and robberies were common in these areas. I had my Buddhas. At the edge of an estuary was a collection of huts on poles. A raft took us to one of the huts. It was a café which served only the jawbone of the tuna and was the only place in the world that did so. I can't remember the taste.

We flew on to Leite. I beat Moynihan at Trivial Pursuit. He blamed it on there being too many science questions. David became ill and blamed the jawbone. Joe slept.

The sequestrators met us at the private airfield and drove us to the summer palace. The garden was an eclectic extravaganza of attempts to ensure an after-life. Statues of Egyptian and Hindu gods peeped out from behind a private

Roman Catholic chapel. Golden Buddhas waited in lines outside a mosque. Inside the palace was resplendent with attempts to delay the onset of any after-life. There was a private intensive-care unit, a room devoted to homeopathic remedies, a gymnasium, and more shoes than one could try on in nine lifetimes.

On the way out, Moynihan pointed to a nearby stretch of land.

'Is that part of the estate?' he asked one of Aquino's sequestrators.

'No, Lord Moynihan, that land must belong to someone else.'

'A pity. It would make an excellent golf course.'

'We would sequester it, whomever it belongs to.'

Corruption did not seem destined to leave the Philippines overnight.

David Embley and myself, however, were. We caught the Cathay Pacific flight to Hong Kong. His stomach upset over, he was having a good time. He had enjoyed Moynihan and the Philippines and was looking forward to Hong Kong. He had not been there since he was in the Forces and wondered how much Wan Chai had changed.

Filing up to the Immigration counter, I got one of those flashes. Although I'd never had trouble in Kai Tak airport, I knew something bad was going to happen.

'David, I think I'm going to get pulled. If I'm not out by tomorrow night, tell Judy. Let me go through first so you can see what's happening.'

David looked shaken. I walked up to the Immigration counter. The Immigration Officer looked up the name in her big black loose-leaf book. She double-checked the entries in my passport and her book.

'One moment.'

She disappeared holding my passport. Three police came to the counter. She returned with another Immigration Officer, again Chinese but more senior.

'Please accompany me, Mr Marks, to pick up your baggage.'

'I have no baggage.'

'You fly to Hong Kong with no baggage?'

'I just have carry-on baggage.'

'Let me see your ticket. Are you travelling alone?'

'Yes.'

'Please come with me to my office.'

'Why?'

'We are performing a routine random stop, Mr Marks. There is nothing to worry about.'

I was led into an office and asked to wait. A television blared away in Cantonese. A secretary bashed away at a computer. Immigration Officers walked in and out but took no notice of me. I chain-smoked cigarettes.

'Mr Marks, I'm Detective Pritchard.'

'Ah, a fellow Welshman to my rescue. What the hell's going on here? Is it my past catching up with me?'

'Why? Do you have a criminal record in Hong Kong?'

'Oh no. But when I was younger, I got busted in England for marijuana.'

'Well, that doesn't concern us here. To tell you the truth, I don't know what's going on. They don't tell me half the time. They do these random searches on people coming in, and if a British bloke is stopped, I just come along and make sure all's fair and proper. Let's go to my office. It's a bit quieter.'

Pritchard's office was a lot quieter. It was done out like a prison cell. Pritchard and I sat at the table for hours. We talked about disasters: the Chernobyl meltdown and the Welsh rugby team's mediocre performance in last season's home internationals (won 2, lost 2). We were waiting for Customs to come and search me.

'I'm sorry, Mr Marks, but the Customs seem to be very busy today.'

'Must be lots of random stops, Mr Pritchard.'

'Aye, I expect so. They shouldn't be too long now.'

They eventually came, searched me very lightly, and took away my briefcase.

Pritchard then disappeared, leaving me with a stonily silent Chinese. After a few more hours, Pritchard returned with my briefcase.

'Sorry about that, Mr Marks. Took longer than I thought.'

'A lot to photocopy was it, Mr Pritchard?'

Pritchard blushed.

'You are free to leave, Mr Marks.'

I found out three years later that the documents had indeed been photocopied. Not that it mattered. My briefcase always contained only what I wanted others to see.

I checked into the Shangri-La, much to the relief of an anxious David Embley. I transferred loads of money from Crédit Suisse to Malik's man in BCCI. I took David to Bottoms Up and other Hong Kong night-spots.

We flew to Bangkok. Customs tore me apart. We flew to Rome. Customs tore me apart. We flew to Palma. No problem. I stayed in Palma for several months. I'd had enough of travelling.

During that summer of 1986, the rest of the ten tons of Pakistani was successfully sold. All the money had been collected by John Denbigh and paid to those who were due. We were very rich. Although it had been a very successful scam, there was no feeling of elation when it was all over. It had gone on for so long, Ernie was in prison, and there had been so many problems. And, of course, we wanted to get richer and do another successful scam.

Gerry Wills, Ron Allen, Flash, and a friend of theirs called Roger Reaves visited Palma. They came by private plane from the French Riviera, where Roger, an escape artist, a fugitive from US justice, and a one-time cocaine pilot and marijuana grower, currently hid. They stayed in Mallorca's luxury hotels and spent fortunes. They wanted to do another load from Pakistan, this time twenty tons. Would Malik oblige?

I met Malik in Seoul. Hyundai, Korea's largest company, was intending to invest several million dollars in Mehar Paper Mills. We could be seen together in Seoul by anybody. It didn't matter. We were well covered. Malik and I answered questions on Malik's paper-mill in Lahore. The Hyundai senior executives seemed impressed. Malik mentioned the necessity of receiving an under-the-counter payment for facilitating Hyundai's investment. The Hyundai senior executives said this was perfectly normal. In the evening, we were lavishly entertained by Hyundai's own private team of geishas.

Malik agreed to do another load, but only if I agreed to set up a central London office for Mehar Paper Mills. I agreed.

After further hectic global travel and money transfers, Gerry's boat was ready to leave Australia, and Malik was ready to complete the production of a further twenty tons. This time Gerry had chosen 'Crumble the Kremlin' as his logo.

Judy and the children had gone back to London to live. She knew through an ultrasound test that she was having a son. She wanted him to be born in Great Britain. On November 16th, the world welcomed our son. I was the first to see him breathe in harmony with the universe. We called him Patrick, after both my great-great-grandfather and Judy's brother.

Two weeks after the birth, I went to answer the door in our Chelsea flat. It was Tom Sunde. I had not seen him since 1980 or talked to him since knowing he was some sort of spook. He was brandishing a sheaf of papers. Without any pleasantries, he launched into his mission.

'Look, these are the names of the people on your boat, the *Axel-D*, in Australia. Check it out. Your phones in Palma, including the ones of your friends and the ones in bars that you used, were all tapped for the first eight months of this year. A DEA agent called Craig Lovato returned to the US with a briefcase full of cassette tapes. They know you just brought in a load from Pakistan. They know you did that Alameda scam. They're going to indict you. Howard, you know I'm your friend. I was on that beach in Scotland with you. Don't forget that. I'm not shitting you.'

'Come on in, Tom. Start again.'

'Ernie's telling the DEA all he knows. Plus, they've got a couple of other snitches close to you. They already know about John Denbigh, a guy called Jim Hobbs, and Malik in Pakistan. By the way, it was he who ripped off that five-ton air-freight scam from Karachi, not me and Carl.'

'How do you know all this, Tom?'

'From Carl.'

'Where does he get it from?'

'You don't ask. But he's got access to what the fuck he wants. He's an amazing guy. He saved my life.'

'So what can I do?'

'If I were you, Howard, I'd disappear right now. Really disappear. But I know you ain't that kinda guy. Carl really has been a good friend to you. He can save your ass again.'

'How?'

'Same way he did last time. Whatever it takes.'

'Will he do it for old times' sake, or will I have to pay him?'

'Money is his only reason for doing it. But he is a good friend.'

'So how much will it cost to stop the DEA busting me?'

'It doesn't work like that, Howard. You just give us what you can. We'll do what we can to stop you being busted and keep you informed of what the DEA know. But at the moment, Carl desperately needs $50,000, and he's giving you something really hot.'

'Tell me what it is, Tom.'

'Oh, I will, don't worry, whether you pay me or not. I'll tell you right now. A radio transmitter has been placed by the DEA on the *Axel-D*. It's functioning now. The boat has left

Australia for Pakistan. The DEA are going to get this one,
Howard. They are so pissed with you it's untrue. You got
that last one through right under their noses, while they were
watching your every move. Man, are they pissed. And the
Alameda scam upsets them because it's the government.
You're not going to get this one through, Howard. Push the
abort button.'

What a challenge.

'Where is this radio transmitter?'

'It's at the top of the main mast, dug into it. Do I get the
$50,000?'

I paid him.

I told Gerry I had to meet him on virgin territory as soon
as possible. We met in Copenhagen. He got through to
Daniel on the boat, who changed direction and headed for
Mauritius. Flash, the electronic genius, flew down. They
found the bug. It would have been stupid to deactivate it and
alert the DEA we were on to them. We'd get rid of it when
we had to.

Gerry felt that too much had been compromised to risk
doing another load from Pakistan to Mexico. He wasn't
giving up, and he still wanted to use the same boat, once the
bug had been safely removed. But he wanted to do a load of
Thai weed from Thailand. No one would expect that
because it hadn't even started to happen. He wasn't quite
sure where he was going to land it. Maybe Mexico again if
he couldn't find anywhere better.

I cancelled the Pakistani twenty-ton load. We had paid a
$1,000,000 non-returnable deposit. We had tons and tons of
the finest hash in a Karachi warehouse. It would probably
come in handy some time.

There was little problem persuading Phil to supply
Gerry's boat with a large load of Thai grass. Details were
thrashed out in seedy Bangkok bars. It was decided to do a
thirty-ton load. This would be the largest scam I'd ever
done.

Another series of global circumnavigations at 30,000 feet commenced. Cash tumbled in and out of my arms in cities throughout Europe and Asia. Wire transfers of several hundred thousand dollars apiece maintained temporary residence in my account at Crédit Suisse, Hong Kong. We all kept moving. We met and discussed plans in strange new places. The DEA would never figure out what we were up to. From the tail end of 1986 to mid-1987, I based myself in both London and Palma and made visits to Bangkok, the Philippines, Karachi, Hong Kong, Kenya, Denmark, Tangiers, Belgium, France, Switzerland, and Canada.

A casualty occurred: Mickey Williams was busted near Bristol attempting to import heroin. I was sad to hear of his arrest but also very upset to discover that he had been dealing smack.

There was a particular reason for visiting Canada. Jarvis introduced me to a friend of his, an American named Bob Light. Some time ago, Bob had been involved in bringing Jamaican marijuana into England. Jarvis had sold it. Bob's problem was simple. He had a source of supply in Vietnam. The marijuana was identical to Thai marijuana in every respect. It was also packaged the same way. It could be taken out to sea and loaded on a boat. Bob also had an ideal landing spot in north-west Canada, near the Queen Charlotte Islands. What he needed was a suitable boat and crew to make the journey across the Pacific.

At about the same time two new characters walked into my fragmented social life in Mallorca. One was a Dutch count named Frederick, half of the well-known, hit-making singing duo, Nina and Frederick. He had long ago given up pop singing and taken up sailing boat-loads of marijuana. He had neither sources of supply nor landing spots. But he did have a fully crewed boat.

The other was Rafael Llofriu, a chief inspector of Palma's Policía Nacional and head of security at Palma's San Juan Airport. I met him at Geoffrey Kenion's Wellies, which had

now become the trendy bar for the hip and the cool to be
seen at. He had heard from regulars in the bar that I was
some sort of successful entrepreneur and made it plain to me
that should I wish to invest in business projects in Mallorca,
he would be most happy to facilitate matters. Rafael was not
offering to do anything illegal. He made that plain. He was
concerned only to promote business among those whom he
felt would enhance the island's prosperity.

I was not suspicious of him for one second and was sure
that the only possibility of any ulterior motive was his
ensuring that his family or friends got some piece of whatever action took place. I liked him and enjoyed his company.
It would be fun to do business in Mallorca with the backing
of the police. If the DEA were making enquiries about me,
maybe he would at least let me know.

Putting together Bob's facilities with Frederick's boat
would be child's play. Bob would put one of his men who
knew details of the loading and unloading parameters on
board Frederick's boat. I would just wait to get paid. I could
do it with my eyes shut. And I did.

I wondered whether Bob's Canadian offload would appeal
to Gerry more than Ron's already used Mexican one. Details
were thrashed out in Vancouver's seedy night-spots.

During one of the very few quiet evenings at home in La
Vileta, the phone rang.

'So I tracked you down, you fucking Welsh cunt. You
think the Kid's some stupid fucking Paddy you can hide
from?'

'I'll pass on that, Jim, but my name is in the phone book,
here and in London.'

'That's fucking stupid. Youse haven't learned nothing I
taught you about security. You won't find my fucking
number in any phone book.'

'No one ever wants to call you, anyway, Jim.'

'Still the same slimy Welsh scumbag. Listen. I need to see
you. I've got something for you. It's real important.'

I turned up for a meeting with Jim McCann in the South of France. Through means not specified, he claimed to be in possession of a ton of the finest Moroccan hash. He needed someone to come to a remote Moroccan beach, pick it up, take it somewhere, and sell it. Regrettably, he knew no one to ask other than me. He'd heard I was doing all right.

Twelve

MR TETLEY, NOT

Gerry's boat sailed from Mauritius to the northern end of the Arabian Sea. Just a hundred miles off shore, one of the crew climbed to the top of the mast, took the DEA's radio transmitter from where Flash had carefully replaced it, and with a certain amount of riotous ceremony hurled it into the sea. It had been packaged by Flash to float. It floated. The DEA would expect the boat to be fairly stationary for a while if it was waiting for a rendezvous with the Pakistani hash supplier. They wouldn't realise until too late that we'd found the bug.

Gerry's fugitive friend and major investor in the Thailand to Canada scam, Roger Reaves, decided Mallorca was also the sensible place for him to live. He had a deep South Georgia accent.

'Howard, let me tell you, boy, you sure got some shit together in these Europe and Asia places. Now with the help of the Good Lord, I've moved tons of cocaine and hundreds of tons of weed from Colombia to the US. I want to do the same over here. This is how I deal. I never rip anyone off or cut them out. No siree. But I gotta meet the guys involved. Like if you wanted me to move gear from Pakistan to

England, I'd have to meet this Malik dude and the guy who offloads me in England. That's the way I operate. If I do business with anyone I meet through you, you get paid, even if you didn't know a damn thing about it.'

'Roger, I have no objections to anyone meeting anyone. But Malik, for example, would definitely object to meeting any American. He doesn't like Americans at the best of times.'

'Well, fuck him then. What about this Lord in Bangkok?'

'You can meet him any time you want. But Lord Moynihan lives in the Philippines, not Bangkok.'

'Do they grow weed in these Philippines?'

'Yeah, Roger, it's just beginning to get commercialised. A friend of mine produced some great stuff last year.'

'Well, I could help you out there. What about this IRA terrorist friend of yours, the one who's always in the newspaper stories about you? I sure would like to meet him.'

'Well, he's got a ton of Moroccan he wants to move. If you've got some money and can take it off him, he'll be very keen to meet you.'

'I'm ready, boy. Do you know good offloading places on the coast here in this Europe?'

'Only in England, Roger.'

'Will you show them to me?'

'Of course. What I'll do is introduce you to a friend of mine, Johnny Martin, in England. He'll take you round them if you like. If you did ever take anything to England, he'd also be the guy I'd suggest to sell it.'

'Do you know people who sell ships?'

'You're on your own there, Roger.'

'I sure would like to meet all three of these friends of yours, beginning with this Lord. Can we meet the Lord right away?'

I arrived in Manila two days before Roger. For reasons that now escape me, I had promised Moynihan to join him at the memorial service commemorating Elizabeth Marcos, sister of ex-President Ferdinand, who had recently died. We duly attended.

Moynihan had opened a hotel in the Ermita area of Manila. Some time ago he had asked if I would put in $50,000. I paid him the money on condition that he would get me a false Philippines passport and allow me and whomever I nominated to stay in the hotel free of charge. With my money and considerably more of other people's, Moynihan converted the Empire Hotel to the McArthur Hotel (motto: 'you will return'). There was a full-on massage parlour on the ground floor called 'The Dawn of Life' and a magnificent luxury suite. It was called the 'Howard Marks Suite'. Moynihan knew my weak spots.

I told him about Roger and his search for a quiet place to grow dope. Flushed with the success of finally screwing some money out of me, Moynihan chartered a private plane to fly around some islands that he felt he could persuade Aquino's government sequestrators to grab and hand over to his control. Roger was delighted with this reception.

We flew to an island called Fuga off the north coast of the Philippines. It had a population of seventeen, no fresh water, and was completely flat. Totally unsuitable for marijuana cultivation. We walked about for a while. The islanders slaughtered a cow, which we ate. Just before the plane took off, Roger dashed out and grabbed a handful of soil.

'I'll take this for testing,' he said.

Back in the 'Howard Marks Suite', I asked Roger if he was serious about growing dope on Fuga. It hardly seemed an ideal spot.

'No, boy, taking that soil was just a show for this Lord. I'll grow dope somewhere else in these Philippines in some mountains he don't know about. I saw some from the plane. But I want that island. I want to live there. It's right on the shipping lanes. Nobody would find me there. And if this Lord thinks I'm growing weed there, he'll make sure no one knows I'm there. With the real Lord's help, I'm made. Does this Lord know anyone who sells ships?'

Via a cluster of one-night stops in Asian capitals, I went to

London to attend to outstanding matters concerning Hong Kong International Travel Centre and Mehar Paper Mills' London office.

Balendo and Orca were handling the travel agency beautifully, but although it was moving from strength to strength, there had been a couple of weeks of slack trade. During this period all the goldfish in the fountain at the front of the shop had died.

'This usually means bad luck,' said Balendo.

'What kind of bad luck?' I asked.

'Can't say.'

'Why do we have to have this bloody fountain in here anyway? It makes an awful noise, it steams up the windows, and kills goldfish.'

'Chinese always have fountain.'

'But why?'

'For good business.'

'But why does a fountain give good business?'

'Chinese word for water is same as Chinese word for money.'

'What is it?'

'*Soy.*'

'What, like in soy sauce?'

'Like in sauce. Today my uncle from Canton will come here and see what is the problem.'

Balendo's uncle perceived the problem immediately. He took one look at the fountain and said, '*Fenshui.*'

'*Fenshui?*' echoed Balendo. 'Ah!'

I smiled knowledgeably.

'This seems strange to you, Howard?' asked Orca.

'Oh no. I know *fenshui* means geometric omen. We've either got to move offices or turn this bloody fountain around.'

Luckily it was the latter. At enormous expense, the twelve-foot-high stone fountain was dismantled and reassembled. It no longer faced outwards. It faced inwards. That way the money would flow into the agency rather than out from it. It made perfect sense to me, but I was beginning to lose it.

Mehar Paper Mills had offices near Hyde Park Corner. Through a firm of head-hunters, I employed a beautiful and intelligent Pakistani lady as a full-time secretary. I had no idea what I was doing. She had no idea who I was. I just gave her and Malik each other's numbers and let them get on with it. Large consignments of everything from ladies' underwear to leather suitcases were regularly delivered. Malik was not concerned to sell them. They were all put into storage. On a visit to Pakistan, I asked him what was the purpose of this procedure.

'D. H. Marks, this is export rebate business. We can make fortune. I will explain you. Government of Pakistan needs to encourage export. Accordingly they will pay exporter a percentage kickback of price that exporter sells his product. Government of Pakistan do not look at what money is actually paid. This would make it too easy for people to cheat. So they send in government official to value product and give export price. Like in your country, D. H. Marks, it is Customs who decide value of all products. I have many Afridi friends in Pakistani Customs. This is in your knowledge. They come and declare big value. We get big kickback. For example, last week I buy two more container full of ladies' knicker. In Karachi, ladies' knicker cost maybe 10 rupees each. I show to Afridi Customs I have order for ladies' knicker from Saudi Arabia. He sign form saying value is 100 rupees each. Government chart show that kickback for ladies' knicker is 30% of export price. Government pay me 30 rupees for each ladies' knicker.'

'So, Malik, you've made a good profit without even selling anything. That's excellent.'

'This is what I am telling you. That is why Mehar Paper Mills' London office has so many boxes of ladies' knicker and other textile product. In Djibouti, where I have cowshit business, I have ten container of ladies' knicker. Nobody wants.'

Gerry's boat, completely free from any DEA surveillance, moved from the Arabian Sea, back through the Indian Ocean, through the Straits of Mallaca, and into the South China Sea.

Moynihan rang me while I was in London. He had just spent several hours being interrogated by Philippine Immigration Officers – a very novel experience for him. Scotland Yard were trying to get the Philippines to deport him so that they could grab him for the old British fraud charges. He'd sorted matters out, and in the process had discovered there was an absolute emergency regarding my security. He suggested that for my own good I come to Manila immediately. I didn't like the sound of this.

Tom Sunde had come round to collect money from me. He was still coming through with interesting information about my past and present associates. He mentioned Lord Moynihan. He said Carl was very interested in this guy because of his closeness to the Marcos family. Carl was currently attempting, on behalf of the CIA, to uncover Marcos's millions. I told Tom about Moynihan's recent warning. He offered to go out to Manila, meet Moynihan, find out what it was all about, and report back to me.

Tom reported that Moynihan had been approached by a Manila-based DEA agent, Art Scalzo, to help him set me up for a bust: a sting operation. Moynihan felt he had no alternative but to play along. But I shouldn't worry. He felt he could handle it without endangering him or me. He had my Philippine passport ready, and he would soon bring it to Europe to give to me.

Tom said not to trust Moynihan. I never did. There had never been any need to.

Gerry's boat was almost motionless in the southernmost part of the Gulf of Thailand. A few Thai fishing boats carrying thirty tons of high-quality Thai weed left a small harbour near Rayong, South Thailand. The voluminous cargo was transferred to the waiting holds in Gerry's boat, which set off through the Luzon Straits between Taiwan and the Philippines and into the Pacific Ocean. It straddled the Tropic of Cancer for a while, then headed for the Bering Sea and the frozen wastes of North Canada.

Some weeks later, the same thirty tons were in a ware-house on Vancouver Island, and Gerry's boat was in Lima, Peru. The scam, my and many others' biggest ever, had worked without a hitch. The DEA were either looking for Gerry's boat in the Arabian Sea or looking for ten tons of hash in California. We'd beaten them again.

Frederick, the marijuana-smuggling Dutch count, had his boat in position two hundred miles west of the Vietnamese port of Da Nang. A Vietnamese smuggling boat left Triton, a small, lawless island under joint Chinese and Vietnamese rule, well known as a safe haven for the world's pirates and their wares. The boats met. Seven and a half tons of Vietnamese grass masquerading as Thai were quickly transferred. Frederick set sail for Canada.

Just after Frederick had picked up the load of Vietnamese weed, I went to Vancouver to pick up the money from the first sales of the Thai weed. Before going, I collected my ticket from Balendo.

'Vancouver makes a change for you from Far East,' said Balendo.

Although my name had never meant anything to him, Balendo had slowly come to realise I was a dope smuggler. It was never stated explicitly, but there was no other explanation for the suitcases of cash that would sometimes pass through his hands.

'Well, I'm going for a good reason, Balendo. I'm going to pick up some money.'

'Ah! So you will be going to Hong Kong afterwards?'

'No, I don't fancy the idea of carrying large amounts of money across borders. I'm too well known. I just give it to someone who gives it to a bank. They transfer it to my Hong Kong account. It costs me 10%.'

'Too expensive for that service. Should be less than 5%.'

'Who does it for that price?'

'Triad. Vancouver is second-largest Chinese community in West. San Francisco, first.'

'I don't know any Triads.'

'All Chinese are Triads.'

Balendo was waiting for me in the lobby of the Sheraton Hotel in Vancouver when I returned with a suitcase containing 300,000 Canadian dollars that I'd just collected from Bob Light. He and Ron Allen were splitting the responsibilities of sales. Within half an hour, Balendo had got rid of the suitcase and returned.

'That was quick, Balendo.'

'The money will be in your Hong Kong account tomorrow.'

'What's the charge?'

'No charge.'

'Can you do this from anywhere to anywhere, Balendo?'

'If there is Chinese community, yes.'

I then realised how stupid I'd been up to now in dealing with money transfers. All those millions of miles of jet travel, those ludicrous hotel bills, those harrowing moments at borders, and the continual fear of being mugged for one's loot had all been unnecessary. If anyone wanted to send me some money, all he really had to do was take it to the nearest Chinese restaurant and tell the proprietor to await a call from Balendo, my friend and business partner of some years. This was doing my head in.

'Balendo, can you stay here and transfer a lot more money over the next few months?'

'Not possible with travel agency in London. I could come over every month and pick up from you.'

Handling the money from this and the next Vancouver load was going to be a great deal easier than I thought. I wouldn't even have to be in Vancouver. I would ask John Denbigh to come over and pick up money from Bob or Ron

whenever either had some to give. When the total reached a
respectable amount, John would give it to Balendo to do his
Chinese magic.

John flew over to Vancouver. I introduced him to Bob
Light. He already knew Ron and Gerry from the Pakistani
scam. I left him totally in charge.

I flew back to Palma via London. I was questioned lightly
by the Special Branch at Heathrow but not searched by
anyone. Chief Inspector Rafael Llofriu met me at the airport
and whisked me through Immigration and Customs. He was
in a bit of a spot. He needed cash. He had a sea-front flat in
Palma Nova that he wanted to sell. Did I know anyone who
wanted to buy it? I bought it.

Judy had seen very little of me since Patrick was born. We
hadn't been away together anywhere for ages.

'Howard, unless you stop tearing around the world and
spend some time with me and the children, I'm going to
freak out. I've booked us all for a two-week holiday in Sicily.
Remember how much we enjoyed Sicily? I thought you
might like it if we all went to Campione d'Italia first, then
took a train from Milan to Rome, and then flew to Palermo.
The children will love it. Masha can come and baby-sit for
us in the evenings. You can get to know your son.'

'It sounds a great idea, love. I can't think of anything
better.'

It was true. I couldn't.

After indulging in some nostalgia in Campione d'Italia,
we travelled to Sicily and stayed in the Santa Domenico in
Taormina, under the shadow of the surprisingly active
Mount Etna. We visited Greek amphitheatres, Roman cities,
and, for my sake, had lunch in Corleone, the inspiration for
Mario Puzo's *The Godfather*. In Palermo, I popped into the
Banca di Sicilia and refreshed my bank account. I had still
not used it to receive payments from anyone.

I kept away from the phones. No one knew how to get in
touch with me. I was really enjoying time with my family. All

Mr Tetley, Not 381

the travelling and scamming had its good points: money and excitement, but I was pushing it too hard. I would have to slow down before I forgot how to be a husband and a father. The resolution stayed with me all the way home.

There was a ton of messages waiting for me when I got home to Palma. John Denbigh was accumulating substantial funds in Vancouver. He wanted someone to give them to in a week's time. McCann was in the Sofia Hotel, Barcelona. If I didn't get there immediately, he'd come directly to my house in Palma. It was urgent. Moynihan was in the Orient Hotel, Barcelona. He had my Philippine passport. Could I come to pick it up? Malik was in London. He wanted to discuss some business proposals, not mother-business. Tom Sunde was in Düsseldorf. He needed some more money. Frederick was still at sea but imminently due to unload his cargo in Canada.

I called Phil in Bangkok and asked if he would go to Canada. The money that John Denbigh was holding would partly pay him off. I made arrangements to fly from Palma to Barcelona and return in a few days. I told Malik to come to Palma. I rang Sunde at the Düsseldorf Hilton. He agreed to fly out to Palma, provided I paid for his ticket.

On the flight to Barcelona, I mischievously thought about introducing McCann to Moynihan. An English Lord having dinner with an IRA terrorist could be quite entertaining.

'So what's a fucking English Lord doing with this Welsh cunt?' said McCann as he shook Moynihan's hand.

'Well, I could well ask you the same question. Prudence forbids,' said Moynihan.

'I'm no fucking Lord,' Jim quickly retorted.

'Well, what I meant was, what are you doing with Howard?'

'Howard fucking works for me. Do you fucking work for him, Lord? Because if you do, you fucking work for me.'

Jim laughed at his own wit.

'Not wishing to offend – no, I wouldn't describe myself as an employee of Howard's. But we do enjoy both a business relationship and friendship. We both went to Oxford. We have a number of mutual interests. We both like good food and good wine. Wouldn't you say so, Howard?'

Before I could answer, Jim interrupted.

'You realise we're at war, Lord Moynihan.'

'Do call me Tony. Who's at war?'

'You and fucking me.'

'I fail to follow.'

'England and Ireland.'

'My dear Jim . . .' Moynihan began.

'I'm not your fucking dear. Don't start that fucking Oxford academic talk with me.'

'Jim, Moynihan is probably one of the most Irish names in the world. I regard myself as Irish. One of my middle names is Patrick. Senator Moynihan is a cousin of mine.'

'But you're a Prod,' objected McCann.

'War is about power, not religion. I am probably more Irish than you, Jim.'

'You won't find me sitting in the fucking House of Lords, that's for sure.'

'You won't find me there now. I was a far greater thorn in their side than you've been. And please bear in mind, I have lived in Roman Catholic countries for most of my adult life. That is not coincidence. I am a vigorous supporter of complete independence for the whole of Ireland.'

'Are you? How many British Army soldiers have you shot? How many Army posts have you blown up?'

And so the conversation continued, each trying to convince the other he was a diehard Irish Republican with the highest of patriotic ideals.

Moynihan told me that he had been entrusted with some of President Marcos's missing millions. It seemed that Carl was right. Could I help him out with my money-laundering connections? I said yes. Moynihan gave me the false Philippine passport. He had another to deliver to someone else in Palma. He was going to ask me to take it, but now his plans had changed, and he and Lady Editha would be visiting Palma themselves. They asked if I had anywhere they could stay. I said they could stay in the Palma Nova flat. I was in the process of purchasing it from Rafael Llofriu. The flat was still in his name, but I had the keys.

McCann's purpose in summoning me was merely to get hold of Roger Reaves. Roger had given Jim the £50,000 he required. Jim was ready to deliver. I felt a bit disgruntled about the two of them just carrying on as if I didn't exist, but I certainly didn't want to get in the way. I told Jim that Roger, his wife, and children were now living in Mallorca. Jim decided he'd better come to Palma after all.

I got to Palma first. Malik rang from Heathrow airport. Iberia were refusing to let him board the flight because he did not have a Spanish visa.

I called Rafael. I explained that a rich investor friend of mine from Pakistan was having problems visiting me. Rafael said to leave it to him. Within twenty minutes, Rafael rang back and said that Malik was on his way. It had been fixed. Rafael was proving to be most helpful.

I went to Palma airport to Rafael's office in the police station. The office had two entrances: one from the public area of the airport and one from the arrivals hall. Rafael said he would meet Malik off the plane and bring him straight to the police station to avoid confrontation with Immigration or Customs. I waited in his office. Minutes later a very frightened Salim Malik was being briskly escorted by Chief Inspector Rafael Llofriu. Malik thought he was being busted. His relief on seeing me was palpable.

'You are bloody limit, D. H. Marks,' was all he said.

Malik stayed at our house. Rafael liked Malik. The next day he introduced both me and Malik to a wealthy Algerian, Michel Khadri, who was living on the island. Enormous deals covering everything from Bangladeshi furniture to luxury hotels in Morocco were fervently discussed. Nothing came from any of them.

Malik's latest proposal for me was to promote the sale of
toothpaste made from the bark of a specific Pakistani tree.
Apparently chewing this bark had for several generations
prevented a particular Himalayan tribe from experiencing
the discomforts of tooth decay. Malik was also concerned
about the pile of hash he was holding in Pakistan on my
behalf. I told him I was working on the latter and would
begin investigating the former.

McCann was next to arrive. I put him up in Hobbs's flat
in Placa del Banc de Loli in the old part of Palma. Then
came Sunde. He told me the DEA were back in Palma.
Through reasons of mischief, I also put him up in Hobbs's
flat. Tom was over the moon with my news of Moynihan's
access to Marcos's missing millions. Finally, Moynihan and
Editha arrived. They stayed in Rafael's Palma Nova flat. I
told Tom where they were staying.

One square mile of this small Spanish island was well out
of control. A Philippine-brothel-owning member of the
House of Lords was staying at the house of a Spanish Chief
Inspector of Police. The Lord was being watched by an
American CIA operative who was staying at the house of an
English convicted sex offender. The CIA operative was
sharing accommodation with an IRA terrorist. The IRA
terrorist was discussing a Moroccan hashish deal with a
Georgian pilot of Colombia's Medellin Cartel. Organising
these scenarios was an ex-MI6 agent, currently supervising
the sale of thirty tons of Thai weed in Canada and at whose
house could be found Pakistan's major supplier of hashish.
Attempting to understand the scenarios was a solitary DEA
agent. The stage was set for something.

The stage was set for disaster, which began with a call
from Phil in Vancouver at the beginning of September 1987.
John Denbigh, Gerry Wills, Ron Allen, Bob Light, and many
others had been busted in Vancouver by the Royal Canadian
Mounted Police. Several tons of marijuana and a few million
dollars had been confiscated. The marijuana had been seized

from a sailing boat attempting to berth in Vancouver. This was the method Bob normally used when transporting the Thai weed from his North Vancouver Island warehouse to Vancouver city.

I was stoical about losing the money and the Thai grass – these things can happen – but the arrest of my dear friend John Denbigh hit me like a ton of bricks: we forget these things can happen.

What about Frederick? Was he sailing into disaster? Was anyone left to meet his boat? Could this have been Frederick's Vietnamese dope the Mounties just busted?

It was. The busted boat had just met Frederick's and was landing the Vietnamese grass when the Mounties stepped in. Frederick had sailed off obliviously. Although John Denbigh, Bob Light, and some others were intimately involved in Frederick's Vietnamese scam, Gerry Wills and Ron Allen were uninvolved and totally unaware of it. The overlap of personnel in the Thai and Vietnamese scams had caused them to be busted for a deal they knew nothing about. They could hardly tell the Mounties that the millions of confiscated dollars were actually the proceeds of a previous Thai importation and nothing to do with the current Vietnamese one. If Ron and Gerry were upset with me, I couldn't blame them. It was my fault.

On the day I heard this tragic news, I visited Moynihan at the Palma Nova flat. He was uncomfortable, flustered, and unable to look me in the eye. I knew he was tape-recording me. I was tempted to say so, but I didn't let on. I tried to turn the situation to my advantage.

'You look worried, dear boy. Is anything wrong, Howard?'

'Yeah, some friends of mine got busted with a load of dope in Vancouver.'

'Oh dear! I'm sorry to hear that. Was it one of your loads?'

'No. Absolutely not. Nothing whatsoever to do with me. I didn't even know it was happening.'

'Which friends? Anyone I know?'

'Gerry Wills. I think I introduced him to you once in Manila or Bangkok.'

'Yes, you most certainly did. A pleasant fellow, I recall. Anyone else I know?'

'No.'

'While we're on the subject, do you mind if I ask you some questions about your business? I mean drugs, of course.'

Moynihan wasn't even attempting to be subtle.

'Go ahead, Tony.'

Moynihan fired all sorts of dumb questions about dope-dealing. I answered them, careful not to admit anything other than what was publicly known about me. He disappeared into the bathroom and came out looking doubly relieved. He asked if I could launder some money from him. It was a lot: several million, currently sitting in Miami. I said I'd put him in touch with my brother-in-law, Patrick Lane. He lived in Miami.

I rang Patrick and explained what I could about Moynihan. He was a fraudster. He was not to be trusted and he had no loyalty to anyone. But he wasn't a dope dealer. And he was an English Lord. And he did claim to have loads of money to launder. There was reason to believe his claim. Patrick told me to give Moynihan his number.

Malik left for London and Karachi. McCann left for Paris. Roger left for Amsterdam. Sunde, suitably remunerated, left for Düsseldorf, promising to ask Carl to find out if anything could be done to get John Denbigh out of jail. I stayed in Palma and made a vow which I have kept to this day: I was not going to do any more dope deals.

This was not a case of my suddenly seeing the light and realising that dope-dealing is a wicked and anti-social crime. I was simply not enjoying myself any more. Most of my close partners were in prison. Some were understandably blaming me for their fate. Others were correctly accusing me of endangering scams by doing too many. I was criticised and ridiculed for not being prepared to deal in cocaine. Some associates were trying to set me up. Others were deliberately excluding me from scams that would not have begun without me. I was under surveillance. I was paying fortunes to the CIA to keep the DEA off my back. I wasn't making any money. I wasn't seeing my family. I broadcast my retirement to Roger Reaves, McCann, Phil, Malik, and Joe Smith, who happened to visit Mallorca on one of his global walkabouts. They received the news with scepticism.

When Frederick finally got in touch, I explained what had happened to his load and announced my withdrawal from any further scams. He took the news extremely well but begged me to get him a false passport. Roger Reaves had asked for the same. I could not refuse these requests and ordered two more passports from Jimmy Newton.

I couldn't decide what to do about the language school in Karachi. Although it was a legitimate business with good potential, it had proved expensive to maintain, and was now losing quite a lot of money. I flew to Karachi. The school was closed down, and George and Assumpta were given money to pack up and leave Pakistan.

Malik said he would get what money he could for the hash he was storing on my behalf. We agreed that from now on we would do only straight business: paper-mills, import-export, and toothpaste.

The Vancouver bust of Thai grass frightened me from ever visiting Bangkok again. The massage parlour, although technically a straight business and quite profitable, had lost its novelty value. Furthermore, I had gathered that before selling their daughters to massage-parlour operators, fathers would often insist on being the first to take away their daughters' virginities. I thought enabling such practices would do little for my karma. I told Phil I wanted to withdraw. He wanted out too. We sold it, but we kept on the Bangkok branch of Hong Kong International Travel Centre.

I called Patrick Lane in Miami. He said he got on

extremely well with Moynihan, but that no business would take place. He was doubtful that any would.

Gerry Wills, Ron Allen, and John Denbigh each got granted bail by the Vancouver court. Gerry and Ron promptly absconded. John stayed. He could never break a promise, not even to a policeman. Gerry and Ron got money to John's excellent Vancouver lawyer, Ian Donaldson.

My life was now very simple. I was a travel agent with a few legitimate trading sidelines. Common enough, but there was nothing for me to do. The business ran itself without me. I became fidgety.

'Balendo, if I was totally at your disposal, able to go anywhere, afford anything, what would you have me do?'

'Simple. Taiwan.'

'Why? What's going on there?'

'Economic explosion. Like Hong Kong and Japan but better. Western companies no foothold. Travel business wide open. Many countries don't send national airlines to Taiwan because of political reason. Scared of China. Good place to investigate. Martial law finished. Your charm good for Taiwan.'

I read up on Taiwan.

Beginning its economic growth with the mass manufacture of cheap and easily breakable plastic toys, Taiwan had moved well up-market into high-quality electronics and nuclear research. Its exports were now valued as greater than China's. Despite its high technology, Taiwan's communications and banking systems were remarkably primitive. Its tourist industry was infantile. There seemed to be little catering for foreigners.

Without too much in the way of business strategy and forethought, I flew to Taipei and checked into the Fortuna Hotel on Chungshan Road. After refreshing myself in the hotel's Jacuzzi, I went for a walk in the area around the hotel. It was a mild night-life area with brightly lit bars and cafés. I called into one for a drink and struck up a conversation with the owner, a Filipino named Nesty. His wife worked in a travel agency. His sister worked in a bar, the Hsaling, which was very popular with Taiwan's few Western visitors. He suggested I meet him and his wife there the following evening. I had an early night. I was very relaxed going to sleep. No one knew where I was except a Filipino I'd just met. I was doing nothing against the laws of any country.

Early next morning, the phone rang.

'Good morning, Mr Marks. Welcome to Taipei,' said a female Chinese voice.

'Who is this, please?' I asked.

'My name is Joyce Lee from Overseas Buyers Centre. We understand you are visiting Taiwan for business, and we are glad to assist you. Would you like to come to our offices and explain your business requirements to us?'

'Yes. When?'

'How about I pick you up from your hotel at 10.30 this morning, Mr Marks?'

'That's fine.'

Joyce Lee was young and attractive. A limousine took us to her offices. I explained that my main purpose in visiting Taiwan was to promote my British travel agency. She quickly made appointments for me to see senior executives of the Taiwanese national airline, China Airlines, and major travel agencies. She was disappointed I didn't come with orders from Europe for Taiwanese goods. I said I might come back with some.

In the evening, I kept my appointment at the Hsaling with Nesty and his wife, Maria. She apprised me of the state of the travel market in Taiwan and the range of prices charged by various airlines and agencies for their flights.

They left the bar, and three New Zealanders squeezed next to me to occupy the two seats vacated. I was drinking whisky and water in separate glasses. Through clumsiness, I knocked over the glass of water on to the lap of one of my new companions. I apologised profusely.

'Are you Welsh?' he asked, brushing off small pools of
water.

'Yes, I am.'

'*Ydych chi siarad Cymraeg?*'

'*Odw.*'

'Roy Richards. Pleased to meet you.'

'Howard Marks. Sorry about the water.'

'Don't worry. Thank God it's only water. Not Welsh
water by any chance, is it?'

'I shouldn't think so, Roy. Mind, a few years ago I was
trying to ship the stuff from Wales to the East myself. Maybe
someone stole my idea.'

'Is that your business then, Howard? Water?'

'No, I'm just a humble travel agent these days, but I used
to dabble a bit in all sorts of trades. What about you? Don't
tell me you're a water man.'

'No way. I left Wales for New Zealand to get away from
the wet. At the moment, I work for the New Zealand
Government. Sounds very grand, but all I and my two
friends here do is interview Taiwanese who want to emigrate
to New Zealand.'

'That's impressive. So you actually decide who can get in
and who can't?'

'No, I wouldn't say that. I don't make the final decision.'

'But you make the first. You can make sure they don't get
in but you can't ensure they do.'

'I suppose that's right. I never looked at it like that.'

'Why do people want to leave Taiwan, Roy? It seems a
nice place, and surely the economy is strong.'

'The Taiwanese are scared stiff of China, especially since
you lot promised to give Hong Kong back to the Chinese in
1997. They think it's only a matter of time before China
marches into here. I don't agree with them for one minute.
But lots of them definitely want out. And if they're of the
right type, we make them welcome in New Zealand.'

'What type do they have to be?'

'Filthy rich, basically. But here that's quite a broad spectrum. We've immigrated university professors, nuclear research physicists, as well as top industrialists. We do several dozen a month. It's a lot of interviews, but the pay's good. And there's no end of profitable sidelines.'

'Like what?'

'Well, the people who want us to grant them New Zealand nationality treat us like bloody gods. They agree to whatever we ask. We can dictate to them what they should invest in when they come to New Zealand, where they should live, and what business they should open. You can imagine there's quite a crowd of New Zealanders with plenty of suggestions. Putting a few of them forward can produce healthy kickbacks for yours truly. We also tell them which hotels to stay in before they settle, even how to travel there. That's all left to us.'

'Do you have a good travel agent?'

'I wonder why you're asking, Howard. We don't actually have a regular travel agent. If your prices are competitive, I'd love to give a fellow Welshman the business. Shall we move on? Have you been to MTV yet?'

In 1988, the streets of Taipei were lined with MTV theatres of all shapes and sizes. I'd noticed them but had not been interested enough to enter. I followed Roy into what appeared to be one of the biggest. After paying some nominal charge, we were shown into a massive room housing the biggest array of music videos and laser discs I had ever seen. We were asked to choose one each and then choose a room. Most signs in Taipei are in one language, Mandarin. Occasionally there would be English ones. In this MTV theatre, there were two English signs leading to the rooms: 'Sex' and 'No Sex'. Shagged-out couples staggered out of 'Sex'. Roy and I went through 'No Sex' and into one of many extremely comfortable private rooms equipped with audio- and video-playing equipment, so highly technical that it looked as if it hadn't yet been invented. We sat on a couch and watched the laser disc of Joe Cocker in *Mad Dogs and Englishmen*. A waiter brought in beer. Roy took out a small joint and lit it.

'I imagine you indulge,' Roy half asked.

'Is it that obvious?'

'I must admit, Howard, I thought it was a safe bet.'

The joint was of excellent-quality Thai grass.

'Roy, would any of these Taiwanese want to emigrate to Wales or Mallorca?'

'They'll go just about anywhere, and they'll bring loads of money with them. But they'll go only where they can get citizenship. If Wales goes independent, you might have a chance, but Britain now is a bit stiff on immigrants. I don't know about Spain. Every country will grant citizenship to absolutely the right type of person. It depends who you know.'

I wondered if Rafael would be interested in letting in a few Taiwanese billionaires through Palma airport and allowing them to spend fortunes in whatever way he thought might benefit Mallorca.

'Yeah, I'd like to see Wales go independent, Roy. There could be some big changes as a result.'

'What would you do if you were the leader of Wales, Howard?'

'I would stop any New Zealanders from entering Wales unless there was an official New Zealand Government statement admitting that the All Blacks' defeat of Wales at Cardiff Arms Park in 1972 was the result of foul play.'

'Welsh rugby has had its day, Howard, I'm afraid. You'll find that out this summer when Wales tour New Zealand. But seriously, what would you do if you were in charge of Wales?'

'The very first thing I would do is legalise marijuana. Anybody would be allowed to smoke it within the country's borders, and growing the plant would be actively encouraged. There would be no ban on importing marijuana into Wales.'

'A lot of people, me included, would go along with that. What about drugs like heroin, though? Would you keep those illegal?'

'No. I'd legalise the lot. But for different reasons. I would still want marijuana to be traded, bought and sold, for what it is: a beneficial herb with no harmful qualities. Substances which are addictive, toxic, or otherwise harmful should be freely available, but accompanied by full and accurate information about the particular drug's effects. If that's how people want to go through life, sick and spaced-out, that's fine, as long as they are fully aware of what they're sticking inside themselves. Society can afford to subsidise the lives of the very few who, sadly, feel there's no other way for them.'

'Would you do anything else, or would legalising dope automatically take care of everything?'

'It would take care of a lot. But for sure I'd abolish nuclear power stations and the armed forces and liberate all those funds tied up in defence commitments. There wouldn't be any very rich or very poor. There'd be full employment. You know, the usual stuff.'

'You'd go down well in New Zealand, Howard. Why don't you try to persuade some Taiwanese to set up a factory or two in Wales, Howard? That would bring some employment to the area.'

'I thought you said the Taiwanese would steer clear of Wales because there's little chance of their becoming Welsh.'

'I did, Howard, but this is a different ball game. Look how many Japanese factories there are in Wales. They aren't trying to be Welsh. The Taiwanese are the new Japanese and want to get themselves in everywhere to make lots of money.'

'Why aren't they in Wales already?'

'Because, Howard, no Welshman has presented the Taiwanese with a proposal embodying attractive terms: tax incentives, residency, and long-term naturalisation prospects. Why don't you become the first person to set up a Taiwanese plant in Wales?'

'How do I find Taiwanese likely to be attracted by such a proposal?'

'I see about twenty every day.'

The next week was spent wining, dining, and engaging in other forms of appointment with senior executives of Taipei industrial organisations and travel agencies.

Armed with several folders of information on Taiwanese business regulations and a host of connections among the Taiwanese power élite, I flew back to London. Balendo was delighted with what I'd achieved and researched. He could better all the prices presently paid for tickets by the New Zealand Government and other visitors to Taiwan. Telexes chattered back and forth between Taipei and London and between New Zealand and London. In a few weeks, Hong Kong International Travel Centre became England's biggest seller of China Airlines' tickets and handled all the air travel arrangements for Evergreen, the world's biggest container-shipping line.

While in London, I engaged a researcher to find out what sort of incentives were being offered to industrialists to open up factories in South Wales. I summarised the information and put it into a presentable report form.

During the course of these researches, I met an American Go player named Michael Katz. He was licensed to practise law in both the United Kingdom and the United States and was vaguely aware of my smuggling history. Over countless Go games, we developed a friendship.

Starting from the time I learned from Tom Sunde that the DEA were on my case, I had determined to do some sort of legal research into the likelihood of my extradition being successfully sought by the Americans, but I had never got round to it. I brought the matter up with Katz. He said he would fly over to America, get hold of all the relevant extradition law, see various lawyers and authorities, and dig out any available files that might relate to my case.

Back home in Palma, I asked Rafael if there was any way

we could take advantage of Taiwanese tycoons' desire to come to Mallorca and build housing estates and factories. He assured me there was. Although he would not consider breaking the Spanish immigration laws, he would be able to help in unique ways. He introduced me to Luis Pina, the *gerente* of Palma's Universitat de Les Illes Balears, who prepared a lengthy report on Mallorca's economic situation, and to Mallorca's Minister of Tourism, who gave me masses of Spanish tourist propaganda.

By June 1988, apart from still smoking over twenty joints a day, I was super-straight and very settled. Although I had visited Taiwan and London, I was spending time at home far more than ever before and enjoying it. Many of my legitimate business plans were now beginning to focus on Palma. I didn't need to fly halfway around the world every time there was a meeting or payment. I toyed with the perverse idea of trying to become incredibly rich through purely legitimate means but soon abandoned it. The people who had succeeded at such endeavours seemed to be unhappy and obnoxious. The only intelligent and happy rich people I knew tended to be criminals and academic aristocrats. I had plenty of acquaintances among the former, but the latter had not really featured in my life since my Oxford student days. It had been silly of me to lose touch with them.

Every seven years past members of Balliol College are invited to a reunion of their contemporaries. I had graduated in 1967 but had ignored the invitations of 1974 and 1981. I accepted the 1988 invitation and flew from Palma to London. Julian Peto met me at Heathrow airport, and we both drove to Oxford.

It was strange to stroll through Balliol's front quadrangle once again. My contemporaries had changed very little in twenty years, and old friendships and alliances were quickly rekindled. There seemed to be no disapproval of my exploits in the hashish-smuggling trade, just interest and polite curiosity. Names and addresses were exchanged. Tentative plans to meet were made. Mac, unfortunately, was not there, but there was news of him. He was in London and appeared not to feel any resentment towards me.

One of my Oxford contemporaries, a fellow Welshman named Peter Gibbins, had become a successful academic. During term-time he lectured university students. During vacations he ran seminars in information technology aimed at managerial audiences from all parts of the world. We talked about Taiwan and the demand there for knowledge of European business practice. Peter asked if I would be able to recruit delegates from Taiwan to attend a seminar series which he would organise and for which he would arrange prestigious academic speakers. It might even be possible to provide accommodation for the Taiwanese delegates in under-graduate rooms in Balliol. I agreed to recruit as many as I could.

I got back to Palma to find that Roger Reaves had been leaving a series of frantic messages for me. We met in a café at Santa Ponsa, a small coastal resort midway between La Vileta and Roger's home in Andraitx.

'Howard, boy, that passport you got me was a dud.'

'What do you mean, a dud? That passport came straight from the Passport Office.'

'Well, wherever the son-of-a-bitch came from, it's a dud. Last week I flew into Amsterdam. The Dutch Immigration took one look at the passport and asked me to come into a room for questioning. It's gotta be a dud.'

'But Roger, there could be any number of other explanations. You could have picked up some heat moving around.'

'Hell, boy, all I've been doing is buying me a boat or two. That don't pick up no heat.'

'Well, it could, Roger. What did the Dutch cops ask you?'

'I didn't stay to find out. No siree. I just prayed to the Good Lord and ran my ass off.'

'What! Did they chase you?'

'Did they chase me! Boy, did they chase me! I had to run across a runway and jump over two real high barbed-wire fences on the airport perimeter. I was cut to shreds. I mean, maybe it ain't the passport, but can you guarantee me it's clean?'

'I can't guarantee it, Roger, no.'

'Okay. Get me another one.'

A few hours later, Roger rang me at home.

'Howard, you're either as hot as the Devil's hell, or you're a cop.'

'What?'

'As soon as you drove off from that café in Santa Ponsa, four plainclothes got out of a car and tried to arrest me. They gave me some bullshit about my car and having to see my documents. I pushed them away and escaped through a bakery. If it wasn't for the Lord's help, I'd be in the can. They're on to you, boy.'

'Then why haven't they arrested me, Roger?'

'To tell you the truth, Howard, that's exactly what I was wondering. I probably won't be in touch for a while.'

'Roger, you don't really think I'm a cop, do you?'

'No, I don't. Damned right I don't. But I feel danger. I feel danger real strong.'

Tom Sunde rang the same day. He wanted more protection money. I told him I was still straight, and therefore skint. I also told him that I thought if I was going to be arrested by the DEA, I would have been by now. He said that a Grand Jury, whatever that might be, was in the process of indicting me. If I paid him $250,000, he would give me all the transcripts. I didn't believe him. He said he would continue whenever he was able, on a purely friendship basis, to let me know if I was in danger of imminent arrest.

The next afternoon, Marie, Roger's wife, came to our house. Shortly after Roger's last conversation with me, he and Marie had gone to pick up their son from his school at the edge of Palma. Several armed police surrounded Roger's car and arrested him. After spending the night in Palma police station, he was taken to the Palacio de Justicia to see the Magistrado, whose rooms were on the second floor. Wearing handcuffs, Roger jumped over the Magistrado's desk, out of the window, and onto the roof of a parked car, severely denting it. He ran down the main street pursued by a horde of policemen. They apprehended him. He was now in Palma prison. His extradition had been sought, not by the Americans but by the Germans.

I had to question Marie for a long time before anything made sense. It appeared that McCann had supplied Roger with a pile of Moroccan. Roger had hired a German cargo boat and German crew to take the hash to England. The German crew were busted when the boat later landed, empty of cargo, at a German port. Very quickly, they told the authorities everything they knew, which included details of Roger. German law prohibits anyone from using a German boat to transport dope anywhere. Roger was indicted in Lübeck, West Germany. Roger thought the Germans would also indict me.

I took the next flight out of Palma. It was clearly no place to be. With me was a travelling bag full of papers and documents relating to immigrating Taiwanese to Palma, information-technology seminars, and setting up factories in South Wales. Once in Taipei I checked into the Fortuna Hotel. Although I had my William Tetley false passport with me (hidden in the cover of a hardback book), I used my real one. I was not hiding. I did not regard myself as being on the run. I felt safe in Taiwan. There wasn't even an American Embassy there.

While I had been in Europe, Roy Richards had been back to New Zealand for a few weeks. He had talked about me to various of his friends in Wellington. One of them had read

David Leigh's *High Time*. Roy had brought the book with him. He wanted me to sign it.

With Roy's help, I obtained China Metal's tentative agreement to open a factory in South Wales and a long list of Taiwanese millionaires wishing to live and invest in Mallorca. A number of industrial managers expressed interest in attending seminars in Oxford. To keep things alive with Malik, I also made arrangements to purchase some empty toothpaste tubes. Everything was working wonderfully well.

Gerry Wills found out my hotel phone number in Taiwan from Balendo. I hadn't spoken to Gerry for almost a year. He said that he had a lawyer with connections in the DEA. This lawyer had told him that a Grand Jury indictment had been returned against him, me, and others in Miami. I was apparently the ringleader. The Americans were about to request my extradition.

It was night-time. I went for a stroll around the campus of the University of Taiwan. Should I go on the run again and use my Tetley passport? Could I possibly survive seeing my wife, parents, and children only in hurried and clandestine meetings? Should I stay in Taiwan? It was, after all, one of the very few countries in the world without an extradition treaty with the United States, and I seemed to survive quite well in the place. My family could at least visit me for extended periods.

I went into Nesty's bar and had a drink with him. The place was unusually empty.

'Where's Maria?' I asked, noticing the absence of Nesty's wife.

'Oh, she's gone to the Dog Temple with her uncle.'

'What the hell is a dog temple?'

'There's only one Dog Temple, Howard. It's on the beach near Tanshui, about one or two hours' drive away. Thirty years ago, a fishermen's sampan was wrecked in a storm, causing the deaths of all thirty-three people aboard. They were all buried in the same grave. One of the fishermen's dogs jumped in the grave and would not come out. It was buried too. The dog has now become a god of loyalty and lies in a temple built on the beach. Loyalty is very important to a criminal. All criminals now worship there for solutions to their problems.'

I asked Nesty for the directions to the Dog Temple and took a cab there. It arrived in the early hours of the morning. The temple had a car park. Vehicles of every conceivable description, from scooters to Mercedes, ploughed in and out. A thousand beggars, gangsters, and hookers milled between the car park and the temple. Inside the temple was an eight-foot statue carved out of black rock. People were on their knees praying to the dog. Others were plastering it with small rations of gold leaf. I made a simple prayer: 'Let me be with my wife and children.' Just thinking of my children made me cry. Myfanwy was coming to spend the summer with us. It was so rare for me to be with all four of my children. In a few days it would be my wedding anniversary. I wanted to be with the woman I loved.

Michael Katz flew from Los Angeles to see me in Taipei. He had a stack of papers on extradition and a file of documents relating to Ernie Combs, which confirmed that there had been telephone taps on my home in Spain. In Katz's opinion, there was no indictment against me; my extradition had not been asked for. Without questioning I took Katz's words as an answer to my prayer to the dog. It was safe for me to go back to Palma, and that's where I should be.

After finalising as much as I could, I flew from Taipei to Vienna and Zurich. At the PTT at Zurich airport, I called Tom Sunde. He advised me not to stay in Palma more than forty-eight hours. I telephoned Rafael, and he met me at Palma airport. We bypassed Immigration and Customs. He drove me home. I showered my children with Taiwanese presents before taking Judy out for a Friday night wedding-anniversary dinner at Tristan's in Puerto Portals, followed by some drinks with Geoffrey Kenion at Wellies. The weekend was spent in the bosom of my adorable family.

Thirteen

DENNIS HOOWARD MARKS

Amber cried from the back seat, 'Daddy, Daddy, don't drive fast. Please, Daddy, don't drive so fast. I'm scared.'

It was almost 1 a.m. on Monday morning, and the five of us were returning from extended eating and drinking sessions at the Taj Mahal and Taffy's Bar in Magaluf. I wasn't driving fast. Amber usually enjoyed the sensation of speed, so I was doubly puzzled by her words of caution. I looked back and saw terror in her lovely blue eyes. What was frightening her? What did her subconscious know that I didn't? Was she foreseeing some disaster that only a child's mind, cluttered with neither prejudice nor preconception, could apprehend? I slowed right down and changed the compact disc from Simply Red to Modern Talking. No other sounds were made during the remainder of the fifteen-minute journey home. The children went quietly to bed. Amber still looked terrified.

I was almost out of hash. Judy's sister Masha and her boyfriend, Nigel, had been staying with us for a few days. They had gone out to buy some hash in Plaza Gomila, but had not yet returned. A small bedtime joint would have to suffice. Judy and I made gentle love and slept peacefully in each other's arms.

At 8.30 a.m. the phone rang. David Embley wanted to play tennis. He said he'd come round in an hour or so. I got out of bed. Francesca was already up, so I made both of us a light breakfast. I checked my dope box. It was no longer empty. Well done, Masha. She'd left a note. She and Nigel had just gone to the Club de Mar to look for work on the boats anchored there.

The phone rang again. It was McCann.

'Get my fucking dope and get my fucking money. My wife and kids have been threatened. It's heavy, man, and it's your fucking fault bringing the heat on everybody.'

'It's not my fault you and Roger carried on without me and it's not my fault Roger's in the nick,' I protested.

'Well, find out from him where everything is. Send someone to Palma nick. It's on your fucking doorstep. You arsehole!'

Coincidentally, or perhaps not, Roger's wife, Marie, was the next to ring. She wanted to come round. She had just seen Roger and had some important news.

As soon as I'd finished talking to Marie, the phone rang again. A long-distance call by the sound of the hiss. No one spoke, and the line went dead. It rang again. This time it was Tom Sunde. He talked about some trivial matters for a minute or so and hung up.

Tom and I had devised a code. If he began his telephone conversation with the words 'how things are', then I should infer that extreme danger was imminent. I went over his conversation in my mind. I couldn't remember how he'd started. Never mind. The authorities never busted anyone halfway through a Monday morning. They preferred Friday evenings, when no lawyers would be available for sixty hours, or dawn on any day, when the victims were suffering from hangovers and unprepared.

I decided to take a quick swim. I looked at the chain of three Thai Buddhas hanging around my neck. Sompop's words rang through my mind: 'Wear in sea but not in bath.'

What was our swimming pool? Was it a small sea or a large bath? It was outside like the sea but enclosed like a bath. I never could work it out. Sometimes I wore the Buddhas when swimming in an outside swimming pool; sometimes I didn't. On this occasion I took them off.

I emerged from the pool to the sound of the entryphone at the front gate. I rarely asked callers to identify themselves. I released the gate lock. It was Marie. She drank some coffee and talked with Francesca while I put on some shorts and a tee-shirt.

The entryphone buzzed again, and I let in David Embley, suitably dressed for tennis. Ten minutes later, he left. He promised he'd be back within the hour.

Yet again the entryphone buzzed. I presumed David had forgotten something and was coming back to retrieve it. Instead three overweight and casually dressed middle-aged men ambled into the courtyard and gazed at the tops of the five palm trees. The night before, Judy had mentioned something about some locals agreeing to trim and tidy up our palm trees. I guessed these were they. I began walking into the yard to greet them.

Suddenly, one of them pulled out a revolver and stuck it into my stomach. His lips were quivering, his glasses were steamed up, his hands were shaking, and his breath stank of peppermint. Twenty years in prison ran through my mind. Francesca let out a scream which I still hear every day. These guys were going to kill her daddy. Instinctively, I put up my hands and said, '*Tranquilo! Tranquilo!*'

My hands were handcuffed behind my back, and I was shoved on to the kitchen sofa. Francesca, trembling violently with fear, ran to me and began kissing and hugging me. One of the intruders pulled her off. In a panic she ran upstairs to where Judy was sleeping. A few more men barged into the kitchen and tore after her as if pursuing an escaped lunatic. Marie turned to stone as one of the cops grabbed her handbag and poured its contents on to the table. One of the three fat intruders made himself at home on a kitchen stool. His eyes were sadistic, and his smile indicated he was having a quiet orgasm. With his open white shirt and Zapata moustache he looked Spanish enough, but he had the unmistakable aura of the DEA. Was this Craig Lovato?

'*Es Policía Nacional?*' I asked.

'*Sí,*' he replied, unconvincingly.

Then David Embley was escorted from outside the gate into the kitchen by two more cops. He, too, was handcuffed. His eyes refused to meet mine. The cops indicated we were leaving. I asked if I could change into more suitable clothes. They refused. I asked if I could say goodbye to my wife and children. They refused. Embley and I were both led out into waiting police cars. I looked up at the bedroom window as I went out of the gate. Maybe I would never see this house again. I heard Judy shrieking as the car door slammed. She'd be all right in a few days, I thought. She'd visit me as often as she could with the children. We still had a fair bit of money. I might be gone a couple of years, but then we'd survived similar problems in the past. And I knew they had no evidence. Spain wouldn't give me up to the Yanks, anyway. They were far too independent to align themselves with America in its phoney drug war. Here they let people smoke hashish in the streets. I'd have a 'lie-down' in a Spanish jail. It would be manageable. I could brush up my Spanish.

At Palma police station I was told I'd been arrested on a drugs charge.

This didn't come as a surprise. I asked for further details. None could be given now. I was given a piece of paper to fill out. Did I want anyone informed of my arrest? I put down Rafael's name. He might be upset to find out I was a convicted drug smuggler, but we'd got on well enough, and he'd be surely able to ease my plight. After all, he was a Chief Inspector of Police. Did I have a lawyer? I put down Julio Morell, Rafael's lawyer. Did I want the British Consul to be informed? Yes, I did.

With a decided lack of ceremony, Embley and I were
relieved of all our personal possessions and put into separate
subterranean holding cells. Mine already had two occupants:
a comatose drunkard and a young Peruvian, who claimed to
be a member of Sendero Luminoso. He was awaiting
deportation and had been there for thirty days. It was rough,
but he assured me that I'd be in the Centro Penitenciario de
Palma tomorrow after the obligatory court appearance. He'd
seen what had happened to prisoners over the last month. He
said I'd like Palma prison: plenty of free time, lots of dope,
and conjugal visits. I lay down on the concrete floor. There
was no furniture, no water, no cigarettes.

I thought of what the police might find at home: the
hashish Masha had scored, half a million pesetas, and my
electronic notebook containing the telephone numbers I
didn't know off by heart. There wasn't too much to worry
about. Even if the British authorities had also raided our
Chelsea flat, there were no dope-dealing accounts or other
incriminating documents lying around.

I wondered if there was any possibility that I had been
arrested as the result of my marginal involvement in Roger
and McCann's chaotic Moroccan scam. I reasoned that the
Germans would have busted me the same time as they did
Roger if they had thought I was involved. On the other hand,
Roger might have suddenly decided to blame me for the
whole thing in the hope of getting himself out of trouble. I
also entertained the possibility that I had been arrested in
connection with the Vancouver bust of Thai grass, but the
Canadians were not known for wasting resources relentlessly
pursuing cannabis offenders. It had to be the Yanks. I drifted
off into a mixture of apprehension, sleep, and dream.

Suddenly, a disgusting sandwich was thrust into my hand,
and I was asked by a jailer if I wanted to use the bathroom.
I was taken to a filthy shower-cum-shithouse. On the way
back I stared through the barred windows of the cell doors,
wondering which one was Embley's. A face came to one of

the windows. This must be Embley's. I hoped he wasn't freaking out too much. The face looked tortured and pained. Tears streamed from eyes full of terrified sadness. The face turned into Judy's. It was Judy's. I wanted it to turn into another face. It wouldn't.

'Oh God! Why have they got you here, love? Where are the children?'

'They're extraditing me to America,' Judy sobbed. 'They're taking me away from my children. Stop them, Howard, please. Stop them, for God's sake.'

'*Silencio! Silencio!*' yelled the jailer. '*No hable!*'

'*Pero es mi esposa,*' I pleaded.

'*Más tarde, más tarde,*' insisted the jailer as he grabbed my arm and led me back to my cell.

This was incredible. How could they possibly extradite Judy? Since my release from prison in 1982, she'd broken no law anywhere, let alone in America. She hadn't stopped nagging me to quit smuggling. No one had even asked her to break the law. What was going on? Where were the children? I lay down and tried to keep calm.

The jailer's watch showed 6 p.m. as the cell opened again. I was handcuffed and taken to an upstairs room. Judy, surrounded by four or five men and stunned by disbelief and sadness, sat crumpled in a chair.

'Look what they're doing to me,' she said, handing me a piece of paper, which indicated that her extradition to the United States was being sought because of her involvement in a series of cannabis importations totalling several hundred tons and dating back to 1970.

'I was only fifteen then, Howard. I didn't meet you until years later, and even since then I've done nothing wrong. I never did anything. What are they doing? I can't leave my children.'

'Where are they, love?'

'Masha's got them. Thank God. Oh! Stop them, Howard. You must stop them. They can't do this to me.'

'They're nuts, Judy. Absolutely nuts. Don't worry, Rafael and his lawyer should be on their way.'

Judy's sobbing became uncontrollable. Some uniformed cops took her away. I was shown a piece of paper similar to Judy's. It stated that my extradition to the United States was being sought because I was the head of the organisation that, since 1970, had smuggled hundreds of tons of hashish to the United States. My Spanish was not good enough to understand the rest.

In the room were two plainclothes policemen who couldn't speak English, a state lawyer who couldn't speak English, and an interpreter who spoke very little English. They all talked to me at the same time. I understood very little of what they were saying but gathered that, because it was a fiesta, Julio Morell's offices were closed. Furthermore, they were not prepared to call Rafael. I would have to make do with this state lawyer, who kept asking me if I wanted to go to the United States voluntarily and make a declaration to that effect. He gave me a stack of papers to sign. I stared at him with disbelief.

'*Puedo fumar, por favor?*' I asked, reaching out for the lawyer's packet of cigarettes. One of the plainclothes policemen was obviously very senior. He looked at me, smiled, and lit my cigarette. In pedestrian Spanish he joked about the book that had been written about me. He said that a number of my friends had also just been arrested. As if to prove his point, the door opened, and Geoffrey Kenion was brought in. The Americans wanted him, too. We were prevented from talking, and I was taken back to the holding cell.

Two hours later, I was taken to the same room and greeted by the policeman who had stuck a gun into my stomach. He motioned me to sit down at a desk.

'Were you really going to shoot me?' I asked.

'I'm sorry, Howard. I'm sorry. *Sólo para la seguridad. Lo siento*, Howard.'

A casually dressed man came to sit opposite me.

'*Tiene cigarrillos, por favor?*' I asked, very politely.

'Sorry, I don't smoke,' he replied in an English middle-class accent.

'Who are you?' I asked.

'Just part of the organisation.'

'Which organisation?'

'You'll see soon enough.'

'Where's Lovato?' I asked.

He jumped out of his seat and tore out of the room. Minutes later, the door opened and in walked the overweight man who'd earlier masqueraded as a member of the Policía Nacional. So this was, indeed, Craig Lovato of the DEA.

'Hello, Howard,' he said with a broad grin.

He then turned his back on me, and his large arse was inches away from my face. He wasn't being rude. He was squeezing himself between a desk and a chair. It wasn't easy.

'I'm Craig Lovato, DEA.'

He held out his hand. I shook it.

'How are you, Mr Lovato? Do you have any cigarettes, please?'

'You know, Howard, I've never smoked in my life. I don't know why people do it.'

'You think it should be illegal, Mr Lovato?'

'That's not for me to say. I'm interested in people who break the laws, not make them. Howard, I gather you knew this was coming, and obviously that's something I'm annoyed about.'

I presumed he was referring to Sunde and Carl.

'I want to establish a relationship with you. Call me Craig. I want you to voluntarily extradite yourself.'

'Give me a cigarette, Craig, and I'll think about it.'

Lovato pulled open a desk drawer, fished out a packet of cigarettes and a lighter, and motioned me to help myself. I took several deep drags.

'What about my wife? Let her go, and you can take me to America today.'

'Bob O'Neill, the Assistant United States Attorney from Miami, Florida, who is in charge of your prosecution, will have to make that decision once you are on United States territory.'

'What's the charge against her?'

'I'm not sure. That's articulated by the Office of the United States Attorney, Miami, Florida. I think it's conspiracy to import a Schedule A controlled substance.'

'She never told me she was doing anything like that. Are you sure about this?'

'A Presidential Organised Crime Drug Enforcement Task Force instructed law enforcement agencies of several countries to investigate certain matters relating to your criminal conduct, and on the basis of the findings, the Assistant United States Attorney, Bob O'Neill, deemed there was sufficient evidence against Judy to go before a Grand Jury in Miami, Florida. The Grand Jury returned an indictment against her.'

'So, what is she actually accused of doing?'

'Using her telephone to further your illegal activities.'

'You mean she might have taken a message for me on our home phone here in Palma? That's illegal?'

'It would be something of that nature, Howard. Yes, it is certainly against United States law. I forget the actual statute.'

'My wife is locked up in this jail for answering her own phone. And you want to extradite her from here to lock her up in America. I'd heard the DEA was over the top. What do you call it? Zero tolerance, isn't it? Going around confiscating people's pleasure yachts if there's the remnants of a marijuana roach on board. You really are completely fucking nuts. Why don't you extradite my one-year-old son? I think he answered the phone on occasion.'

'Howard, I merely enforce the law.'

'Whatever it is, Craig?'

'Whatever it is, Howard.'

'You don't even have to think. It must make life a lot easier.'

'Of course it does, Howard.'

'What are the charges against me?'

'Again, they are articulated by the Office of the United States Attorney, but I'm given to understand that there are fourteen charges against you, of conspiracy, money laundering, and RICO.'

'What's RICO?'

'In the United States you will be assigned a lawyer who will explain this to you.'

'I'm obviously going to fight extradition, unless you let my wife go.'

'You might just beat extradition on a technicality. But I'm a betting man. I'm from Las Vegas. I bet I'll get you. What's the code for these databanks of yours?'

'I can't remember.'

'Howard, we can always get Washington to do it.'

'Yeah, they should find it pretty easy, though they might fuck it up. How's Lord Moynihan?'

The question threw him a little, but he quickly recovered. 'I think, Howard, he'll come out of this smelling like a rose. By the way, he thinks you have a contract out on him. He's under our protection. I think I'm also authorised to inform you that Patrick Lane has just been arrested by my DEA colleagues in Miami. He is now in MCC, Miami Metropolitan Correctional Center. Chi Chuen Lo, or Balendo Lo, as you know him, was this morning arrested by my Scotland Yard colleagues. Hong Kong International is going down the tubes, Howard. Still, I'm sure you have plenty of money buried somewhere.'

'I've never had any money in my life. Why has Balendo been arrested? What is he meant to have done?'

'He was part of what we refer to as the "Marks Cartel". He worked for you, Howard. We know that.'

'He's a bloody travel agent. Nothing else. What's the "Marks Cartel"?'

'The Office of the United States Attorney has reason to believe that Balendo Lo, or Chi Chuen Lo, which is his real name, knowingly facilitated the international travel arrangements of cartel members. The "Marks Cartel" is your organisation, Howard. You've not heard of the Colombian "Medellín Cartel"? Come on.'

'I thought a cartel was a group of people who agreed on things like commodity prices. With whom am I meant to be agreeing in the "Marks Cartel"? Myself?'

'It's a bit like General Motors, Howard. It's all connected.'

I was losing his drift. Either he or I was insane.

'You might like to know, Howard, that Malik, too, is about to be arrested in Karachi.'

'You think Pakistan are going to give him up to you guys?'

'He'll be the most difficult, especially given his close relationship with President Zia, which we know all about. But we'll get him, somehow. He's part of the "Marks Cartel".'

'Why have you arrested David Embley? Is he another extraditable "Marks Cartel" member?'

'It was the Spanish authorities' decision to arrest David, and it's their decision when to let him go. However, I shall say to them that, in my opinion, he was simply at the wrong place at the wrong time: your house when we arrested you. I must say you have beautiful children.'

'Can you talk to Judy, please, and let her know that there's some chance of her being released if I voluntarily extradite myself?'

'I don't like talking to distraught persons. Judith is very distraught.'

'That must limit your conversations quite a bit.'

'I'll see you in prison tomorrow, Howard. I must let my Spanish colleagues return to their families. They must be missing them.'

Back in my holding cell, the drunkard had finally woken up. He was screaming protests in Catalan. The Peruvian terrorist had buried his face in his hands in a gesture of 'Do Not Disturb'. I lay on the floor and began to feel very sad. Things looked bad, and there seemed little I could do other than collect my thoughts together, summon up whatever inner strength I might have, and let the worst day of my life slip away.

At dawn the next morning, I was fingerprinted, photographed, and asked questions about my particulars. Invariably, jailers and prison employees engaged in processing new arrivals have a propensity for misspelling names and addresses. They are most reluctant to make corrections. These mistakes often cause no end of problems further down the line. Is it deliberate? From the processing room I was taken to a reception area where Judy and Geoffrey had already arrived. David Embley was nowhere to be seen. Lovato must have let him go. Judy was in a terrible state, weeping uncontrollably and being fed tranquillisers. A jailer began to put handcuffs on her.

'*Hombre, es mi esposa,*' I protested. '*No necesitan estos.*' I couldn't bear to see her in them.

'*Todos son iguales. Todos tienen esposas. Esposas, también, tienen esposas,*' said the jailer, much to the amusement of a growing group of his colleagues. (It took a while for me to realise that the source of the humour lay in *esposas* being the Spanish word for both wives and handcuffs.) The three of us were then quite roughly handcuffed.

Geoffrey, although looking quite bemused, was absolutely silent. We were put in the same prison van and driven to Palma's impressively quaint Palacio de Justicia. Geoffrey remained silent during the five-minute journey to court. Judy sobbed continually.

Emerging from the prison van was like walking on to a film set in full swing. Dazzlingly bright searchlights and thousands of camera flashes illuminated throngs of noisy journalists. We were quickly taken through them to the Palacio's holding cells and then led one at a time to the corridor outside the

rooms of the Magistrado. This must have been the second
floor that Roger Reaves had jumped out of just a few weeks
ago. For sure, he had balls.

The Magistrado was a young man with a kind face.
Through an excellent interpreter, he explained that as a
result of a United States Government extradition request, I
was to be held at the disposition of the Audiencia Nacional,
Madrid. I could volunteer myself for extradition anytime I
wanted. I had the right to fight extradition, and I would have
the full protection of Spanish law if I did so. I asked the
Magistrado if I could telephone my children. He handed me
the phone immediately. I rang. Masha answered. The
children sounded okay. I told them I'd get me and Judy back
home as soon as I could. It was the truth, but it took a while.

We had several hours' separate and solitary wait in the
Palacio's holding cells. A local Spanish lawyer came and, in
excellent English, introduced himself as Luis Morell.
Although a distant relation of my initial lawyer of choice,
Julio Morell (who, it seemed, did not want to be remotely
involved in this matter), he had been independently engaged
by Bob Edwardes to represent me and Judy. I liked him
immediately. He gave me some pesetas, a carton of
cigarettes, and a change of clothing. He said he'd be over to
see us at the prison as soon as he could.

The media crowds were still there as the three of us were
taken back to the prison van. I assumed they were all
members of Palma's newspapers and broadcasting
companies. Mallorca was, after all, a small island. Local
interest was understandable. Judy was looking stronger. She,
too, had been allowed to talk to the children. We looked at
each other as the prison van drove up to the Centro
Penitenciario de Palma, and each of us knew that the other
was recalling the time Rafael once pointed it out to us and
remarked that its location had been carefully chosen as one
in which there was no escape from the hot sun. We got out
of the van and were greeted by friendly, smiling prison

funcionarios and trusty prisoners (prisoners trusted by the authorities), smoking cigarettes and drinking cans of beer. They relieved me of my wedding and engagement rings. I never saw them again. They debated which cells to assign us to.

'Can I have the same cell as my husband?' asked Judy with a humour that came from God knows where.

The *funcionarios* roared with laughter.

'May as well try it,' said Judy, with a glimmer of a smile. She was walked off to the women's section, Geoffrey and I to the men's.

We were taken to an empty prison walking yard.

'Sorry, Geoffrey. I didn't expect anything like this to happen. I'm sure you'll be released soon.'

'Don't worry. There's no evidence of any wrongdoing of mine. And I would hate to be in your shoes with my wife locked up. This might be very serious for you, Howard. Very serious, indeed. And I really believe David Embley is behind this. Think about it.'

I couldn't think about it.

Surprisingly, I was put into the same cell as Geoffrey. Within minutes, a trusty banged the door, pushing under it a variety of items. It was a care package from Roger Reaves. It contained cigarettes, cosmetics, writing materials, food, beer, magazines, prison money tokens, and a note in Roger's handwriting. He'd seen our court appearance on the news. He had some dope to smoke if I needed it.

The cell door opened. I was told to pack up my stuff. I was being taken to the *tubo*, whatever that was. The escorting *funcionarios* stopped outside a cell door over which was written in huge block letters *MUY PELIGROSO*. Inside the cell was a very empty cage of slightly smaller dimensions. I was locked in the cage. The cage was locked in the cell. The cell was locked in the prison. I watched two large cockroaches cautiously emerge from a filthy toilet hole. They were a lot bigger here than in Brixton or Wandsworth prisons. It would be difficult to bond with these creatures. Night fell. I lay on a filthy mattress and chain-smoked until daybreak.

I heard a trolley wheel to a stop outside the cell door.

'I am the morning *funcionario*. Would you like some breakfast, sir?'

Sir! This was different.

'Yes please,' I answered.

The cell door was opened, and a tray containing a sumptuous breakfast, good enough for a condemned man, was pushed through.

'I will be back later, sir, to see if you need any more.'

He didn't come back, but it was a nice thought.

I spent all the morning being interviewed by a series of prison officials and prison social workers. After the usual fingerprinting and photographic session, I was taken back to my cage and given another first-class meal. I fell asleep for a few minutes.

'Dennis Hooward Marks,' yelled a voice from beyond the cage.

I jumped up from the floor.

'*Sí.*'

'*Tiene visita.*'

The cell and inner cage were unlocked, and I was escorted from the *tubo* to the visiting area, which was a row of very low-walled cubicles seating prisoners on one side and visitors on the other. The prisoners all seemed to know each other's visitors, who kept dashing from cubicle to cubicle, shouting at never-ending streams of screaming children. The noise was unbelievable. At any moment, each prisoner had an average of six visitors and was separated from them by a sheet of almost opaque bullet-proof glass. At the bottom of the glass were a few cigarette-sized holes through which conversation was meant to take place. One could see and hear everyone except one's visitor.

'*Cabina número uno. Sólo cinco minutes*, Hooward.'

Only five minutes! This was no conjugal visit. I sat opposite Masha. She seemed very much in control. The children were okay. She had seen Judy. The lawyer had just seen Judy and was currently having a meeting with the prison director. The police had taken away our cars. They had also removed many items from the house, but they had missed my personal dope stash. The Palma Nova flat, the one I'd bought from Rafael, had also been busted. That worried me because hidden somewhere in the ceiling was a large can of Mallorquian home-grown grass and one of my false passports. I explained to Masha where the hiding-place was. She would check. She had brought me some clothes, books, and the last three days' British and Spanish newspapers. The package had been given to the *funcionarios*.

We had been talking for just two minutes when I felt someone tugging at my trouser leg. I looked around and saw Roger Reaves. He was on all fours, looking up at me and brandishing a can of beer and three ready-rolled joints.

'Drink the beer and hide the joints down your crotch. I hate to see you all like this. Man, I couldn't believe what I saw on TV. Why did those sons of bitches pick Judy up? I've been praying for her. You know they did the same thing to me in Georgia all them years ago. They picked Marie up. The dirty sons of bitches. But now I've got me a way outa here. I've been praying to God for it. Marie's going to fire a rope over the wall into the exercise yard. She'll use a crossbow. I've got me a few *funcionarios* paid off. I can get you out of your cell at night. You can come with me. We'll come back for Judy. Then we can go to South Africa and grow pot. Marie and Judy would love it there. Lord, it's a wonderful country. There's a guy here from Rotterdam. He can ship the stuff from South Africa to Holland. You know how much good weed goes for in Holland now? By the way, that Irish friend of yours definitely ripped us all off.'

I was finding this all a bit hard to take.

'Roger, I must talk to Masha. I've only got another couple of minutes more.'

'Oh! Lord! Howard. I'm sorry. Please excuse me. I'll see you all later. God bless you.'

'Michael Katz has come over,' said Masha. 'He's going to try to see you with the Spanish lawyer.'

'*Termina, Hooward, por favor, ahora.*'

Masha was asked to leave. The visit was over. I was given the package of clothing and reading material she had brought and taken back to the *tubo*, and then immediately back to the same visiting cubicle. This time it was my Spanish lawyer, Luis Morell. He gave it to me straight. The Americans wanted me badly. The media was giving my arrest maximum publicity. It would be almost impossible to persuade Spain not to extradite me. Judy had a much better chance. Eventually, we would both have to be transferred to Madrid prisons in good time for the Audiencia Nacional's final decision. He would try to get Judy bail or, failing that, keep her in Palma for as long as possible so she could keep in touch with the children. He and Michael Katz would come to see us later for a long visit.

Back in the cage at the *tubo*, I looked at the newspaper reports of yesterday's court appearance and the day before's arrest. They were unreal. Both broadsheets and tabloids reported official statements from the Florida United States Attorney's Office that they had just busted the 'biggest marijuana operation the world has ever seen'. It was 'the biggest drug bust in history'. According to Thomas Cash, official spokesman for the DEA, I was the 'Marco Polo of drug trafficking' and shipped in 'thousands of tons'. According to the *Daily Express* and *Daily Mirror*, I ran a '£200,000,000 cannabis empire', using as part of my *modus operandi* 'undersea hollows and hideaways marked by oceanographic buoys'. One of these hideaways, a cave on the Costa Brava, had just been busted and inside was discovered a 'huge hashish supermarket', well stocked with fifteen tons of the finest

Lebanese, several fast boats, and a cache of machine-guns. I owned a fleet of freighters. I owned finance houses. I had homes all over the world. I had connections with top gangsters, secret services, and terrorist organisations. I had boasted I was 'too smart, too sophisticated for any law agency to catch'. The *Daily Mirror* described me as the head of 'a multi-billion pound international empire' and as 'one of the most sophisticated drug barons of all time, with a ruthless organisation matching anything operated by the Mafia or the feared Colombians'. One of my terrorist underlings, James McCann of the Provisional IRA, had also been arrested in Palma.

What the hell was Jim doing in Palma?

The report of McCann's arrest prompted the Republican Press Centre in Belfast to make what I believe was the IRA's first official statement concerning McCann's links with them. It read: 'The Irish Republican Army repudiates any suggestion by the media that James McCann, arrested for involvement in drug smuggling, has ever had any connection with our movement or our struggle. Our attitude to drugs and drug trafficking is well known.'

The newspaper reports also revealed that my organisation had been stumbled upon when Scotland Yard and the FBI were jointly investigating the whereabouts of the proceeds of the November 1983 Brinks-Mat £26,000,000 gold bullion robbery at London's Heathrow airport. Finally, proof of my ingenuity had been provided by the discovery in my home of empty toothpaste tubes used for concealing messages carried throughout the world by my couriers.

I was vainly attempting to grasp all this when I was again taken from the *tubo*, this time to the director's office. Inside were Joaquín Mejuto, director of Centro Penitenciario de Palma, Luis Morell, and Michael Katz. Katz was wearing one of my shirts, one that Amber had given me. Luis explained that due to the high-profile nature of my arrest and its presumed legal complexity, Señor Mejuto had been kind enough to allow us to use his offices for visits from my lawyers. Señor Mejuto would now leave us in private, but was there anything that I needed? I said I would like to see Judy. Señor Mejuto nodded and left.

'Thanks for coming, Michael,' I said. 'Who else has been arrested?'

'The only names I have are Roger Reaves, John Denbigh, Ernie Combs . . .'

'Wait a minute, Michael. These guys have already been in prison for ages.'

'I suppose they've been re-arrested for this charge. The other names are Patrick Lane, Balendo Lo, James Newton, Teresita Caballero, John Francis, Brian Daniels . . .'

'Those last three names mean nothing to me.'

'I believe they're charged in the indictment. There are other arrests. Altogether there were arrests in nine different countries: England, Spain, Philippines, Thailand, Holland, Pakistan, Switzerland, America, and Canada.'

'What exactly has everyone been charged with?'

'No one will tell us at this stage, but I'm pretty sure you have been charged with conspiracy and RICO.'

'What's RICO?'

'I don't know. I'll ask a friend of mine who is a drugs lawyer in Michigan.'

'Where are they holding McCann?'

'James McCann was not arrested, Howard. The Spanish authorities have officially stated that the report of his being arrested in Palma was erroneous. They have also officially stated that the fifteen tons of Lebanese found in a cave on the Costa Brava did not concern you. Have you seen any of the DEA?'

'Yeah, I saw Craig Lovato at the police station. He said he was coming to see me again today. I'm hoping to fix up a deal to voluntarily extradite myself to set Judy free.'

'Well, that's up to you. But I'd advise against it. Was this the same DEA agent who arrested you at your house? Did this DEA agent question you?'

'Yes, a bit. He was the only cop who did.'

'Aha! He's broken American law!' Katz yelled excitedly.

'Which law?' I asked.

'The Mansfield Amendment. It was enacted a few years ago to deter DEA agents from further engagement in torture/interrogation sessions held in Mexico. The DEA had been having a great time down there stubbing cigarettes on American dope dealers' balls. Accordingly, United States law enforcement agents are no longer allowed to participate in a foreign arrest or question those arrested in another country. Lovato has goofed badly. You can beat your extradition on this.'

I perked up at this possibility, but Luis Morell looked singularly unimpressed.

'You know Lord Moynihan set you up,' said Katz.

'I know he was trying to. But I never did anything with him and never said anything to him I shouldn't have.'

'Well, he's the star witness against you, but the point is that co-conspirator evidence, especially from an *agent provocateur*, is not admissible in a Spanish court. Neither are phone taps. In order to extradite you, a prima-facie case, governed by Spanish court rules, has to be established. What can they present? They don't seem to have anything usable. As for Judy, she'll be released almost immediately. She's been charged with conspiracy. There's no offence of conspiracy recognisable in Spanish law. All extradition treaties have a dual-criminality clause. Judy can't be extradited from Spain to America unless what the Americans allege she did is recognisable under Spanish law. For example, if the Saudi Arabians accused me of drinking alcohol while praying in Mecca, no country where alcohol is legal would allow Saudi Arabia to extradite me. Judy's been charged with conspiracy. That doesn't exist in the Napoleonic legal code, which forms the basis of Spanish law. The Spanish have to let her go, or at least give her bail until the court in Madrid denies her extradition. It is my opinion

422   **Mr Nice**

that a similar lack-of-dual-criminality argument might be able to be made in your case, depending on the exact nature of the charges, of course.'

I looked expectantly at Luis Morell.

'Do you agree, Luis?' asked Katz.

'For Judy, yes, maybe. But the Spanish do not want to upset the Americans. It will be hard to stop you from being extradited. I think we should go now. Señor Mejuto, the director, is coming back. We will come to see you again tomorrow.'

They left after thanking Mejuto. With Mejuto was a trusty prisoner, who spoke perfect English and Spanish. Mejuto wanted to ask me some questions. The trusty interpreted.

'The director wants to know if you will now speak to the press.'

'No.'

'The director understands you wish to see your wife.'

'Yes. Can I?'

'The press are friends of the director. The director would like you to see them. Then, afterwards, he will leave you alone with your wife for twenty minutes.'

Clearly, Joaquín Mejuto was getting a backhander from some journalists.

'Okay, I'll see them.'

'The director is going to fetch your wife.'

Completely unescorted, I followed the trusty to a room containing a few chairs, table, and a sofa. I sat down. A few minutes later, Judy came in and sat beside me. She looked awful. She was very upset.

'Howard, what's happening? I'm not talking to the press. Have you seen the garbage they wrote about us in the papers?'

'Judy, this was just a way of seeing you. But people should know what's being done to you. Public sympathy can only help.'

The door burst open, and at least thirty journalists barged in. They jostled each other for the best seats, setting off flashes and placing tape-recorders in strategic positions. They threw us cigarettes and barraged us with questions.

I trotted out the same statements that I'd given the Old Bailey and the Inland Revenue. I said that I had not been involved with marijuana smuggling since 1973. Sure, I maintained friendships with people in the marijuana business and strongly campaigned for its legalisation, but my money, what little there was, was straight. It came from my travel business, my various trading companies, and other financial projects that I'd participated in throughout the world. I accurately described the details of my arrest and strongly proclaimed Judy's innocence, publicly pleading with the Spanish authorities to let her go.

The incessantly repetitious questions wore us down. Judy was on the point of collapse, far too weak to hold back her tears. The journalists left. Judy and I were alone for twenty minutes. We were both far too exhausted and shattered to do anything other than look into each other's eyes and hold hands.

'Get me out of this mess, Howard,' she said as the *funcionarios* came to take us away. 'For God's sake get me back to the children.'

One of the journalists had kindly commented that I stank of stale sweat. This must have got around. The *funcionarios* took me straight to the showers. I was certainly very grimy. There was no soap, but the shower felt good. Dodging the spray, I smoked one of the three joints Roger had given me. I thought of Bangkok massage parlours and Taiwanese bathhouses. Things change.

The next morning, after another politely served and first-class breakfast, I was taken to Mejuto's office. The same interpreter was there.

'The director wants to know if you are prepared to be interviewed by some television companies. They are his friends. You will be able to see your wife again. The director will take you there now.'

Judy looked worse than ever as the TV-AM crew entered the room. The interview was a re-run of yesterday's press conference. We both made impassioned pleas for Judy's release, emphasising her complete innocence and the totally unnecessary suffering she and our children were undergoing. We did the same for Spanish TV immediately afterwards. And then the same for another crowd of journalists. We were shown the day's newspapers. Some accounts were stupidly sensational; others were very sympathetic. Bob Edwardes, good friend that he was, had given a long interview to the *Daily Mirror* in which he described me as being a quiet and devoted family man with a modest lifestyle. Some accounts were really bizarre. A couple of the tabloids reported Geoffrey Kenion as having hosted Prince Charles and Princess Diana to a slap-up dinner at Wellies. *The Times* carried a report of how the DEA had failed in an attempt to kidnap me from the Philippines and take me to America without going through extradition formalities. I wondered how they'd managed to fail. The British authorities, apparently, had refused to condone the kidnap on foreign soil of a British subject.

Judy and I again had twenty minutes to ourselves, but we were still too numb and stultified to have any sort of rational communication. I had never seen anyone more overcome by misery. We were escorted back to our separate quarters.

In the early evening, my lawyers came to visit me. Katz was able to give more names of those arrested. They were Patty Hayes (Ernie's girl-friend), Wyvonna Meyer (Gerry's wife), Ronnie Robb, and Philip Sparrowhawk. Katz was also able to give names of others the DEA were trying to arrest: Jim Hobbs, George Lane, Salim Malik, Bradley Alexander (whom I'd never met or heard of), Gerry Wills, and Rick Brown. He was making a personal appeal to Assistant US Attorney O'Neill to allow Judy bail. Four days was long enough to be locked up without knowing what the charge was. He was going to insist on getting a copy of the indictment. Katz's drug-lawyer friend in Michigan was going to get hold of a RICO expert, but Katz still didn't know what RICO was. Both Katz and Morell would be back again to see me tomorrow. They were going to see Judy right away.

That night, back in the cage, I managed to get a good few hours' proper sleep. I woke up refreshed. It was Friday, July 29th. I was hungry. I waited for the sound of the breakfast trolley. Instead, the cell and cage were opened by a very senior prison official, who spoke reasonable English.

'Howard, please get your things. You are leaving.'

'Where am I going?' I asked.

'We are not allowed to say.'

'Can I see my wife?'

'No. This is not allowed.'

'Can I phone my children?'

'I'm sorry, Howard. No.'

'Can I inform my lawyer?'

'No. But I will inform your family and your lawyers once you are at your destination.'

I was handcuffed and taken to the front gate. Roger Reaves was there, also in handcuffs.

'Howard, it's good to see you, but I've got the most godawful news. The Americans have charged me with the same shit they laid on you: RICO.'

'What is RICO, Roger?'

'God knows. They say I grew pot in the Philippines.'

'But you didn't, did you?'

'No, but I was going to. Yes, siree. With the Good Lord's help.'

'What's that got to do with America, Roger?'

'That's where I would have sold it. You know how much good weed goes for in the US these days?'

'But you didn't grow any weed, and you didn't sell any. How can they convict you?'

'Howard, let me tell you something about the US.

Whatever those sons of bitches charge you with, they convict you. I'm talking about the Feds. If it's a state charge, you can maybe beat it. I beat a bunch of them back home in Georgia. But our charges now are all federal charges. You can't beat the Feds. The only chance is to plea-bargain a sentence you can handle.'

'So you're going to plead guilty to RICO even though you don't know what RICO means and even though you didn't grow any weed.'

'You bet. If they get me to the US, that's what I'll do. For sure. But I'm praying I don't go to the US. It looks as if I'm going to get extradited to Germany. With God's help I'll get my freedom there, or maybe even before. I almost got away last night. I'll tell you later.'

We were both piled into a police van. I couldn't get my wedding and engagement rings back. I was told they'd be sent to wherever I was going. At breakneck speed we were driven to the ferry terminal in Palma docks. Glimpses of familiar landmarks such as the imposing Belver castle, the magnificent cathedral, and the windmill discothèques hanging off the cliffs made me feel desolate. Would I ever enjoy them again with my wife and children?

Fourteen

SEÑOR MARCO

The van drove straight onto the ferry. Several armed police pointed at us with automatic rifles. There was no one else around. We were tightly gripped and marched down rickety gangways into the ship. At the end of a narrow corridor was a prison-type cell. We were pushed inside. The guards pointed to their rifles and wagged their fingers at us, indicating that any nonsense from us would result in our being shot. They threw in a brown paper bag of *bocadillos* and shut the door with a bang.

'Why all this heavy stuff, Roger? Are we meant to be mass murderers?'

'I think I know why. Last night I offered the prison director, Mejuto, a million dollars if he'd help me escape. He said he would. I'd have been gone tonight. I guess the son of a bitch got scared and snitched on me.'

That would certainly explain it. I wondered what sort of accommodation we could look forward to now.

We sat in silence for a couple of hours, then the ferry started to move. We knew that ferries left this terminal for either Valencia or Barcelona. It would be an eight-hour trip. Roger read loudly from his pocket New Testament. He prayed and prayed. He asked the Lord for a sign of His ever-present help. None was forthcoming. We ate the *bocadillos*. Roger began to look angry.

'That son of a bitch Moynihan must have been setting me up all this time. You did say not to trust him, but I didn't think he'd do this to me. I'm gonna kill him. I'm gonna kill the no-good son of a bitch.'

'That's not very Christian of you, Roger.'

'Hey! I still want him to go to Heaven. I just want him to go now. Right now.'

The security precautions that veiled our departure from Palma had dissipated by the time we disembarked at what we recognised to be Barcelona. I saw Michael Katz surrounded by an excited crowd of TV cameramen and newspaper photographers. How did he get here? We were driven to Barcelona's notorious Modelo prison. Every Spanish gangster has been there. There was none of the customary fingerprinting and photographing procedure, but watches and other personal property were taken from us. Roger and I were each given a plastic bottle of water and locked up in separate holding cells out of earshot of each other. Apart from me and my bottle, the cell was absolutely empty. There wasn't even a stone bench or hole in the ground to use as a toilet. There was no daylight. There was no noise. No one responded to my yells for cigarettes, food, writing materials, and access to a bathroom. Using the plastic bottle as a pillow, I law on the tiled floor and caught a few snatches of sleep. I pissed in the corner. This was a very hard way of doing time, but I knew it couldn't last. I just held on.

It lasted just over twenty-four hours, after which I was led out to a small exercise yard, brilliantly illuminated by massive searchlights, and told to walk around by myself for half an hour. I was allowed my cigarettes and watch. After the walk, I was given an excellent meal of roast chicken, taken to one of the prison's cell blocks, and locked up, alone, in a normal cell. There was a bang on the door.

'*Cómo está*, Howard?'

'*Bien, gracias. Y usted? Habla Inglés?*'

'*Sí*. I speak English, Howard. I am the night *funcionario*. Roger is in another cell in this unit. He sends you his best wishes. Tomorrow, my friend, one of the day *funcionarios* will put the two of you into the same cell. Okay? Good night, Howard.'

'Marco Polo, *quieres chocolate?*'

The DEA's name for me was beginning to take root. Did I want some hash? Of course I did. My best ideas came when I was stoned. I needed some now. Day had just broken.

'*Sí, por favor. Muchas gracias.*'

A piece of Moroccan and a packet of cigarette papers appeared from under the door.

'*Tienes cigarrillos y cerillas?*'

'*Sí. Tengo.*'

I rolled a small joint. Suddenly, all the cell doors were opened and over two hundred prisoners were running down the gangways and out through a large door into the sunshine. Each was carrying a chair from his cell. I figured it was some kind of mass break-out. So did Roger, whom I saw tearing along clutching his chair, his eyes darting in all directions. I grabbed my chair and did the same. It was not an escape. It was merely a rush to find a shady spot in the exercise yard. It was a Sunday, and prisoners could stay out of their cells all day. Roger and I sat next to each other in the sun. Within minutes, we were surrounded by gangs of other prisoners bringing us cups of coffee, cigarettes, and croissants. They knew all about us. We were pummelled with questions. Was I really the biggest dope dealer in the world? Had I really worked for the British Secret Service, the IRA, and the Mafia? Had Roger really offered a Spanish prison director a million dollars? They made us extraordinarily welcome and explained how much we would like Modelo. Everything was available here: alcohol, all manner of dope, hookers on conjugal visits, and even remote telephones. Looking around the exercise yard confirmed the existence of a somewhat *laissez-faire* regime. Groups of Moroccans, Nigerians, and Spanish gypsies were openly gambling with real money and smoking joint after joint. Ghetto-blasters boomed away. Mainlining junkies brandished syringes. Roger asked if there was any way of escaping from the prisons. The prisoners warned him to keep quiet as there were many *chivatos* (snitches/grasses) around. Roger questioned away regardless. My name was called on the Tannoy. I had a lawyer's visit.

Katz was sitting in a lawyer's visiting cubicle. I sat opposite him. Glass separated us, but it was not as sound-proof as that in Palma. Katz explained how he and Morell had been stonewalled when they had attempted to visit me the previous Friday. Katz had guessed I had been shipped to the mainland and had flown to Barcelona, rented a car, met the ferry, and followed the prison van to Modelo. It had taken forty-eight hours of hassling with the British Consulate, prison authorities, and judges to be allowed to visit me. Not easy at the weekend. Judy was still in Palma prison, but she and the children were as well as could be expected.

Katz's briefcase lay facing me. He leaned over and opened it. I stared inside and looked into the lens of my JVC camcorder.

'I smuggled it in,' said Katz. 'They're very loose here. I'll switch it on, and then you can give a video message to the children.'

I managed a few words.

Katz thought I would soon be moved to Carabanchel prison in Madrid. He'd come to see me there. He still didn't know precisely what Judy and I had been charged with and was still unable to find out what RICO meant. He had been too busy trying to locate and see me. He intended to get on to it right away.

At the end of our conversation, another prisoner just terminating his legal visit came up to me.

'Are you the Marco Polo?'

'I'm rapidly becoming so, yes. But my real name is Howard.'

'I know. My name is Jacques Canavaggio. I am from Corsica. We have not met, but everybody now thinks we are old partners. A week ago they arrested me in the Costa Brava with fifteen tons of hashish. The newspapers said it was yours. I am sorry if I make your problems worse.'

We shook hands.

'Jacques, it's hardly your fault. For my part I'm very pleased and honoured to meet you.'

'The honour is mine.'

The prisoners were still gathered around Roger when I was returned to the exercise yard. He was continuing his loud enquiries into escape possibilities and extolling the virtues of South Africa as a headquarters for marijuana farming. The weekend's Barcelona and Mallorca newspapers were given to us to read. One of them, quoting a report in *The Times*, stated that I had been moved from Palma prison because of fears that I might be released by a Mallorquian magistrate. Most accounts explained our secret transfer as being due to Roger's attempt to bribe his way to freedom. All reported we were going to end up in Alcala-Meco prison just outside Madrid. A prisoner explained to us that this was bad news.

There are two men's prisons in Madrid. The main one is Carabanchel, run, apparently, along the same lines as Modelo. You can get whatever you want. It houses a few thousand Spanish and foreign prisoners, including extradition cases. The other prison is called Alcala-Meco and is situated just outside the ancient university settlement of Alcala de Henares. It was recently built, with help from the Germans, to house ETA terrorists. The regime was Spartan.

The crowd thickened around both of us, and we were again inundated with small gifts of coffee, cigarettes, and food. Several *funcionarios* then broke through the crowd and frog-marched Roger and me to a double cell on the third floor and locked us up. Roger became irate and tore the wash-basin and fittings from the wall. Water gushed into the cell.

It took a good half-hour for the *funcionarios* to unlock us, by which time there was a waterfall down several landings. With our possessions, we were taken to another cell block and locked up there until the next morning. I had stamps and writing materials. I took the opportunity to write to my parents, sister, and eldest daughter. They were heartbreaking letters to write. I imagined my parents' deep unhappiness and distress on hearing the news of the arrest of Judy and myself. They really thought I had straightened out completely. The current allegations would flatten them. My sister, at the age of thirty-seven and against medical advice, had become pregnant for the first time. She didn't need this mess. Myfanwy was meant to have stayed with me in Palma from tomorrow until her sixteenth birthday later in August. She'd seen so little of her father. Now she would see me less, maybe much less.

Then we were moved to another cell. Then another. I lost count. We weren't allowed to make telephone calls or speak to other prisoners. We didn't even get our legally mandated daily outdoor exercise period.

On Tuesday, August 2nd, we were hastily unlocked, handcuffed, and firmly marched to a waiting prison van that resembled a tank. Parked in front of the vehicle was a Policía Nacional saloon car, stuffed full with uniformed cops and guns. Another was parked behind, and at least four police motorbikes were noisily revving up. Two police helicopters hovered above. Roger looked pessimistic.

Inside the van Jacques Canavaggio and two of his gang were waiting. A crew of three armed police van drivers were checking their handcuffs.

'We meet again, Marco Polo. I think we are travelling together to Madrid. One day we are drinking champagne; the next day we wear the handcuffs. It is the nature of our business. We will drink champagne again. That is sure.'

When the drivers were satisfied we were all safely hand-cuffed, the procession left Barcelona and began the nine-hour journey to Madrid. By noon, the five of us were feeling as if we were trapped in a sardine can on fire. We yelled and screamed for a break, some cool, fresh air, something to eat, and some cold water. The prison van and escorts pulled into a service station. The doors were opened, and we felt a welcome breeze. Roger looked everywhere. There was nowhere sensible for him to run.

'*Podemos comer? Tenemos hambre.*'

We were hungry all right. The drivers bought us a selection of *bocadillos*.

'God, I could murder a beer,' said Roger.

'We could ask,' suggested Jacques Canavaggio.

We pleaded with the police to get us some cans of beer. To our surprise they relented and purchased a case. The eight of us, five top-profile prisoners and three armed police drivers, opened cans of beers and had an amiable conversation on a number of topics while a veritable commando force of hovering helicopter pilots and other armed escorts patiently waited. Things like that happen in Spain. They could never happen in England or America.

Somewhere near Madrid, we turned off the *autopista*. We drove on hilly roads through a few exquisite Spanish villages. Then the landscape suddenly changed. It was eerie, bare, and exposed. We saw a sign for Torrejón, a huge American airbase, before turning off on to a road leading to the ugliest prison I had ever seen, surrounded by gun towers, high-rise barbed wire, and elevated perimeter walkways. After stopping at innumerable check-points, we piled out of the van to have our handcuffs removed by a reception *funcionario*. He was very cordial.

'*Ah! El Marco Polo de las drogas. Bienvenido a Alcala-Meco. Conoces a Jorge Ochoa? Es mi amigo.*'

'I know Jorge Ochoa,' said Roger, before I was given a chance to answer the *funcionario*. 'The son of a bitch still owes me ten million dollars. He was in this prison? I thought they only kept terrorists here.'

Jorge Ochoa was the son of Fabio Ochoa, a Colombian cattle-breeder, who began exporting cocaine to the United States during the mid-1970s. Jorge transformed his father's family business into a multi-million-dollar cocaine corporation but did not come to the DEA's attention until 1977, when sixty pounds of cocaine, allegedly his, were busted at Miami airport.

In November 1981, the Colombia guerrilla movement M-19 (Movimiento 19 de Abril) kidnapped Jorge's sister Marta. In response, Jorge, his father, and others formed MAS (Muerte a Secuestradores), a vigilante organisation devoted to killing kidnappers. MAS were very successful and killed dozens of M-19 members. Marta Ochoa was released.

MAS had unintentionally brought together and united under a common purpose cocaine exporters who until then had competed with each other for chunks of the world markets. Jorge Ochoa, Carlos Lehder, and Pablo Escobar formed an alliance that became known as the Medellín Cartel. Shortly afterwards, Roger began working for Ochoa as a pilot. Roger felt he'd been badly cheated by Ochoa on their last deal.

During 1984, following the murder of Colombia's pro-American Minister of Justice and under intense pressure from the United States Government, Colombian President Betancur tried to rid his country of cocaine exporters by threatening them with extradition to America. Jorge Ochoa and other Medellín Cartel leaders were given refuge in Panama by President Manuel Noriega. Together with Gilberto 'The Chess Player' Rodriguez, who was then the leader of the all-powerful Cali Cartel, Ochoa travelled from Panama to Madrid. On the basis of a US extradition request, Spanish authorities arrested both of them in November 1984.

Ochoa avoided extradition by persuading the relevant authorities in Colombia to charge him and seek his extradition from Spain. The US had charged him with importing cocaine. Colombia charged him with exporting the same cocaine. The charges were essentially identical. If two countries request a person's extradition for similar offences and one of the countries is that person's country of citizenship, that country's request will be given preference. Spain had little choice but to deny the US's extradition request and, in 1986, extradited Ochoa to Colombia, where he walked out of prison and remains free.

The reception *funcionario* explained to me and Roger that although Alcala-Meco housed plenty of Basque separatists, it was by no means a prison exclusively for terrorists. The prison had housed not only Ochoa and Rodriguez but also Gaetano 'Don Tanino' Badalamenti, the Sicilian Mafia boss, who was extradited from Spain to America on the basis of running the Pizza Connection, a nation-wide heroin distribution ring. (The *funcionario* seemed most pleased that his prison, having already extradited Ochoa and Badalamenti, the world's biggest cocaine and heroin smugglers, was now going to extradite Marco Polo, the world's biggest cannabis smuggler.) Many high-profile, physically dangerous, and escape-prone criminals were currently here, as well as prisoners who had proved uncontrollable in other institutions. There were three different regimes operating within the prison: normal, restricted, and Artículo 10, the most severe form of incarceration imposed in Spain. For reasons unknown to the *funcionario* Roger, Jacques Canavaggio, and Jacques's two gang members had been assigned to normal regime; I had been assigned to restricted regime. I felt sick. We shook hands and parted company.

The single cell was certainly Spartan. The only moveable objects were a small plastic stool and a foam-rubber mattress. The wash-basin and toilet were plastic. Everything else was concrete or steel. A window looked out on to a towering white wall. I had no possessions. They were being scrutinised by prison security personnel. I was assured that in due course I would get all I was allowed. Every two hours, to the sound of a *funcionario* yelling '*Recuento*', I had to stand up to be counted through a pinhole in the steel door.

After a day and two nights' total isolation, a normal procedure in most countries' high-security prisons, I was permitted to have a few hours in the *patio* (exercise yard) with the other restricted-regime prisoners. Virtually all were Spanish, but there were a few Nigerians and a couple of armed robbers from Marseilles. The Frenchmen and a Spaniard named Zacarias, who looked like Frank Zappa, introduced themselves to me. They gave me the usual prison care packages of food and cigarettes, as well as some very welcome Moroccan hash.

I cabled my whereabouts to Masha in Palma. I filled in visiting application forms for all my family, Masha, Bob Edwardes, and David Embley. I smoked a joint and went to sleep.

Michael Katz came to see me early the next morning. The visit was through glass. From top to bottom, he was wearing my clothes. He was carrying my briefcase. I didn't really mind, but it was odd behaviour. He had visited Judy in Palma prison. She had just been seen by the children and had been completely torn up by their visit. Katz had the impression Judy didn't think much of him. He was right. Geoffrey Kenion was also still in Palma prison. Katz had been too tied up with matters in Barcelona and Palma to do any research into RICO. The Americans had still not informed him of the precise nature of the charges against us. There had been loads of media coverage. He was going to leave the newspapers with me, as well as some money to credit my prison account. I asked him to please find Madrid's best extradition lawyer and send him to see me as soon as possible. I completed a power-of-attorney form for him to access my funds in Zurich.

Lying on the bare foam mattress back in the cell, I went through the newspapers. Both the *Observer*, where David

Leigh still worked, and the *Sunday Times* offered the beginnings of a cogent explanation for my high-profile arrest. It went something like this.

In early 1986, Craig Lovato was one of several DEA agents working in Spain with the Spanish drug police. The Spanish drug police were tapping my phone in Palma. Lovato listened to my conversations and figured I was dope-dealing. The Spanish didn't believe I was breaking Spanish law. Overcoming the resistance of his superiors, Lovato investigated my background and read all that had been written about me.

Lovato's wife, Wendy, also worked for the DEA. At the time she was in Florida assisting Scotland Yard in their investigation of the whereabouts of the proceeds from the Brinks-Mat gold bullion robbery. She had her nose buried in David Leigh's *High Time*, Lovato's book-of-the-month. The British police were intrigued to learn that I was her husband's current target. They offered to help. As a result, the DEA and Scotland Yard launched a combined operation against me called Operation Eclectic. In no time, law enforcement agencies from Canada, Holland, Pakistan, Philippines, Hong Kong, Thailand, Portugal, and Australia joined the operation in a massive orgy of international co-operation.

Although I found it hard to understand why the Spanish police were tapping my phone in the first place, the rest of the account made sense.

There was also a mention in the press of RICO: it stood for Racketeering-Influenced Corrupt Organisations. There was no further explanation.

A full-page article in *Newsweek* mentioned that I kept the loyalty of others by not killing people. The *People* stated that there was a £1,000,000 contract out on the life of Lord Moynihan, who was living under the protection of the United States authorities. Another report stated that Detective Superintendent Tony Lundy, Scotland Yard's

most controversial detective and soon to be forced into
retirement, had been responsible for turning Moynihan
against me. This was completely at odds with my previous
understanding of overtures made to Moynihan by Art Scalzo
of the DEA.

A *funcionario* returned my visiting applications. Bob
Edwardes and David Embley would not be allowed to visit
me. Family and in-laws only. I smoked a joint.

In an interview with the *Sunday Times*, Lovato said he had
disdain for me and that I had a weak character. He was
getting very personal. Perhaps this could be his undoing. I
wondered if there was much to what Katz had explained
about Lovato's illegal questioning of me. I filled out a
visiting application for him. He wouldn't be able to resist
coming to question me, further breaching American law and
bending the Spanish visiting rules in the process. It was
worth a shot. I gave his address as the American Embassy,
Madrid.

Unexpectedly, I was called again for a visit. Behind the
glass this time was Gustavo Lopez Munoz y Larraz, one of
Spain's finest criminal lawyers. His English was absolutely
fluent, and many of his mannerisms were more English/
American than Spanish. Both Bernard Simons and Katz had
independently asked him to come and see me. Gustavo said
he was quite expensive but definitely the most experienced
extradition lawyer in Madrid. He would come to see me as
often as I wished. He would liaise with Michael Katz and
Bernie Simons in London and with Luis Morell in Palma.
He was originally from Cuba, and his family practised law in
Florida. Next week he was going to Miami for a ten-day
holiday. He spent a lot of time in the United States. If I
wanted to by-pass the prison mail procedures to communicate with Judy, or indeed anyone else, we could write to
him, and he would forward the mail. I engaged him.

I spent most of the next few days in the *patio* with Zacarias
and Claude and Pierre, the two Marseilles bank robbers.

The weather was really hot, but there was a cold shower cubicle to cool off. Nigerians huddled in shelters, gambled, and smoked dope out of sight of the solitary *funcionario*. A few Basque terrorists played chess. Young and fit Spaniards exercised strenuously. We walked.

'Are you interested in escape, Marco Polo?' asked Claude, the best English speaker of the three.

'Aren't we all? Why do you ask?'

'The three of us have a plan to leave here at the end of this month. We would like you to join us. Quite a few people have escaped from here. It is not that hard. We don't want money, but maybe you could help us after our escape with false passports. Zacarias knows where we can hide in Spain.'

Zacarias passed me a joint. He rarely took part in conversation. When he did, he spoke Spanish with a coarse Madrid accent.

'*Sí, Marco Polo. Fuga es posible, chavalo. Es muy fácil.*'

'Will anyone get hurt?' I asked Claude.

'Only if they do something very stupid. In time I will explain everything. You don't have to answer now, Marco Polo. But please think about it.'

Zacarias bit off two chunks of his piece of Moroccan hash. One he gave to me; the other he tied to an AA battery with an elastic band and threw it out of the exercise yard and over the roof of the cell block.

'The other side of that roof is the *patio* for prisoners under Artículo 10,' explained Claude. 'We take care of them as best we can. It's really hard there.'

The same battery came flying over the roof back into our *patio*. A note was tied to it. The hash had been received. It was safe to send another missile.

The lack of both incoming letters and replies to my telegrams was puzzling me. All the other prisoners were receiving mail of some kind. Someone other than lawyers would surely be trying to contact me by now. I had been there over a week. I was beginning to build up some anxiety about this when I was called for a visit.

As I walked to the visiting cubicles, I expected to see Katz or Gustavo. Instead, through the smudgy glass, I saw the heartbreaking sight of my parents' faces, with their devastated eyes belying their welcoming, relieved smiles. We couldn't touch each other. Quivering and trembling, we stared at each other. I was struck by the horrific reality that, failing either their extreme longevity or my ability to get out of this mess, I would never, as a free man, be able to see them again. Tears rolled down my face.

'Howard *bach, cadw dy ysbryd*. Keep your spirit. We've just talked to Masha, and Judy and the children are all right. Well, not all right, but bearing up,' said Mam, also unable to hold back the tears.

'We'll do whatever we can,' said Dad.

'Mam and Dad, I'm so sorry.'

'Did you get our letters, *bach*?'

'No, Mam.'

'Howard *bach*, I have to ask you one question. Dad and I will do what we can whatever you did, but did you have anything to do with hard drugs or guns?'

'No, Mam, of course not. I hate those businesses. The Americans and the media have both gone mad.'

'Well, the newspapers, I don't bother with, ever. I know what they're like. They'll write anything to sell a story, whatever comes into their heads. There was a man from the *Daily Mirror* outside the prison when we were coming in. He was wanting to talk to us. I said "No." I'll never forgive them for what they did to us in 1974 when you were kidnapped on bail. No, I won't talk to the newspapers, ever,' said Mam.

'I've got my doubts about the Americans, too. Never mind the newspapers. All that tripe about you being the biggest in the world, owning ships and banks,' added Dad.

'Now with cannabis,' Mam went on, 'we know you're a bit

penstyff about it. You've always had a bee in your bonnet, for some reason. If I know it's just that, I'll feel a lot better.'

'It is just that, Mam.'

'Talking about Americans, who is this Katz fellow?' asked Dad. 'He's a weird bird, that one. He asked me for some money. I said I wanted to see you first.'

'Yeah, he is weird, Dad. I've made arrangements to pay him.'

'Do you still have some money, Howard?'

'I think so, Dad, but I don't know how much.'

'Now Gustavo we thought was very nice,' said Mam. 'He brought us here this morning to make sure we had no problems seeing you. There's a lot of red tape, isn't there, *bach*? He's talking to the director of the prison now to see if we can leave some things we brought: books and Welsh cakes, Howard *bach*. He said what they were doing to you and Judy was outrageous, but he said there was hope. Dad liked him, too.'

'Yes, I liked him, too. I gave him a cheque for £5,000. And Bob Edwardes and I are making arrangements to give Luis Morell some money.'

'I'm sure I've got enough to cover that,' I said.

'Well, Mam and I wanted to do it. We've also put some money in your account here. We'll make sure Masha and the children won't go without, while we can. Who is this Nigel fellow?'

'He's Masha's boy-friend.'

'Is he all right?'

'I think so. I hardly know him.'

The twenty minutes were quickly over. My parents were visiting again the next day. I was taken to the *patio*. The authorities let the Welsh cakes in. I shared them with Zacarias and the two Frenchmen. I complained about the shortness of the visit and not being allowed to embrace my parents. Zacarias said he could arrange for me to have a contact visit for two hours tomorrow. One of the senior visiting guards was his friend, and Zacarias himself was having a contact visit early the next morning. He would arrange things then. I thanked Zacarias profusely.

Zacarias was as good as his word. The next day, I was not taken to the visiting cubicles. I was taken to a large room with chairs and tables. My parents were sitting down, surrounded by groups of Spanish prisoners and visitors. After hugs and kisses, I sat down with them. The noise was deafening. I exchanged watches with my father. Wearing an Audemar Piquet in prison seemed silly. Dad would take care of it for me. Zacarias, quite openly smoking a joint, came up and asked if we wanted one of the bedrooms upstairs. One was free. It would be a lot quieter. Zacarias's friendly *funcionario* took us upstairs to an enormous bedroom. I looked at the king-size bed. If they let Judy out of Palma, she could come to see me here. What a civilised prison system. We sat on a sofa and talked and went over everything. We talked about old times. They would come to see me as often as they could, at least once a month, health permitting.

'Bye, Dad.'

'Goodbye, *bach*. Stay strong, and remember to try to help others here as much as you can.'

'Cheerio, Mam.'

'Cheerio, Howard *bach*. *Cadw dy ysbryd.*'

Instead of being escorted back to the *patio* or to my cell, I was taken to the office of the Jefe de Servicios, the person in charge of the prison's security. With him was a young bespectacled *funcionario* who spoke English.

'*Los periodistas están aquí. Quieren hablar con usted,*' said the Jefe.

The young officer interpreted.

'Men from newspapers are here. They wish to speak with you. You do not have to. You have no obligation.'

'Which newspapers?' I asked.

'*El País* from here in Madrid and the *Daily Mirror* from England and the *Paris-Match* from France. You are not required to speak with them.'

'Oh, I don't object to seeing them,' I said.

'But you have no obligation,' he insisted.

'I understand, but I agree to see them.'

'*Firma acquí*,' said a very disgruntled Jefe, giving me a form to sign.

In a well-furnished meeting room, I spent three hours being rudely interrogated by the *Daily Mirror*, gently questioned by *Paris-Match*, and heavily sympathised with by *El País*, who at first simply could not believe that the charges against me involved nothing other than cannabis. Each of the journalists found Judy's incarceration outrageous. The *Paris-Match* lady said that in France I was already a hero. The *El País* interviewer explained that her newspaper colleagues were taking a great interest in the case, and I would be asked many times to be interviewed and photographed while here in Alcala-Meco.

Once again, I was starting to get turned on by the glamour of publicity, but this time I resolved to use it to advantage. Maybe if I kept Judy's plight long enough in the public eye, either the Spanish or the Americans would be shamed into letting her go. I made several pleas for her release.

With a parting gift of a carton of cigarettes, the journalists left me in the meeting room. The Jefe, his English-speaking sidekick, and four *funcionarios* walked in. I was stripped of all my clothes and possessions. I assumed it was to check the journalists hadn't given me anything they shouldn't have, but I was wrong.

'Howard, you are to be placed under Artículo 10. This is effective immediately and will remain effective until the next meeting of the *junta* [a national panel of senior prison bureaucrats], when there will be a review of all Artículo 10 prisoners. You will now be taken to the Artículo 10 *modulo*. You will be kept in complete isolation for a week. You will be allowed twenty minutes' exercise a day, alone in the *patio*. You are not allowed to look at or make signals to other prisoners. After a week, you may exercise in the *patio* one hour a day with other Artículo 10 prisoners and receive one ten-minute visit through glass each week. There will be no contact or conjugal visits. You are permitted six books, a daily newspaper, and a weekly magazine. You are permitted cigarettes. You are permitted to write and receive letters and telegrams. Once a month you may receive from your family one small parcel of food and clothes. You are not permitted to sit on your bed between 7 a.m. and 11 p.m. Do you understand these conditions?'

'Why am I placed under Article 10? What have I done wrong? Is it because I spoke to the journalists?'

'The *junta* will explain to you at their next meeting. Do you understand the conditions?'

'And when is that?'

'The *junta* will meet in December. Do you understand the conditions, Howard?'

'No, I do not understand the conditions.'

'I will read them again for you, Howard. If you still do not understand them, we will have to put you in Artículo 10 *celdas*, where you have no cigarettes, no books, no visits . . .'

'I understand the conditions.'

'Good. Sign here.'

The Artículo 10 cell block was grim, bare, and dark. The cell was filthy and full of cockroaches. Inedible and disgusting food was thrown in twice a day by some ill-tempered and nasty *funcionarios*, who wielded riot sticks and pocket tear-gas sprays. The window gave an oblique view of the *patio*, in which handfuls of prisoners took turns to exercise. Besides me, at least two Artículo 10 prisoners were prohibited from association with others. As I did my turn of solitary exercise, I was stared at by dozens of pairs of eyes looking out from their cells. A couple of guys waved and smiled. I waved back and was yelled at by the *funcionarios* for doing so.

Each day dragged. One of them was my forty-third birthday. No mail was delivered. It was obviously being held back. My mother would have sent at least three birthday cards well in advance. There was no visit or word from Katz or Gustavo. I was miserable. I had no idea why I was held under Artículo 10. I didn't know what I had been charged with. Where was Judy? How was she? Were the children okay? Was Katz able to get hold of my money?

The week's complete isolation ended with a delivery of a large parcel of newspapers, letters, and cards, mainly from family and friends. Judy was still in Palma. Bail could not be applied for because the Palma court dealing with such matters was closed for August. Geoffrey Kenion had been moved to Alcala-Meco and placed in the same cell block as Roger. The President of Pakistan, Zia ul-Haq, had been killed in a mysterious mid-air explosion. This wouldn't be good news for Malik. He might lose some of his protection.

A large envelope came from Katz. He had got hold of the American indictment specifying the charges against me. Reading it was an unnerving introduction to United States law.

A British indictment is normally a straightforward one-page document clearly stating the allegations. My American indictment was forty pages of incomprehensible bureaucratese. Essentially, I had been charged with running, from 1970 until 1987, an enterprise devoted to cannabis dealing and money laundering. I had been separately charged with conspiring to run such an enterprise. These were the so-called RICO charges. I had also been separately charged with an enormous variety of specific acts and conspiracies, ranging from the 1973 rock-group speaker scams to money laundering in 1987. Much of the conduct in question seemed totally innocuous, such as my travelling from London to Rome in 1973 and my receiving telephone calls at my Palma home in 1986. The indictment said these acts, in themselves, were illegal because they 'furthered a racketeering enterprise'. Judy and virtually all the other twenty co-defendants had been charged with conspiring to import 15,500 kilos of hashish into the United States during 1986. A few of us had also been charged, in the American indictment, with conspiring to import several tons of Thai marijuana into Canada.

Although the charge against Judy and some others was absurd, the formal accusations against me, in general terms, were true, despite being a little over the top. I had been dope-dealing and money-laundering since 1970. I felt hard done by in being charged yet again for the 1973 speaker scam and felt puzzled by the inclusion in an American charging document of an importation to Canada scam, but presumably a good American attorney could get me some relief on these particular matters. The rest was down to what sort of evidence was needed to support the charges and how much of it they had. I would have to examine the evidence and concoct a story consistent with it. I had done it before. Until I saw the evidence, I could do nothing in this regard. It was important now to study American law and Spanish extradition law. I wrote to my sister requesting some basic books on American law and wrote to Katz requesting details of the statutes mentioned in the indictment and of the penalties for their infringement.

Each hour, five Artículo 10 prisoners took their exercise in the *patio*. To discourage friendships, the individuals were continually varied. Throughout my time on Artículo 10, I befriended just two prisoners: Juan, a Spanish gypsy from Andalusia, who was in the cell adjacent to mine, and Darin Bufalino from Boston, Massachusetts. They had both recently escaped from Spanish prisons. Darin was the grandson of Russell Bufalino, the head of one of New York's five major crime families and the man accused of ordering the murder of Teamster boss Jimmy Hoffa. Darin was being extradited to the state of Massachusetts for the armed robbery of an armoured car and didn't think it worthwhile even attempting to fight extradition. He didn't know much about RICO but had heard it was a hard rap to beat.

Towards the end of August, Gustavo visited me. Judy had been transferred to Centro Penitenciario de Yeserias, Madrid's prison for women. Gustavo would see her later that day and be registered as her lawyer. The prison authorities had told Gustavo I was put on Artículo 10 because I planned to escape. He was furious and planned to get me reclassified. He, too, had managed to get a copy of the indictment, as well as a copy of the United States Sentencing Reform Act. He explained that the Sentencing Reform Act, which abolished parole, allowed for only 15% remission for good behaviour, and provided for vastly increased terms of imprisonment for drugs offences, had been in force since November 1987, almost a year. However, it had been a rather controversial piece of legislation, and its constitutionality was currently being examined in the United States Supreme Court.

Back in the dim light of my dirty cell, I read the Sentencing Reform Act. It made for chilling reading. If Judy was convicted of the solitary charge against her, she would be sentenced to a minimum term of ten years' imprisonment with no possibility of parole. If I was convicted of any of the main charges against me, I would be sentenced to a mandatory term of life imprisonment with no possibility of parole. Life meant life. If the new Sentencing Reform Act applied to me, if I couldn't beat extradition, and if I got convicted, I would never be a free man again. Even if I lived to be a hundred, I would die in a federal prison. I would never again be able to go to a bar, a restaurant, a disco, a concert, a party, a shop, an office, or a house. No more country walks, sea views, or loud music. No more hashish hilarity with old friends. No more drunken nights in Europe's and Asia's capitals. I wouldn't be able to bring up my children, or even see them being brought up. No more cuddles and excitement. None of that joy. Nothing to look forward to. I would never make love again.

That night I heard my children screaming. I jumped out

of bed and ran to their bedroom door. It turned into cold
steel.

I spent a few weeks of almost sleepless nights pathetically
freaking out in my misery, sadness, and madness. A letter
from Judy didn't help. Where would the children go to
school? How would little one-year-old Patrick manage
without his mummy? Why wouldn't they let her out on bail?
Did one have to be a real criminal to be granted such relief?
Her isolation from the children, Masha, and Palma friends
coupled with the atrocious conditions in Yeserias prison
were taking their toll. She was questioning her ability to
survive any longer in these circumstances. I could not begin
to let her know that she might be looking at a minimum
sentence of ten years.

There was nothing but disappointment, uncertainty, and
loneliness. George Bush was to become President of the
United States, so there would be no change for the better in
American drug policy.

At his first attempt Gustavo was unable to get Judy bail.
He failed to get me off Artículo 10 and failed to get
permission for Judy and me to see each other. Scotland Yard
would not return to Katz the truckful of possessions they had
seized from our Chelsea flat and my office at Hong Kong
International Travel Centre. The Spanish court would not
order the Palma police to return the cars and other
possessions to Masha in Palma.

The Americans amplified their extradition process to
include a further extradition request specifically for the 1973
speaker scam. This came from the Federal District of
Nevada, making it the fourth separate authority to charge me
with precisely the same offence. Lovato did not grab the bait
I had offered. He did not come to see me surreptitiously and
illegally question me. Instead, he and US Attorney Bob
O'Neill formally applied to the Spanish authorities through
Comisión Rogatoria, a legal device used by co-operating
countries' law enforcement bodies for purposes such as

obtaining witnesses' sworn testimony, obtaining documentary evidence, or questioning nationals held on foreign soil. The Audiencia Nacional readily granted the application. Gustavo countered by applying for permission to question Lovato and O'Neill while they were in Madrid. The Audiencia Nacional quickly denied that request without saying why.

After being granted an extension of a further forty days, the United States Government finally served the extradition papers. These included evidence seeking to establish a prima-facie case against Judy, Geoffrey Kenion, and me. Lovato had written some of the accompanying affidavits, swearing statements that were models of DEA ungrammatical hyperbole. He had apparently personally identified over 160 members of my organisation. One of them, Roger Reaves, was my 'agronomist'. According to Lovato, Judy had 'instructed members of the organisation in the furtherance of their illegal activities. These instructions included money transfers, co-ordinating travel and communications between the members of the organisation. JUDITH MARKS has full knowledge of all alias' [sic] and codes utilised by the organisation and such [sic] can pass instructions in the absence of her husband, DENNIS HOWARD MARKS, with the same proficiency as he.'

There were dozens of summaries of investigations, tapped telephone calls, and surveillances carried out by the DEA in Palma, New York, Bangkok, California, Manila, Florida, and Karachi (where they were enthusiastically assisted by Michael Stephenson, Her Majesty's Customs and Excise man in Pakistan). HM Customs had also carried out extensive observations in London. It seemed that no actual illegal activity had been seen or overheard in any of these places, but this obstacle had been overcome by Lovato's long-winded explanations of what lay between the lines and behind the scenes. As far as he was concerned, we were all dopers; therefore, all our conversations were about dope deals, all our activities were scams, and all our financial transactions were money laundering. A rather circular argument, but in most cases he had correctly guessed what was going on. But certainly not always. There were loads of mistaken identifications and off-the-wall conjectures and speculations.

US Attorney Bob O'Neill had also written a sworn affidavit purporting to explain the appropriate American law. It failed miserably to do so, largely by assuming that words and phrases such as 'felon', 'Grand Jury', 'racketeering enterprise', 'pattern of racketeering activity', 'interstate transportation of wagering paraphernalia', 'wire fraud', 'laundering of monetary instruments', and 'lending money at a usurious rate at least twice the enforcement rate' were common parlance in Europe. Gustavo and I still did not understand what RICO really was.

The Audiencia Nacional, however, didn't have these problems of non-comprehension. As far as they were concerned, the papers were perfectly in order, and unless we objected at a forthcoming court appearance, they were happy to proceed with our extradition. Should we object, there would be a court hearing sometime in the New Year. We objected.

In October, Judy's youngest brother Marcus and his wife packed up their home and carpentry business in the Dordogne. In return for a living wage, they had agreed to move to Madrid, visit Judy and me as often as permitted, and liaise between us, our lawyers, our co-defendants' lawyers, our friends, and our families. They brought Amber, Francesca, and Patrick to visit me. Although I was relieved to see them alive and well and very comforted to hear of the support being given them by Bob Edwardes and their school, a ten-minute meeting through glass left me deeply depressed. A visit from my parents intensified the depression. I was being brought to terms with what I was missing. I had lost control of everything. I didn't want any more visits. didn't want to reply to the scores of letters I was now receiving from known and unknown well-wishers. Even when I saw Judy at the extradition hearing, I just felt numb and couldn't speak. I saw despair and accusation in her eyes. Why hadn't I stopped smuggling when she told me to? How could I let them do this to her? Why had I ruined our children's lives? All was now lost.

I curled up in my cell. The winter had started. Artículo 10 prisoners were not allowed heating or hot water. I shivered in my misery and fear. What was going to happen to my family? What was going to happen to me? Life in the cell forever. I'd had enough of this life if this was what it amounted to.

I'm not going to do myself in, but there's nothing for me to look forward to now. I'm never getting out of prison. No one's going to come and save me. I can't have hope, like a hostage. I can't even help anyone; I don't see anyone. There's no one I can love and touch. I suppose I'll just live it out. I could read lots of books. But what would be the point? I could never apply what I learned. I could become fit and do a million push-ups a day, but why? I would only become healthier and have to live through more of this. The next meaningful experience would be death. Maybe after that, things would look up. Oh, God! Why hadn't I still sorted out whether or not this life was all we had? All those stone circles, cathedrals, monasteries, and temples I'd visited in my travels had been no help. If there was a better time ahead, I could handle this one. Elvis and John Lennon were still kind of around somewhere, weren't they?

And what about Jesus Christ? Sweet Jesus, if you really did beat this death rap and if you really do know there's lots of good times to come, please, please, make sure we, whom I sincerely believe you love, also know.

I read the Bible. The Old Testament was upsetting. Lots of wars and killing. God was much nastier than they'd told us in Chapel in Wales. Was He American? St Paul was a disappointment. I didn't like the bit about always obeying authority. But Jesus was great.

But what about all the Hindu and Buddhist stuff? Weird gods and monsters and lots of lives to live. That would be handy. I could get into that. Jesus didn't say there wasn't any reincarnation. I could prepare myself for the next lives while just being a remote spectator of this one.

My sister had sent me a book on yoga. I remembered how the same book had helped me during my last time in prison. This time, the conditions were infinitely worse, but it might still help. I spent several hours a day contorting myself, breathing deeply, and meditating. I fasted on many days and ate very little on the others. My strength and spirit began to return.

Juan, the Andalusian gypsy, and I were in the *patio*. We were spending our exercise period watching large ants. We needed some hashish. Neither of us had smoked any for weeks. The flying battery service did occasionally operate, but it never had anything for me, Juan, or Bufalino. Juan said it was easy to smuggle hashish into the cell block by hiding it in books. He had no money, but if I wanted to arrange to send him a book concealing some hashish, he would take the risk of receiving it this end, and we could split it between us. Marcus sent him a suitably doctored copy of the Spanish translation of James Clavell's *Whirlwind*. We had enough top-quality Moroccan to get stoned every night for a few weeks.

I enjoyed the next visit from my parents, but my father had a strange tale to yell through the glass. Bob Edwardes had received a booking at his La Vileta restaurant from someone claiming to be the aide of Prince Khalid of Saudi Arabia. The aide was staying at the Valparaiso Hotel, Palma. On some pretext, Bob rang up the hotel, who confirmed that Prince Khalid was a guest and that his aide had indeed made a booking at the La Vileta restaurant. The phoney Prince, the aide, a bodyguard, and an attractive American blonde turned up and ate a Sunday lunch. Amidst brief courtesies, Bob was asked to join the table. Prince Khalid's stand-in told

Bob that he was under orders from his uncle, the brother of King Fahd and Minister of Defence in the Saudi Government, to do what he could to release me and Judy from prison. He claimed to be able to use the Saudi Arabian royal family's good offices within the Spanish Government as a way of solving the problem as well as having several million dollars available for any expenses. Meetings at the Valparaiso Hotel followed, including one in which Masha and the children were invited to a private tea. The normally public terrace had been especially closed off for the occasion. Bob was asked by the aide to go to Geneva and pick up funds to use for my present needs. They met at La Réserve. The aide began prevaricating, and Bob smelt a rat. Bob flew back to Palma and heard no more.

'I'm darned if I can work it out,' said Dad. 'You know some odd fellows, you do.'

'I've no idea what it's about, Dad.'

I still haven't worked it out.

Fifteen

MARCO POLO

Yoga, meditation, hashish, and the bizarrely unexpected are an invigorating combination, and I was in fairly good mental shape when I was summoned to the Audiencia Nacional for the Comisión Rogatoria with Lovato and O'Neill. They were accompanied by El Fiscal, the Spanish prosecutor, and looking confident, smug, and contented. Gustavo sat close by looking solemn. The judge explained that they had the right to ask me questions. I had the right not to answer. Did I intend to answer any questions? I said I did not. The judge said the proceedings were closed. Lovato whispered a few sentences to El Fiscal, who then asked if Lovato and O'Neill could have an informal talk with me. The judge stood up and said his function had finished. He washed his hands of any further proceedings and walked out of the court. El Fiscal told the guards to leave and wait outside the door and then asked Gustavo if he wanted to stay. Gustavo refused to answer, but he stayed. Lovato and O'Neill extended their hands. I shook them. Lovato seemed to have put on weight. O'Neill was young, good-looking, and short. Lovato spoke.

'Howard, I don't blame you for not answering questions in front of the judge. My intention was to have a private talk with you in response to the note you wrote asking me to visit you. In the past, the Spanish authorities would allow me to visit incarcerated individuals, but now we have to do it this way. Your lawyer submitted a request to the court to ask Bob and me some questions you had. Bob and I will now answer them if you wish.'

'Gustavo, what shall we ask them?'

'I advise you not to say anything, Howard. This is most irregular.'

'I've read some of the newspaper reports of your pleas for Judith's release,' continued Lovato, 'and I feel I have to inform you that we, as the United States Government, cannot negotiate any matter involving her release. Plea-bargaining is illegal in this country and will have to wait until you are on United States territory. However, it is undoubtedly in both your and your wife's interests to cease opposing extradition and come voluntarily to Florida. The United States Government would not oppose Judith being granted bail if she came to Miami. We could plea-bargain both your sentences. Judith could visit you while you remained incarcerated in Miami Metropolitan Correctional Center. She could have the children with her. All this prison time you're both doing in Spain is just dead time. None of it will be deducted from the prison sentences you will receive. Isn't that right, Bob?'

'I believe that is correct, yes, but I'm not a sentencing expert,' said O'Neill.

'Is that right, Gustavo?' I asked.

Gustavo said nothing. He carried on writing, taking down every word that was said.

'Why have you charged me with the 1973 speaker scam?' I asked. 'I've already done a sentence for that.'

'We, the United States Government, don't recognise foreign convictions,' answered Lovato.

'Why is that load of marijuana in Vancouver anything to do with America? Have you stopped recognising foreign countries as well?'

'Well, Canada is close to us. But besides that we have evidence to show that the same product was sold in California. It is the United States Government's belief that the consignment was destined for distribution within its borders. This gives us jurisdiction. We have long arms, Howard.'

'Mr O'Neill, does the Sentencing Reform Act apply to these charges?'

'Call me Bob, Howard. I feel more comfortable that way. It's a good question. The simple answer is "I don't know." I wouldn't want to mislead you. But if the Act did apply, your mandatory sentence would, of course, be life. If it did not apply, then you would be subject to a maximum of 145 years.'

'It's a long time either way, Howard,' said Lovato. 'Come to the United States now and start making it shorter, maybe a lot shorter.'

'I don't think Spain is going to extradite me. With due respect, I don't think you're too confident of it either; otherwise you wouldn't be trying to persuade me to come voluntarily.'

'It's just for your own good, Howard. I hate to see you doing dead time.'

O'Neill broke in. 'Howard, I'll be frank with you. One of the reasons we want you there quickly is that the trial of your co-defendants is scheduled to begin early next year. For reasons of economy, we'd like to try you at the same time. If I was you, I'd want a multi-defendant trial, too, rather than be the only one facing the jury. But I'm not going to even attempt to coax you. It's your decision. But I'm interested why you don't think Spain will extradite you. Why won't they?'

'Because I'm charged with RICO, money-laundering, and conspiracy. None of these are crimes in Spain.'

'That's irrelevant. They are in the United States,' said Lovato.

'But for Spain to extradite,' I argued, 'it has to recognise them as crimes.'

'Howard, I'm not commenting on the advice you may have received from your excellent attorney Señor Gustavo Lopez Munoz y Larraz here, but you have to do the time, not him. Forget the legal bullshit that happens in these courts. You will be extradited. Spain already upset us by not extraditing Ochoa. Spain realised it made a mistake. Spain will not upset the United States Government in that way again. Rely on it.'

'Still the big guy on the block, Craig?'

'You better believe it, Howard.'

'Unless there are further questions, I think we'd better leave, Agent Lovato,' said O'Neill.

El Fiscal brought the guards back, and they took me to a lawyers' visiting cubicle to see Gustavo.

'Howard, I have never seen anything like that in my life. The judge's behaviour was atrocious. I will ensure that an official complaint is made. I will tell the newspapers today. But forget that, for I have good news for you.'

'What?'

'I am sure we can now get Judy bail.'

'Why? What has changed?'

'A number of your co-defendants, including all the females, have been granted bail by the American authorities. Even Judy's brother, Patrick Lane, has been offered release on bail for a $1,000,000 bond. Another co-defendant, James Newton, has been released on bail by the British authorities. I have received many compelling letters from doctors, psychiatrists, and residents of Mallorca expressing concern about the plight of your children. It will soon be Christmas; even judges can be human. I have excellent reason to believe Judy will be granted bail. The application may prove to be a little expensive, but it will succeed.'

'That's great news, Gustavo. Thank you.'

'There is more good news. A short time ago France

requested the extradition of a man found in Spain. The offence was international credit-card fraud. Spain denied extradition on the basis that he could be tried equally well in Spain.'

'Presumably, though, Gustavo, he had been charged by the Spanish authorities for the same offence. Spain hasn't charged me with anything. We can't make them charge me, can we?'

'That is where you are wrong, Howard. We can ensure you are charged through *acción popular*, a method by which Spaniards can petition a court to force the police to prosecute. There has been a great deal of coverage of your case in the Spanish newspapers. Everyone knows Marco Polo, believe me. There were plenty of references to caves of hashish in the Costa Brava. Your headquarters were in Palma de Mallorca. You must have broken Spanish law, so why send you to Florida rather than try you here? My professional colleagues resent what they see as an example of judicial colonisation: America administering our system of justice. Spain's legal system is perfectly adequate, yet it is treated like that of an incompetent banana republic.'

'If I was charged here, what sentence would I get?'

'You would not even get convicted, but the maximum sentence in Spain for any cannabis offence is six years. You would be out after serving two.'

'What about Judy?'

'She would be immediately released.'

'What's the next step, Gustavo?'

'We get forty signatures from people outraged at the extent of drug trafficking taking place within Spain and furious with the Spanish Government for abrogating its responsibility to deal with the problem. They demand that you, Judy, and Kenion be charged for the crimes you have committed in Spain. On the strength of this, a lawyer will submit an *acción popular* to the court. It mustn't be me, obviously, but it will be a very good friend. The arguments will be mine. He will simply sign and submit it.'

'Okay. Let's do it. It sounds wonderful. Anything else?'

'Yes. I have tried and tried to understand RICO. I cannot. If I cannot, the Audiencia Nacional will not be able to. But they will pretend to understand and say it's perfectly proper to extradite you for such a charge. I suggest we bring to next year's extradition hearing an American lawyer, one sympathetic to your position, who is a qualified expert on RICO. The Audiencia Nacional will then be forced to accept that RICO has no equivalent whatsoever in Spanish law and is an unextraditable charge. I could probably find such a lawyer, but maybe you know of one.'

'That's a good idea, Gustavo. I'm sure I could find one.'

'Also, Howard, I think we should ask the Audiencia Nacional to allow us to present Bernard Simons at the extradition hearing so that he can explain to the court that you have already done a sentence for the 1973 speaker scam.'

'Okay. What about this rule about not extraditing from Spain someone who might end up with a sentence of more than thirty years? I'm apparently facing the possibility of life, or with a bit of luck, 145 years.'

'The United States Government will give an assurance to the Audiencia Nacional that you will not receive a sentence greater than thirty years, but it doesn't mean very much. If the Americans get you across the Atlantic, it's a different ball game, as they themselves say. But, Howard, you will not be extradited. The *acción popular* will work, if nothing else.'

'I hope so, Gustavo. Is there any other news?'

'Yes. I received a call from Marcus yesterday. He had spoken to Katz, who is now in Miami. Katz has got copies of all the evidence the prosecution intend presenting against your co-defendants. He is bringing it here soon.'

'I'll go through it with a toothcomb, Gustavo. Anything else?'

'That's it.'

Gustavo's lawyer friend submitted the *acción popular* to the court. To add more force to the petitioners' arguments,

I capitalised on my newsworthiness and wrote long letters to Spanish newspapers complaining how the Americans had thwarted my plans to turn Mallorca into the Hong Kong of the Mediterranean. Fabulously wealthy Far Eastern businessmen and Saudi Arabian princes had approved plans to invest colossal sums of money building final-stage assembly plants, leisure parks, and luxury hotels. The letters were published on a couple of front pages. As expected, they were interpreted as proof of my wicked desires to flood the country with drug money. I gave interviews to the Spanish magazine *Panorama*, stating that Spain was a paradise for drug users and traffickers and that I had personally smuggled into Spain large quantities of dope. Gustavo got a few more 'enraged citizens' to submit these newspaper and magazine articles to the court as further evidence of the dire need for me to be busted by the Spanish.

The next time we met, Juan and I were running low on hashish. He suggested that I arrange to get some sewn into a pair of trousers and mailed to him. I asked Marcus to do it. A couple of nights later, some *funcionarios* marched into Juan's cell. A scuffle broke out. There was the hiss of tear-gas spray, and whines of pain echoed down the metal corridors. Other prisoners banged their doors with their shoes. The *funcionarios* marched back, still scuffling.

'Juan, Juan. *Qué pasa?*' I yelled.

'*No lo se, Marco Polo. Son unos hijos de puta. Todos. Pero no se preocupe. Asi es la vida. Adiós, mi amigo, y suerte.*'

Poor Juan. They'd obviously busted the dope, and he'd given the *funcionarios* some lip when he'd been confronted. I never saw him again.

My first wife, Ilze, had a friend, Gerard E. Lynch, who was Professor of Law of Columbia University, New York. He was an expert on RICO and had published extensively on the subject. He sent me articles. I understood RICO. For an appropriate consideration, he would be delighted to come to Madrid and explain RICO to the Audiencia Nacional.

Katz brought in the documents of evidence from Miami. There were over ten thousand papers, two thousand of which were transcripts of telephone taps on my phone. It didn't make for comforting reading, but there didn't seem anything there that clinched it for the prosecution. The evidence made it obvious that most of those charged had been up to some sort of skulduggery, but exactly what was open to interpretation. No major player was grassing, and I felt sure that none would. Numerous defences were leaping to mind. This could even be fun. Let's beat them again.

At the beginning of December, I was called in front of the *junta*. Although my walks with Juan had made my Spanish quite proficient, a Nigerian junkie prisoner had been summoned to act as my interpreter. Each member of the *junta* rose and shook my hand.

'*Ah. Señor Marks. El Marco Polo de las drogas. El famoso. Cómo está?*'

'I am well,' I replied, 'but why have I been put on Artículo 10, and why am I still on it?'

'Because, Señor Marks, the DEA say you are the leader of an armed gang.'

'I am not,' I protested, 'and never have been. I hate violence.'

'We have made our own investigation and drawn our own conclusions,' said the head of the *junta*. 'We agree with you. In one week you will be released from Artículo 10 and sent to a normal cell block. Good luck, Señor Marks.'

I was thrilled. I wrote excitedly to my children and my parents. No more visits through glass. The tide was beginning to turn.

Well, it was trying to, but the elation was short-lived. Just before Christmas, Gustavo came to see me. In an unprecedented and deeply suspect move, the judges appointed to hear our extradition had all been replaced. Gustavo's friend was no longer on the panel of three. The head judge would now be Orbe y Fernandez Losada, a strongly pro-American look-alike to General Francisco Franco, whose daughter had lost her life through a drug overdose. We couldn't have been landed with anyone worse. Gustavo explained that Judy should still get bail, but he had lost much of his confidence. He suspected that the Americans were somehow behind the appointment of Judge Orbe y Fernandez Losada.

Judy's bail was denied. She and the children would not be able to share Christmas together. Deep sadness threatened again, but instead I was besieged by furious anger, the like of which I'd never experienced. I could understand the DEA wanting to give me a hard time: I had decided to pit my wits against them, and I was fair game. But why do this to my children and to my wife, whose only crime was to be mine? Why is the DEA so sadistic and inhuman? How can they happily and deliberately cause innocents to suffer? In the name of what? I must always remember that the DEA are evil. They began as President Nixon's Mafia, in many cases not even agreeing with the crazy drug laws they so zealously enforced. But these laws gave them, and continue to give them, the excuse to be cruel and powerful bullies. Lock up the women and make them cry. Make the little children scream.

The DEA can't be forgiven for this. They know what they're doing. I hate them. I'll fight them until I fucking die.

My children came to visit me. I could touch them, hug them, and kiss them. They seemed to be holding up so well and displaying such resilience. They gave me strength. Masha and her boyfriend, Nigel, were with them. There was something strange in Nigel's eyes. Something wasn't right. Maybe he was just unhealthily stoned or tired.

I was out of Artículo 10 and housed in a clean cell in a normal cell block. There was a view of fields and mountains and fences and gun towers. Daylight poured through, and there was a light to use at night. I knew no one, but many of the prisoners and *funcionarios* had heard of me, and I quickly made friends. There was plenty of hashish. Personal possessions of all kinds were permitted. Each day I'd spend a few hours walking in the *patio*, improving my breathing and my Spanish. Most of the time I spent doing yoga and examining the ten thousand pages of evidence from Miami. Marcus and Gustavo came to see me frequently. These visits were always through glass. Once Gustavo came accompanied by someone I'd not met.

'Howard, this is the lawyer of Roger Reaves. This visit of ours gives you and Roger the opportunity to talk to each other. He will be here any second.'

Roger ran up to me.

'Boy, I wanna snitch on you. Do you mind if I snitch on you? I'm sorry to come out with it just like that. Lord! I'm sorry, Howard. It's so good to see you. Man! You look healthy. Thank the Lord. How's Judy and the kids? I think Marie's going out with another fella.'

'Everything's okay, I guess, Roger, but Judy didn't get bail.'

'She didn't! Man, those sons of bitches ought to meet their Lord.'

'What's this about snitching?'

'Here, let me explain to you. I'm going to tell you right now. I'm going to be extradited to Germany before the US can put a finger on me. Thank the Lord. It's true. Ask my lawyer. That's good for me. I've been talking to some Germans here in my cell block and once I'm convicted there, provided I plead guilty and get a light sentence, I get put into a prison that's real easy, I mean real easy, to escape from.'

'So why do you need to snitch on me?'

'To get a light sentence. I'll snitch on McCann too. I'd like to do that. You could do the same deal, Howard. Get extradited to Germany, and snitch on me and McCann. We could escape together and go to South Africa to grow pot. Then we could sail it to Canada. Forget the US. I have good buddies in Canada. We'd get a good price. That's for sure.'

'But I didn't really do anything in that scam, not that

concerns Germany, anyway. I haven't been charged by the Germans.'

'You will be once I snitch on you.'

I burst out laughing.

'Okay, Roger, snitch on me, but only if none of my other plans work.'

'What! You have a plan to escape from here! Funnily enough, I've been thinking the same thing. Ain't that something? We need to get some jewellers' string, that stuff which cuts through bars. I asked Marie to put one in the next food parcel. I don't know if she will. She's weird these days.'

'I was thinking of my plans to beat extradition in court, not escape.'

'You won't beat it, Howard. Not the US. You have to deal with them. Make them think you're giving them something. Then they give you something. That's the way it goes. The Feds don't lose. They get whomever they want. Believe me.'

Gustavo, who was unashamedly listening to all this conversation, interrupted.

'Mr Reaves is wrong, Howard. The Americans do not always succeed in extraditing who they want. They did not get Ochoa. They will not get you. And (this is good news for you, Howard, I know) they will not get Balendo Lo. I have just called Bernard Simons. A partner in his firm represents Mr Lo. The British authorities have refused to extradite Mr Lo. Today, Mr Lo is a free man.'

'That's great news, Gustavo. Is it for sure?'

'Bernard himself told me. Bernard is, of course, only too glad to testify for you at the extradition hearing.'

'I still think the Feds will get him,' said Roger. 'They always do.'

Gustavo indicated he wanted to see me privately. Roger and his lawyer went their separate ways.

'The Audiencia Nacional have agreed to allow you and Judy to have a conjugal visit. She will be brought to this prison at the beginning of next month. She will stay two hours.'

Every Monday at about 11 a.m., a prison van brings five or six female prisoners from Centro Penitenciario de Yeserias to Alcala-Meco to meet their incarcerated husbands and boy-friends. The males patiently wait in a holding cell, clutching a pair of freshly laundered sheets, a pack of prison-issue condoms, and a thermos flask. Each couple is taken to a bedroom and left to their own devices. Judy looked well and wonderful. The cancer of despair had gone, and her humour had returned. She seemed fairly optimistic about her chances of beating extradition, and daily life in Yeserias had been made more bearable by her having made a couple of good friends. Marcus's visits were keeping her in touch, as well as providing her with what comforts were allowed. Much was discussed but little decided. We made love. It was amazing. Just as well. It was going to have to last for several years.

Gustavo came to see me the same evening. I was still full of my visit with Judy and didn't notice his glum demeanour at first.

'We might have to try completely different tactics, Howard.'

'Why? What's happened?'

'The *accíon popular* has been denied. It is possible to appeal, of course, and I have asked my friend to do so, but no one understands how the court could have ruled against us. During the proceedings it emerged that the DEA had formally complained about the way you were manipulating the Spanish press for your own ends. The Audiencia Nacional responded by making an order preventing you from being interviewed by journalists. So much for the freedom of the press.

'As if that isn't enough, the Audiencia Nacional have refused to allow Professor Lynch, the RICO expert, to address them at our extradition hearing and are not permitting Bernie Simons to testify that you have already served a sentence for one of the charges. The Audiencia Nacional have even refused my most harmless and reasonable request to have a stenographer present to transcribe the proceedings at our expense. We are appealing, but the situation is quite out-rageous. You are not being given the protection of the extradition law of this land. I have never heard of such a thing before in all my years of practising law in Spain.'

'That means I've had it, Gustavo. I'm going to be extradited, aren't I? And Judy. There's nothing else to do.'

'Howard, as I've said all along, Judy's case is very different from yours. These court rulings do not significantly affect her position. And you must not lose hope. We still have much we can try.'

'Like what?'

'We must initiate an *antijuicio*. This is a formal denunci-ation of the judges who have denied your constitutional rights by not allowing you to present evidence to dismiss the extradition warrant and by not protecting you from being questioned by the DEA in their own courtroom last November. Once you commence the *antijuicio*, provided it's not frivolous (and this certainly isn't), the court is legally bound to call its proceedings to a halt. Eventually, the higher courts at least will rule that you must have your consti-tutional rights and be allowed to present your case against being extradited. It will take time, but in the meantime you cannot be extradited, and if we can keep the courts tied up until two years after your arrest, you will be set free anyway.'

'It sounds good, Gustavo, I agree. Is it bound to work?'

'No. There is a chance that the *antijuicio* won't be looked at by the courts in time. If that happens, you must publicly refuse to recognise the jurisdiction of the court. This will give you another avenue of appeal against any decision of the Audiencia Nacional to extradite you. Please don't worry, Howard. We will win. But I must admit, there's an awful lot of pressure from the Americans, and they are corrupting our justice system. It won't be easy.'

'Why doesn't Spain have the balls to stand up to the Americans?'

'It's not just Spain, Howard. I am leaving some papers with you, and you will see what has happened in Pakistan, the Philippines, Holland, and your own country. The Americans are having it all their own way in this case. No country has the balls to stand up to them. But don't lose hope. We will do whatever has to be done.

'I will probably not see you again until the extradition hearing, which takes place at the Audiencia Nacional in one week. Remember not to recognise the court's authority to deal with you. Oh, by the way, the Audiencia Nacional has ordered Roger to be extradited to Germany.'

Gustavo was right. The Americans were really throwing their weight around. The *Sunday Times* reported that Benazir Bhutto, Pakistan's newly elected prime minister, had explained the country's problems as a legacy of the previous Zia ul-Haq regime's tolerance and encouragement of drug trafficking. The United States was considering giving Bhutto a $4.02 billion aid package. Robert Oakley, the United States Ambassador to Pakistan, met Benazir Bhutto and emphasised America's desire to put Salim Malik on trial. America wanted him to be the first man ever extradited from Pakistan to the United States. Benazir knew the deal: no Malik, no aid. In a shameful abandonment of its justice system, Pakistan agreed to give up Malik. Those DEA megalomaniacs Harlan Lee Bowe and Craig Lovato had got their own way.

After learning that there wasn't in fact an extradition treaty between the Philippines and the United States, the DEA persuaded the Manila authorities to deport Ronnie Robb to Amsterdam. The Dutch police promised the DEA to grab him on arrival at Schiphol Airport. They did, and he joined Hobbs in an Amsterdam prison. Extradition proceedings were begun.

In England Jimmy Newton's bail had been revoked, and he was in Miami prison. He holds the distinction of being the only non-American person ever to be extradited to America for the crime of supplying within non-American territory another non-American with a non-American passport. Worse still, Balendo Lo had been re-arrested as the result of a renewed United States extradition request for precisely the same charge. The British, after deeming that Balendo should not be extradited, were prepared to lock him up and give the DEA another chance.

I was beginning to see what Roger meant. The Feds do not give up.

The Audiencia Nacional was packed with the world's press. Judy, Geoffrey Kenion, and I stood in a bullet-proof glass box in the middle of the court. We had microphones. Geoffrey went first. He had agreed to be voluntarily extradited. At the holding cells below he had explained to me that his lawyers had worked out a deal for him to plead guilty and tell the DEA the little he knew. He would then be released. I believe he made the right decision. He did not participate in any dope scam. He did a money run for me about which the DEA already knew.

Judy went next. She said she was innocent and did not want to be extradited. She wanted to present her reasons through Gustavo.

I got up and denounced each of the judges by name. They had violated my constitutional rights. They were the subject of an *antijuicio*. They should be dismissed. I did not recognise their authority to deal with me. The judges' faces angrily flushed to a deep red. They yelled at the defenceless court interpreter. They told me to keep quiet. The case would continue despite my protests.

Gustavo spoke at length about the suffering Judy had experienced. Lovato had arrested her and rudely interrogated her in her nightclothes. She had been needlessly and mercilessly locked up hundreds of miles away from her young children, who were undergoing deep traumatic stress. There was no evidence presented that she had broken any law. She had a completely spotless record. There were scores of the most complimentary testimonials from highly respectable members of Spanish and British society. The DEA were charging her with the crime of being my wife. This was repugnant to the Spanish system of justice.

After about an hour, the judges became restless and uncomfortably bored. They adjourned the hearing for a week.

At the lawyers' visiting cell, Gustavo was furious.

'The judges aren't even listening to me. They have made up their minds.'

'What, with Judy, too?'

'Well, Judy still has a good chance, but they will certainly rule for you to be extradited.'

'I'm kind of resigned to that, Gustavo. I'm presuming you can keep battling in the appeal courts until the two years are up.'

'I can, and I will. But this hearing may be your last public appearance. The appeal courts do not require your presence.'

'So?'

'Given the way things are going, perhaps you should employ the tactic of the last resort.'

'Which is?'

'At the end of the hearing, you will be asked if you have anything to say. If you verbally insult the King of Spain or the country of Spain, this is a serious crime with which the court will have to proceed. I'm not suggesting you do this, Howard, you understand. I'm just explaining the law.'

'I understand, Gustavo. If I did publicly insult King and country, what would happen?'

'The guards on duty at the Audiencia Nacional would grab you. The court would close. The press would have a field day. There would be court cases. The injustices you've suffered would become publicly aired. The whole episode would become Spain's biggest scandal. It would waste a lot of time, which would be useful.'

I wasn't looking forward to this one little bit. I'd rehearsed the speech in Spanish. It was just a few lines: 'Spain is now an American colony. The King of Spain has no balls. He is no better than a whore, bending his body and his morals to his American master. I spit in his face and shit on the Spanish flag.'

As the prison van drove from Alcala-Meco to the Audiencia Nacional, I saw hundreds of Madrileños going about their business on this glorious early spring morning. They stopped to talk and laugh with each other. They sat in cafés, shamelessly chain-smoking and drinking their pre-breakfast coffee and brandy. Children were skipping past them, bubbling with the joy of life. The faces of the men were proud but friendly. The women were either kind mothers or sex goddesses. I loved these ordinary Spanish people, with their healthy contempt for regulation, their inability to get stressed, and their devotion to having a good time. They're Europe's best. Newspapers and magazines carried photographs of King Juan Carlos and Queen Sofia engaged in ordinary activities like drinking beer and playing a one-armed bandit. I couldn't offend these people. It wasn't their fault. I didn't believe in what I was going to do, so I chickened out. I sat in silence throughout the court hearing, knowing that, in one way, I had given up. How could I possibly fight the DEA if I wasn't even ruthless enough to insult the people who were locking me up on the DEA's behalf?

The Audiencia Nacional ruled that Judy and I should be extradited on the Florida federal charges. We did get one victory: I was deemed non-extraditable on the 1973 Nevada rock-group-scam federal charges because too much time had elapsed. It was a hollow victory, as my Florida federal RICO charges included the 1973 rock-group scam. (One of RICO's prosecutorially endearing qualities is its ability to circumvent statutes of time limitation.)

I lodged an appeal. Judy felt very strongly that she had lost her last chance to beat extradition. Equally strongly, she felt that no court in the world could possibly convict her of dope smuggling. She wanted to go to Florida and establish her innocence in front of a trial judge. Geoffrey Kenion went to Florida, where the trial of those co-defendants already in America was soon to start. Panic messages from Patrick Lane begged Judy to continue resisting extradition until his trial was finished. He was afraid the DEA would force her to testify against him. Reluctantly, she joined me in my appeal against the extradition order.

The interest I had in the Miami trial prevented me from sinking too low. Also helpful was a rearrangement of the housing arrangements in Alcala-Meco: all non-Spanish prisoners were now in the same cell block. It wasn't exclusively for foreigners, but largely so. Roger Reaves, Darin Bufalino, and Jacques Canavaggio were pleased to see me. Zacarias was also there. He had too many connections to be locked up in the same cell block as other Madrid gangsters. The first day I was there, he did nothing but smile and feed me strong joints of Moroccan.

The second day, we were not let out from our cells until early evening. Everyone was excitedly huddled around the day's copy of *El País*. The news was mind-blowing: Esteban Zacarias Sanchez Martinez had escaped from Alcala-Meco, from this very cell block. Zacarias, probably stoned out of his head, had sawn through his cell bars, climbed on to the roof, climbed in the shadow of gun towers over at least three perimeter walls and fences, and escaped from Spain's top-security prison. Roger was seething with envy.

'I told you it could be done from here. Good Lord, you know I did. I bet he used that jeweller's string to cut through the bars. Marie never sent it to me; otherwise, I'd be in South Africa growing pot. Goddamn it! Why wouldn't she send it? I'm going to appeal against being extradited to Germany. I'll stay here awhile. If that stoned hippie Zacarias can get out of here, you bet your arse I can.'

Jacques Canavaggio approached.

'This is good news about Zacarias, Marco Polo, no? What is happening in your case? Are they going to try you in Spain? I think this *acción popular* was a very good idea. My trial, of course, will be in Spain. I am glad it is nowhere else.'

An idea struck me.

'Jacques, the *acción popular* so far has not worked, but maybe you could make it work.'

'Whatever I can do, my friend.'

'Tell the Spanish police that the fifteen tons of Lebanese dope in your cave in the Costa Brava came from me. Then the Spanish will have to try me here.'

'Marco Polo, I am Corsican. We tell the police nothing. But maybe I can persuade one of my co-defendants from France to give the police your name. Would that help?'

'Thanks, Jacques.'

'It is my pleasure, Marco Polo.'

More helpful than any of this was the arrival in Alcala-Meco of John Parry, the alleged launderer of the Brinks-Mat millions. He had been picked up by the Spanish police in the Costa del Sol and transferred to Madrid for extradition proceedings. Scotland Yard wanted him badly. Within two minutes of conversing with him, I knew I had met one of the very few life-long friends one makes during years of prison. His compassion, intelligence, humour, and ability to keep himself and others cheerful continually uplifted my spirit. We spent all our out-of-cell time with each other. My parents and his wife befriended each other on their monthly visits to see us. The *funcionarios* moved him to the next cell to mine. We discussed our cases at length and worked on each other's defences.

Most of my creative defence work had to wait until the outcome of the Miami trial of Patrick Lane, Ernie Combs, and others. The trial began in April. Reports were sent to me via Judy's sister, Natasha Lane, now living in Florida, and Marcus. Jimmy Newton, Geoffrey Kenion, John Francis (who had allegedly assisted John Denbigh in money transfers), and Wyvonna Wills (Gerry's wife) did deals pleading guilty for immediate release. All except John Francis agreed to be witnesses for the prosecution if called. Staunch attempts were made by the defence lawyers of those pleading not guilty to throw out the telephone-tap evidence. To everyone's surprise, including that of the prosecution, Judge James C. Paine ruled the telephone taps to be admissible. Ernie, his girl-friend Patty, and Patrick were convicted by a jury. Rick Brown, Ernie's long-term dope-mover, and Teresita Caballero, a girl-friend of Patrick's whom I'd never met, were acquitted. Sentencing of those convicted would take place in a couple of months.

The trial transcripts, together with copies of the actual cassette recordings of the taped phone taps and taped conversations with Lord Moynihan, were sent to me from Miami. None of the defendants had taken the witness stand to speak in their own defence. No constructive defence had been offered. I knew this was a mistake. Only guilty people decline to be cross-examined and rely on prosecutorial incompetence to obtain their freedom.

The DEA had made one enormous boob. Presumably not knowing of the existence of Jarvis, they had incorrectly assumed that it was I who had delivered the crates of hashish to the American President Line at Karachi Wharf in 1984. DEA agent Harlan Lee Bowe and Her Majesty's Customs and Excise Officer John Stephenson were so convinced of this that they had managed to persuade various Pakistani employees of the American President Line to positively identify me. I knew I wasn't in Pakistan at that time. There would be plenty of records to establish that fact and show to a court, yet again, that Michael Stephenson didn't always get things right. This time, unlike at the Old Bailey, the accusation would be correct.

I listened to the cassettes and searched for the recording of my denial to Moynihan of involvement in the Canadian scam or any recent American scam. It was missing. I searched for

reference to it in the trial transcripts. A DEA agent testified
that his secretary had inadvertently erased twenty minutes of
recordings, but that Moynihan had confirmed that during
that twenty minutes I had admitted involvement in Canadian
and American scams. So the DEA were prepared to destroy
evidence that didn't suit them and commit perjury to explain
its disappearance. No big surprise.

The original reel-to-reel recordings of the telephone taps
no longer existed. The Miami court was given the rather
pathetic explanation that the Spanish police were forced
through reasons of economy to re-use the reel-to-reel tapes.
It apparently did not occur to the DEA that an extremely
small fraction of the several million dollars they were
expending on this case could have equipped the impoverished Spanish police with a fully functional, state-of-the-art
recording studio, let alone with a few blank reels.

Craig Lovato had, however, managed to copy his own
carefully chosen selection of five hundred conversations and
bits of conversations before the Spanish ran out of tape.
From these he compiled a set of 'composite duplicates', a
kind of cut-and-paste auditory collage. Lovato was confident
he knew the identity of each person speaking, whereas, in
fact, he had made almost thirty misidentifications. Some
were understandable. Others weren't: Chi Chuen Lo's very
Cantonese accent was once identified as the voice of Lord
Anthony Moynihan, while the cockney twang of Mickey
Williams was continually identified as Salim Malik's voice.

I spent hours every day making my own transcripts of the
tapped telephone calls. The transcripts provided by the
United States prosecution were laughably inaccurate. Most
of the errors were clear evidence of perceptual bias, making
me think they had been prepared by Lovato. 'Tight' was
transcribed as 'Thai', 'eight o'clock' as 'Bangkok', 'drag' as
'drug', 'cats' as 'cash', 'of course' as 'at the coast', 'fits in
with your' as 'that big shipment of yours', and 'overlapping'
as 'mobile operative'.

At the Miami trial, Lovato explained several suitably selected snippets of telephone conversation in terms of smuggling dope from Pakistan to America. It wasn't difficult because the conversations were so vague and almost never referred to anyone's real name or any specific place. They were consistent with almost any scam happening anywhere. Lovato might testify that 'over there' meant California and 'Mozambique' meant Mexico, but equally, if not more, plausible interpretations were always possible. After all, when the Spanish began their investigation in 1985, they maintained I was smuggling into Spain. The Dutch, who it turns out were tapping Hobbs's Amsterdam switching-station telephone at the same time, thought they'd stumbled on to a plan to smuggle dope into Holland. Each of the two countries had plenty of evidence, aided by its own interpretations of the vague telephone conversations, to support its belief. Perhaps many of the countries involved could have made a case for believing they themselves were the countries to receive the dope.

My defence was beginning to take root. I felt excited. It might not be as intriguing a defence as being a secret agent, but it could work. I couldn't begin to pretend I wasn't a hashish smuggler, but I could make out I would never dream of smuggling it to America, not with the penalties being dished out these days. I'd be crazy even to think about it. Even Americans don't smuggle to America any more. There are better places where you get a better price for the dope, where it's not so easy to get caught, and where you don't get much prison time if you do. Other than Lovato's interpretations, there wasn't much evidence to show I had imported hashish into America. Since 1973, the only consignment that had been busted in the United States was the two tons in the naval station in Alameda, California, the one shipped by the US Government on the American President Line. The DEA, with the help of Michael Stephenson, had already shot themselves in the foot on that one. Which country should I choose? To where could I pretend I'd smuggled ten tons of Pakistani hash?

It would have to be Western Europe, Canada, or Australia. Nowhere else could handle such a load. I began to construct three separate scenarios, one for each country, and tested them against the prosecution evidence. Each would require a lot of contextual research, but each had potential. Explaining away the evidence of millions of dollars in America might pose a problem, but money laundering was a global activity, and cash would transit through the most unlikely places. There might be all sorts of reasons why whoever purchased the hashish (at whatever destination) would want to pay for it in America in dollars, the currency of every international black market. As long as no one grassed, I would be all right, even if I was extradited.

Marcus came to see me with some most disturbing news. To give them a bit of a break, the children had been sent to Britain to spend time with some friends and relatives. While there, Francesca visited our family doctor, Basil Lee. She broke down in front of him and gave a horrific account of her living circumstances. Nigel was a hopeless junkie and drunkard. He was squandering my money. He was censoring all her letters to me and Judy. His pastimes included battering Masha and locking the children in their rooms for hours on end. Little Patrick had been discovered lying in a gutter in the middle of the night while Nigel had passed out in a nearby bar. Francesca's life was nothing but screams and torment. She was desperate. She was eight years old.

Dr Lee wrote a very strong letter to Judy. Nigel and Masha had to go. Marcus explained that Natasha Lane and her two children were coming over to Palma. As long as I paid all expenses, they would stay there until Judy was home. I was shocked into deep silence. I knew there had been something weird about Nigel, but I had not suspected this. I suppose the problem had been given the best solution. Natasha would be fine. There was nothing I could do. But during the nights the pain of my children revisited me with a vengeance.

Marcus's next visit also brought bad news. Johnny Martin had died of a heart attack in Brighton. Although towards the end he had become an unhealthy junkie and lost much of the character I loved, I had lost an old friend with whom I had shared no end of good times and adventure. My heart went out to his wife, Cynthia, and his children.

At last Marcus brought some excellent news. Although Patrick Lane had been facing a possible life sentence or 120 years, he had just been sentenced to a grand total of only three years.

Only three years! Is this what we were all worrying about? Had Judge Paine seen through all the DEA sham? He must have realised that we weren't that bad or that big and decided to let us out before all the nasty guys took over the hashish business. If Patrick got three years, what could I expect? Maybe twice as much. I could manage that. I'd be free in a few years. As for Judy, if Patrick got three years, she should be looking at a maximum of three minutes. She could no longer be forced to testify against Patrick, and it was clearly unwise for her to stay here in Madrid fighting extradition. The United States has a Speedy Trial Act. Judy could be extradited and acquitted within a few weeks. Even if she was convicted, and that seemed impossible, Judge Paine would hardly want her to spend any more time in prison.

The lawyer who obtained Rick Brown's acquittal was Don Re from Los Angeles. In 1984 he had successfully represented John De Lorean, the Belfast car manufacturer who had been set up in a cocaine sting operation. His credentials were first class. I wrote asking if he would fly over to Madrid to see me and Judy. He would. It would cost $25,000. It had to be done.

Don Re was equally certain that the best strategy was for Judy to go to America. He would take care of her as soon as she arrived and get her home as soon as possible, for a deposit of a further $25,000. It had to be done. American lawyers were clearly expensive. Don Re had already received as much as Gustavo.

The more I studied, the more I realised that Australia would be the ideal country to pretend to have swamped with dope during the time of the 1986 telephone taps. Among the ten thousand pages of evidence were all sorts of references to Australia. There were documents showing that Ernie Combs had smuggled dope from India to Australia during the 1970s and that Philip Sparrowhawk had smuggled Thai dope into Australia during the 1980s. I was refused an Australian visa in 1985. The DEA and Australian police had put the bug on Gerry's trawler while it was berthed in Australian waters in 1986. Carl had an Australian passport. I had a false passport which carried an Australian visa. Moynihan was documented both as having smuggled heroin to Australia and as having been an Australian intelligence agent. Judy visited Australia at the same time as I visited Moynihan in Manila. Joe Smith was Australia's first big marijuana smuggler. Several co-defendants visited Australia during the critical period. The telephone taps were full of references which, creatively interpreted, related to Australia. I could weave a plausible tale on the basis of that lot.

Through Marcus, I obtained detailed published chronologies of events in Australia. I linked suitable ones to vague references in the telephone taps. I studied Australian politics, crime, drug consumption, drug trafficking, and banking systems. I came across the tale of Nugan-Hand Ltd., a private Australian bank.

In 1973, a new banking business was opened in Sydney by Frank Nugan and Michael Hand. Frank Nugan was an Australian playboy whose family fruit business was centred in Australia's marijuana-growing region. Michael Nand was a New York CIA agent. He was a former Green Beret who had participated in the CIA's mass assassination Phoenix Program in Vietnam. He had been an employee of Air

America, the CIA-owned airline responsible during the
Nixon era for taking tons of opium from the Golden
Triangle to lucrative markets. The declared source of the
new bank's funds was money invested in real estate by
American soldiers taking a break from slaughtering
Vietnamese women and children.

In 1977, a branch was opened in Chiang Mai, Thailand.
Its office had connecting doors with the DEA's. In no time
the bank expanded its interests to include financing Las
Vegas casino projects, handling some of the Shah of Iran's
fortune, dubious international arms dealing, and laundering
the proceeds of opium and heroin traffic. The governing
body of the bank was peppered with high-ranking US brass.

In 1980, Frank Nugan was found dead. He had either
been murdered or performed a suicide requiring the skills of
a professional acrobat. Michael Hand disappeared. The
bank collapsed. A large chunk of the cream of America's
military personnel had lost their money. The US Senate
investigated the whole matter. The CIA gave sworn
testimony in secret. The investigation closed.

Carl had once been wrongly accused of assassinating
Frank Nugan. The *Sunday Times* had reported that Lord
Moynihan was linked to Nugan-Hand Ltd.

This was great. I could throw in all the exciting stuff that
juries love to hear. I could maybe even resurrect a part of my
MI6 mythology. I was just a gentle pot smuggler, doing my
business in various parts of the non-American world and
keeping an eye open for anything really evil to tell my Oxford
chums at MI6. I used Gerry Wills to land a load of hashish
in Australia and used Jacobi and Sunde to launder the
proceeds. Australian currency controls were unbelievably
stiff. Jacobi knew CIA agents who held vast cash hoards in
the United States and would happily exchange it for cash
within Australia's borders. We had ways of getting cash out
of the United States, so we would take it from there and pay
all concerned. No dope ever saw America. I had given a full

report of the affair to my non-existent MI6 superiors, who were most interested in the details of CIA agents holding suitcases of dollars. In a desperate attempt to cover up, the CIA/DEA, with the help of the Australian police, turned to their Nugan-Hand banking associate Lord Moynihan and asked him to help them set me up. They were keen to convince the world that the dope was purely an American scam which had not involved the CIA's Australian money-laundering activities.

I was convinced this Australian defence could work. It wasn't even as bizarre as the successful Mexican secret agent defence. But did American juries have a sense of humour?

In 1989 summer heat began to stifle Alcala-Meco. I religiously adhered to my daily yoga sessions, worked on my defence, smoked joints, and walked the *patio* with John Parry. Roger was working on an escape plan. My fight against extradition was now totally in the hands of Gustavo and the courts. A plethora of time-consuming issues was before the Audiencia Nacional's appeals division, the slow-moving Spanish Supreme Court, and the almost stationary Spanish Constitutional Court.

At the end of July, a forty-minute documentary about me was shown on Spanish national television. It was sympathetic to my plight and was followed by dozens of letters from Spanish citizens offering everything from paying my legal fees to the best shag I could ever imagine. They all expressed shame at the way the Spanish were giving me up to the Americans.

After the television programme, Judy and I were separately visited by Amber, Francesca, and Patrick. They knew this would be their last visit before Judy left for America, and the girls were very frightened. Patrick was happy but still hadn't spoken a word since our arrest a year ago. Amber and Francesca spent the whole visit sitting on my knee and sobbing.

'Will we see you here, Daddy, when Mummy's gone?'

'Of course, my loves. You'll probably come to see me every couple of months. We'll see each other soon enough.'

I was wrong. It took almost five heartbreaking years before I saw them again.

Jacques Canavaggio came up to me in the *patio*.

'Marco Polo, I cannot help you. I have been told by someone whose business it is to know that if any of my people say you were involved in my Lebanese load in the Costa Brava, the American pigs will extradite me for being part of your organisation. These DEA bastards are crazy people.'

'I understand, Jacques. Please don't worry.'

'You always have a friend in Corsica, Marco Polo. Remember that.'

Jacques walked off. Darin Bufalino approached.

'Hi, Limey. What's happening?'

'I'm not a Limey,' I protested. 'I'm Welsh. You Yanks are all the same.'

'I'm no Yank. I'm half-Irish and half-Italian.'

'What's the difference?'

'You got me there, Limey. But listen. They're extraditing me to the good old US of A in a few days. Is there anything I can do for you over there? I'll be in prison, but I got connections, Howard, you know that.'

I had been worrying about keeping my Australian defence secret and had already resolved to send out via Gustavo all my research materials. I also wanted to lead the DEA to believe that I was going to try another, completely different defence, so that I could take them by surprise.

'Darin, would you be prepared to leak some information to the DEA? It would be false information. It would only hurt them and no one else, and it would really help me.'

'Hey, I don't doubt you, man. But if I did that, I'd be down on record as a snitch. That could seriously damage my career prospects. I'll do anything else to help, I promise.'

The criminal ethic was proving inconvenient. I had to think of another way. John Parry joined us. I explained the problem to him.

'It's easy, Howard. If they take you to America – please God they don't – but if they do, take your phoney defence notes with you. Those DEA bastards are bound to grab them when you get to Florida. They'll photocopy the lot, give them back to you like nothing had happened, and think they've got one over on you. Then you can stick it right up them with your real defence.'

That would work.

Judy left. Just before she was taken on the plane at Madrid international airport, she was allowed to send me a telegram. 'Pray for me,' it said. I prayed and cried and heard the wails of my children.

Darin Bufalino was extradited to Boston. Other fellow-prisoners were extradited to various countries. Roger had requested them to write to him giving full details of the travel procedures they had to undergo. Some of the letters had arrived.

'Let me tell you something, boy. Escaping from that airport in Madrid is a piece of piss. If I did it in Amsterdam, I'm damn sure that with the help of the Good Lord I can do it here.'

'But, Roger, you'll have handcuffs on. You didn't in Amsterdam.'

'Hey, I had handcuffs on when I jumped out of the court in Palma. They don't mean shit to me. But that don't matter anyway because the cops take the handcuffs off at the departure lounge. I bet you ain't ever seen a guy with handcuffs on in a departure lounge or a plane. No siree you ain't. I'll just get on another plane. Maybe go straight to South Africa. I can't wait to hit that Madrid airport.'

Shortly after this conversation, Roger was extradited to Germany. He was driven all the way by car. As planned, he pleaded guilty and snitched on me and McCann. The German authorities gave him a seven-year sentence and housed him in a maximum-security prison in Lübeck.

On Friday October 31st, Gustavo came to see me. He was flustered and angry.

'Its incredible. Absolutely incredible. The Audiencia Nacional appeals court and the Constitutional Court have dismissed our cases against extradition. The *acción popular* appeal has also been dismissed. Usually these cases take years to resolve. In your case they have acted almost immediately. It's completely without precedent.'

'Do I have any chance left, Gustavo, or am I on my way to Miami?'

'The Supreme Court still has to rule. They shouldn't extradite you while that is pending. I have some other ideas which I will discuss with you on Monday. Just try to relax over the weekend.'

The next day, Saturday, I worked on my false defence, the one to mislead the DEA. The papers relating to my real Australia defence and my detailed analysis of every item of the prosecution evidence had been given to Gustavo. I created the sort of phoney defence the authorities would believe to be mine: after I had worked for the Mexican Secret Service and been acquitted of any involvement in marijuana smuggling, MI6 posted me to the Khyber Pass. It was declared United States and United Kingdom policy to support the *mujaheddin* against the occupation of Afghanistan by the Soviet Union. Some financial aid was officially given, and covert encouragement was given to illegal fund-raising such as that resulting from the export of Afghan hashish. It was clear that the 1986 hashish load came from the *mujaheddin*. The stamp on each slab said as much. It was clear that the 1984 American President Line load involved the CIA. I was not breaking American law. I was carrying out in Pakistan the work assigned me by MI6 and the CIA, helping to rid the world of the Communist scourge. It was monstrous even to charge me.

In a file headed 'Try to use if possible', I put in newspaper reports on CIA hot money finding its way to the Afghan rebels, the IRA purchasing Stingers from the *mujaheddin*, the September 1986 hijack by the PLO of an American airliner on the runway of Karachi airport, *mujaheddin* bases in the Khyber Pass being used to train Arab and Filipino terrorists, and theories of who assassinated President Zia ul-Haq. For good measure, I also threw in some stoned nonsense about a Communist cell in Nepal controlling the world's hashish supply.

Just the sort of defence the DEA would expect.

I spent all of Sunday morning and most of the afternoon lying on my bed smoking joints. At four o'clock, when we were locked in to eat our meal, there was a polite knock on the cell door. It was one of the friendly young English-speaking *funcionarios*. He called from the other side of the metal door.

'Marco Polo, pack up your things, if you please. You are leaving now. I will be back in twenty minutes when all the cells are opened. Please be ready then.'

The *funcionario*'s footsteps receded. I went cold. I started to tremble. Shakily, I started to put my phoney defence notes and other possessions in a pillowcase.

'Did I hear that right, Howard?' asked John Parry from the next-door cell. 'If so, you'd better roll yourself a good strong joint of that Moroccan hash. It might be your last for a while. Don't worry. You'll be okay. Keep your chin up. Think of all them hamburgers and hot dogs. Beats this paella.'

I finished packing my bag, rolled a huge strong joint and put what hashish I had left in my underpants. I puffed away frantically. The cell doors opened. Hashish smoke and fumes billowed out and enveloped the *funcionario*. He burst out laughing and walked away. John Parry went running after him.

'*Funcionario, funcionario*, look at Marco Polo. He is smoking *chocolate*. You must bust him. He must do some time in prison here. You can't let him go to the United States.'

'No, no,' said the *funcionario*. 'Marco Polo can do what he likes. Only America will make him pay. I allow him to smoke the hashish. But he must hurry. Interpol is waiting.'

'I don't think that'll cause Marco Polo too much bother,' said John. 'He doesn't really like Interpol. And anyway, I have to carry his bag. I always used to carry his bag.'

'Yes, okay, you can carry his bag. But please be quick.'

John Parry carrying my pillowcase and I smoking my massive joint were led down the corridor. We were met by about ten uniformed guards and a few serious-looking men in sober suits.

'This is where I say so long, Howard. Stay strong.'

We were both in tears. We hugged and said our goodbyes.

Very quickly I was bundled into a van, taken to Madrid police station, and placed in a holding cell. Although very firm in denying me the opportunity to communicate with anyone, the police were more than friendly, almost apologetic, and plied me with food, coffee, and cigarettes. When locked up for the night, I swallowed the lump of hashish and fell asleep.

Very early the next morning, I was brought up from the cells. Alongside the Spanish police stood three very obvious Americans, one Hispanic, one Black, and one Irish.

'Are you Dennis Howard Marks?' asked the Hispanic.

I nodded.

'We are the United States of America Federal Marshals Service. We have a warrant to take you to the United States of America. You will now be relieved of all your possessions other than the clothes you are wearing. I will now perform a strip-search on your person.'

'He has already been searched,' lied one of the senior plain-clothes Spanish police.

'I would have preferred to search him myself. Please note that for the record. Mr Marks, kindly hand over those cigarettes of yours, and slip your hands into these handcuffs.'

'I'm a heavy smoker, particularly on planes.'

'We will administer you cigarettes when you require them.'

'I want one now.'

'You will have to wait until we get to the airport. We are pressed for time. We have been waiting for you since Friday. There was a lot of paperwork to do. In any event, I doubt if my Spanish colleagues would allow you to pollute their office with your cigarette smoke.'

'*Por favor, hombre!*' said the Interpol man, and handed me one of his cigarettes.

At breakneck speed, the three marshals, the Interpol man, and I were driven to Madrid airport. After an hour in a holding cell, I was taken at gunpoint aboard an absolutely empty Pan Am 747. A marshal sat each side of me, one behind. Regular passengers were beginning to board. The Hispanic marshal suddenly looked very proud of himself.

'This is American territory. An American aircraft is on American territory wherever it is. Read him his Miranda rights.'

And they did, like they do in the movies.

Sixteen

41526-004

I hated every minute of the journey. Once we landed at New York, the Hispanic US Marshal put a chain around my waist and led me like a pet chimpanzee through a maze of corridors. At first the US Immigration and Naturalisation Service wouldn't let me through because I did not have a US visa and was a convicted, drug-dealing felon. Then the US Marshals were prevented from boarding because they had lost the onward flight tickets to Miami and had overlooked getting permission for the firearms they were carrying in order to kill me if I decided to jump out of the plane. Shortly before midnight, we arrived at Miami International Airport, where we were greeted by another US Marshal, a very young, very big, bald Black wearing a hideously multi-coloured Mickey Mouse tee-shirt. The four US Marshals and I got into a large limousine driven by yet another US Marshal and drove down a freeway to a large complex containing apartment blocks, factory, chapel, and a lake. It looked like a garden village. A notice indicated that it was Miami Metropolitan Federal Correctional Center (Miami MCC), United States Federal Bureau of Prisons. An obese female sporting a semi-automatic and a grotesquely short mini-skirt waved us through to the reception area. I was the only arrival. The prison guards, called hacks rather than screws, took away all my personal possessions, stripped me naked, looked up my arse, and made me pull my foreskin back. I was assigned a number, 41526-004, had my photographs and fingerprints taken, and marched to a solitary cell. I couldn't sleep. Two hours later, at three o'clock in the morning, a guard shouted through the door.

'Name?'

'Marks,' I answered.

'Number?'

'I don't know. I've only just got here.'

'Number?'

'I don't know.'

The guard disappeared and came back with three more. They took me to a cold holding cell full of Colombian and Cuban cocaine dealers. I gathered we were all being taken to Miami Courthouse. Most of the Colombians and Cubans were on trial and were absolutely shattered. Each day they were woken at 3 a.m., kept in holding cells for five hours, handcuffed and shackled by US Marshals, taken by bus to the courthouse, produced in the actual courtroom for a maximum of four hours, held in the courthouse's 'bullpen' holding cell for several hours, and taken back to prison. They never got to sleep before midnight and were not allowed any books or papers during the hours they were awake. In these conditions, they fought the US Government for their freedom.

I was in the courtroom for a mere few minutes. The magistrate told me to come back tomorrow. For four or five days I was shunted between the prison and the courthouse, each day appearing for a few minutes. There was no DEA and no press. On the last occasion, I saw Robert O'Neill, the prosecuting Assistant United States Attorney I had seen in Spain. He told me I had now been arraigned. I had been assigned a lawyer, a federal public defender whose fees

would be paid by the US Government. O'Neill advised me
to pay for a better one.

After this last court appearance, I was taken back to
Miami MCC. Having completed the first few days of
mandatory isolation, I was now taken to dormitory accommodation in the main compound of the prison complex. The
next morning was beautifully sunny, and at the permitted
time I took a walk around the lake. There were ducks on the
surface and a plastic alligator on the bank. Concrete tables
and benches were scattered around. Racket-ball courts,
tennis courts, outdoor gymnasium, jogging track, football
field, horseshoe-throwing pitch, basketball court, bowling
pitch, cafeteria, shop, library, outdoor cinema, pool rooms,
television rooms, vending machines, lay conveniently close
at hand. A man came running towards me. It was Malik.

'D. H. Marks. So we are here together. It is wish of Allah.
And this, American bastard say, is God's country, land of free.'

'How the hell did they manage to extradite you, Malik?'

'Political reason. With Zia, it would not happen in blue
moon. But Benazir, she is now in charge. She wants
American dollar. Appeal Court judges in Pakistan extradite
me. Next day American pig give them US visa and Green
Card. Now they live handsome life in Washington. They
think they have left Third World for better life. DEA ask me
to plead guilty and co-operate and become snitch. Then they
will send me back to Pakistan. I say "Why not?" I will tell
them the bullshit.'

'Malik, you're not going to testify against me, are you?'

He smiled.

'If I do, D. H. Marks, then you can do the cross-examine.
You will see what harm I do. I am just going to tell them the
bullshit. We are in paper-mill business.'

'What's happened to your nephew Aftab?'

'He has become snitch against me.'

'Will he testify against me, too?'

'If DEA ask, he will do.'

Jim Hobbs and Ronnie Robb joined us. Both had been unceremoniously extradited from Holland and then offered immediate freedom if they agreed to plead guilty, become snitches, and grass up everyone they knew. They had declined the offer and were awaiting trial. Then I saw Ernie for the first time in ten years. He had lost all his excess weight and looked exactly like he did in 1973.

'Ain't this some shit?'

'Ernie, I'm sorry about all the goofs I made,' I said.

'Aw! Forget it. I made a few myself. Prison don't bother me, but I can't stand the thought of my Patty being inside for seven years. I'll do anything to get her out. Anything.'

Patrick Lane joined us. It had been five years since I'd seen him. Like Ernie, he looked remarkably healthy and suntanned.

'You must be pleased getting only a three-year sentence. That's close to an acquittal.'

'That's where you are wrong, Howard. The prosecution are appealing.'

'What! On what grounds?'

'Because I carried on doing business with Lord Moynihan after November 1st, 1987. That means I should have been sentenced under the Sentencing Reform Act, which demands a higher sentence than the one Judge Paine gave me. The prosecution say I should get fifteen years without parole. That makes it a worse sentence than Ernie's. At least he'll get the chance for parole before that. I won't. I'll be in prison until well into the next century. I can't do this to my wife and kids.'

The six of us sat around discussing old and present times. I hadn't had a joint for almost a week.

'Can we get any dope here, Ernie?'

'Forget it.'

In the afternoon I interviewed a number of Miami attorneys, all wearing the trappings of dope-dealing wealth and most claiming to have close friends within the prosecution with whom they could negotiate a favourable snitching deal. One of the lawyers, Steve Bronis, behaved very differently from the others. He was cold as ice and didn't smile.

'Mr Marks, let me make one thing clear before we start. If you intend to plead guilty or co-operate with the US Government, I am not your lawyer.'

'You're my lawyer. As long as I can afford you. What will you charge?'

'I'll get the papers from the court and read them. Then I'll let you know.'

In the evening, I talked to some other prisoners, again mainly Cuban and Colombian. The message was obvious. Unless one was absolutely as innocent as the driven snow and could prove it without the remotest shadow of a doubt, one would get convicted. The only way to avoid the resulting heavy sentence was to become, or pretend to become, a snitch.

My mind was troubled when I tried to get some sleep. No way can I become a snitch, a grass, a *chivato*, a stool-pigeon, a squealer, a rat, a traitor, a wrong 'un, a betrayer, a Judas, and lie at the bottom of Dante's hell for all eternity. I wouldn't be able to look my kids or my parents in the eyes if I did that. If Patty was convicted and got seven years, what would happen to Judy, presently languishing in a nearby jail? She was equally incapable of grassing and might have to spend years in prison. I might have to spend forever inside. How would our children survive without us? But then I mustn't give up. When I asked the US Marshals in court what had happened to my personal belongings, they said the DEA had them. John Parry's idea had worked. The DEA are now reading my phoney defence. I'll stick it right up them in trial. If I can get acquitted at the Old Bailey, surely I can manage it in downtown Miami. I'll talk to Hobbs and Malik in the morning and get them to agree to say the Pakistani load was for Australia, not America. I drifted off.

'Name?'

'Marks.'

'Number?'

'41526-004.'

'You're going to court, Marks. Leave everything behind in your locker.'

Thirteen hours later, in the Miami Courthouse's bullpen, the court proceedings finished for the day. I had not been called. I managed to get a US Marshal's attention and asked him what was happening.

'What's your number?' asked the Marshal.

'41526-004.'

'You are being transferred to another facility.'

'Where?'

'North Dade.'

I'd heard that name before. That was where Judy was being held. I turned round to face the other prisoners.

'They're sending me to a women's prison,' I exclaimed. 'North Dade. That's where my wife is. Fantastic.'

'That's not just a broads' joint,' said one of the prisoners. 'It's where they put stool-pigeons. You're getting a break, Limey.'

North Dade Detention Centre is a Florida state jail rather than a federal prison. State jails normally house offenders against that state's law. International dope smuggling is a federal offence, but the US Federal Government has taken to renting state jails from the state authorities and using them for its own purposes. Some of North Dade was used to house the increasing number of female federal prisoners; the rest was used to cultivate snitches and protect them from those who would wish them ill. The jail itself conformed somewhat to the American movie stereotype, with metal-grilled, electronically controlled cell entrances. Facing the array of cells were televisions that were never switched off. There were telephones. The outside recreation area was a small cage containing a table-tennis set-up and a weightlifting machine and could be used by only a handful of people at a time. There were no facilities other than those required for basic hygiene. Almost every male prisoner was a self-confessed snitch who had been caught smuggling cocaine. They had agreed to testify against their business partners and friends in return for lower sentences. One man was giving evidence against his mother. Each had his own justification: he'd been ripped off, it wasn't his fault he was busted, he told them to stop, he couldn't stay in prison for years because it wouldn't be fair to his family, everyone would have to become a snitch soon, there was no other way. The American 'War on Drugs' was fulfilling some hidden and sinister agenda. Demand for confessions had been a characteristic of political repression in many countries at many times. It probably reached its peak during the Cultural Revolution in Communist China. Loyalties to families and friends have to be replaced by loyalty to country. Forget individual ethics and obey the laws and regulations. Enjoy yourself, but do it our way: watch TV for as long as possible, then practise using your firearms. If you don't do it our way, we'll kill you. If your brother is doing something illegal, you should stop him. If you don't, you're as bad as him, and we'll get both of you.

The jail regime was loose. The guards had been instructed not to upset the snitches; they were valuable government property. Not all of the inmates were Hispanic. One was of Italian extraction. His name was Anthony 'Tomak' Acceturo, the once-reputed boss of the New Jersey Lucchese crime family. We discussed our loathing of snitches and the US Government which had created them. At the same time, it was obvious we each suspected the other of being a snitch. Why else would we be here?

Judy and I were able to talk to each other on the phone. She was twenty yards away. Although keeping up her strength, she had been bitterly upset by the treatment meted out to her by her brother Patrick's wife. Their home was within a twenty-minute drive of North Dade, and it had been understood that at least someone would visit her. No one did. Not even her lawyer, Don Re, had been to see her. She was very, very lonely and cried for her children.

Steve Bronis came to see me the first morning, and I said I had not become a snitch. He said he knew and explained that the likely reason I had been transferred was to remove any possibility of my persuading Malik, Ernie Combs, and Patrick Lane not to become snitches. These days there were more snitches than non-snitches. Soon they'd have to build very small special prisons just for stand-up guys.

Bronis had already reviewed the transcripts of the trials of Ernie, Patrick, and others. He felt that the defence lawyers had not put enough effort into getting the telephone taps thrown out of court. He had contacted the DEA and Gustavo in Madrid. Gustavo had sent Bronis the papers I'd left with him. The DEA claimed that there were no defence notes in my personal belongings. Read your heart out, Lovato.

Bronis arranged to have Judy accompany us during his legal visits. I hadn't seen her for six months. She looked different: more worried and more strained. Judy's choice was simple: admit to something she'd never done, get a sentence of time already served, and go home as a convicted felon; or wait for months, maybe years, in a county jail and attempt to establish her innocence before a brainwashed jury. She chose the former. A few weeks later, Don Re's able assistant, Mona, represented Judy in front of Judge Paine, who convicted her and set her free. The relief was the greatest I have ever known. Her and our children's intense pain and suffering were over. We might not see each other for a while, but Judy's plea agreement made provision for US Government assistance to be granted to help her to enter the country in the future and visit me.

Talking to the snitches, I quickly discovered what small fry I was. I had been charged with somehow being involved with a grand total of about a hundred tons of dope over a period of almost twenty years. Now I was associating with Cubans who had done more than that in a single shipment and had documentary evidence to prove it. Lovato and his DEA buddies had certainly done a remarkable job in getting the world to believe I was its biggest-ever marijuana dealer. Part of me really loved the attention I was getting because everyone thought I was the greatest smuggler in the universe. American media, journalists, and authors began to take an acute interest in me. I had been the mystery cartel leader, absent from a trial having all the ingredients that Americans yearn for: a British Peer of the Realm running knocking-shops full of Filipino whores and snitching on his buddy from James Bond's organisation, MI6, who had been smuggling dope in Pink Floyd's equipment and banking in Hong Kong and Switzerland. It was really international: not just a bunch of Hispanics from south of the border, but real foreigners from Europe and Asia. ABC's peak-viewing news programme, *Prime Time Live*, wanted to interview me. I said yes, of course.

Paul Eddy and Sara Walden were former members of the *Sunday Times* Insight team and now lived near Washington, DC. They had just written a book called *The Cocaine Wars*, which covered cocaine smuggling from Colombia to Miami, and now wanted to write a book about my arrest and trial. Paul Eddy had written to me in Madrid advising me of his intention and asking if I would agree to be interviewed by him. I did so on the condition that I would not answer questions if I felt that I might mess up my defence by doing so. They interviewed me a number of times at North Dade Detention Centre's visiting room, providing a welcome break from the tedium of the television-flooded cell block and enabling me to have an objective viewpoint of the evidence against me. BBC Television wanted to make a documentary of Paul's book about me. The director, Chris Olgiati, interviewed me at North Dade. BBC Wales were

making their own special documentary about me. They
interviewed me too.

The fame I'd longed for ever since I was a weak swot in
school was now well and truly mine. I loved it. But the
fortune I had also longed for had disappeared. I wasn't
completely skint: Judy still had the Palma house and its
contents. The Chelsea flat was also still in her name, and the
Palma Nova flat I'd bought off Chief Inspector Rafael
Llofriu was still mine. Some or all of this property could be
sold to support Judy and the children. But I had no cash or
healthy bank accounts, and Bronis wanted $150,000. My
parents sold their smallholding in Wales, now worth a dozen
times what it cost them, and liquidated their savings. I was
forty-five years old and apparently the biggest dope dealer in
the world, yet my modest-living and modest-earning parents
were the only ones able to pay for the best dope lawyer in
America. Humiliation and shame took their grip of me.

I explained my defence theory to Bronis. Apart from the
rock-group scams, I hadn't smuggled any dope to America.
I wasn't Mr Dennis, and I could prove I wasn't in Pakistan
when DEA Agent Harlan Lee Bowe said I was. The
Alameda scam did not concern me. But I was a dope
smuggler. The Pakistani scam in which I participated was to
Australia. The Vietnamese scam was to Canada. The United
States was not involved. No one in their right minds would
smuggle dope to the US these days. Bronis himself worked
like a demon. He hired a private investigator to collect
documentary back-up for my defence. We obtained
meteorological data from Australia showing that comments
made by us and tapped by the DEA clearly referred to a
particularly severe storm off the Australian coast. We
obtained reams of statistics about money-laundering and
dope-trading in Australia. Every word of the 500 phone taps
could be explained. There was enough to convince a jury
that what actually happened was a Pakistani scam into
Australia. Showing that the Vietnamese scam was a

Canadian affair was much easier because the DEA were accusing me of precisely that. Additionally, however, the DEA were claiming American jurisdiction of the Canadian scam on the basis of some weed the DEA had found in California which had been packaged in precisely the same manner as that busted by the Royal Canadian Mounted Police in Vancouver. Each half-kilo bag of Vietnamese weed masquerading as Thai weed carried a label bearing the words 'Passed Inspection' and a logo of an eagle. The Californian and Vancouver weed obviously originated with the same supplier in Vietnam, but the DEA had no other proof of my participation in any importation to America. DEA Agent Lovato had gone well over the top in trying to prove the Californian Vietnamese weed was mine. He maintained that the logo on all the packages was of a sparrowhawk. As Sparrowhawk was Philip's surname and Philip worked for me in Bangkok, it was obvious that I was smuggling dope into America. Bronis and I acquired ornithological texts demonstrating the physiological differences between sparrowhawks and eagles. Lovato would look a fool in court.

Matters were made considerably easier when, to my enormous joy and consolation, Old John was freed by a Vancouver court. The DEA had intentionally withheld favourable evidence, and the outraged Vancouver judges acquitted Old John of the Canadian charges and denied the United States' extradition request. He was free. The DEA were shown, again, to be cheats. There was other good news: Arthur Scalzo, the DEA's man in the Philippines, the one who dealt with Moynihan, had fled Manila under threat of a multi-million-dollar lawsuit for damages. His credibility would be easily attacked. Also we had accumulated all sorts of dirt on Moynihan. He would be no problem, and he knew nothing. I was going to enjoy this trial. I would make it the most entertaining and colourful trial Miami had ever seen. I would win. I'd be a star.

The prosecuting authority in any US federal case is the
Assistant US Attorney for the particular federal district. He
has an obligation to resolve any prosecution quickly and
cost-effectively. This is achieved by plea-bargaining. The
prosecutor offers a maximum sentence for a plea of guilty to
some charge plus some other considerations. Craig Lovato
and Assistant US Attorney Bob O'Neill came to see me and
Bronis in North Dade. They gave us two choices: go to trial
against overwhelming evidence and spend the rest of my life
in an American prison, or plead guilty, become a snitch, and
go home in a few years. They strongly recommended the
second choice. Bronis told them to get fucked. I was
innocent. We were going to trial.

O'Neill left North Dade a disappointed man. Then he left
his job and went to work for a firm of civil litigators in New
York. He was replaced by a lightweight who knew nothing
about the case. Things were looking up.

My confidence continued to increase as the July 1990 trial
day approached. Just before my Old Bailey trial in 1981, I
had received a poem from Patrick Lane which had given me
a great deal of support. This time I received a letter from
him.

Dear Howard,
    I have just spent the past eight hours with agents
Lovato and Wezain here at Oakdale and I have agreed to
tell them everything that I know about you and about
this case. Consequently, I will be testifying against you at
your trial in August. I am informing you of this partly to
ease my conscience by forewarning you, but also in an
attempt to persuade you to plead guilty now and to make
a deal with the Government before it is too late.
    After serving my time for the past two years in stoic
silence, you can well imagine how painful and difficult
a decision this has been. I am all too aware that little
Amber, who has always treated me with such

reverence as her favourite uncle, will now only think of
me as the man who betrayed her Daddy and sent him
to jail for life. But I have had to weigh my loyalty to
you as an old friend and brother-in-law against my
love and duty towards Jude, Peggy, and Bridie. I am
facing the very real probability of a new 15/20-year jail
sentence, and I have no right to impose that on my
family when I am offered a way out. In return for the
Government's agreement not to pursue the extra jail
time, I have become a co-operating witness.

Co-operation is a bit like pregnancy: there are no
half-way measures. Having agreed to tell the truth, I
will have to tell the whole truth; from when I first met
you till when I last saw you and everything in between.
They started asking me questions today, slowly and
methodically, and they will be back again tomorrow,
and the next day and the day after that until they are
satisfied that they know everything that I know. As I
answered their questions, part of me felt detached,
listening to my voice as though it belonged to
somebody else, speaking in the courtroom. As I
listened to that voice, speaking slowly, telling only the
truth, I finally realised that you do not stand a chance.
If you go to trial, you will be destroyed and I will be
one of the instruments of destruction . . .

[M]y evidence alone will sink you. We have been
good friends too long, you and I, and I know too much
about you . . . I do not care how imaginative or
resourceful you are, and I have never underestimated
your abilities; this time you will not pull it off . . . For
you to spend the rest of your life behind bars will not
only be a shameful waste of all your gifts but will be a
terrible tragedy for all the people who love you and
need you and whom you will leave behind . . . So, as a
lapsed Catholic to a Welsh Baptist, I am recommending submission to a greater power. *Extra ecclesiam*

nulla salus – no salvation outside the church. I'm afraid
it involves a humiliating loss of face and a painful
swallowing of pride, but if you wish to rejoin your
children while they are still little children, I see no
alternative to a complete and utter surrender. You are
surrounded, outgunned and outnumbered – there is no
dishonour in such a defeat. But as a father, as a
husband, as a son, and as a brother, you have no right
to throw away your life in a futile gesture of bravado . . .

I want little Patrick to be proud of his name. I do
not want to have to stand in a Florida courtroom and
point my finger at you and reveal to the cold scrutiny
of strangers all the secrets of twenty years of
friendship. Please don't make me do that. Whatever
you decide, all my prayers are with you.
Patrick.

I had been grassed up by my own good friend and brother-
in-law, the person after whom I'd named my dear son.
Where was all that loyalty, unity, faith, trust, camaraderie,
and romance? Where had it gone? Was it all bullshit? Of
course it was. We weren't the Mafia. We weren't the IRA.
We weren't even Robin Hood and his Merry Men. We were
just a bunch of easy-going guys who took the easy way out
when the rest of the world went mad and ruthless. Alcatraz
and Sing Sing weren't meant for the likes of us.

We all have our breaking points, don't we? Put a gun to
the head of any one of my children, and I'll tell you all I
know. But threaten me with a prison term, and I'll tell you
to fuck off. So why, Patrick? You're definitely no wimp: you
took suitcases of hashish from a locked car outside
Hammersmith police station when the owner was inside
being grilled by the cops; you drove a car full of hashish from
Ireland to Wales; we unloaded a ton of hashish in a German
gravel pit; we've been together with loads of money and dope
in loads of countries. Can't you fight your way through a

prison term? I've spent the last nine months with snitches. They're human. I don't blame you, Patrick. But I can't do it. I'll never help the DEA do any of their evil work. I'm not going to put anyone behind bars and obtain my happiness through someone else's tears. You may be doing the right thing, Patrick. It's just my expectations of you that were wrong. And that's not your fault.

Patrick knew nothing about any of the scams to Canada. He collected the money from the Pakistani scam but had no proof that the hashish had been imported into America. I was going to maintain that the cash in America resulted from a complicated money-laundering system used to move Australian currency. Patrick could not refute that. His testimony wouldn't matter. Bronis would destroy him anyway. Sorry, Patrick. You've got to go through the public humiliation of unsuccessfully betraying me. You can't sink me. Only one person can do that: Ernie Combs, who had handled every ounce of dope I'd imported to America over the last twenty years. No way would he roll over and become a government snitch.

The DEA and the newly appointed prosecutor wanted another meeting with me and Bronis to make a final offer. This time the offer was go to trial and get banged up forever or plead guilty and get a maximum of forty years (with possibility of some parole) with no requirement to grass anyone up or even talk to the DEA. Again Bronis rejected the offer. I was innocent. The DEA said I might like to change my mind: Ernie Combs had agreed to testify against me. He did not do it to lessen his own forty-year sentence by one day. He did it to secure immediate release for his old lady, Patty.

I love you, Ernie, but no more dope deals.

In West Palm Beach Courthouse on July 13th, 1990, I pleaded guilty to racketeering and conspiracy to racketeer. The Canadian charge had been dropped. It was specified I could never be subpoenaed at anyone's trial or any Grand

Jury proceeding to testify against them. The judge accepted
the agreement not to impose a sentence greater than forty
years. The sentencing date was set for October 18th.

From West Palm Beach I was taken to Miami MCC
rather than to North Dade. Having been convicted, I wasn't
any problem and could no longer adversely influence my co-
defendants to irritate the system. Jim Hobbs and Ronnie
Robb had finally given in and pleaded guilty. As in the case
of Judy and of several other co-defendants, the judge agreed
to set them free once they'd admitted some non-existent
crime. Miami MCC was much the same as when I'd left it
nine months previously but was now frequently in the news
because of the DEA's capture and forced extradition of
Panamanian leader Manuel Noriega. Apparently the
American invasion of Panama was nothing to do with
grabbing the strategic Panama Canal. The US were just
doing a drug bust. Noriega was housed in Miami MCC
prison in special prisoner-of-war quarters. I saw him a few
times but never conversed with him.

Shortly after I arrived, Balendo Lo turned up. The British
had finally given in to DEA pressure and extradited him. He
had been charged with facilitating my racketeering enterprise
by supplying me with airline tickets. His business and
marriage to Orca had been ruined. He was not a happy man.

A pre-sentence investigation report was prepared by a
United States Probation Officer, Michael Berg. After an
exhaustive enquiry into the whole case and into me, he
concluded:

> In essence, Marks has pled guilty to facilitating the
> importation of vast quantities of marijuana and
> hashish into the United States while living in Europe.
> This 45-year-old British subject has remained in
> continuous confinement since July 25, 1988. An
> Oxford fellow, he is regarded by many as an
> intelligent, fascinating, and charismatic individual.

Aware of this reputation, this writer must confess to not being disappointed.

Marks is a devoted husband and father. He has been described in glowing terms by friends and relatives and all of their letters have been reviewed and considered. Much has been written about Dennis Howard Marks and much will continue to be written. Acknowledging this, this investigation attempted to separate fact from fiction. Dennis Howard Marks has, to some extent, become a victim of his own legend. By what the Government now alleges, he is not the world's biggest cannabis trafficker and he certainly is not responsible for 15% of all the marijuana that has entered the country, as DEA once claimed. He is not the biggest trafficker ever prosecuted in the United States, nor, for that matter, in the Southern District of Florida. However, make no mistake, Dennis Howard Marks is a major trafficker. It is astounding that he operated so long, that so many loads successfully entered this country, and that he did it all while remaining in Europe.

Early one morning, I heard over the prison compound's Tannoy, 'Inmate Marks, 4-1-5-2-6-0-0-4, report to the lieutenant's office immediately.' Inside the lieutenant's office, I was handcuffed behind my back, taken to 'the hole', the prison within the prison, and locked up alone all day with no privileges. No explanation was given for a week. Then I was told I was being locked up because I had attempted to escape. Bronis got on the case and a week or so later I was out of the hole. We couldn't find out who was behind the escape allegation. Bronis suspected Lovato. It was a typical DEA move.

Roger Reaves's sister, Kay, lived in Miami and eventually obtained permission to visit me. She had exciting news. While I was in the hole suspected of making escape attempts, Roger actually did escape. He had fulfilled his plan to the letter. He snitched on me and McCann, got a seven-year sentence, and escaped from his German prison, despite its being a maximum-security one. He sent his love and promised to pray for me.

The world's press turned up at West Palm Beach on October 18th. So did a clutch of DEA agents, US spooks, and law enforcement representatives from every corner of the globe. Because of my high profile, I wasn't woken up at 3 a.m. with all the other prisoners attending court. The US Marshals picked me up in a limousine at 11 a.m. Notoriety has its advantages. The courtroom was packed. Julian Peto had especially flown over from London just to say a few words to the judge on my behalf. Kay Reaves was also there, praying like mad. So were Patrick Lane and his family. He, too, wanted to say a few words on my behalf, but the judge wouldn't let him. The new prosecutor, Assistant United States Attorney William Pearson, said: 'Your Honour, it is clear that Mr Marks was and is a very highly educated person. I think he has thrown all the gifts he was given to the wind. He has abused the trust, not only of his friends and family, but of his colleagues, the people that taught him in school, and of those people who respected him along the way. He has completely self-destructed and was probably motivated by his greed. While it is true that the United States and other police agencies have not been able to locate as much of Mr Marks's properties as we would like, we are certain, and the Court should feel very certain and secure in the fact, that Mr Marks made an enormous amount of money through his drug-dealing for those twenty years.

'As for specific recommendations from the United States, it is our position a forty-year sentence is appropriate. This is a pre-guideline sentence. Mr Marks will be eligible for parole after a percentage of that forty years. Based on those activities, and thumbing his nose at the United States as well as at the United Kingdom since 1980, we think it appropriate that the Court impose a forty-year sentence.'

Stephen J. Bronis, attorney-at-law, had a different slant: 'If someone asks me to describe in one word the case of United States of America versus Dennis Howard Marks, I would have to say bizarre. No other word better describes a man so complex, fascinating, and so intellectually gifted as Mr Marks allowing himself to be put in a situation that he faces today, and no other word more aptly fits what this case has become. Bizarre is the best way to describe some of the things that I have heard agents of the Government say about Mr Marks, and to Mr Marks. I know this, Your Honour: I have practised criminal law for eighteen years, I have represented the spectrum from murderers and rapists to Judges and Generals, but I have never witnessed anything like this.

'Agent Lovato has been awash in glory since the day he handcuffed Mr Marks. Next Tuesday, PBS will air a broadcast, a docudrama, and in that drama Agent Lovato will be re-enacting his crime-stopper techniques, and after you do what he hopes you will do with Mr Marks, he will leave the courtroom for the awaiting journalists, who will splash his picture in the national media and European papers.

'I am sure, Judge Paine, you have sensed the Government's urgency for you to unflinchingly execute the severe punishment they want you to put upon Mr Marks. They have recommended that you sentence him to forty years in prison. Forty years in prison on a guilty plea to a marijuana offence. It is bizarre that we are giving any credence whatever to the notion of a forty-year sentence. Forty-year sentences should be reserved for the thoroughly evil and violent of our species. Intellectually, they know that. I know that, and I believe you know that, Judge Paine. Judge, I myself have represented scores of marijuana smugglers on a scale much larger than Mr Marks, and I know many other such defendants. None that I am aware of has received the Draconian punishment after pleading guilty that the Government wants you to inflict in this case. For a marijuana smuggler who has pled guilty, forty years is inconceivable.'

The Honourable Judge James C. Paine said: 'Mr Marks, would you please come forward and receive your sentence. Mr Marks, there is no doubt you are a person of superior intelligence, and you had an excellent education. It is apparent that you enjoy an enviable relationship with relatives, business, academic associates, and friends. Your biographical data discloses a personality which enjoys intellectual challenge, games of strategy coupled with a general feeling of disenchantment with conventional society.

'The letters of support for Mr Marks do not proclaim his innocence. They do cite his many admirable qualities so as to counter-balance his errors. After defining the defendant's many and varied talents, some of the letters of support indicate that it would be a shame to require him to expend many years of his life in prison at a cost to the public when he could contribute greatly to society. No doubt, that would be a shame. The problem is that on the basis of past experience, society cannot count on his making commendable contributions. On balance, his contributions have been negative rather than positive.

'It is apparent, Mr Marks, that you regard the use of marijuana and its derivatives as consistent with sound moral principles, and it is also apparent that you have been quite willing to violate laws which prohibit or control use, possession, or commercial transactions with respect to marijuana. You have been quite willing to ignore, or studiously violate, the laws of many countries. You have demonstrated that you have little respect for the rules of society as expressed by criminal laws which do not conform to what you believe to be acceptable conduct. While there is a large body of opinion that use of marijuana is not addictive, does not impair health in an unacceptable way, and should not, therefore, be illegal, there is, also, a large body of opinion to the contrary as to these matters. Further, and more important, federal statutes prohibit trafficking in marijuana. These statutes have been enacted by the Congress of the

United States, and are enforced by the executive branch of the Government by initiation of court action and otherwise. I have taken an oath to administer justice, perform all duties agreeable to the laws of the United States. So, even if I agreed that laws controlling use and sale of marijuana are inappropriate, even foolish, I would have to abide by them until Congress has repealed them. These are rules of society which the courts are bound to apply – whether you agree or not that these laws should be in place.

'The fact that the governments of many European countries and people of Europe are more tolerant of marijuana than is the Government and population of the United States is irrelevant to the matter at hand. Should the foregoing actually be a fact, it seems strange, Mr Marks, that you didn't confine your activity to the European market, thereby reducing your risk of harsher punishment. You were apparently willing to accept this risk.

'I must say I have some difficulty in characterising as candid the information you have offered with respect to your current financial condition. It is true the Government has offered no documentation that you are able to respond to a substantial fine. Despite this, I find it difficult to conclude that your net worth is zero.

'Having considered the foregoing, I impose this sentence. As to Count 1 of the indictment, it is adjudged that the defendant is hereby committed to the custody of the Attorney General of the United States or his authorised representative for imprisonment for a term of ten years. As to Count 2, the defendant is hereby committed to the custody of the Attorney General of the United States or his authorised representative for imprisonment for a term of fifteen years. The sentence as to the second count is to run concurrently with the sentence as to the first count. I will recommend that because you are a citizen of the United Kingdom, it is recommended within the policies and procedures within the Bureau of Prisons that you be considered for a transfer to serve an appropriate portion of your sentence in an institution in the United Kingdom.'

In stunned silence I was taken from the courtroom to the court's holding cells. What a wonderful judge! I'd been given a total of fifteen years, not the forty years that the might of the US Government was demanding. With maximum parole, I'd have to do a total of only five years. I'd already done almost half of that. A year or so more in American prisons plus a year or so in a British nick and I'd be a free man. End of story. What on earth had we all been panicking about? I knew that at that very moment, Julian Peto would be ringing my wife, children, and parents with the news. They would be ecstatic with joy.

The cell gate opened, and I was taken back before Judge Paine. He said: 'Let the record show that I asked for all interested persons to be reassembled because I simply made a very serious error in stating this sentence. I said that the sentences as to each count were to run concurrently. I misspoke without realising I had done so and should have said consecutively. I said concurrently and I meant consecutively, and that was my clear intention within my mind. Somehow I substituted the word concurrently for consecutively when I stated the sentence. I am quite embarrassed about it. I apologise to each of you. There were a number of people in the courtroom who are not here, and it is undoubtedly going to be the source of confusion in newspaper reports about the matter. The fact is that I simply used the wrong word. It seems inconceivable I have done that, but I did. I must restate the sentence. There is no change in it whatsoever except the word consecutively must be substituted for concurrently.'

A surreal nausea overtook me. I'd suddenly been given another ten years. Now I was serving a twenty-five-year sentence. God! For a few minutes, I'd been so happy.

Hours later, at Miami MCC, I settled down. The sentence wasn't that bad. With maximum parole, I should be out in just over six years, and most of that six years might be served in Britain.

The media descended on the prison. Cameras, microphones, and lights littered my cell. I gave dozens of interviews and continued to get off on the glamour and notoriety. As Bronis had told the judge, the BBC documentary, *The Dream Dealer*, was screened by PBS. The entire prison watched it. I loved it and thought it well done. It became Britain's entry for the Montreux TV festival, but won no prizes.

Lovato had been interviewed extensively and didn't come across as a nice guy. I did, to the prisoners, anyway. Lovato accused my wife and children of uttering anti-American vulgarities at him when he arrested Judy and me. He said that I was so ruthless I even laundered money through a foreign charity. What in fact he was referring to was the few thousand dollars I had given, at Sompop's request, to the charity for handicapped children in Bangkok.

A written confirmation of the judge's sentence quickly followed. He added a $50,000 fine and a recommendation that I serve the American portion of my sentence in a special prison in Butner, North Carolina, which was particularly suited to prisoners wishing to study when incarcerated. It was affiliated with North Carolina University and Duke University and was probably the best joint in the federal system. Doing time there was known to be easy. I just had to wait in Miami MCC for a month or so until the authorities were ready to move me.

The regular guard came into our cell early one evening.

'Marks. Get your shit together. You're leaving. You're an escape risk, so we're processing you first. You'll be black-boxed.'

There was no point arguing. A black-boxed prisoner was chained, shackled, and handcuffed. Hands were rendered further immobile by a black metal box. He was segregated from other prisoners while being transported.

'I don't think you'll appreciate Indiana, Marks.'

'Indiana? I thought Butner was in North Carolina.'

'It is. But United States Penitentiary, Terre Haute, is definitely in Indiana. I've been there.'

'I'm not going to Terre Haute. I'm going to Butner.'

'Marks, you're going to Terre Haute. It's a very rough joint. Someone in the US Government obviously doesn't like you. You've been no sweat to me, though. Good luck, buddy.'

Seventeen

DADDY

There are fifty states in America. Each has its own administration of justice. So does Washington and the rest of the anomalous District of Columbia. So do Guam, the Virgin Islands, and other US overseas possessions. These combined authorities keep well over a million people incarcerated for offences such as murder, possession of drugs, rape, and child molestation. No other country imprisons anything like that number. In addition, the United States Government has created its own federal justice system, which envelops all the above jurisdictions and imprisons a further 100,000 individuals. Typical federal offences are crimes which threaten national security, involve federal employees, involve institutions which are federally insured, are committed on Indian reservations, involve two or more states of the United States, or are related to drug smuggling. Sixty per cent of federal prisoners are drug offenders. Generally, federal offenders get housed in federal prisons. Exceptions occur for short stays during the federal prisoner's court appearances, when the Feds want to isolate a prisoner to turn him into a snitch, or when the Feds want to inconvenience a prisoner by subjecting him to 'diesel

therapy' (continual shunting around from one state jail to
another for no reason). To accommodate these circumstances, some sections of some state prisons (including
county jails) are permanently designated for the use of the
federal authorities. North Dade was a typical example.
Similarly, state offenders are generally housed in state
prisons. The only exception is when a particular offender is
too troublesome for the state authorities to handle. The Feds
will take care of him. A federal prison, therefore, will house
Indian braves, terrorists, bank robbers, presidential assassins,
spies, interstate hooker transporters, dope smugglers, and
any state convict too butch for the state authorities to handle.
To house its broad spectrum of offenders, the United States
Federal Bureau of Prisons operates institutions of several
different security levels, based on such features as the
presence of external patrols, gun towers, walls, fences,
detection devices, staff-to-inmate ratios, and the conditions
of confinement. Of its more than one hundred institutions,
six were classified as the highest security level, built to house
America's most violent and dangerous criminals. They are
referred to as United States Penitentiaries (USPs). One of
these six, the one with the worst reputation for slaughter and
gang rape, was at Terre Haute, Indiana. Known as 'Terror
Hut', it was America's 'gladiator school' and provided an
arena for tough redneck US Government hacks, Black inner-
city gang leaders, bikers, and psychopaths. Half of those
imprisoned there would never be released. It promised to be
different. I was terrified.

Fear is an emotion best not displayed, so I was putting on
a brave face as one of ten chained and shackled federal
inmates shuffling on board the prison bus in below-zero
temperatures at Hulman Regional Airport, Indiana, on
January 10th, 1990. An identical bus was alongside loading
a handful of prisoners bound for one of the other USPs,
situated at nearby Marion, Illinois. We were 200 miles from
Chicago. Six weeks had elapsed since I had left Miami MCC

on a sixteen-hour bus journey to Atlanta, Georgia. In the USP at Atlanta, I was stuck in the hole for five weeks because my record stated I was a high escape risk. Then, along with a hundred others, I was flown by a United States Federal Bureau of Prisons aeroplane from an air force base in Georgia to Oklahoma City Airport. After a night on the floor in the snowbound federal prison at El Reno, another prison aeroplane had brought me here. There was one other 'black-boxed' prisoner. We sat together. He was Gennaro 'Jerry Lang' Langella, the Mafia boss of New York's Colombo crime family. Despite doing a life sentence in prison, he was ranked the fifth most powerful crime figure in the world. Jerry had no release date. The US Government had buried him alive. As he was telling me this, the bus drove slowly past the first of USP Terre Haute's facilities: the cemetery, the graveyard of those who are forgotten before they die.

At the reception's holding cells we were, for the seventh time that day, thoroughly searched. Yet again we were photographed, fingerprinted, and medically examined. We were give plastic cards to serve as identification. They could also be used to buy junk food from vending machines if one had money in one's inmate account. We were led to our respective cells.

Built in 1940, and holding a twenty-year escape-free record, USP Terre Haute resembles an enormous insect whose outside skeleton is razor wire, whose body is the main thoroughfare, whose legs are cell blocks for prisoners, whose claws are holes for administering torture, whose arms are mindless facilities for its 1,300 inhabitants, whose compound eyes are TV cameras, and whose head is a gymnasium. The razor-wire insect sits in a razor-wire-enclosed adventure playground containing tennis courts, basket-ball courts, at least a hundred tons of weightlifting equipment, racquetball courts, handball courts, bowling pitches, football pitches, baseball pitches, throwing-horseshoe pitches, jogging track, outside gymnasium, covered casino-type card-playing area,

and an eighteen-hole crazy golf course. Close to the casino
was the Native American Indian sweat lodge and sacred area.
Close to the totem pole was a prison industry factory, Unicor,
where prisoners slaved away for pittances making govern-
ment-issue materials and surreptitiously fashioning 'shanks',
home-made but lethally sharp knives and swords. Facilities
provided inside the insect included a chapel accommodating
every conceivable religion, a law library with photocopying
machines and typewriters, a leisure library, a cafeteria, a pool
hall, two recording studios, a cinema, a school, a hobby shop,
a supermarket, and thirty television rooms. Each cell block
differs from the others in terms of type of accommodation:
dormitories, single cells, multi-prisoner cells. Movement
between cells within a cell block was permitted most of the
day. Movement between one's cell block and common areas
was allowed for ten-minute periods at specific times. My
assigned cell already had three occupants: a redneck who was
dying of liver cancer, a Lebanese heroin smuggler, and a Black
crack distributor. Conversation was surprisingly easy. They
were incredibly friendly and considerate towards me.

USP Terre Haute had one major advantage: one couldn't
be transferred anywhere worse. At a non-penitentiary, one
could be threatened with transfer to a penitentiary. At one of
the other penitentiaries, one could be threatened with Terre
Haute. Apart from the hole, which had long lost its bite due
to frequency of imposition, there was no threat available to
the Terre Haute prison authorities other than dishing out
more prison time. For those doing life without parole, this
was hardly relevant. There was plenty of illegally distilled
alcohol, plenty of dope brought in by bent hacks, and large-
scale gambling was endemic. Although most of the time the
prisoners were content either to play basketball or to watch
it on television, the lack of any effective deterrent often
resulted in periods of mindless mayhem. At least one
prisoner was 'shanked' every day. There would be several
vicious and messy fights every day. There were plenty of

murders and immeasurably more maimings. Most were gang-related, but some would result from petty individual squabbles.

Most of the gangs were Black Muslim-based. One of the most formidably powerful street gangs ever is the El Rukhn gang of Chicago. Originally the Black P. Stone Nation, formed in the 1960s by an amalgamation of the Blackstone Rangers and other Chicago street gangs, and shrewdly financed by Libya's Colonel Gaddafi, the El Rukhn gang had a membership in the tens of thousands and large real-estate holdings acquired through a wide range of criminal operations. Other Chicago gangs had sprung off from the Blackstone Rangers, including the Vicelords, who under the leadership of Roosevelt Daniels, later to be brutally murdered in the prison cafeteria, had, at that time, the stranglehold on prison life in Terre Haute. Sometimes the Vicelords got on with the El Rukhns at Terre Haute. Sometimes they didn't. Many members of Los Angeles's two notorious rival street gangs, the Bloods and the Crips, were too much for the Californian authorities to handle: they were sent to Terre Haute. In Washington, DC's infamous Lorton prison perennially fighting Blacks had proved to be uncontrollable: they were sent to Terre Haute. Neither the Vicelords nor the El Rukhns got on with the Crips or the Bloods or any of the DC gangs. Each gang had its own peculiarities of vocabulary, its own colours, and its own system of elaborate hand signals. Different from the American city street gangs and hating them with a passion were the Jamaican Posse gangs, some with dreadlocks, some without.

There were White prison gangs too: the fanatically racist Aryan Brotherhood, the equally racist Dirty White Boys, the rednecked Dixie Mafia, the Mexican Mafia, innumerable Cuban, Puerto Rican, and Colombian syndicates, and various biker gangs. Although rival biker gangs such as the Hell's Angels, the Pagans, and the Outlaws would kill each other almost on sight in the street, in prison they would sensibly call a truce and allow their conflicting ideologies to coexist peacefully. One of the most famous bikers ever, James 'Big Jim' Nolan of the Outlaws, resided at Terre Haute, scheduled for release in 2017.

Rules of prison gang initiation varied. Some would require the carrying out of a random killing within the prison. Being British and a famous non-rat, I could avoid most conflict by being nice, charming, and eccentric; but I never felt safe. I would have to choose my friends carefully.

Terre Haute boasted quite a few notable *mafiosi*. Apart from Gennaro 'Jerry Lang' Langella, the most senior Mafia member, one found John Carneglia, Victor 'Vic the Boss' Amuso, and Frank Locascio, high-rankers in New York's Gambino crime family, the facilitators of my New York airport hashish scams. There was Anthony 'Bruno' Indelicato, son of Alphonse 'Sonny Red' Indelicato and a *capo* in the crime family of Joseph 'Joe Bananas' Bonanno. Also in Terre Haute were Sicilian Antonio Aiello of the Pizza Connection case and Joey Testa of the Philadelphia Mafia. I made friends with them all. The Italian Mafia, like the bikers, 'truced up' against the common enemy when inside and postponed their differences, seeming very resigned to doing their time. The outside operations they still headed were continuing and prospering through the prison's telephones and visiting room. Their main concern was the quality of the prison pasta and availability of keep-fit facilities. Classified somewhere between the Italian Mafia and a street gang are the Westies, a no-nonsense New York Irish criminal organisation. A few of its members resided at USP Terre Haute, including its highly intelligent and charismatic boss, Jimmy Coonan. The rest of the prison population was made up of psychopaths, spies, perverts, and sophisticated, high-profile individual criminal personalities serving decades of time.

One of them, Corsican Laurent 'Charlot' Fiocconi, became one of the best friends I have ever had. Charlot's case was the last of a series that became immortalised as the French Connection. In 1970 he was arrested in Italy, extradited to the United States, convicted of heroin smuggling, and sentenced to twenty-five years. In 1974 he escaped from a New York jail and went to the middle of the Brazilian jungles to mind his own business. He stayed there for seventeen years. He met and married a beautiful lady from Medellín, Colombia. In 1991 they were both arrested in Rio de Janeiro in connection with cocaine charges. The United States locked him up in Terre Haute to finish his sentence.

Another prisoner with whom I developed a strong friendship was Veronza 'Daoud' Bower. He had been a Black Panther in the 1960s. In the early 1970s he killed a cop. He had been in penitentiaries ever since. Daoud had grown waist-length dreadlocks and had devoted his twenty-odd years of continuous prison life to playing chess and Scrabble, perfecting his own physical fitness, and studying and practising various healing techniques. He could do several thousand push-ups non-stop and relieve or cure virtually any ailment. Daoud was the only non-native American Indian who participated in religious sweat-lodge rituals.

The prison staff varied from fat military megalomaniacs to fat and demented local Ku Klux Klan rejects. Indiana is the state with the highest incidences of illiteracy and obesity and traditionally has been host to many fervent Ku Klux Klan supporters. The hacks' hobbies included shooting animals and brawling in bars. One hack was busted for running around bollock naked, another for bringing in dope, and another was dismissed for participating in a convicts' pornography racket. The prison chaplain was busted for bringing heroin into the prison.

A new arrival at the prison must find himself alternative official employment within forty-eight hours to avoid being forced to work in the kitchen for $25 a month. There are scores of different jobs available in the libraries, laundry, classrooms, and other common areas. While Desert Storm

was in full swing, I presented myself to the prison's
Department of Education and was interviewed by a likeable
and intelligent hack named Webster. His teenage sons were
fighting in Desert Storm. He gave me the job of teaching
English grammar to prisoners studying for their General
Education Diploma (GED), a qualification regarded as
equivalent to a high-school diploma. My pay was $40 a
month. On my first day I faced a classroom of seventeen
young Blacks, most of whom were looking at the rest of their
life behind bars. Correctional Officer Webster sat at the back
ready to step in if there were problems. There had been in
the past, like the time a mutilated and bloody corpse was
found in the bathroom. It had always been difficult for a
prisoner, even with the protection of a hack, to teach other
prisoners because he dared not display any authority or
superiority and could not even begin to appear to be
administering any kind of discipline. An inmate teacher, if
not cautious, could find himself regarded as a semi-hack or
jailhouse snitch. I was scared, but I applied the usual rule:
never show your fear.

'My name's Howard Marks, and I hope to be able to help
you study for the English grammar section of the GED exam.'

'Hey! Hey! Hey! Webster! Webster! I ain't trying to learn
no motherfucking thing from no motherfucking cracker.
There ain't nothing no motherfucking White dude can tell
me. Nothing. You know what I'm saying? There ain't
nothing no motherfucking White dude can tell me.'

'Now, now, this is an equal-opportunity prison,' said
Webster, in an attempt to pacify and control Tee-Bone
Taylor, cop killer and second-in-charge of the Vicelords.

'Webster, it ain't like that. You be welling, man. Don't be
laying no racist government crap on me. I ain't trying to hear
that motherfucking shit. This cracker don't be knowing more
than me. He ain't chilling in no projects like me and my
brothers. What does he know? Hey! Hey! Hey! Teach! Teach!'

'Call me Howard, please.'

'I said Teach, Teach. You want to teach. I call you Teach. You know what I'm saying?'

'Okay, call me Teach.'

'Teach, what gives you the motherfucking right to teach me English?'

'I am English, Tee-Bone,' I lied. I usually corrected those who called me English. I was Welsh. These guys would have never heard of Wales.

'So? Is you saying that makes you speak better English than us niggers here?'

'Of course. We invented the language.'

'We has our own language, Teach.'

'I accept that. And it's no better or worse than English. But if you want to pass this English examination, I honestly want to help you.'

'What motherfucking use is English going to be to me, Teach? I ain't trying to be disrespecting your language or dissing you about no motherfucking thing, but I ain't trying to be no writer, Teach. You know what I'm saying? I ain't trying to be no writer, Teach. I don't be seeing no streets again, Teach. This motherfucking Government got us homeboys here till we die, Teach. We niggers ain't trying to be no badass Americans. If it wasn't for you crackers, we wouldn't be here. Our ancestors was brung here against their will from our own country in chains.'

'So was I. And you know who brought me over? A Black US Marshal.'

Tee-Bone stood up.

'What the fuck is you saying, Teach?'

'You know what I'm saying. Whoever we are and however we got here, we all want to get out. Look, guys, I've only just got into this system, but I've already worked out that there's only three ways out of here: you pay a lawyer a few million dollars, which none of us have; you get over the fence and give government lunatics like Webster here some target practice; or you write your way out.'

'How is you going to write your way out?' asked a young Washington, DC crack dealer.

'Listen. Most of us got more time than we deserved. Some of you shouldn't even have been convicted. The Government lied and cheated about how much dope you did so they could bang you up forever. Blacks get hit harder than Whites. A lot of people out there want to put a stop to this government racial harassment. A lot more people don't even know it's happening. Even some of the judges don't believe it's going on. It's only judges, a few honest politicians, and some powerful individuals can change things. I don't mean to be rude, but most of you can't even write a letter that these guys could understand. And they're the only ones who can get you out of this shit. Don't tell me you're going to lie down that easy. I meant it when I said I was brought here in chains. The DEA came to my house in Europe, dragged me and my old lady over here, and left our three children without a mum or dad. I hate your fucking Government more than you ever could.'

'Okay, Teach. Chill out. You're not a bad dude. I know where you be coming from,' said Tee-Bone. 'Teach us some cracker rap, Teach.'

'Sure. Now why did you guys choose to speak English rather than Spanish, Portuguese, or French? These guys fucked you around just as much as we did.'

'Give it to us straight, Teach.'

'Because you have good taste. You gave us the music. We gave you the lyrics. Now we'll start with punctuation marks. Do you know what they are? What's this?'

I wrote a full-stop on the board.

'That's a period, Teach.'

A Rastafarian Posse member objected.

'Wapen him, Teach. Him say "period". Me say "full-stop". Ah Jamaica me come from. In Jamaica a "period" mean a bitch bleeding.'

The head of the Department of Education summoned me to the next room.

'Marks, you're teaching GED, right.'

'That's right.'

'You don't appear to have one.'

'One what?'

'A GED, Marks. I have no record of you having a GED or a high-school diploma.'

'I don't have either. That's right.'

'Now the powers that be might consider it inappropriate for a prisoner without a GED to be teaching other prisoners how to get one. You see what I'm getting at?'

'But I've got a Master's degree.'

'There are plenty of people with Master's degrees who can't teach GED. The haircutting school in this prison gives Master's degrees to people who can't read.'

'But I got my Master's degree at Oxford.'

'Oxford, Wisconsin. Who was your inmate supervisor?'

'Not Oxford, Wisconsin prison. The University of Oxford in England.'

'Well, no disrespects, but the United States Government is a bit wary of foreign qualifications. Generally, it doesn't recognise them.'

'It recognises foreign convictions.'

'Maybe. I'm not a criminologist. I'm an education specialist, and I take the view that if the foreign qualification is meaningful, then the holder will have no objection to being re-tested by a more appropriate body. Shall I put your name down to sit the next GED examination?'

I passed. Wearing a radiant blue gown and mortar board, I was presented with a certificate by a smiling, tongue-in-cheek Webster.

In conjunction with a local university the prison's Department of Education also funded and ran evening classes. I wanted to attend, but they weren't available to non-American citizens. This really infuriated me. The US Government were tearing around the world extraditing people and then refusing them an education in prison because they were aliens. I went to see the head of the Department of Education to complain.

'Yes, Marks, what's the problem?'

'This is straightforward discrimination. Why aren't we aliens allowed to pursue further education?'

'You have to remember, Marks, that each course a prisoner takes costs the American taxpayers $2,000. Have you paid much in the way of American tax?'

'It costs the American taxpayer $25,000 a year to keep me here. Don't you think it would make economic sense to spend 10% more and enable me to emerge as a useful community member rather than a biker or crack dealer?'

'I don't know, Marks. I'm not an economist. I'm an education specialist.'

'It seems insane to me. And unconstitutional. Don't you have something called the Fifteenth Amendment which prohibits discrimination on the basis of nationality?'

'I don't know, Marks. I'm not a lawyer. I'm an education specialist. Anyway, Marks, you should have thought of that before you came to America and broke our laws.'

'I didn't want to come here. I was brought against my will.'

'Well, you shouldn't have broken any laws after arriving here, whichever way you were brought.'

'I haven't.'

'Then take it up with your lawyer, Marks. I can't help you. I'm an . . .'

'I know.'

A correspondence course was possible. I applied to the University of London to do an external law degree. I was accepted and began some preparatory study in the prison's law library. There was plenty of overlap between American and English law.

Forty dollars a month is not much, even if one is provided with free accommodation, food, clothes, and leisure activities. I had significantly greater expenses than the average American prisoner because of the costs of making international telephone calls, the only way I could talk to my family. Furthermore, prisoners who had unpaid fines (I had one of $50,000) would be forced to make substantial monthly contributions to the debt under the guise of 'The Inmate Financial Responsibility Program'. The only jobs that paid really well ($200 a month) were at the prison industry factory making army blankets for the US troops in Iraq. Fuck that. Everyone not helping the war effort had to find a 'hustle', an illegal way of making money within the prison system from those lucky enough to have funds or getting paid for doing their bit for Desert Storm. Possible hustles included stealing food from the kitchen, stealing knives from the factory, stealing all manner of stuff from the stores, making and selling alcoholic beverages, taking sports bets, doing other prisoners' laundry, making customised greetings cards, painting portraits, giving blow-jobs, enforcing debt payment, and interior decorating of cells. Some prisoners became jailhouse lawyers, helping people attempting to obtain post-conviction relief from the courts. It was an ideal hustle for me, and I busied myself articulating other prisoners' presentations to judges, lawyers, and Congressmen. A couple of early successes were achieved – a conviction overturned and a sentence reduced by ten years – and these ensured that I was heavily in demand. I never actually charged for my work, but I was almost always given something: food stolen from the kitchen, a tennis racquet, a Walkman, a hand-stitched Marco Polo jogging suit, a leather briefcase. Money Orders from New Jersey and Florida, all marked 'remittance to inmate from family', dribbled into my account. I made an average of $300 a month. It was more than enough.

Hunting Marco Polo, by Paul Eddy and Sara Walden, was published and sent to me in Terre Haute by the *Mail on Sunday*, who wanted me to review it. I did. The book was written rather like a police manual but was accurate enough in its coverage of material with which I was familiar. One feature irritated me: its presentation of my arrest as the culmination of a chess-type battle of wits between equally armed opponents (me and Lovato). Lovato had a colossal federal budget and had the co-operation of fourteen different governments' law enforcement agencies; I had a bunch of nice guys.

Much had taken place outside the prison walls between my departure from Miami MCC and my receiving of a GED diploma at the end of 1991. In a sickening display of bullying and cowardice, the DEA persuaded the Dutch authorities to re-arrest Old John after his arrival in Amsterdam. They extradited him to Miami. He appeared in front of Judge Paine, refused to say anything other than plead guilty, was sentenced to time served, and set free. Balendo Lo pleaded guilty to money laundering and was immediately set free. Philip Sparrowhawk was extradited from Bangkok to Miami. He told the DEA everything he knew and was set free. Of the ten people extradited at enormous expense from all over the world, nine of them were almost immediately released once they had appeared in front of Judge Paine and pleaded guilty. I was the only one the US Government wanted to keep locked up.

After his release, Malik went back to Pakistan. Then he went to Hong Kong, where he was arrested and extradited back to the United States. I have no idea why, or where he is now. But for sure, Lovato was involved.

McCann was arrested by the German police in Düsseldorf. They found some hashish and a false passport in his car. For some reason the Germans did not charge him with the 1973 bombing of the British Army base in Mönchengladbach for which they had been obsessively seeking his extradition for almost two decades. Instead, through courtesy of information supplied by Roger Reaves, they charged him with supplying a German boat and captain with a ton of Moroccan dope bound for England. Perhaps, like the Americans, they thought of it as a more serious offence. A German judge, McCann's prosecutor, and McCann's defence lawyer eventually came to question me in Terre Haute. I swore that I had nothing to do with any Moroccan hashish deal and that as far as I knew neither had McCann. McCann was acquitted, despite the German prosecution taking the extraordinary step of paying Lovato to make an eleventh-hour appearance at a German court to discredit my testimony. Fucking McCann. He still hasn't got a dope conviction.

By placing a notice in *The Times*, Lord Moynihan faked the death of his baby son to ensure that his even younger son would sit in the House of Lords. DEA Agent Craig Lovato was godfather to at least one of his sons. Then Moynihan actually died of a heart attack in the Philippines. Or so the world's press would have us believe. There's no corpse.

In clouds of secrecy, Tom Sunde voluntarily surrendered to the DEA to be debriefed. He pleaded guilty to a dope charge and was sentenced to five years' probation. His mentor, Carl, continued to search for President Ferdinand Marcos's millions. In doing so, he stepped on the toes of the Swiss authorities, who sought his extradition from Germany. The Germans refused to give him up. Immediately afterwards Jacobi was arrested in Hong Kong pursuant to a United States extradition request based on DEA allegations that he had sold me information. Hong Kong declined to extradite.

Roger Reaves was re-arrested. After escaping from Lübeck prison, he had decided to become a fugitive in America. The authorities recognised him and put him in a county jail. A tunnel was discovered in his cell. He was transferred to USP Lompoc, California. Ron Allen, the Chicago dealer who was with me in Pakistan, was finally caught. He pleaded guilty in exchange for a short sentence. Only Gerry Wills remained unbusted.

Judge Robert Bonner, the head of the DEA, visited

London. In response to questions asked about my 25-year sentence, the *Daily Telegraph* quoted him as saying: 'I don't know how we keep people like Marks out of drug trading unless you put people like him in the slammer. I'm not troubled by the length of the sentence. He should serve it.'

The *Daily Telegraph* also made reference to a report that I had £50 million tucked away. I wrote to the editor:

It was such a wonderful and much needed Christmas surprise to read in your columns that I am the owner of £50 million concealed in Caribbean and/or Eastern bloc bank accounts. I was totally unaware that I had this loot. All they say about the damaging effects of cannabis on the memory must be true.

Federal Bureau of Prison rules preclude my sensibly and responsibly using this money. Providing, therefore, you undertake to pay my federally imposed fine, settle my wife's mortgage, keep my family from starving, and pay for my children's school fees, I would be delighted to transfer these funds to any purpose you choose.

Please let me know whether or not you are interested. If so, I will send you a duly notarised power of attorney form granting you access to any and all funds of mine held in any bank account in any country.

Incidentally, there were a couple of errors in your report. I am incarcerated in a federal penitentiary, which is in Indiana not Florida. Also I was fined $50,000 not £100,000. Still, that's all the more for you if you take advantage of my offer. Trusting and hoping these were the only inaccuracies.
Howard Marks.

My letter was published, but no one took up my offer. Things looked up for a while when Bill Clinton announced he was standing for office. An Oxford-educated, dope-taking, philandering, draft-dodging leader was just what this ridiculous country needed. Then he said he stuck joints in his mouth but didn't inhale them and that he definitely wouldn't legalise any dope. The *Mail on Sunday* came to interview me. They said they had proof I lived with Clinton in Oxford. (Maybe he was just a passive stoner.) I didn't remember living with Clinton anywhere, but I didn't deny it. Perhaps one day I could use this strange rumour to my advantage. I declined to answer any questions about my old mate Bill. It wouldn't be fair to him. Clinton had been at University College, Oxford, failing his B.Phil. when I was doing postgraduate work at Balliol and living at Garsington. I never met anyone who smoked joints without inhaling.

Much was made plain to me during the same year (1991), all thoroughly depressing. My assumption that I would be released on parole as soon as I was eligible (November 1996) provided I behaved myself was totally wrong. Whether or not one is granted release on parole in the United States is not determined by one's institutional conduct, as it is in the British parole system, but by the current political perception of the offence committed. I didn't know this. I had not met anyone who had been granted parole. Drug smuggling was considered to be responsible for all of America's worst problems. Large-scale smugglers of any drug didn't get parole. The news hit me hard. Instead of release in 1996, I had to get used to the idea of getting released a few years into the next century. I checked the law books on parole cases. Parole had been refused to marijuana smugglers on the basis of the excessive quantities involved, the unusual sophisti-cation of the scam committed, the seniority of the particular parole applicant within the scam, the number of people to whom he gave orders, its international character, and the case's notoriety. I wasn't optimistic. In the law library, I also discovered a Parole Commission policy statement taking an official stance of discouraging prisoners from pursuing careers in law. Such plans for release would be unfavourably reviewed. I dropped out of the University of London's external law degree course.

Also incorrect was my assumption that I would be smoothly transferred to a British prison. At first my application was lost for several months, then resubmitted, then rejected on the basis that my offence was too serious. This didn't make much sense. Murderers and heroin smugglers had already been transferred to or from the United States. I was sure Lovato was behind these refusals, but I had no proof, yet.

The governing body of USP Terre Haute could see I was not US penitentiary material. They recommended to their national superiors that I be transferred to a less stringent facility with greater opportunity for education. The Federal Bureau of Prisons' bosses said no. Again I suspected Lovato's sadistic hand. Again I had no proof, yet.

Lovato formally requested the British authorities that Judy's flat in Chelsea be confiscated. British law prevented further proceedings. Lovato then requested the Spanish authorities that our home in La Vileta be confiscated. The DEA's justification was not that the house had been purchased with the proceeds of dope money. It hadn't been, and that was easily proven. It was because I had used the home telephone, thereby rendering the house as an instrument of my racketeering enterprise and as such for-feitable to the United States and/or Spain. An embargo was placed on the property and remained there for four years, after which time even the routinely accommodating Spanish authorities couldn't bring themselves to throw Judy and the children on to the streets because her husband had used the phone.

But the worst thing that happened to me that year was the news that my four-year-old son, Patrick, had jumped off the roof of a tall building. The impact of his little body hitting the concrete floor shattered both his legs. No one knew why he did it. Did he think he was Superman? Was he trying to fly? Did he throw himself into the jaws of death to resolve some indescribable inner torment? Was he trying to do himself in because he had no dad? The hard reality of being a prisoner hit me like never before. I couldn't be there to help absorb Patrick's pain. By the time I got out, he wouldn't need a dad. How many more accidents and tragedies to my dear family would I be unable to prevent? Please God, no more.

To make matters even more depressing, the next year, 1992, got off to a very bad start. My father was rushed to hospital with severe bronchial pneumonia. God, I'd been dreading this: one of my parents getting seriously ill. God, please don't let any of them die before I get out. The first and last verses of Dylan Thomas's poem swam through my brain:

Do not go gentle into that good night,
Old age should burn and rave at close of day;
Rage, rage against the dying of the light.

And you, my father, there on the sad height,
Curse, bless, me now with your fierce tears, I pray.
Do not go gentle into that good night.
Rage, rage against the dying of the light.

Dad survived.

Outside my window, construction work had begun on the one and only federal Death Row. Although most individual states regularly electrocute, gas, and otherwise murder those convicted of particularly heinous crimes, the Federal Government has not executed anyone for a federal offence for decades. They just locked you up. That had changed with the Reagan/Bush federal death penalty for drug offences. Now eight people, all Black, had been sentenced to death by federal courts. There was nowhere specific to house them, and they were scattered all over the country. The US Government decided to build their very own execution chamber (lethal injection) and waiting rooms (Death Row). The location was Terre Haute. I could see it through my window. It brought me down.

It was a most heartbreaking day when I was informed that my dear friend Old John, within months of freeing himself from the clutches of the DEA, had been diagnosed as suffering from cancer. Before he became the scourge of the DEA and the world's most honest dope smuggler, he had been an electrician. The asbestos that got to him then was slowly but surely killing him now. I felt so sad.

Doing time began to get hard. The absence of my family was tearing my heart out. I'd been down for four years, twice as long as last time. I had more than another twelve to do if, as seemed certain, I would be denied parole. Judy couldn't wait for me that long; no one could. At the age of sixty, I would re-enter the world, skint, full of hate and completely unemployable and useless. No one would want to listen to my boring tales of woe, gore, violence, and depression. I'd be old and ugly. No one would want to shag me. And my dreams weren't about sex; they were about prison. That's when you know you are locked up: when you know you can't escape by nodding off. When I get out my kids will all have left home and been replaced by my grandchildren. We'll visit my parents' graves. I'll smile benignly at the children of Judy and her new husband when I pay them a social call after collecting my dole or my pension. I'll walk past discos and try to remember when I last danced. Was it worth waiting for? I became ill. I caught shingles and had several bouts of 'flu. Smoke and phlegm filled my lungs. I couldn't piss properly. I couldn't bend my left leg. I had pains everywhere. Abscesses filled my gums. Eleven teeth were extracted. Any other dental treatment would have been deemed cosmetic rather than curative. An ill-fitting plastic denture plate dangled from my mouth. I needed glasses to read.

Whenever I get really down, I start getting religious. The American Christian Right had thrown me off Christianity. If God was a Republican, forget it. But for weeks I read the Bible and many works of other religions. I realised what I was doing wrong: I was taking myself too seriously. I should just help people as much as possible, keep fit and well, and take what comes. I can't control what happens to me anyway. I can only control my attitude to it. So I spend the next decade in prison. Big deal. So what? What next?

I had my own cell now. Next to me on one side was Big Jim Nolan's cell, on the other side lived Bear, another Outlaw. I gave up smoking after thirty-five years. Being constantly summoned for urine tests had frightened me off taking any kind of dope. A dirty urine meant more prison time. Marijuana stayed detectable in urine for thirty days, heroin for one day. There was no marijuana. There was lots of heroin. I looked forward to a big fat joint in twelve years' time.

I got up every morning at five, did a series of dynamic yoga exercises followed by a callisthenics routine taught me by Daoud, drank fresh orange juice, read some religious writings, taught inner-city Blacks how to write for three hours, missed lunch, played tennis with Charlot for two hours, taught for another three hours, ate a healthy meal, played tennis again, walked for a few miles round the track, worked in the law library, did an hour of yoga and meditation, and read classical novels before going to sleep. I did that every day for over a thousand days. Charlot also worked at the Department of Education teaching mathematics to Hispanics. We persuaded the Head of Education to let us teach voluntary evening classes in French and philosophy. The Black Muslims appreciated hearing about how the Islamic philosophers Avicenna and Averroës had preserved the Ancient Greek wisdom while the Europeans were busily being barbaric. The Italian gangsters loved hearing about how many of the Ancient Greek philosophers and mathematicians, such as Pythagoras and Archimedes, would in fact have been modern Italian and that the Renaissance was definitely an Italian affair. Not only did they have the Roman Empire, the Catholic Church, and the Mafia, they also had culture by the balls.

I was slim, fit, healthy, mellow, and seemed to be happy and enjoying life. I was like everyone else there. The minutes dragged, but the months and the years flew by. I was becoming institutionalised.

I realised this after I had been visited separately and successively by my parents, my daughter Myfanwy, and my two daughters Amber and Francesca during 1993. It was brought home to me what I had been missing. My father had resolved after his last illness to make the effort to cross the Atlantic come hell or high water. I had seven wonderful visits with him and my mother. Myfanwy wanted to share her 21st birthday with me. She did so in the Spartan confines of USP Terre Haute visitors' room. When I finally saw Francesca, she looked like my memory of Myfanwy. I thought Amber was Judy. I had five days of heavenly visits. I loved them so much. Amber wrote this:

> It was like reopening a wound,
> As I sat there.
> Waiting.
> Knowing that any minute
> I would see him again.
> Him I hadn't seen for so many years.
>
> Him who meant the world to me.
> I should have been happy,
> But I could feel the tears brimming.
> It had been so long.
> I was beginning to feel the pains again.
>
> No one could understand why I was crying.
> I was about to see him.

I should be smiling.
The sorrow felt by his absence
Was creeping out from deep inside
In long-kept tears.

And then he came.
Like I'd seen him only yesterday.
That hug said nothing
Of the years I'd longed to hold him.
We sat down.
They chatted and laughed.
I was oblivious to the conversation.
I kept looking at that hand
That I hadn't felt for so long.
And marvelling at the fact that it was in mine.

I remember leaving him,
Having to go, to say goodbye.
It was too much.
I'd turned my back,
Ashamed of the tears,
Trying, trying to control my pain,
Like I'd managed all those years.

But I couldn't.
So I walked.
One last glance at the man I loved most in the world,
And quickly ran out.
I wanted to go back,
Hug one last time,
But the pain was too much.
Had to get out.
Control myself.
Re-bury those tears.
Hide the pain.
Forget the sorrow.

And later,
When I peered out of that aeroplane window,
And watched his world
Slip further away,
I looked down at my hand,
Where his had once been,
But now was gone,
And wondered
If I'd ever have it there again.

Julian Peto had so kindly brought Amber and Francesca over to see me in America. He is the most unfailing friend. Judy couldn't come. Despite previous assurances to the contrary, the US Government refused to let her into the country because she had a conviction, the one she'd accepted in order to be reunited with her children four years ago.

What was I doing? I was clapping myself on the back for being able to survive contentedly in the world's worst penitentiary while my real life was proceeding without me. And I was accepting it. The US Government was preventing my being transferred to a British prison and simultaneously preventing my wife from visiting me. They were going too far. Those evil bastards had already gone too far. Amber's poem and Judy's inability to see me for the next twelve years rekindled an almost dead fighting spirit. I had to get out of here.

I reasoned that despite some bureaucrat's constant rejection of my application to be imprisoned in Europe, my best way out lay in that direction. By now I was receiving about fifty letters a week from family, friends, lawyers, journalists, those who wished me well, and those who had been interested in what they had read about me. I wrote letters to all of them. There was clearly a lot of support out there for me to be transferred to a British nick. Everyone thought that the Americans were being pigheadedly harsh on me. They collected signatures supporting my transfer application. My wife and children toured the schools and bars of Palma accumulating signatures. My parents went to almost every house in Kenfig Hill doing the same. Britain's greatest champion of legalised marijuana, Danny Roche, got half of Liverpool to sign petitions begging for my return to England. My parents' Labour Member of Parliament, Win Griffiths, took up the cause with a vengeance and worked unceasingly to obtain my transfer. The outstanding British charity organisation, Prisoners Abroad, whose admirable efforts to comfort those imprisoned overseas have saved lives and families, vigorously campaigned on my behalf. They were joined by the Prison Reform Trust, Release, Justice, and the Legalise Cannabis Campaign, all of whose support had been co-ordinated by a wonderful lady I have never met, Judy Yacoub from Lancashire. BBC Wales interviewed me and aired a sympathetic broadcast. Duncan Campbell wrote an equally sympathetic piece in the *Guardian*. *Wales on Sunday* carried the following editorial:

> Time for Marks to return
> HOWARD MARKS has been sitting in an American prison for over two years and could still be there in the year 2003. Because his wife has a drug conviction she is banned from re-entering the country and cannot visit him. Three times, applications have been made to let him complete his sentence in a British jail. Three times, the Justice Department has said no.
> This newspaper does not condone what Howard Marks has done, but twelve years is a long time between visits. Surely the Americans, who put such great store in home, Mom and apple pie, could show a little compassion and allow the move to a country which his family can visit.

Even the British Home Office went so far as to formally request my repatriation. American organisations helped. Prisoner Visitation and Support, a multidenominational charity which had visited and comforted me and hundreds of other prisoners without visitors in US prisons, wrote compelling letters to the relevant government agencies. Families Against Mandatory Minimums, by far the most effective prison reform organisation in the US, did the same. Thousands and thousands of signatures piled up on Attorney General Janet Reno's desk. Still no answer, but this time it was taking a long time for them to say no.

Balliol College, some of whose members hold high positions in the United States Government, had also made relentless and impassioned pleas to wherever they could. I had never expected Balliol to support me to the extent it did when I was in Terre Haute. Christopher Hill, the old Master, and John Jones, the current Dean of Balliol, regularly corresponded with me the entire time I was there. John had even attempted to get the prison authorities' permission to allow me to proof-read the College Register before its publication. They refused.

The United States has a Freedom of Information Act. Through it one is meant to be able to acquire all government files referring to the individual making the request. It takes forever. The application is passed from one agency to the other. It gets lost. It's going to cost. There's a horrendous backlog. There are countless exceptions preventing some documents being released. Large chunks of documents finally released are blacked out under the guise of hindering DEA investigations. More often than not, one has to take the government agency to court to get anything remotely revealing. But with tenacity and motivation, documents will dribble through, and it's always worth the effort. I got all sorts of stuff.

Lovato had written the following letter to Joe Meko, a Regional Director of Prisons:

SUBJECT: Request for Denial of Transfer of Inmate No. 41526004, Dennis Howard MARKS from a High Security System (Terre Haute, Indiana) to a Medium Security System.

Dear Mr Meko:

As per our telephone conversation this date, October 7, 1992, I am requesting that the consideration of the transfer of Inmate No. 41526004 Dennis Howard MARKS be denied.

Mr MARKS is an Oxford graduate (Graduate level degree). He was recruited and utilized briefly in the service of Her Majesty as an MI-5 operative. This service was discontinued when it was determined that Mr MARKS was a major international drug dealer.

As case agent on the investigation code-named [Eclectic], I worked with the police departments of eleven different countries in an effort to dismantle Mr MARKS' organization. Mr MARKS' organization was world-wide, with offices in Pakistan, Thailand, Hong Kong, Manila, Australia, Canada, the United States, England, Spain and the Netherlands. During the principal year of investigation, Mr MARKS had five separate loads of cannabis being shipped to Europe, the United States and Australia. Mr MARKS netted 3 million dollars profit from just one of these loads (ten tons to Los Angeles, CA).

No monies were ever recovered from Mr MARKS. Mr MARKS has, in my opinion, several million dollars awaiting him should he escape. Mr MARKS, in my opinion, lacks the personal courage to attempt any type of physical escape. However, he would utilize his superior intellect to encourage the 'System' to open the doors for him. The first step in this procedure would be the transfer to a less secure facility than the one he is currently incarcerated in. Mr MARKS has a history of drug dealing dating back to 1970. More importantly, he has a history of evading or escaping law enforcement authorities. Mr MARKS was arrested circa 1973 on drug charges emanating out of the United States in England. Mr MARKS posted bond, then became a fugitive for a

period of (7) seven years. Mr MARKS fled Spain on this
investigation on two separate occasions when he felt he
was about to be arrested.
When apprehended in Spain in July 1988, Mr MARKS
fought extradition to the United States for one year
before the courts ordered him extradited. Mr MARKS
has a documented life style which includes false
passports and identities. Mr MARKS has a family in
England. Mr MARKS has absolutely no reason to
remain in prison for the next 25 years if given the
opportunity to RUN!
I request that this opportunity not be afforded him.
There are several police and Justice Department
agencies, both in the United States and abroad, who
would provide similar letters such as this if needed.

This explained why I was being kept in America's toughest
penitentiary.

To the government agency responsible for deciding
whether or not I should be transferred, the DEA didn't try
any persuasive tactics. They just lied: 'It should be noted as
part of the plea agreement that the Assistant United States
Attorney stated before the court that Mr MARKS would
have to serve a minimum of twelve years in a US prison
before any consideration be given for a request for a
transfer.' This explained why I was not, as requested by my
sentencing judge, transferred to a British prison.

To the Case Manager at Terre Haute, the DEA wrote:

Enclosed please find information concerning an inmate
in your institution, Dennis Howard Marks. Should
MARKS file any further requests for parole, transfer to
England, his native country, or any other actions
influencing his incarceration, please contact:
Group Supervisor Craig Lovato.

To me Group Supervisor Craig Lovato of the DEA wrote:

Howard,
I hope this communiqué does not offend you. If it does,
just let me know and I'll cease and desist. I think that
Paul's book personalized our relationship to a certain
degree. As a result of that, I do find myself, on occasion,
wondering how you are doing.
What prompted this missive was two things actually.
Terry Burke had called to inform me that you had once
again made application for transfer to England and the
second was an article in the *Arizona Republic* regarding
the execution of murderous drug kingpins. No, I know
you don't fall into this category, but the site for these
events is Terre Haute! I suppose this is not news to you
but it was to me. It's difficult, to a degree, to write to
you, without giving the appearance of superciliousness. I
trust that you will know that is not my intent. The truth
is, that because of your imprisonment, your opinions and
viewpoints on certain matters are a point of curiosity to
me. The fact that you plead guilty allows me the latitude,
with your permission, to communicate with you on
matters of mutual interest. Unlike with Ernie, who
continues to pursue avenues of quiet desperation.
I am sure that your viewpoint, as a stranger to our land,
must at times be contrary to that of John Doe citizen. If
you wish to continue with our correspondence, drop me
a line, and we will continue.
Craig.

Lovato was not only ensuring that I stayed in this hell-hole
of a prison for another twelve years, but he was also taunting
me about dope dealers getting executed outside my window,
letting me know that he knew I was trying to get to England,
and wanting to play some sick cat-and-mouse pen-friend
game with me. I had no proof that he was also responsible

for persuading the Immigration authorities to prevent Judy
from visiting me. Neither did I have proof to the contrary. I
was convinced he was.

After my conviction in Miami, Bronis had submitted a
Motion to Reduce Sentence. This was invariably done in all
cases to give the judge the opportunity to modify a sentence
after further reflection. Such a motion has to be filed within
120 days of conviction. The judge can take as long as he likes
to rule on the motion. Judge Paine had sat on mine for four
years. While it is pending, supplemental material relevant to
the motion can also be filed for judicial consideration, and
we had submitted a variety of letters from people concerned
about the psychological damage to my children and the
unfair way I was being treated. Somehow, Bronis managed
to force the judge to grant a hearing in open court to
consider, among other matters, the DEA's malicious,
sadistic, and mendacious behaviour with respect to my
incarceration. The basis of the motion was that the sentence
was turning out to be harsher than the judge had intended.

For the first time in four years, I left USP Terre Haute.
Chained and shackled, I was air-freighted via a week's stop
in El Reno, Oklahoma, to Miami MCC. There I got the
usual escape-risk treatment and was put into the hole. The
hearing took place at West Palm Beach. Lovato had flown
down to make sure the judge got his message. Julian Peto, as
ever, was there to speak on my behalf. Lovato took the stand.
He limped from an obviously painful knee injury. I felt sorry
for him. Was I going mad? Lovato testified. Bronis destroyed
him. Then Lovato said it wasn't the case that Judy and the
kids were short of money, because only a few weeks ago it
had been reported to him that Judy could still afford to wear
her Rolex watch. I had bought it for her on our second
wedding anniversary together in 1981, twelve years ago. I
knew the judge was on my side on this one. But Judge Paine
didn't rule. He said he'd let us know. I was taken to a West
Palm Beach County Jail, where for five weeks I was the only

White in a cell block full of Blacks rapping and hip-hopping. I felt completely at home. Then back to Miami MCC for another week in the hole as a high-profile escape risk. Then to El Reno. Then back to Terre Haute. My good friend Charlot Fiocconi had been transferred to another penitentiary. I was going to miss him so much. I had been there a month before I was informed of Judge Paine's three rulings: my sentence had been reduced by five years from twenty-five to twenty years; I was to be considered for immediate transfer to England; if any government agency prevented my transfer, I was to be imprisoned in a regular joint, not a penitentiary. No huge victory, it seemed. I'd only knocked a few years off, but it looked as if I might be leaving America.

The reduced sentence meant that my parole eligibility date was now in a few months. There was still no reason whatsoever to think that anything had changed with respect to big dope dealers never being granted parole, but I went through the motions and turned up in the prison's parole hearing rooms to present my case on the last day of January 1995. Webster came with me and told the parole examiner I was the best teacher he had ever had and for sure I was going straight. I expected Lovato to be there. He wasn't. I was waiting for the bullshit about how high-profile, international, gangster-like, and terrorist my evil dope empire had been. Instead the parole examiner began: 'Please don't mention anything to your family yet, but, Mr Marks, I am recommending to the United States Regional Parole Commissioners that you be released on parole on March 25th. It is their decision, which you will receive within three weeks, that is final. This hearing is terminated.'

I simultaneously experienced every emotion I had ever experienced in my life. I had been given maximum parole. This was unheard-of. I would be home in two months. Contrary to the examiner's advice, I told my wife, children, parents, and sister. They all cried. I cried.

So did Lovato, I expect. I still don't know for sure what

happened, but I think there are two possibilities. Either Judge Paine had a word with someone in the Parole Commission to cut me loose, or the USP authorities had failed (deliberately or incompetently) to inform Lovato of the parole hearing as the DEA had instructed them, so he was unable to raise official objections. I was terrified Lovato would find out, get to the Regional Commissioner and put a spanner in the works, but on St Valentine's Day I received the heaven-sent confirmation. I was being paroled. I would be deported to England as soon as possible after my release date. I wouldn't even have to abide by my parole conditions, there being no appropriate jurisdiction to enforce them, but if they wanted me to piss in a bottle every day and mail it to the nearest United States Embassy, I would.

No one leaves Terre Haute for freedom. They leave for court cases or are transferred to lower-security institutions on the long, gradual road to the prison gate. I felt sad and guilty about leaving these guys behind. Most of them would never see the outside world.

'Just do one thing for me, Howard,' said Big Jim Nolan. 'Send me some of those European magazines of broads cat-fighting each other. That way I can jack off twice before breakfast. You know the Outlaws got a Chapter in England now. Go and say hello from me. I'll be there one day.'

'If we can ever do anything for you, Howard, let us know,' said Victor 'Vic the Boss' Amuso.

'A part of us is free, Howard, when you get home. God bless you,' said Bear the Outlaw.

'Keep this stone, Howard,' said Daoud the Rastafarian ex-Black Panther. 'It's a sacred American Indian one. It goes invisible during shake-downs. No one will find it. This means a part of us will always be with you.'

Goodbye, guys. There's a lot of you that will always be me, not just with me. I'll never forget you, your courage, your sadness, your kindness to me, your suffering, your families, your patience, your strength, your goodness. I love you.

And so I left the United States Penitentiary, Terre Haute, still clad in escape-proof chains, to begin the seven-week journey that would end up with my sitting on a Continental Airlines plane rapidly losing altitude over Surrey. At Gatwick, Passport Control gave a two-second look at my emergency passport and waved me through. With this piece of paper, my plastic US Penitentiary Inmate Account card, and a copy of *Hunting Marco Polo*, I persuaded the airport's Post Office to give me a British Visitors' Passport valid for three weeks. I changed my US dollars to pounds and phoned all of my family. I bought a ticket to Mallorca. At Palma airport, I saw a beautiful eight-year-old boy. Seven years ago he had been struck dumb for eighteen months as his mother lay weeping in a Florida county jail. Then he cast his fate and his body to the winds not knowing what or who he was, and busted his bones. His blue eyes shone, and his soul smiled. He ran towards me.

'Hi, Dad.'

penguin.co.uk/vintage